You may be reading the **wrong way!!**

IT'S TRUE: In keeping with the original Japanese comic format, this book reads from right to left—so action, sound effects, and word balloons are completely reversed. This preserves the orientation of the original artwork—plus, it's fun! Check out the diagram shown here to get the hang of things, and then turn to the other side of the book to get started!

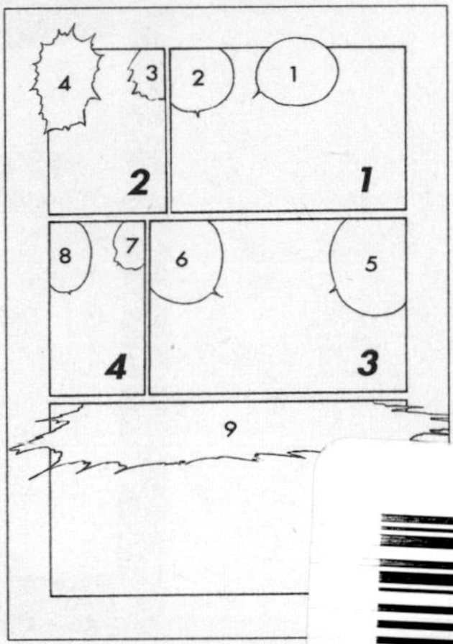

1
1
2
2
3
4
3
5
6
4
7
8
9

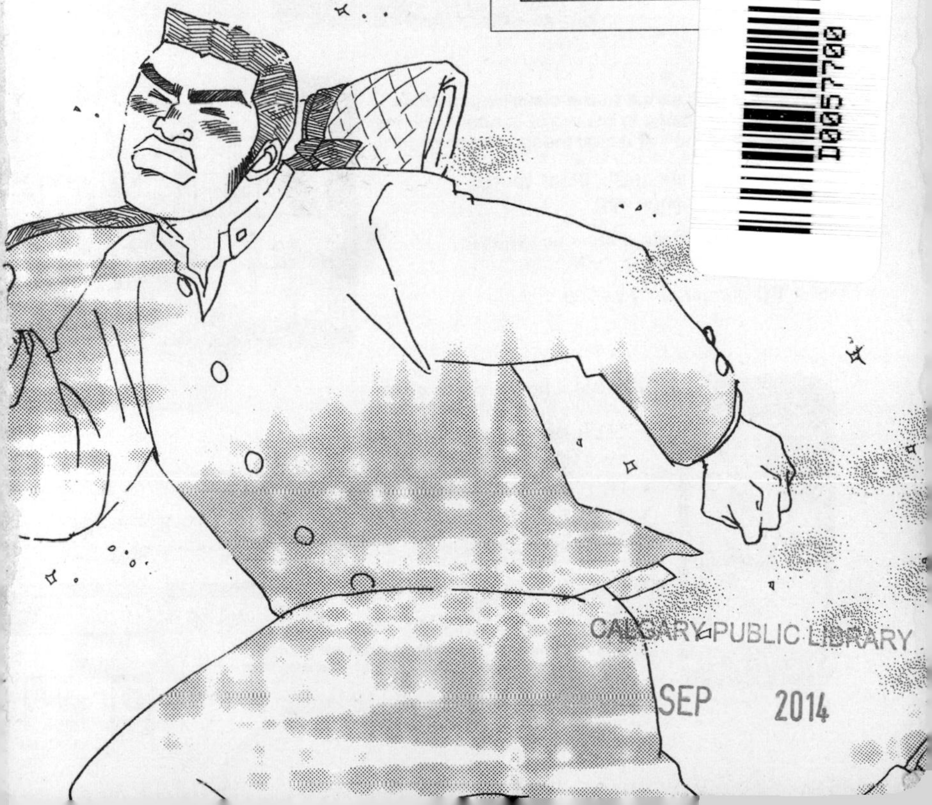

VIZMANGA

Read manga anytime, anywhere!

From our newest hit series to the classics you know and love, the best manga in the world is now available digitally. Buy a volume* of digital manga for your:

- iOS device (**iPad®, iPhone®, iPod® touch**) through the **VIZ Manga** app
- Android-powered device (**phone or tablet**) with a browser by visiting VIZManga.com
- **Mac or PC computer** by visiting VIZManga.com

VIZ Digital has loads to offer:

- 500+ ready-to-read volumes
- New volumes each week
- FREE previews
- Access on multiple devices! Create a log-in through the app so you buy a book once, and read it on your device of choice!*

To learn more, visit www.viz.com/apps

* Some series may not be available for multiple devices. Check the app on your device to find out what's available.

RATED **T** FOR OLDER TEEN
ratings.viz.com

VIZ MEDIA
viz.com/apps

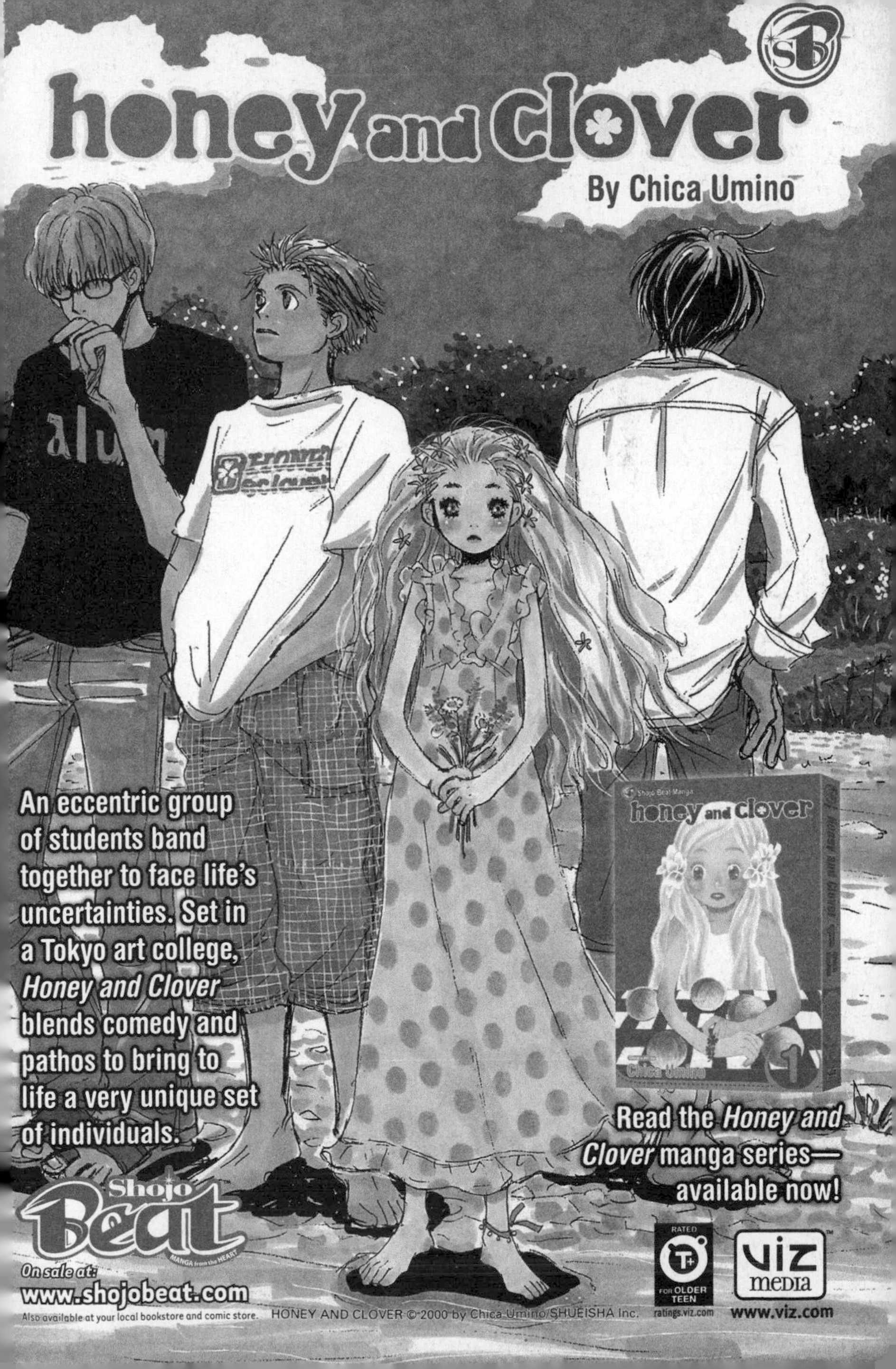
honey and clover
By Chica Umino
An eccentric group of students band together to face life's uncertainties. Set in a Tokyo art college, Honey and Clover blends comedy and pathos to bring to life a very unique set of individuals.
Shojo Beat Manga
honey and clover
Chica Umino
1
Read the Honey and Clover manga series—available now!
Shojo Beat
MANGA from the HEART
On sale at:
www.shojobeat.com
Also available at your local bookstore and comic store.
HONEY AND CLOVER © 2000 by Chica Umino/SHUEISHA Inc.
RATED T+ FOR OLDER TEEN
ratings.viz.com
VIZ media
www.viz.com

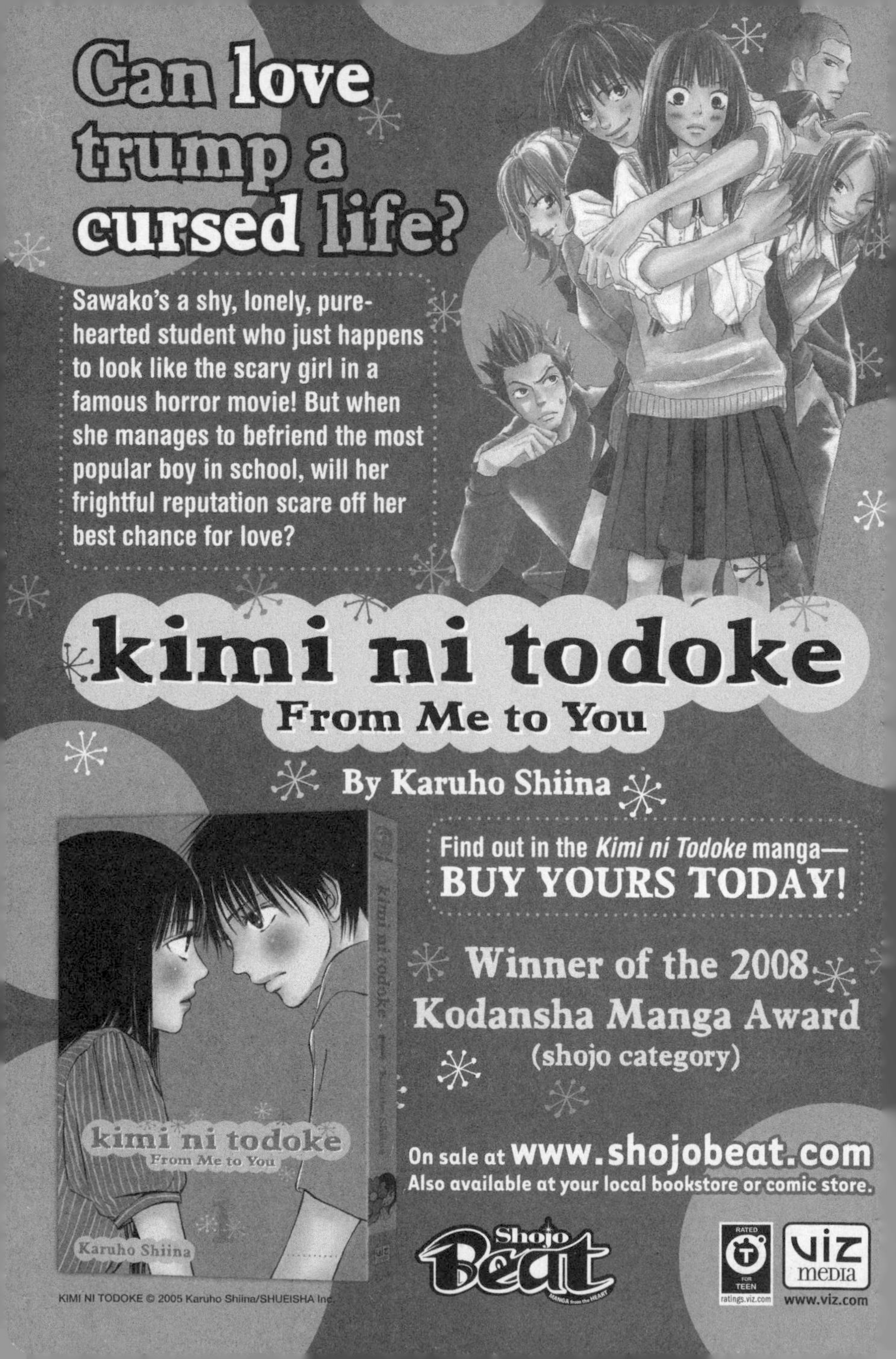

Can love trump a cursed life?
Sawako's a shy, lonely, pure-hearted student who just happens to look like the scary girl in a famous horror movie! But when she manages to befriend the most popular boy in school, will her frightful reputation scare off her best chance for love?
kimi ni todoke
From Me to You
By Karuho Shiina
kimi ni todoke
From Me to You
Karuho Shiina
Find out in the Kimi ni Todoke manga—
BUY YOURS TODAY!
Winner of the 2008
Kodansha Manga Award
(shojo category)
On sale at www.shojobeat.com
Also available at your local bookstore or comic store.
Shojo Beat
MANGA from the HEART
RATED T FOR TEEN
ratings.viz.com
VIZ media
www.viz.com
KIMI NI TODOKE © 2005 Karuho Shiina/SHUEISHA Inc.

MY LOVE STORY!!

Volume 1
Shojo Beat Edition

Story **KAZUNE KAWAHARA**
Art by **ARUKO**

———————— // ————————

English Adaptation ♡ **Ysabet Reinhardt MacFarlane**
Translation ♡ **JN Productions**
Touch-up Art & Lettering ♡ **Mark McMurray**
Design ♡ **Fawn Lau**
Editor ♡ **Amy Yu**

———————— // ————————

ORE MONOGATARI!!
© 2011 by Kazune Kawahara, Aruko
All rights reserved.
First published in Japan in 2011 by SHUEISHA Inc., Tokyo
English translation rights arranged by SHUEISHA Inc.

The stories, characters and incidents mentioned in
this publication are entirely fictional.

Printed in the U.S.A.

Published by VIZ Media, LLC
P.O. Box 77010
San Francisco, CA 94107

10 9 8 7 6 5 4 3 2 1
First printing, July 2014

Shojo Beat

My love STORY!!

1

Story KAZUNE KAWAHARA

Art ARUKO

MY love STORY!!

1

CONTENTS

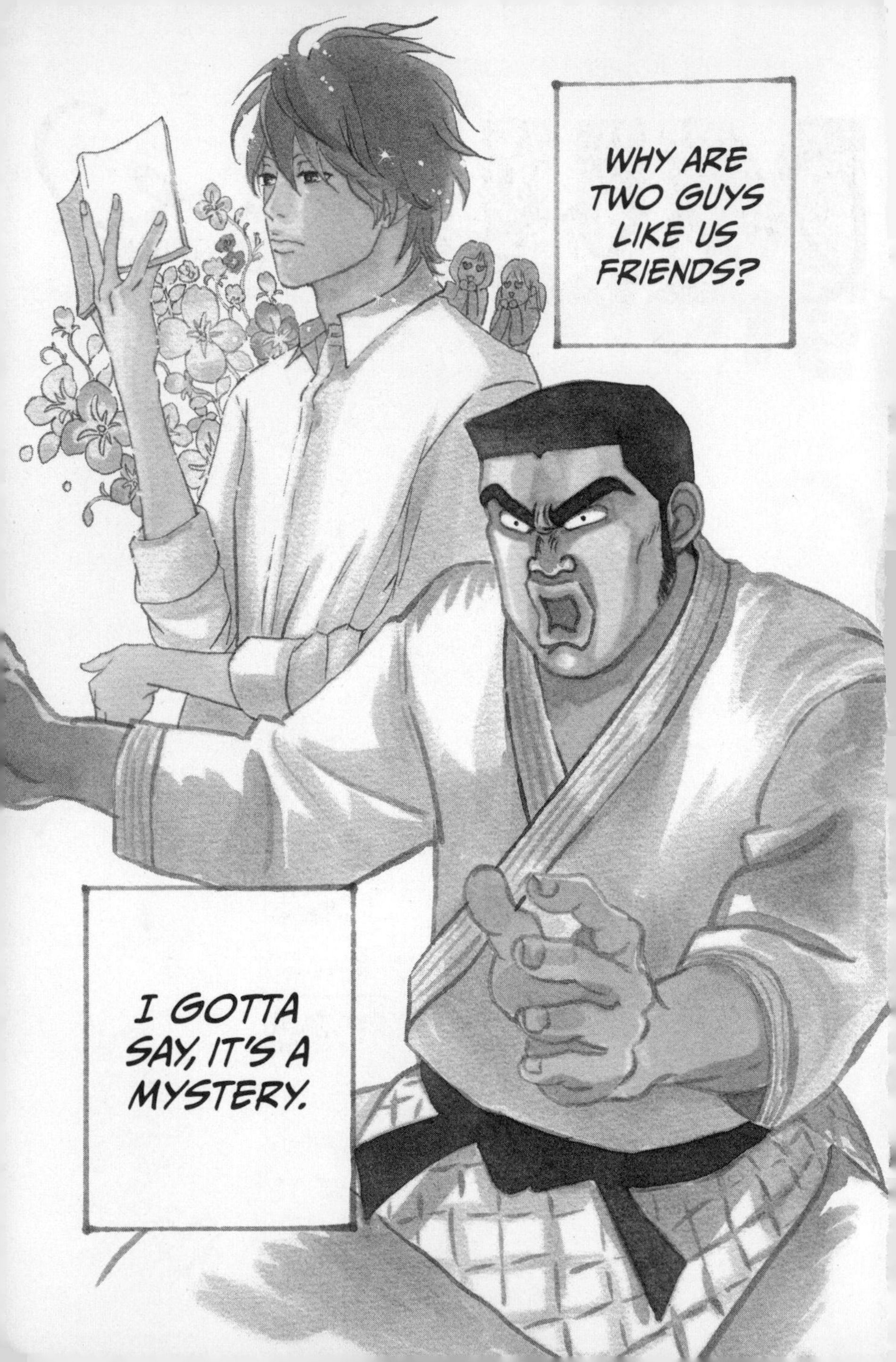
WHY ARE TWO GUYS LIKE US FRIENDS?
I GOTTA SAY, IT'S A MYSTERY.

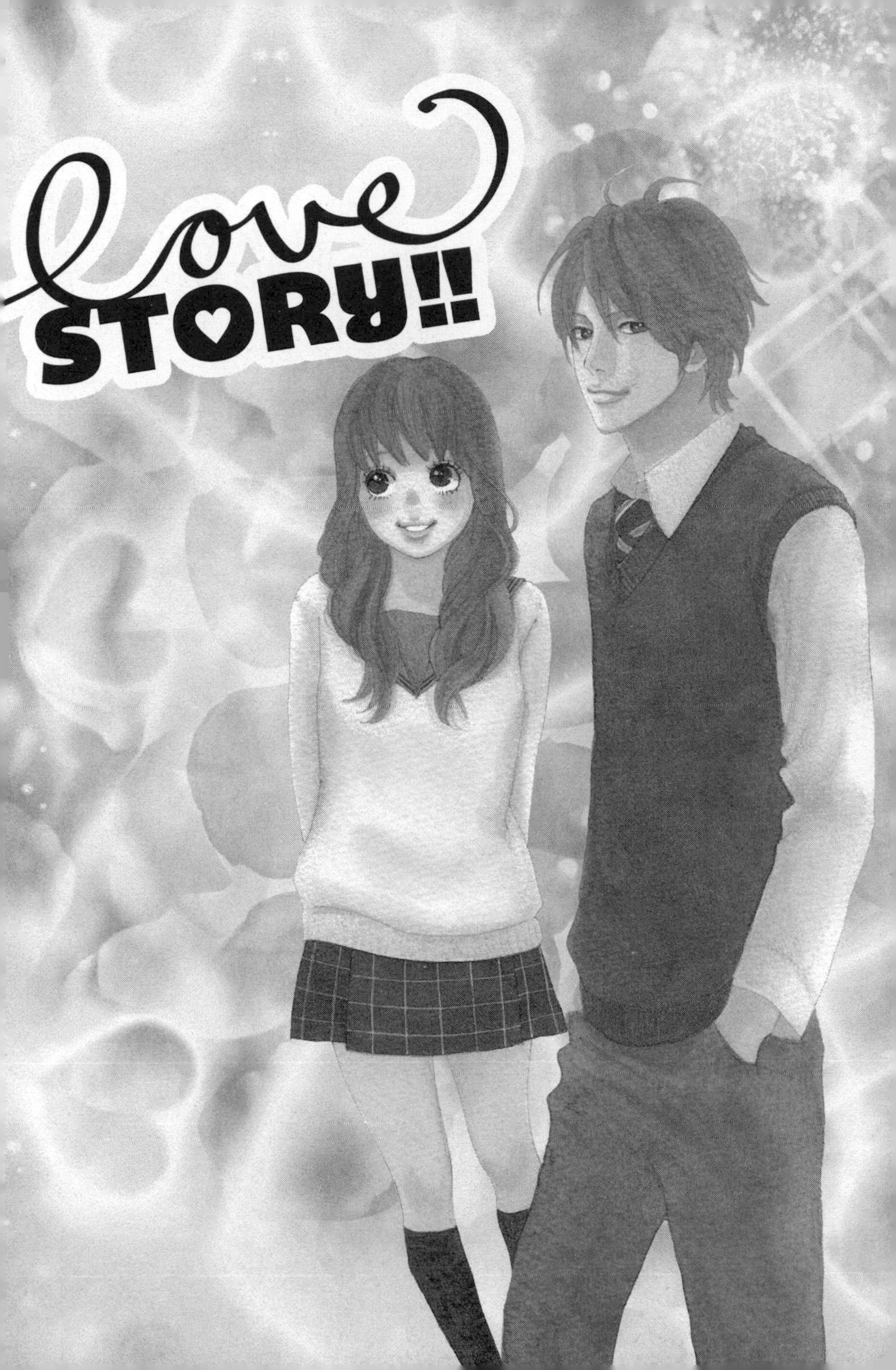
love
STORY!!

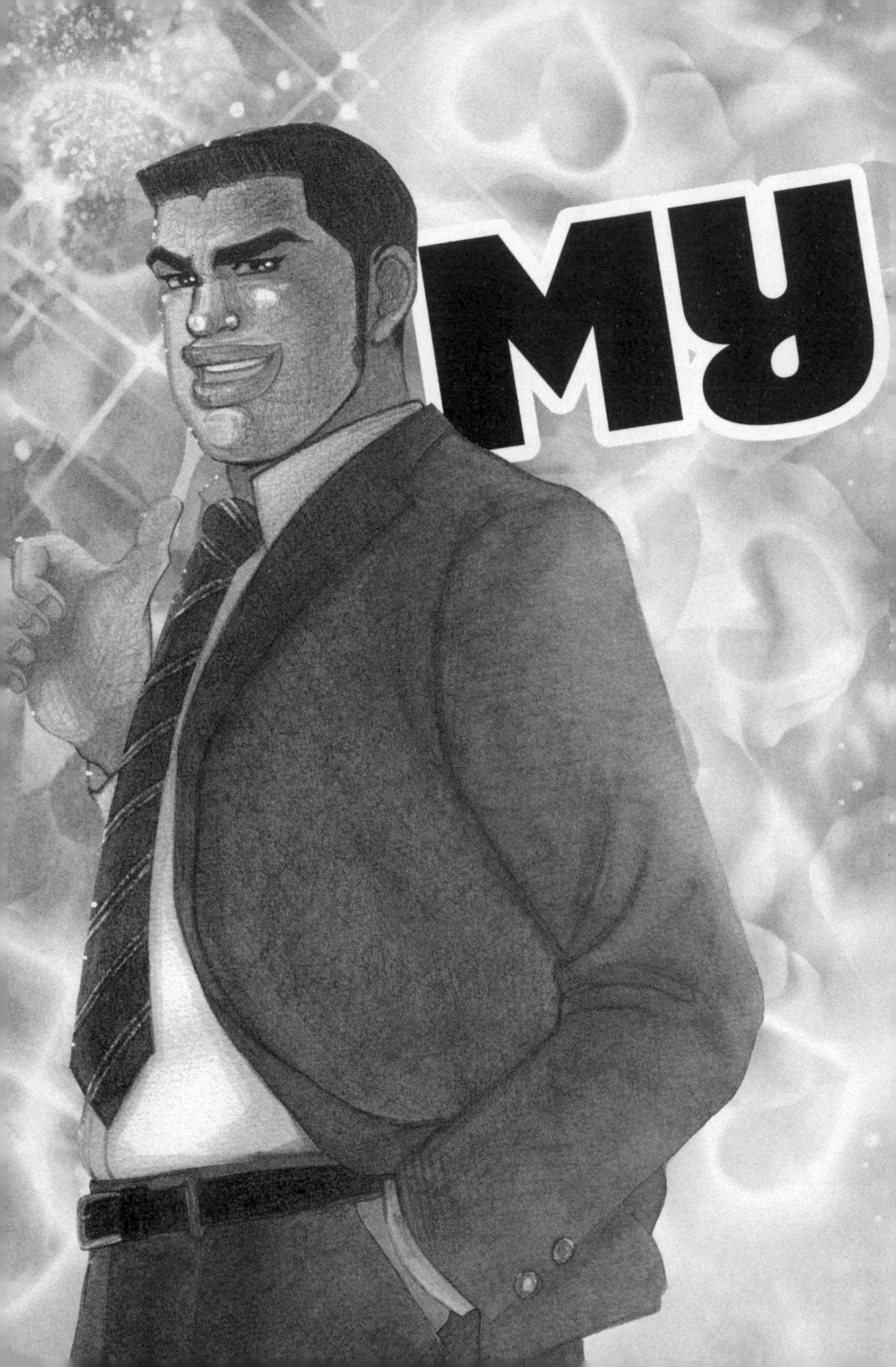
MY

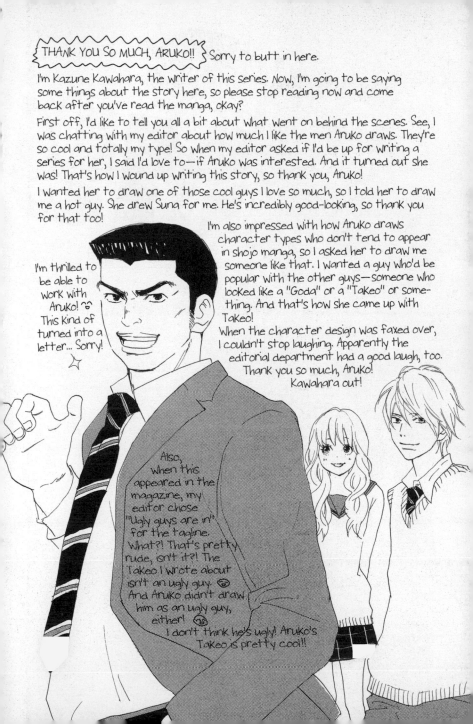

THANK YOU SO MUCH, ARUKO!! Sorry to butt in here.

I'm Kazune Kawahara, the writer of this series. Now, I'm going to be saying some things about the story here, so please stop reading now and come back after you've read the manga, okay?

First off, I'd like to tell you all a bit about what went on behind the scenes. See, I was chatting with my editor about how much I like the men Aruko draws. They're so cool and totally my type! So when my editor asked if I'd be up for writing a series for her, I said I'd love to—if Aruko was interested. And it turned out she was! That's how I wound up writing this story, so thank you, Aruko!

I wanted her to draw one of those cool guys I love so much, so I told her to draw me a hot guy. She drew Suna for me. He's incredibly good-looking, so thank you for that too!

I'm also impressed with how Aruko draws character types who don't tend to appear in shojo manga, so I asked her to draw me someone like that. I wanted a guy who'd be popular with the other guys—someone who looked like a "Goda" or a "Takeo" or something. And that's how she came up with Takeo!

When the character design was faxed over, I couldn't stop laughing. Apparently the editorial department had a good laugh, too.

Thank you so much, Aruko!

Kawahara out!

I'm thrilled to be able to work with Aruko! This kind of turned into a letter... Sorry!

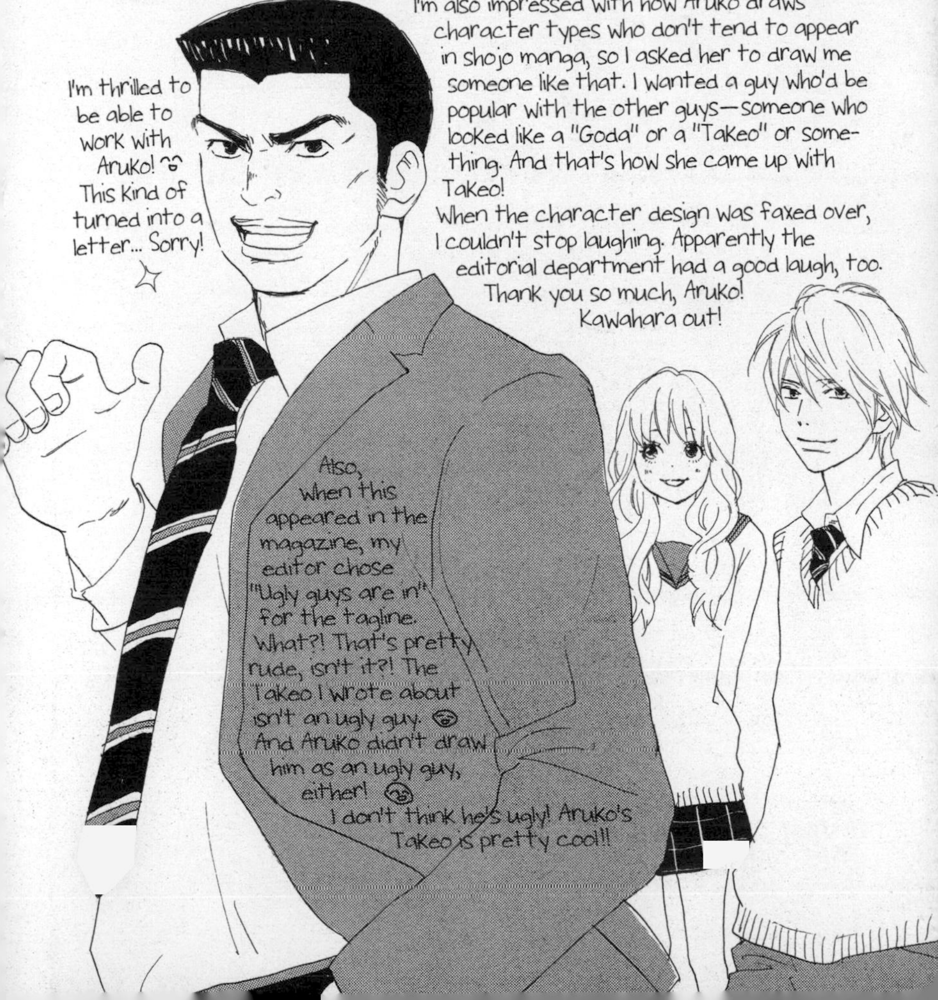

Also, when this appeared in the magazine, my editor chose "Ugly guys are in" for the tagline. What?! That's pretty rude, isn't it?! The Takeo I wrote about isn't an ugly guy. And Aruko didn't draw him as an ugly guy, either! I don't think he's ugly! Aruko's Takeo is pretty cool!!

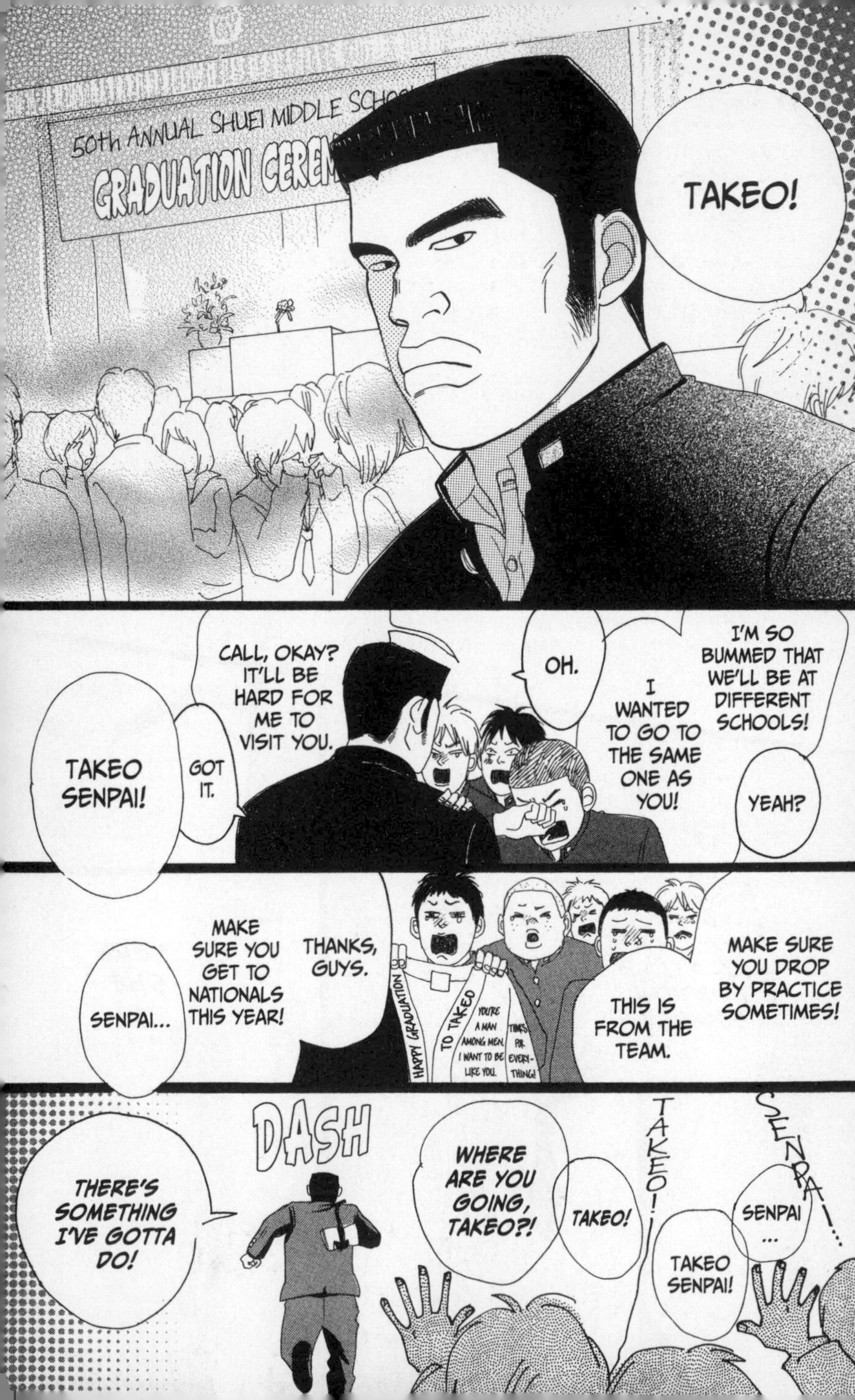
TAKEO!
I'M SO BUMMED THAT WE'LL BE AT DIFFERENT SCHOOLS!
YEAH?
I WANTED TO GO TO THE SAME ONE AS YOU!
OH.
CALL, OKAY? IT'LL BE HARD FOR ME TO VISIT YOU.
GOT IT.
TAKEO SENPAI!
MAKE SURE YOU DROP BY PRACTICE SOMETIMES!
THIS IS FROM THE TEAM.
THANKS FOR EVERYTHING!
YOU'RE A MAN AMONG MEN. I WANT TO BE LIKE YOU.
TO TAKEO
HAPPY GRADUATION
THANKS, GUYS.
MAKE SURE YOU GET TO NATIONALS THIS YEAR!
SENPAI...
SENPAI...!
SENPAI ...
TAKEO SENPAI!
TAKEO...!
TAKEO!
WHERE ARE YOU GOING, TAKEO?!
DASH
THERE'S SOMETHING I'VE GOTTA DO!

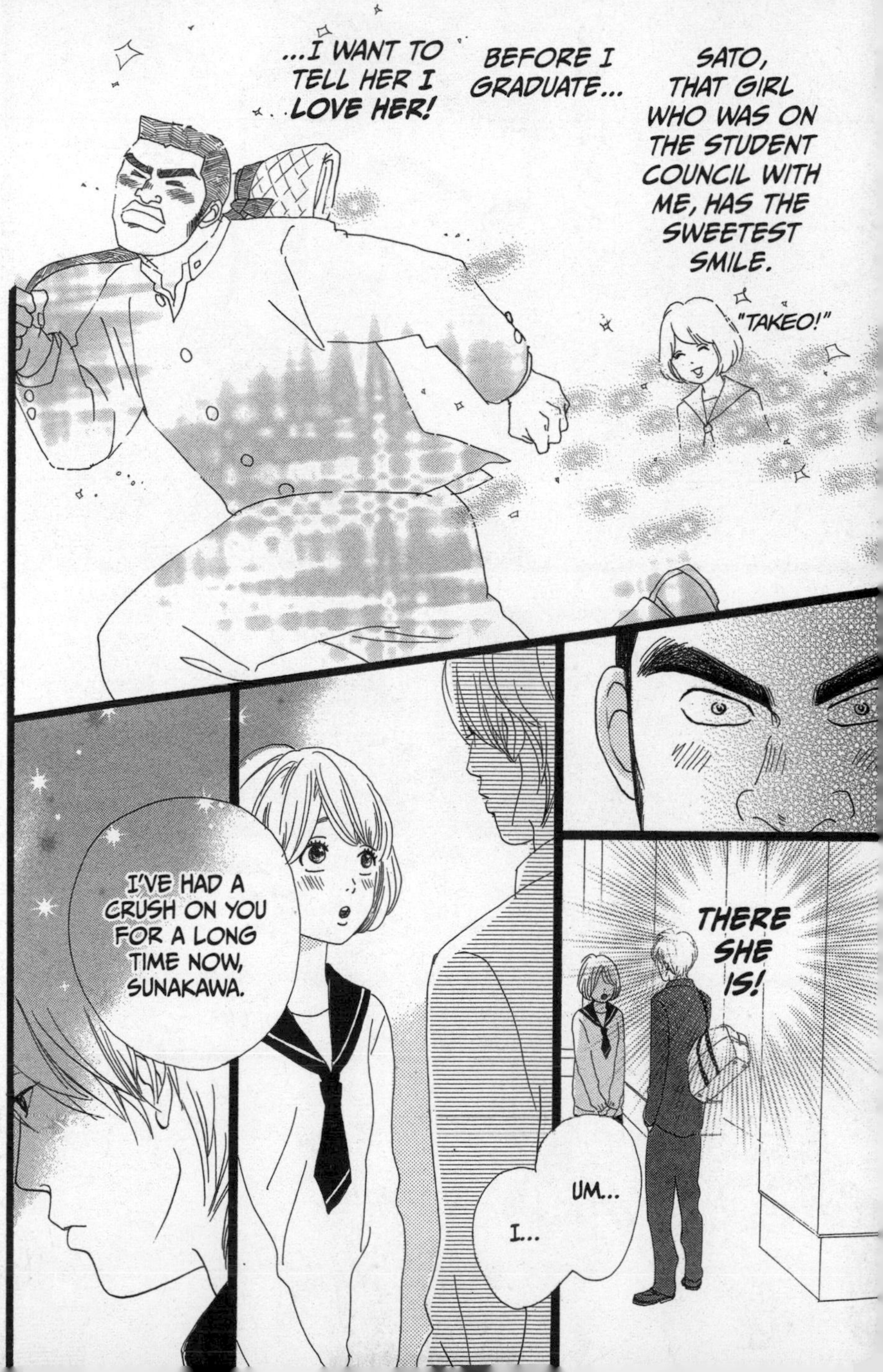
SATO, THAT GIRL WHO WAS ON THE STUDENT COUNCIL WITH ME, HAS THE SWEETEST SMILE.
"TAKEO!"
BEFORE I GRADUATE...
...I WANT TO TELL HER I LOVE HER!
THERE SHE IS!
UM...
I...
I'VE HAD A CRUSH ON YOU FOR A LONG TIME NOW, SUNAKAWA.

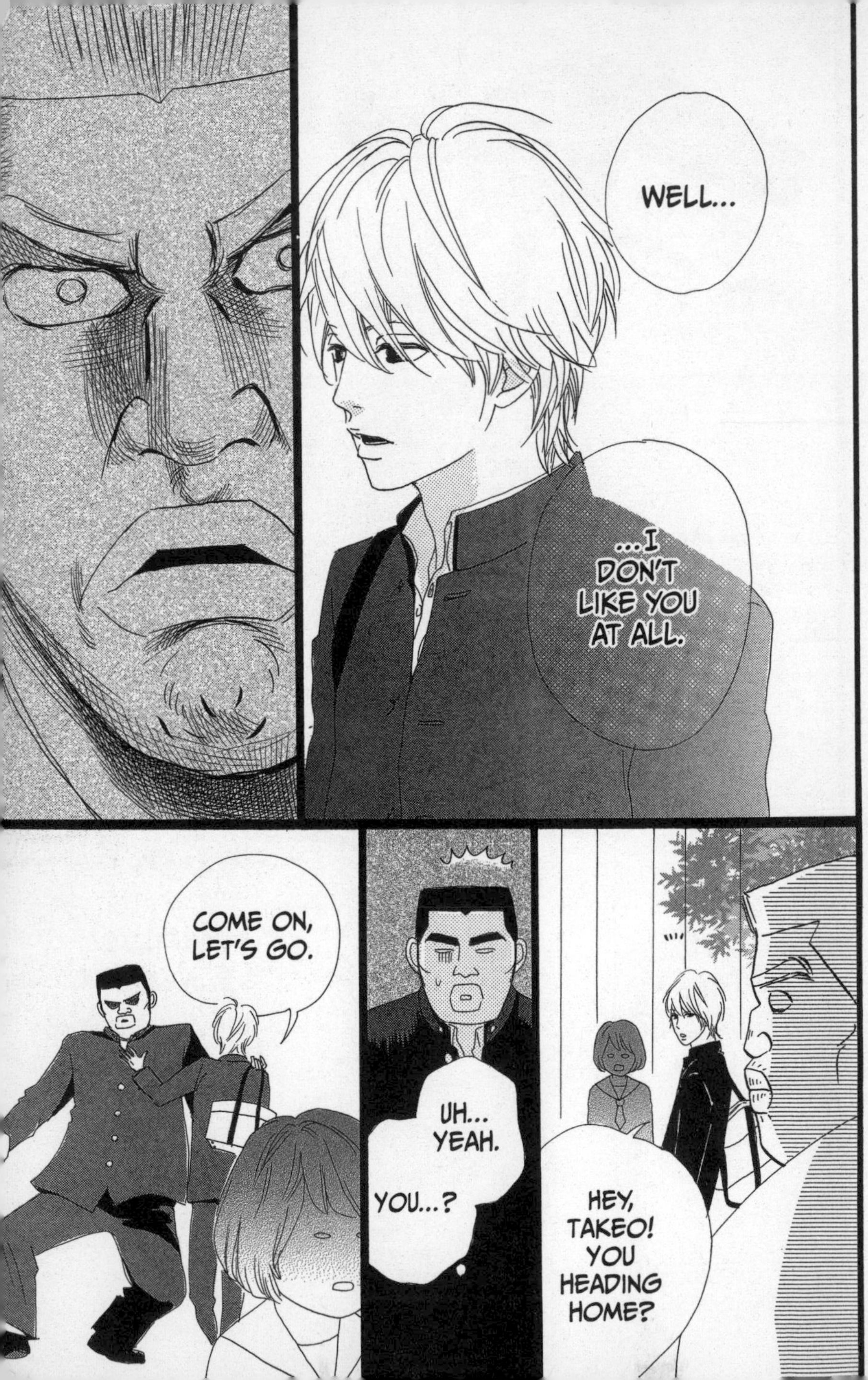
WELL...
...I DON'T LIKE YOU AT ALL.
HEY, TAKEO! YOU HEADING HOME?
UH... YEAH.
YOU...?
COME ON, LET'S GO.

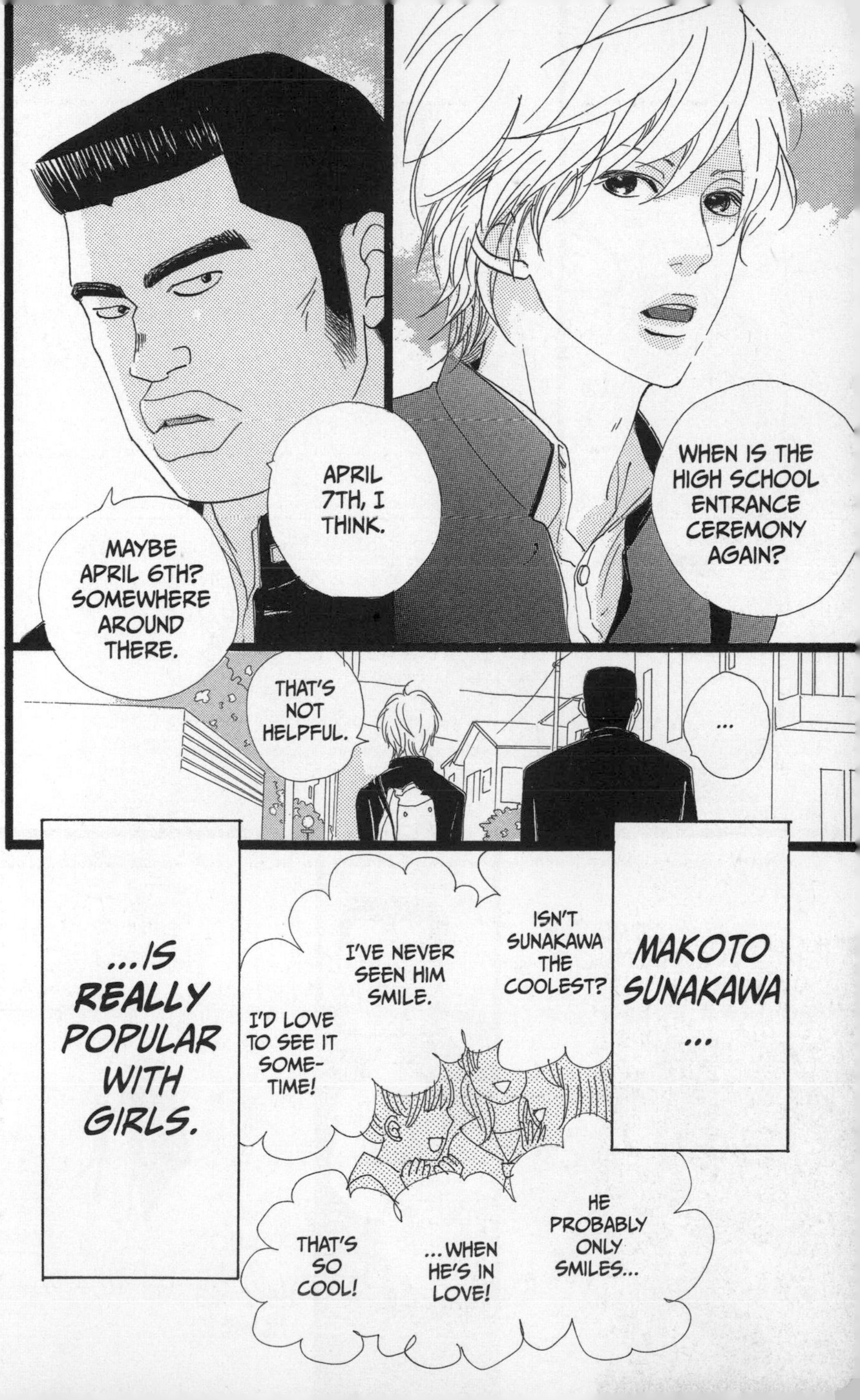
WHEN IS THE HIGH SCHOOL ENTRANCE CEREMONY AGAIN?
APRIL 7TH, I THINK.
MAYBE APRIL 6TH? SOMEWHERE AROUND THERE.
...
THAT'S NOT HELPFUL.
MAKOTO SUNAKAWA...
ISN'T SUNAKAWA THE COOLEST?
I'VE NEVER SEEN HIM SMILE.
I'D LOVE TO SEE IT SOME-TIME!
HE PROBABLY ONLY SMILES...
...WHEN HE'S IN LOVE!
THAT'S SO COOL!
...IS REALLY POPULAR WITH GIRLS.

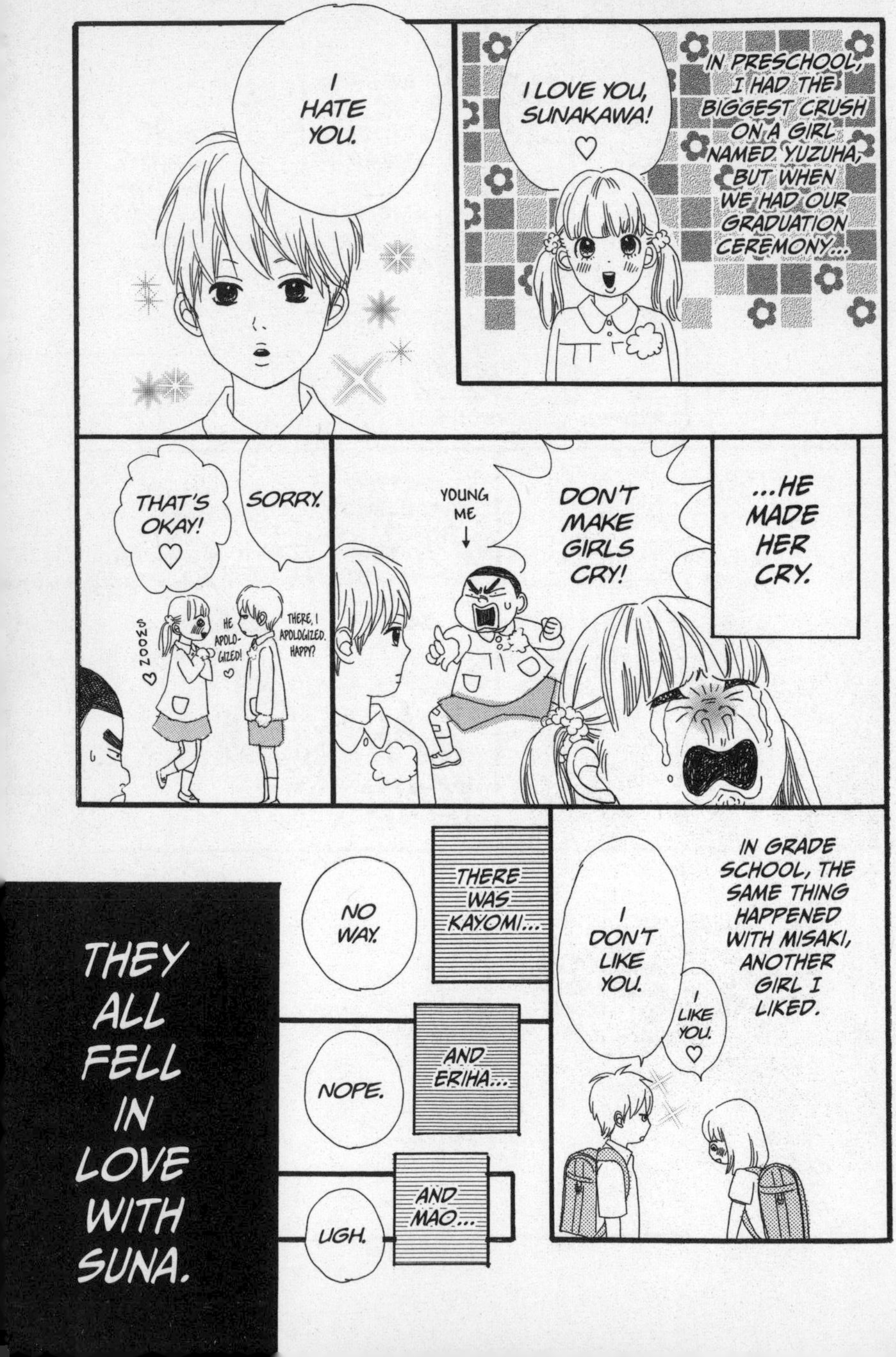
IN PRESCHOOL, I HAD THE BIGGEST CRUSH ON A GIRL NAMED YUZUHA, BUT WHEN WE HAD OUR GRADUATION CEREMONY...
I LOVE YOU, SUNAKAWA! ♡
I HATE YOU.
...HE MADE HER CRY.
DON'T MAKE GIRLS CRY!
YOUNG ME
SORRY.
THAT'S OKAY! ♡
THERE, I APOLOGIZED. HAPPY?
HE APOLOGIZED! ♡
SWOON ♡
IN GRADE SCHOOL, THE SAME THING HAPPENED WITH MISAKI, ANOTHER GIRL I LIKED.
I LIKE YOU. ♡
I DON'T LIKE YOU.
THERE WAS KAYOMI...
NO WAY.
AND ERIHA...
NOPE.
AND MAO...
UGH.
THEY ALL FELL IN LOVE WITH SUNA.

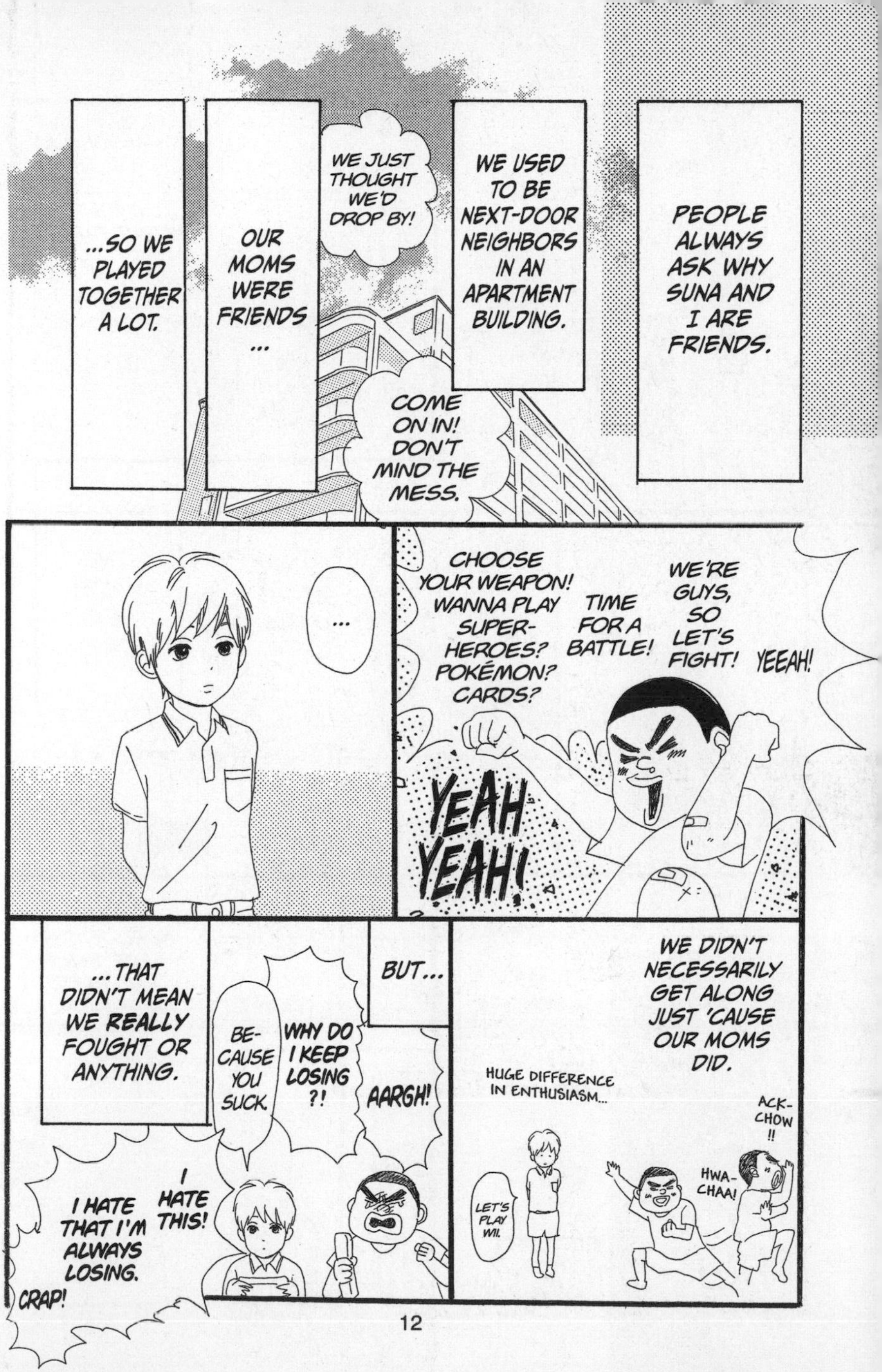
PEOPLE ALWAYS ASK WHY SUNA AND I ARE FRIENDS.
WE USED TO BE NEXT-DOOR NEIGHBORS IN AN APARTMENT BUILDING.
WE JUST THOUGHT WE'D DROP BY!
COME ON IN! DON'T MIND THE MESS.
OUR MOMS WERE FRIENDS ...
...SO WE PLAYED TOGETHER A LOT.
YEEAH!
WE'RE GUYS, SO LET'S FIGHT!
TIME FOR A BATTLE!
CHOOSE YOUR WEAPON! WANNA PLAY SUPER-HEROES? POKÉMON? CARDS?
YEAH YEAH!
...
WE DIDN'T NECESSARILY GET ALONG JUST 'CAUSE OUR MOMS DID.
ACK-CHOW !!
HWA-CHAA!
HUGE DIFFERENCE IN ENTHUSIASM...
LET'S PLAY WII.
BUT...
AARGH!
WHY DO I KEEP LOSING ?!
BE-CAUSE YOU SUCK.
...THAT DIDN'T MEAN WE REALLY FOUGHT OR ANYTHING.
I HATE THIS!
I HATE THAT I'M ALWAYS LOSING.
CRAP!

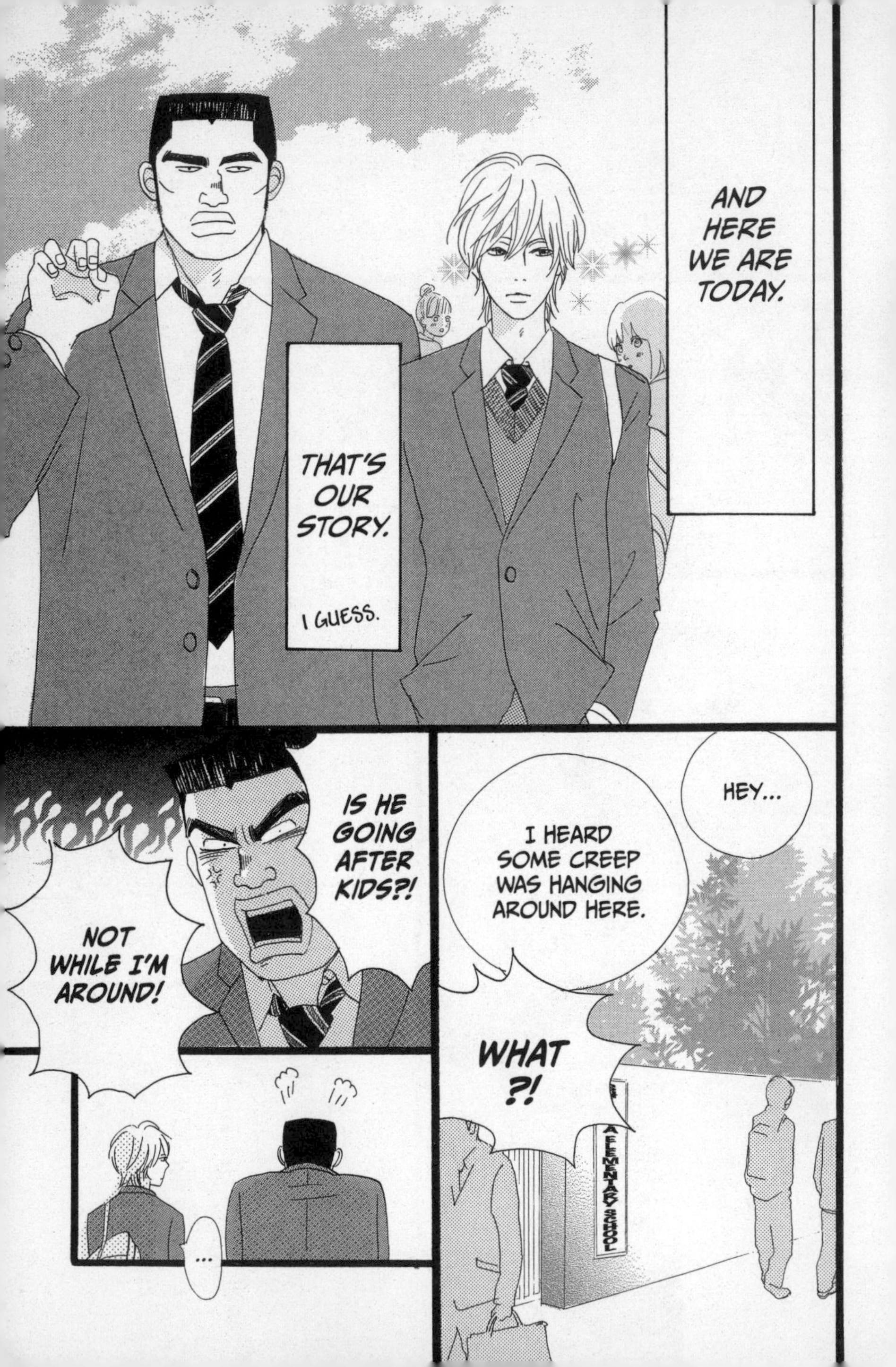
AND HERE WE ARE TODAY.
THAT'S OUR STORY.
I GUESS.
HEY...
I HEARD SOME CREEP WAS HANGING AROUND HERE.
WHAT ?!
A ELEMENTARY SCHOOL
IS HE GOING AFTER KIDS?!
NOT WHILE I'M AROUND!
...

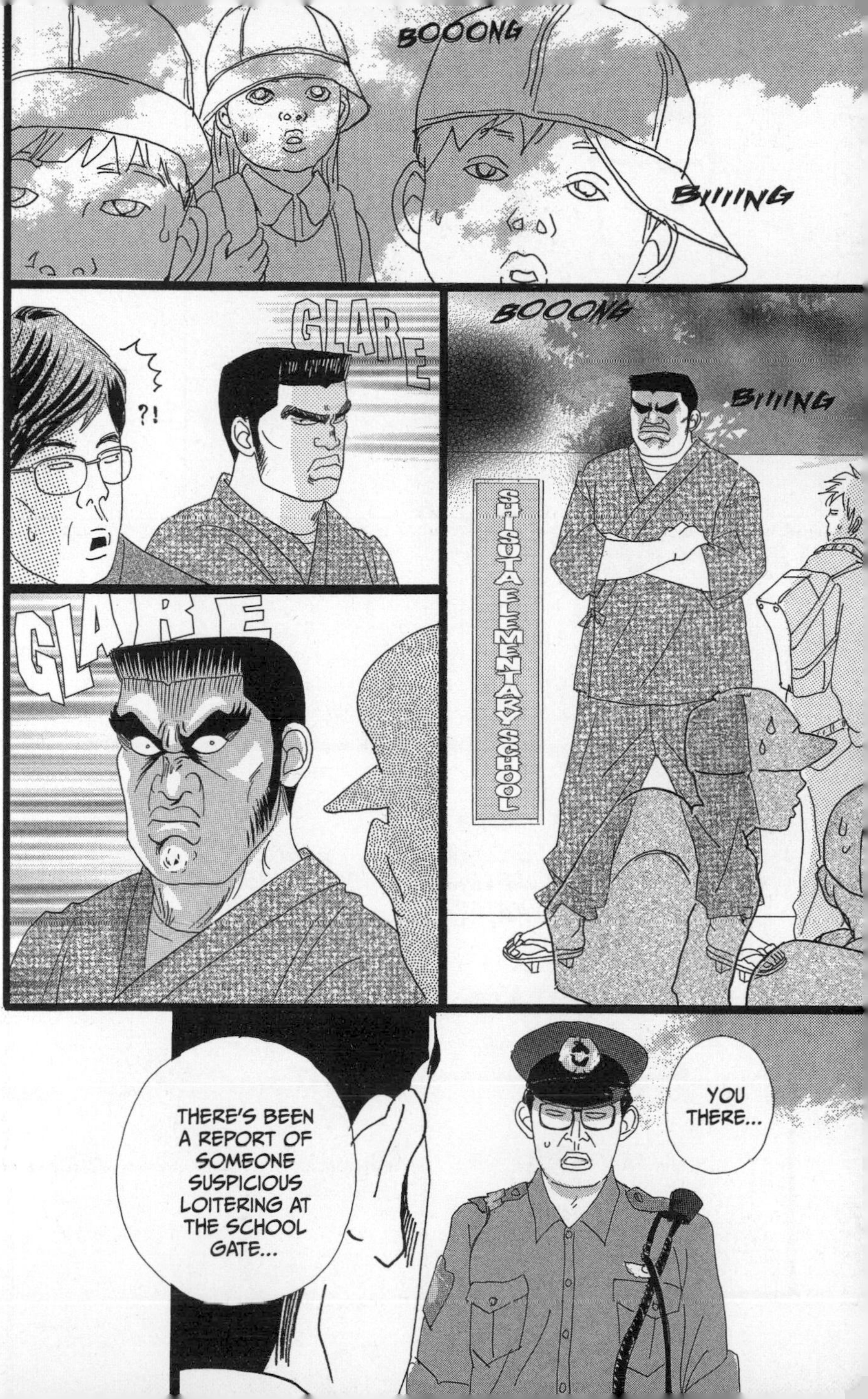
BOOONG
BIIIING
BOOONG
BIIIING
SHISUTA ELEMENTARY SCHOOL
GLARE
?!
GLARE
YOU THERE...
THERE'S BEEN A REPORT OF SOMEONE SUSPICIOUS LOITERING AT THE SCHOOL GATE...

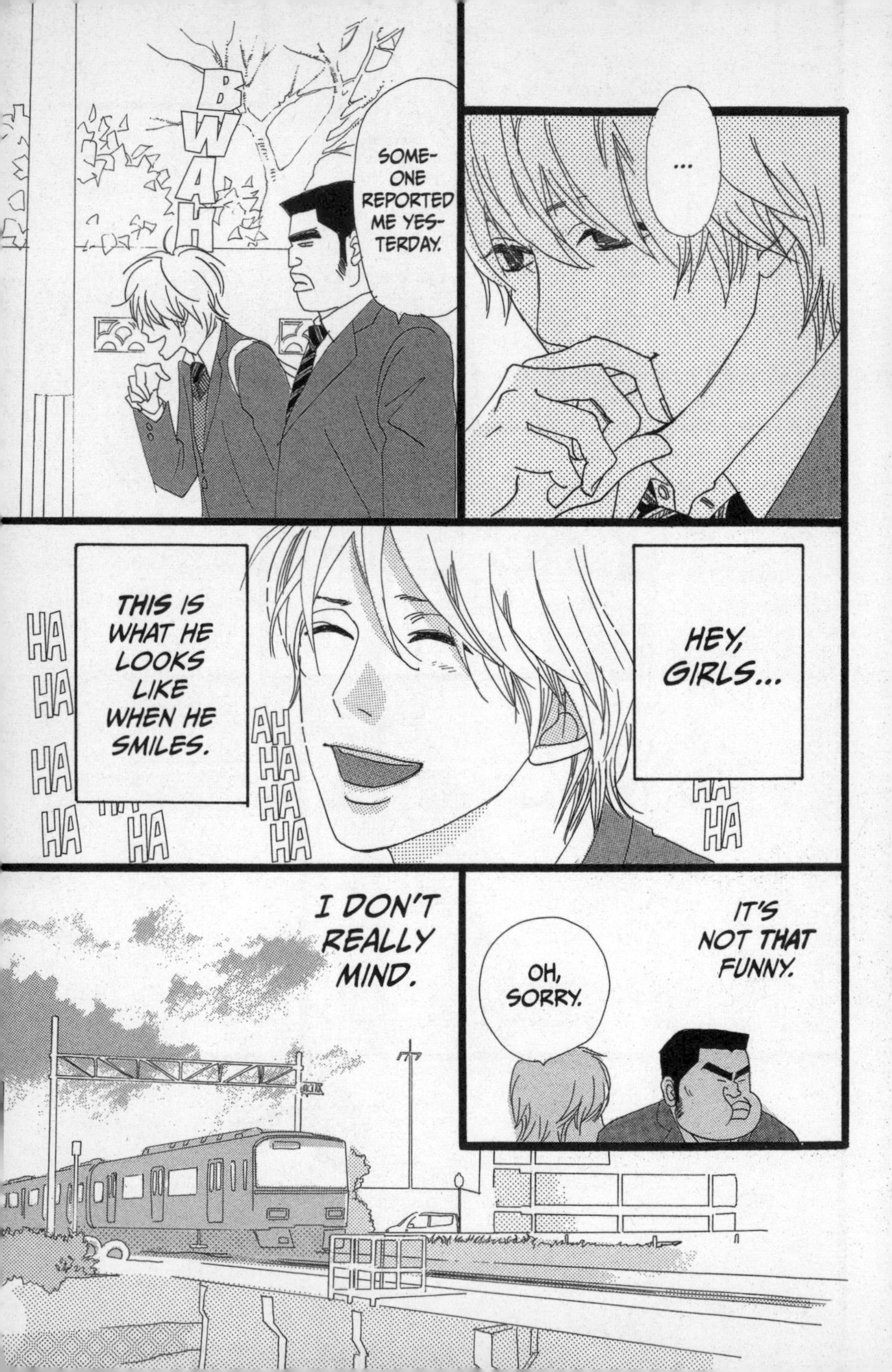
...
BWAH
SOME-ONE REPORTED ME YES-TERDAY.
HEY, GIRLS...
THIS IS WHAT HE LOOKS LIKE WHEN HE SMILES.
HA HA HA HA HA
AH HA HA HA HA
HA HA
IT'S NOT THAT FUNNY.
OH, SORRY.
I DON'T REALLY MIND.

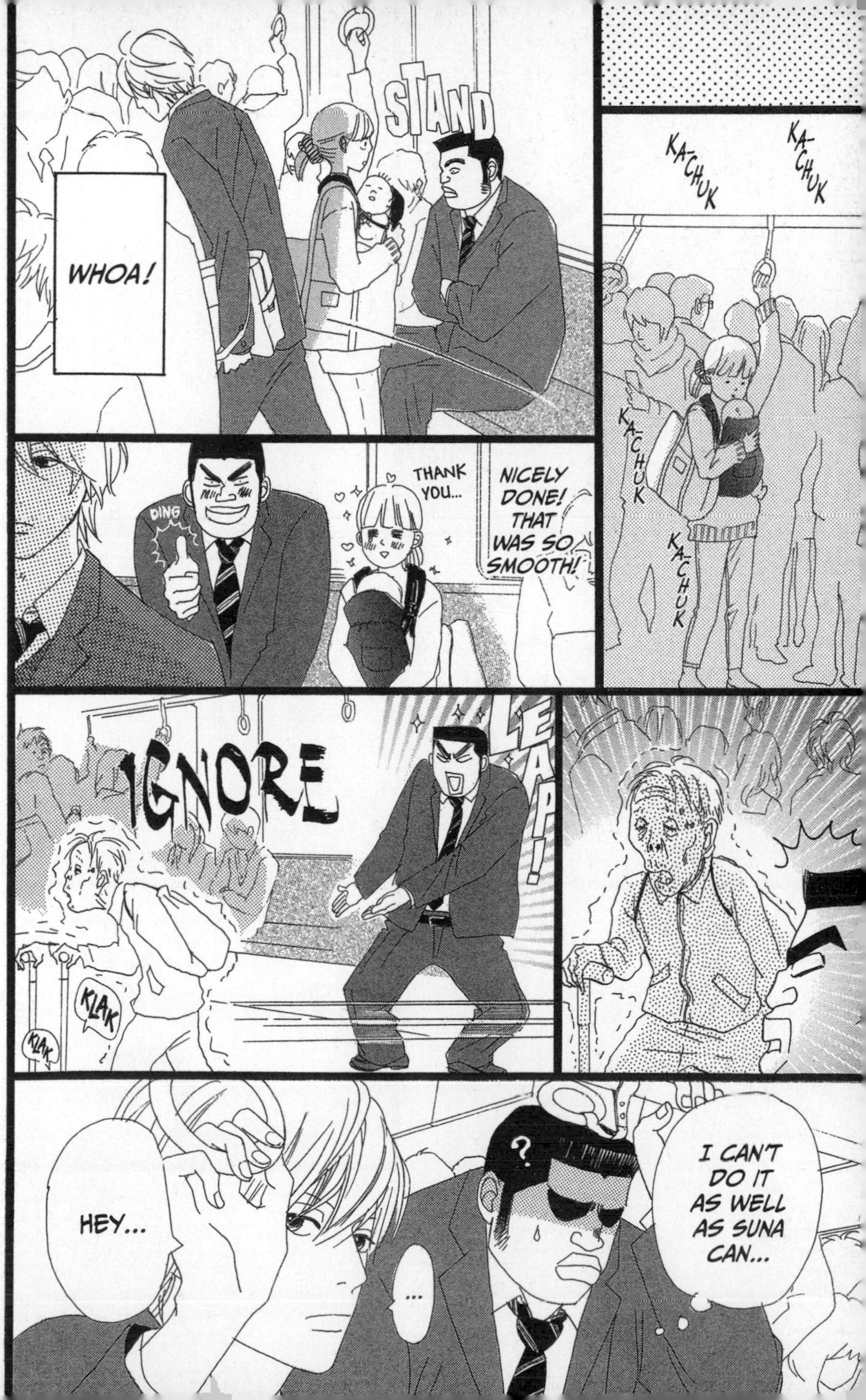
KA-CHUK
KA-CHUK
KA-CHUK
KA-CHUK
STAND
WHOA!
NICELY DONE! THAT WAS SO SMOOTH!
THANK YOU...
DING
LEAP!
IGNORE
KLAK
KLAK
I CAN'T DO IT AS WELL AS SUNA CAN...
...
HEY...

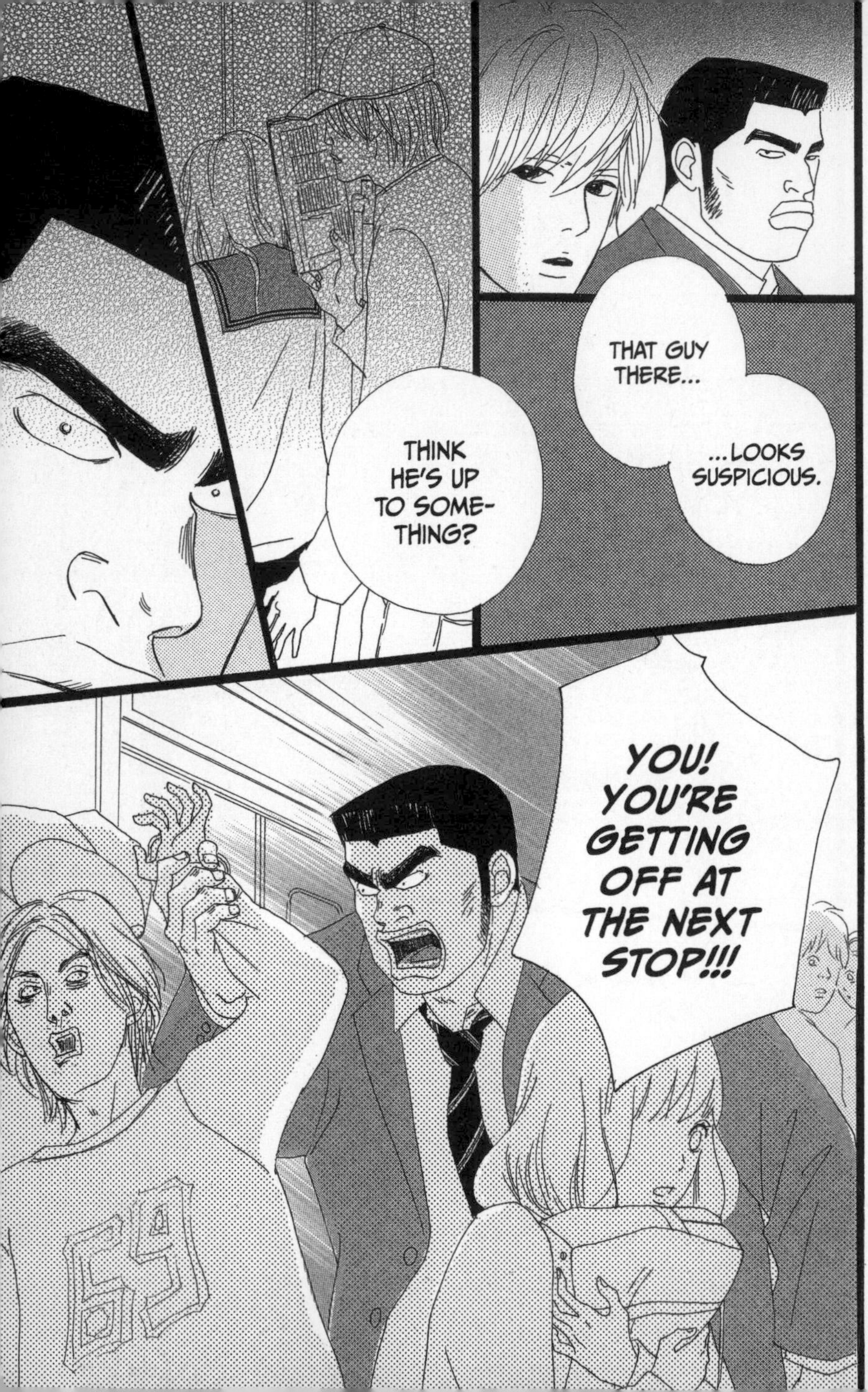
THAT GUY THERE...
...LOOKS SUSPICIOUS.
THINK HE'S UP TO SOME-THING?
YOU! YOU'RE GETTING OFF AT THE NEXT STOP!!!

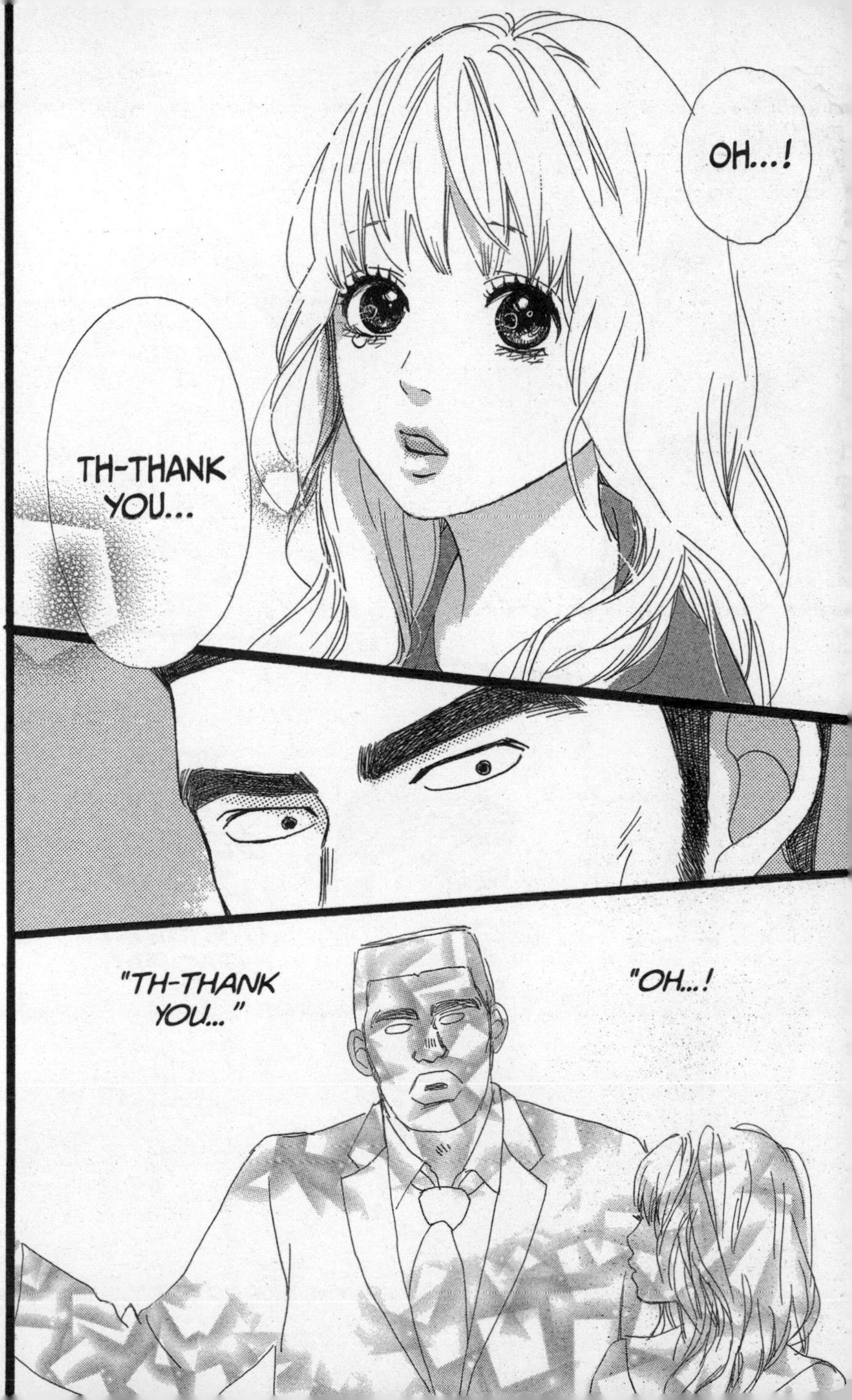
OH...!
TH-THANK YOU...
"OH...!
"TH-THANK YOU..."

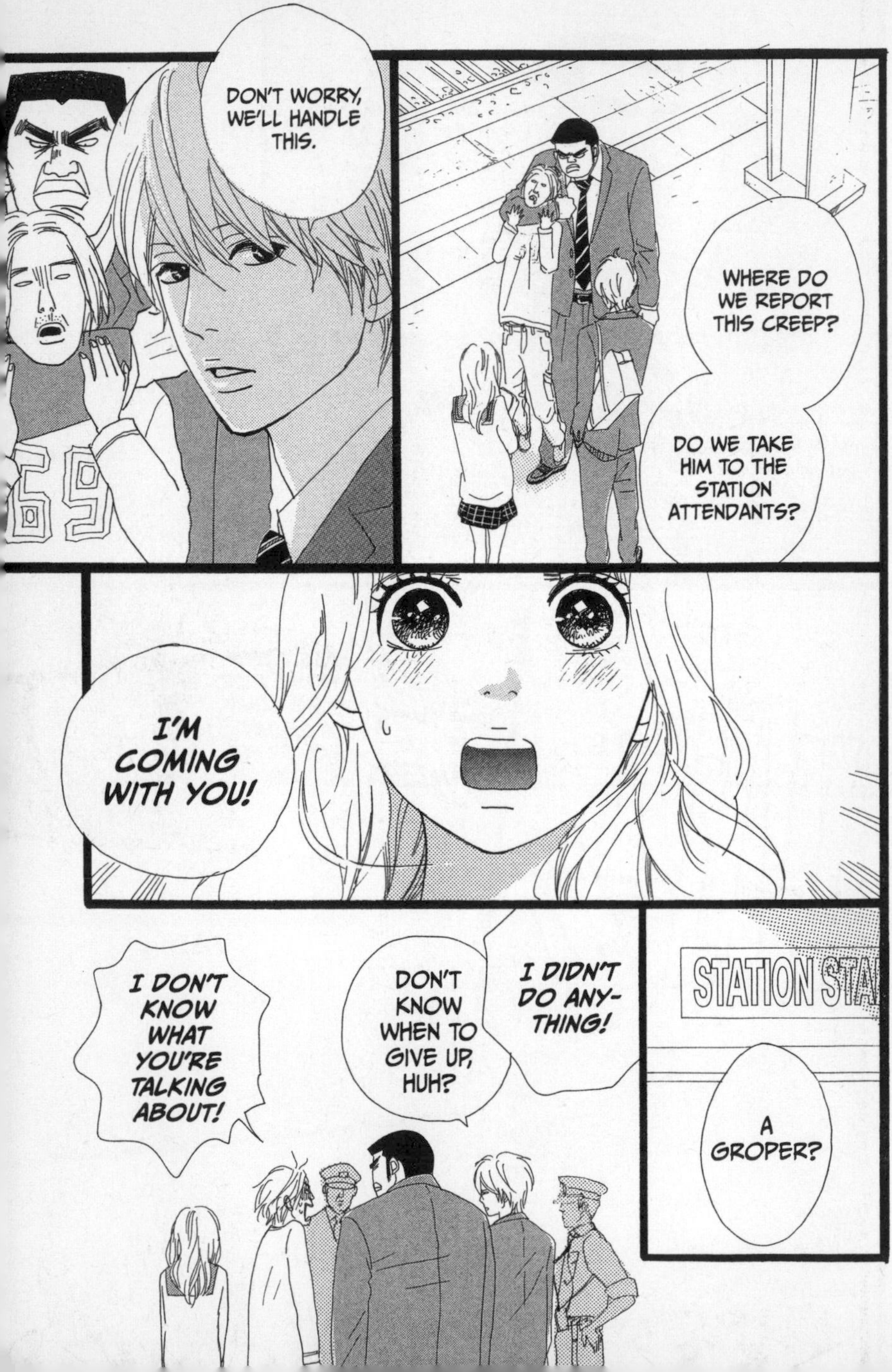
WHERE DO WE REPORT THIS CREEP?
DO WE TAKE HIM TO THE STATION ATTENDANTS?
DON'T WORRY, WE'LL HANDLE THIS.
I'M COMING WITH YOU!
STATION STA
A GROPER?
I DIDN'T DO ANY-THING!
DON'T KNOW WHEN TO GIVE UP, HUH?
I DON'T KNOW WHAT YOU'RE TALKING ABOUT!

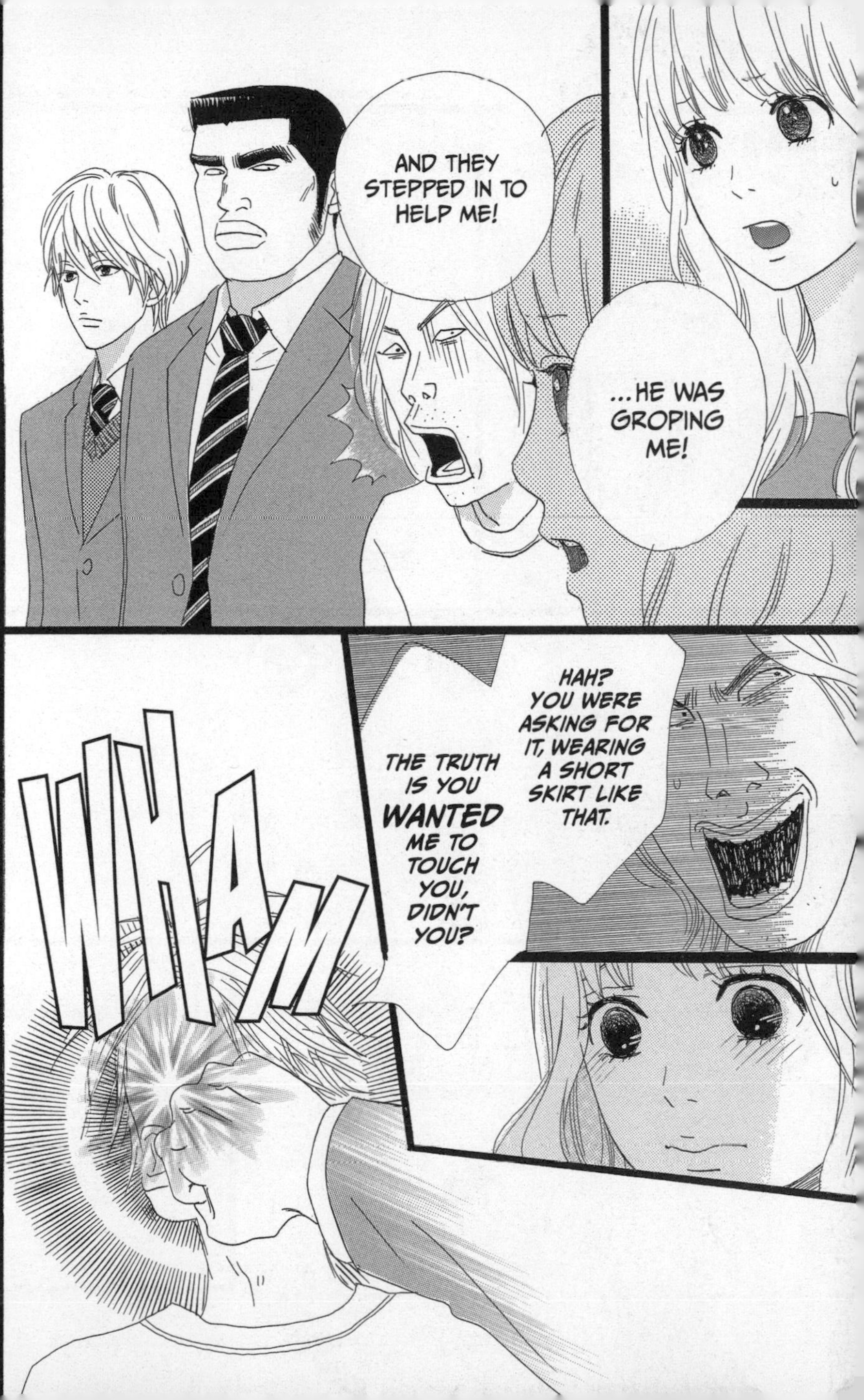
...HE WAS GROPING ME!
AND THEY STEPPED IN TO HELP ME!
HAH? YOU WERE ASKING FOR IT, WEARING A SHORT SKIRT LIKE THAT.
THE TRUTH IS YOU WANTED ME TO TOUCH YOU, DIDN'T YOU?
WHAM

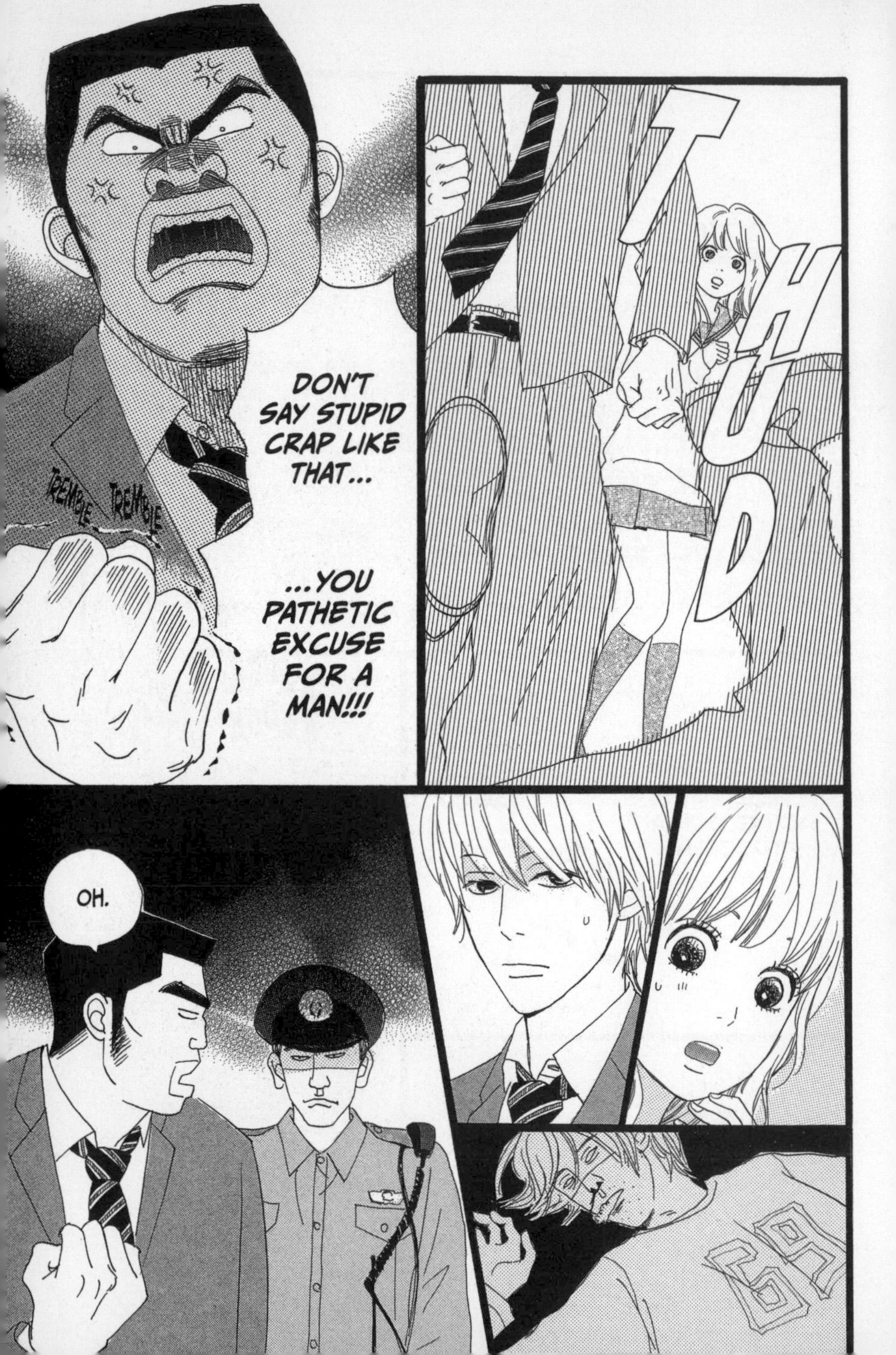
THUD
DON'T SAY STUPID CRAP LIKE THAT...
TREMBLE TREMBLE
...YOU PATHETIC EXCUSE FOR A MAN!!!
OH.

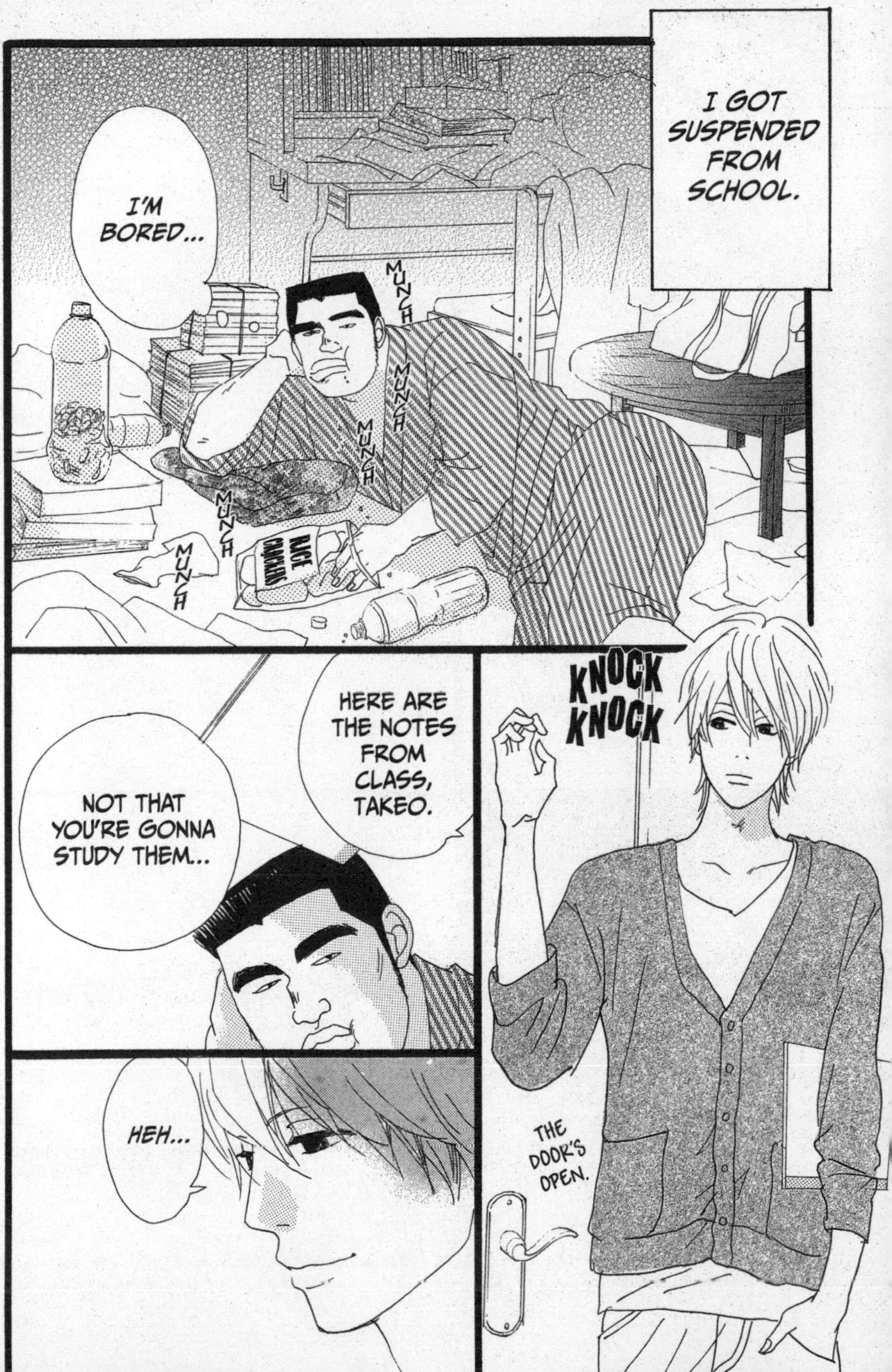
I GOT SUSPENDED FROM SCHOOL.
I'M BORED...
MUNCH
MUNCH
MUNCH
MUNCH
MUNCH
RICE CRACKERS
KNOCK KNOCK
THE DOOR'S OPEN.
HERE ARE THE NOTES FROM CLASS, TAKEO.
NOT THAT YOU'RE GONNA STUDY THEM...
HEH...

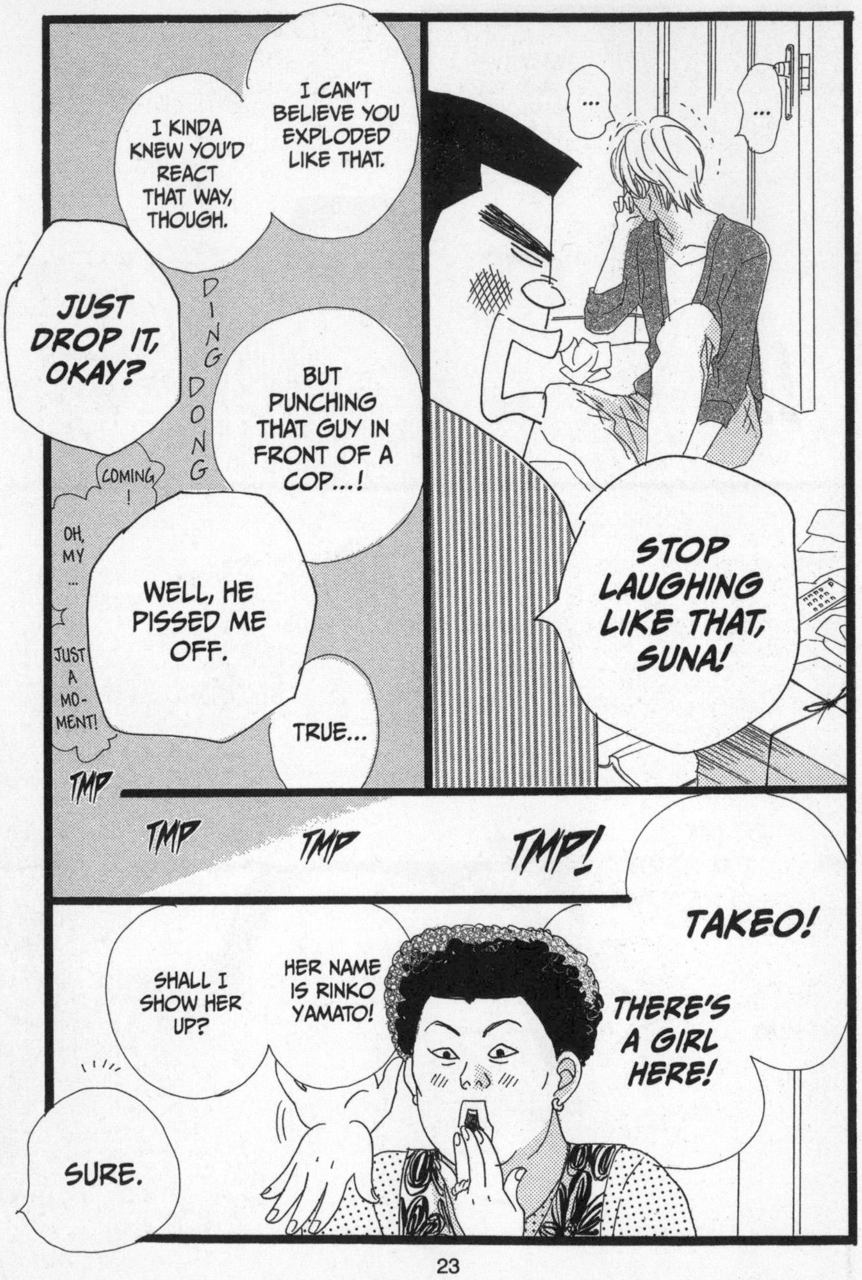
...
...
STOP LAUGHING LIKE THAT, SUNA!
I CAN'T BELIEVE YOU EXPLODED LIKE THAT.
I KINDA KNEW YOU'D REACT THAT WAY, THOUGH.
JUST DROP IT, OKAY?
BUT PUNCHING THAT GUY IN FRONT OF A COP...!
WELL, HE PISSED ME OFF.
TRUE...
DING DONG
COMING!
OH, MY...
JUST A MO-MENT!
TMP
TMP
TMP
TMP!
TAKEO!
THERE'S A GIRL HERE!
HER NAME IS RINKO YAMATO!
SHALL I SHOW HER UP?
SURE.

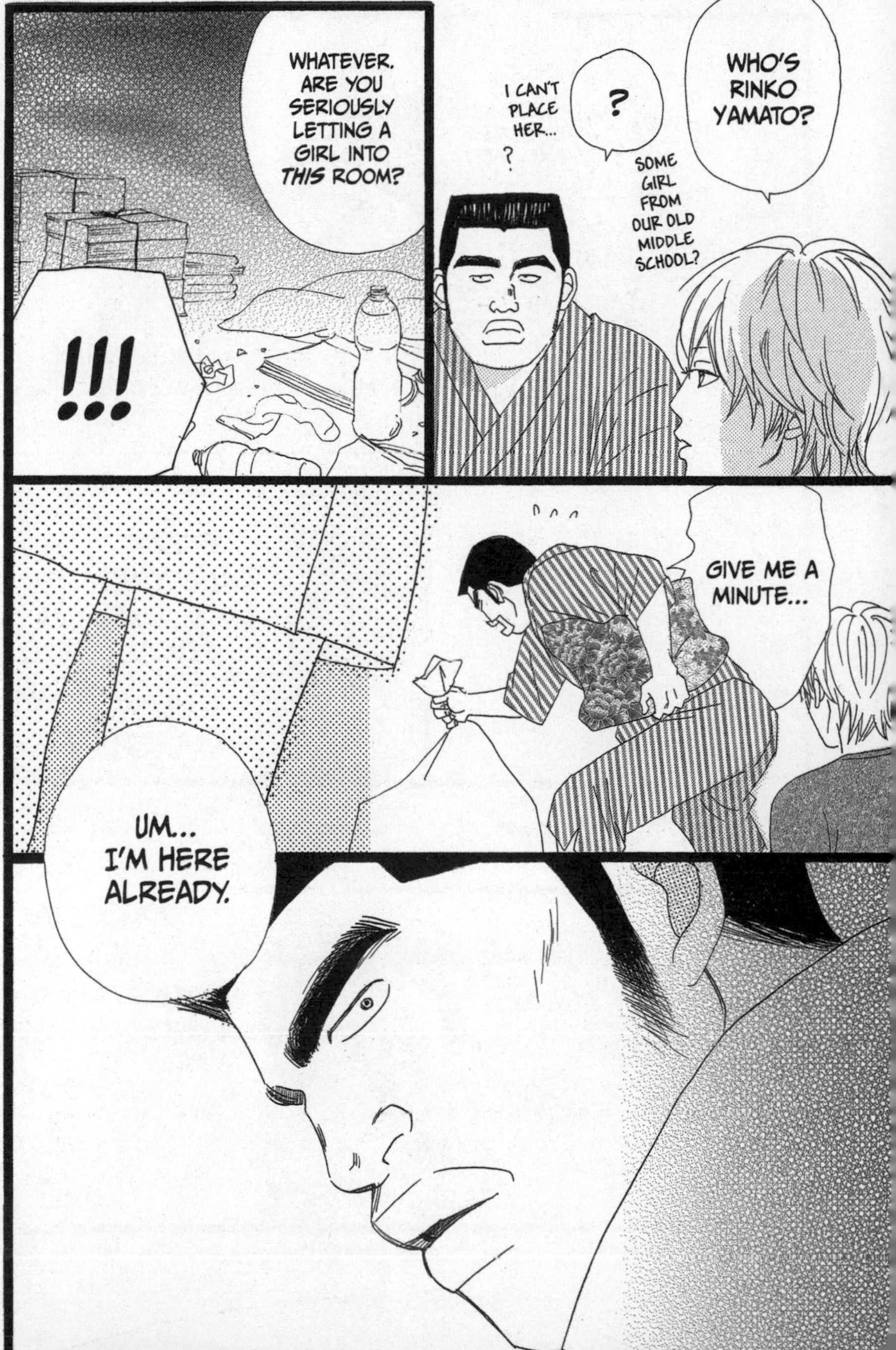
WHO'S RINKO YAMATO?
?
SOME GIRL FROM OUR OLD MIDDLE SCHOOL?
I CAN'T PLACE HER...
?
WHATEVER. ARE YOU SERIOUSLY LETTING A GIRL INTO *THIS* ROOM?
!!!
GIVE ME A MINUTE...
UM... I'M HERE ALREADY.

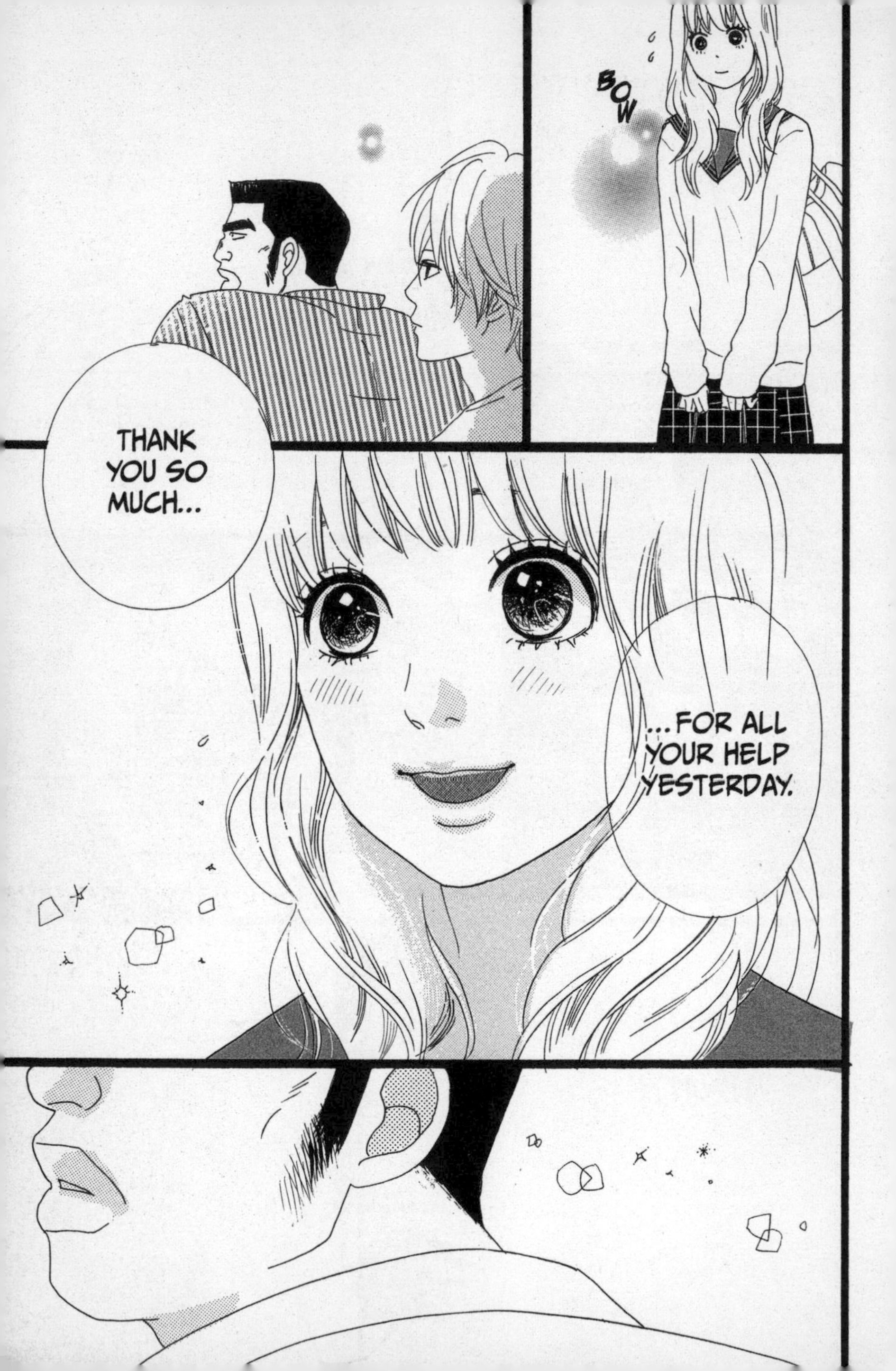
BOW
THANK YOU SO MUCH...
...FOR ALL YOUR HELP YESTERDAY.

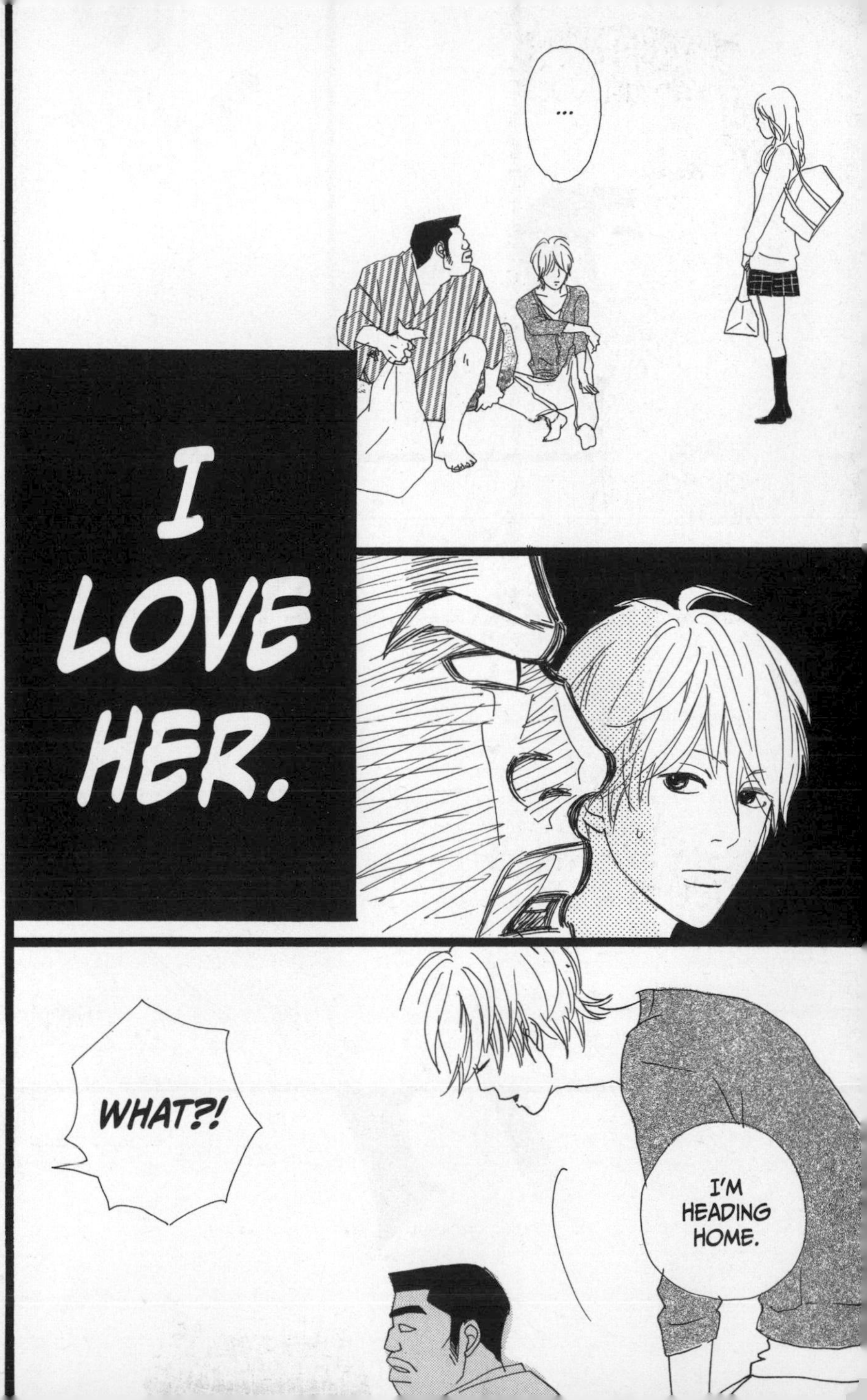
...
I LOVE HER.
I'M HEADING HOME.
WHAT?!

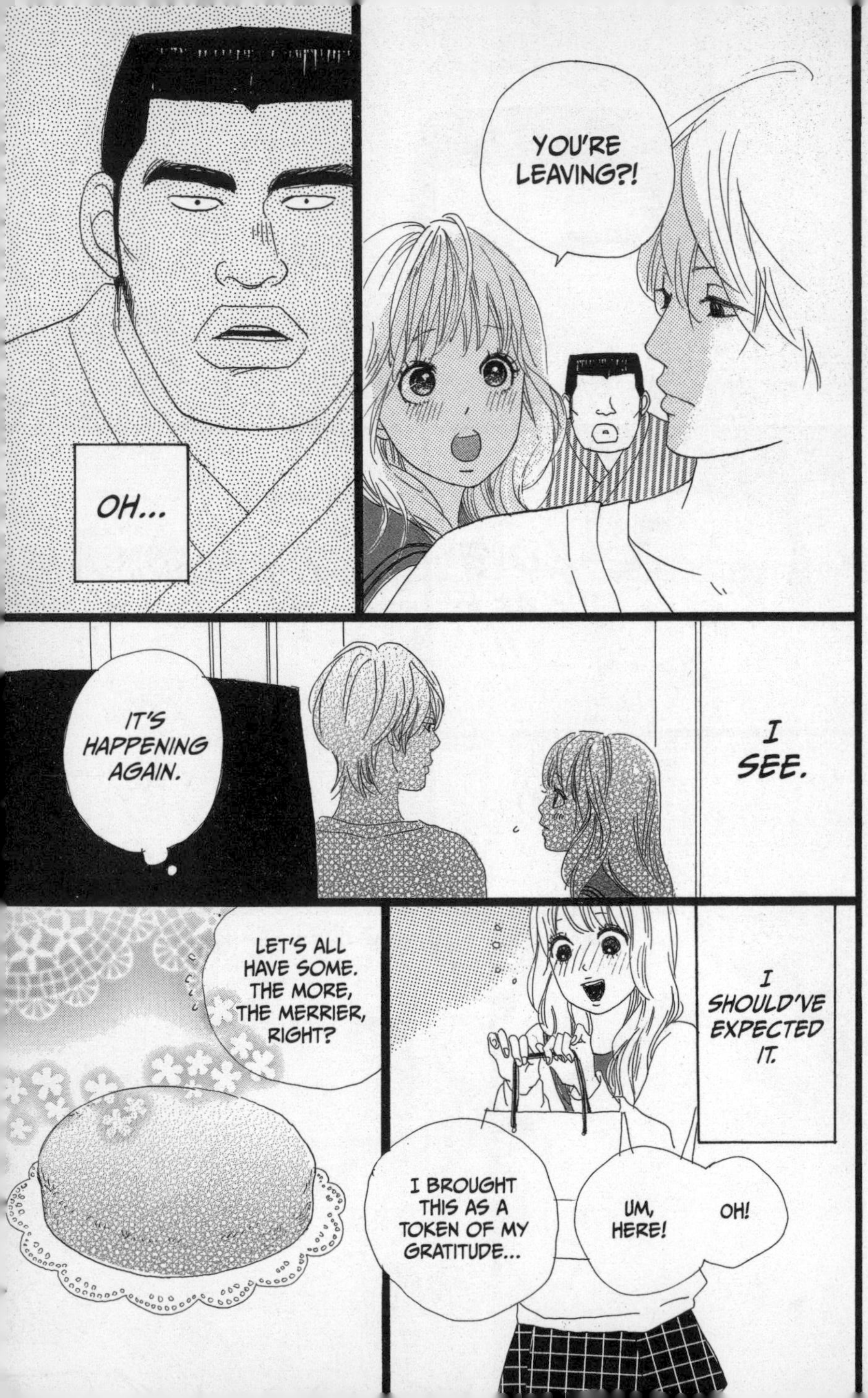
YOU'RE LEAVING?!
OH...
I SEE.
IT'S HAPPENING AGAIN.
I SHOULD'VE EXPECTED IT.
OH!
UM, HERE!
I BROUGHT THIS AS A TOKEN OF MY GRATITUDE...
LET'S ALL HAVE SOME. THE MORE, THE MERRIER, RIGHT?

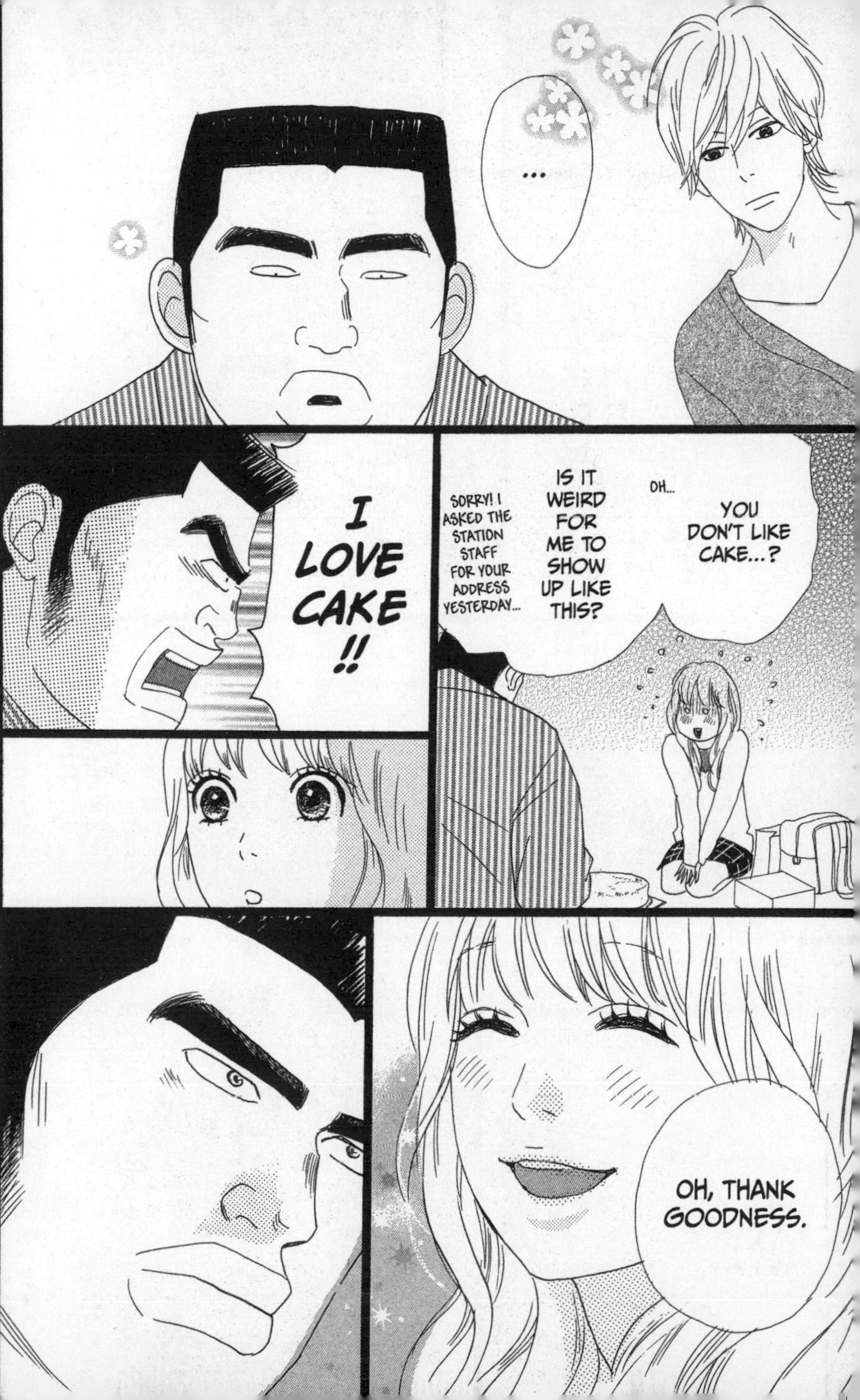
...
YOU DON'T LIKE CAKE...?
OH...
IS IT WEIRD FOR ME TO SHOW UP LIKE THIS?
SORRY! I ASKED THE STATION STAFF FOR YOUR ADDRESS YESTERDAY...
I LOVE CAKE!!
OH, THANK GOODNESS.

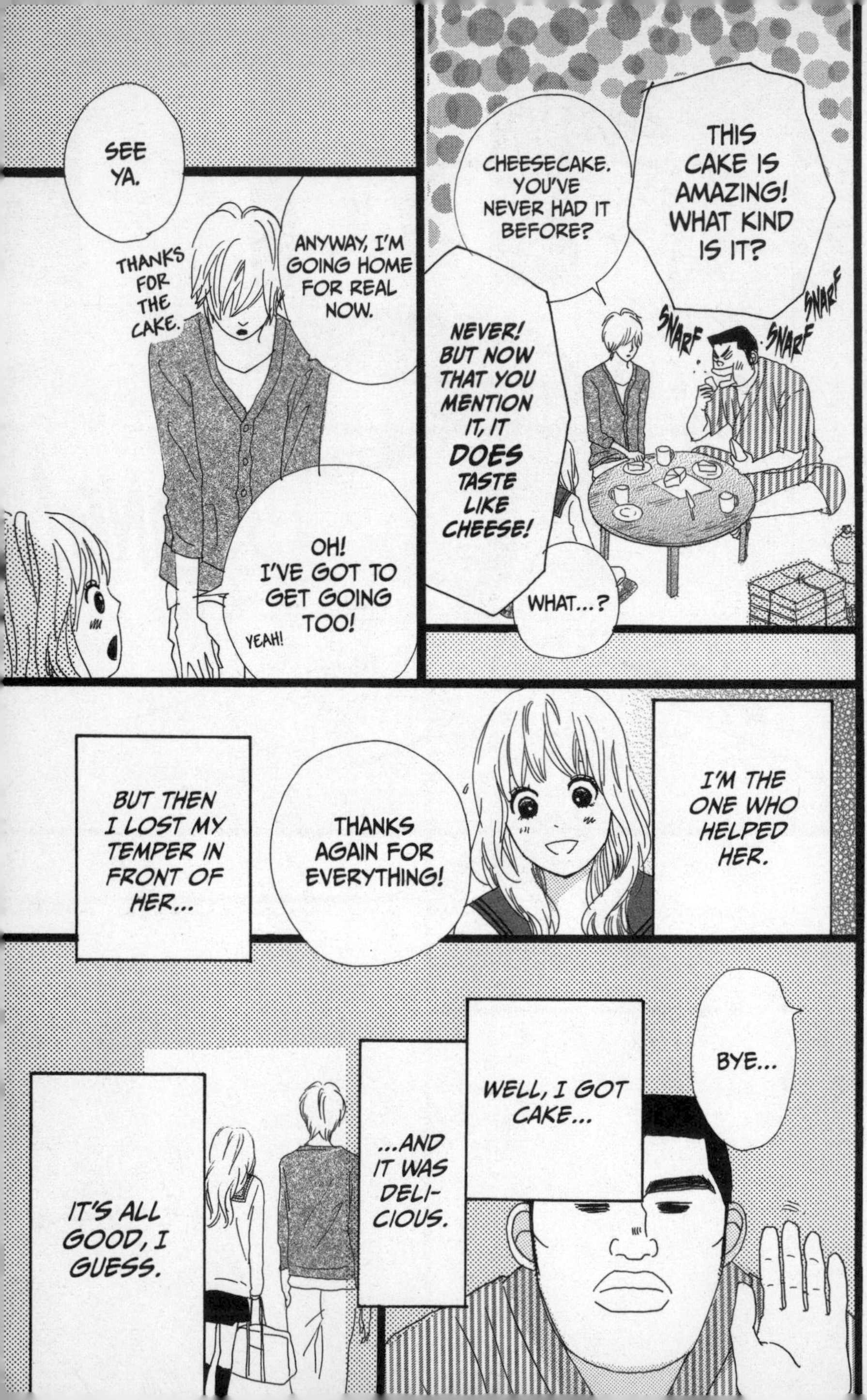
THIS CAKE IS AMAZING! WHAT KIND IS IT?
SNARF SNARF SNARF
CHEESECAKE. YOU'VE NEVER HAD IT BEFORE?
NEVER! BUT NOW THAT YOU MENTION IT, IT DOES TASTE LIKE CHEESE!
WHAT...?
ANYWAY, I'M GOING HOME FOR REAL NOW.
SEE YA.
THANKS FOR THE CAKE.
OH! I'VE GOT TO GET GOING TOO!
YEAH!
I'M THE ONE WHO HELPED HER.
THANKS AGAIN FOR EVERYTHING!
BUT THEN I LOST MY TEMPER IN FRONT OF HER...
BYE...
WELL, I GOT CAKE...
...AND IT WAS DELICIOUS.
IT'S ALL GOOD, I GUESS.

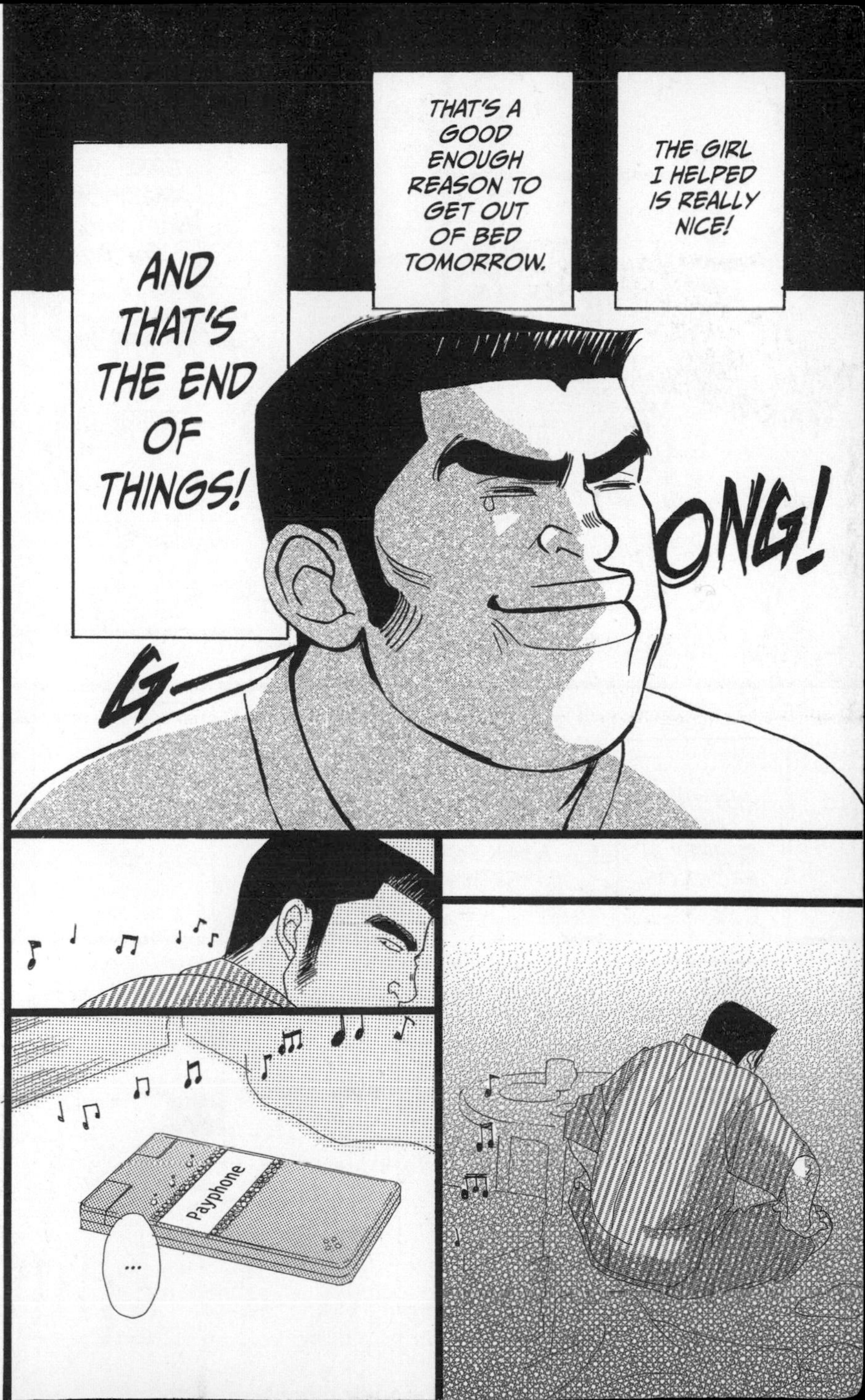
THE GIRL I HELPED IS REALLY NICE!
THAT'S A GOOD ENOUGH REASON TO GET OUT OF BED TOMORROW.
AND THAT'S THE END OF THINGS!
G— ONG!
Payphone
...

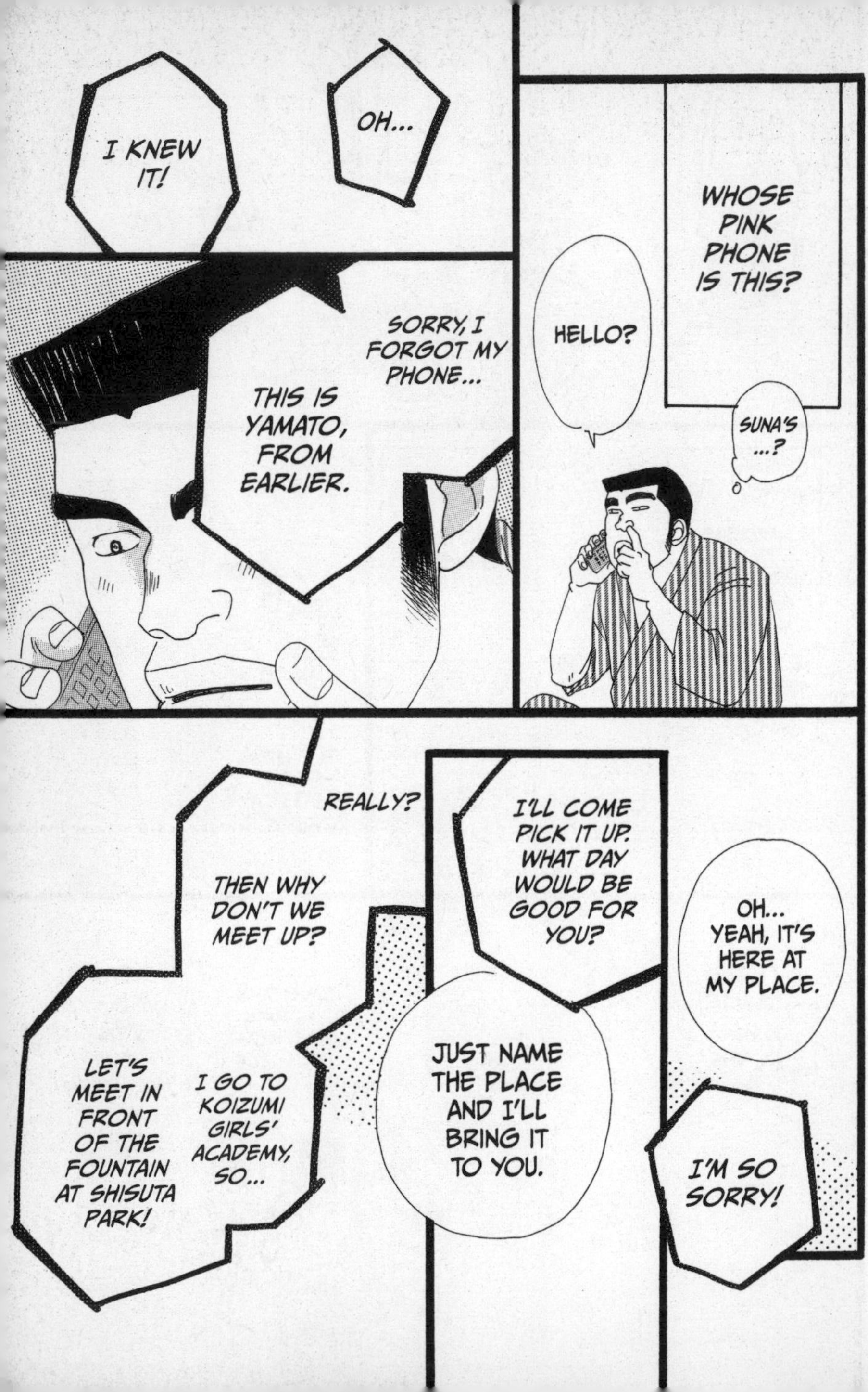
WHOSE PINK PHONE IS THIS?
HELLO?
SUNA'S ...?
OH...
I KNEW IT!
SORRY, I FORGOT MY PHONE...
THIS IS YAMATO, FROM EARLIER.
OH... YEAH, IT'S HERE AT MY PLACE.
I'M SO SORRY!
I'LL COME PICK IT UP. WHAT DAY WOULD BE GOOD FOR YOU?
JUST NAME THE PLACE AND I'LL BRING IT TO YOU.
REALLY?
THEN WHY DON'T WE MEET UP?
I GO TO KOIZUMI GIRLS' ACADEMY, SO...
LET'S MEET IN FRONT OF THE FOUNTAIN AT SHISUTA PARK!

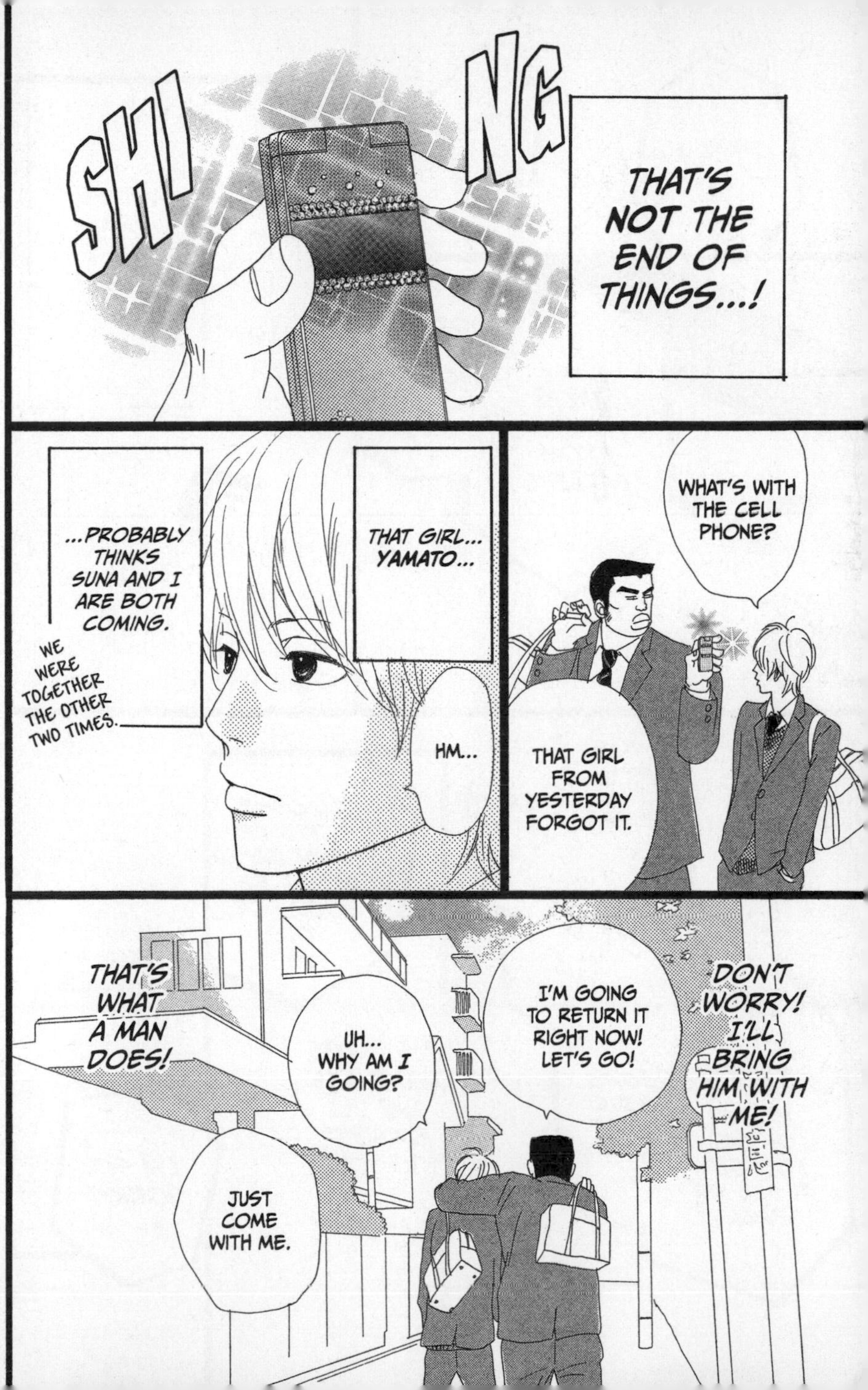
THAT'S NOT THE END OF THINGS...!
SHING
WHAT'S WITH THE CELL PHONE?
THAT GIRL FROM YESTERDAY FORGOT IT.
THAT GIRL... YAMATO...
HM...
...PROBABLY THINKS SUNA AND I ARE BOTH COMING.
WE WERE TOGETHER THE OTHER TWO TIMES.
I'M GOING TO RETURN IT RIGHT NOW! LET'S GO!
DON'T WORRY! I'LL BRING HIM WITH ME!
UH... WHY AM I GOING?
JUST COME WITH ME.
THAT'S WHAT A MAN DOES!

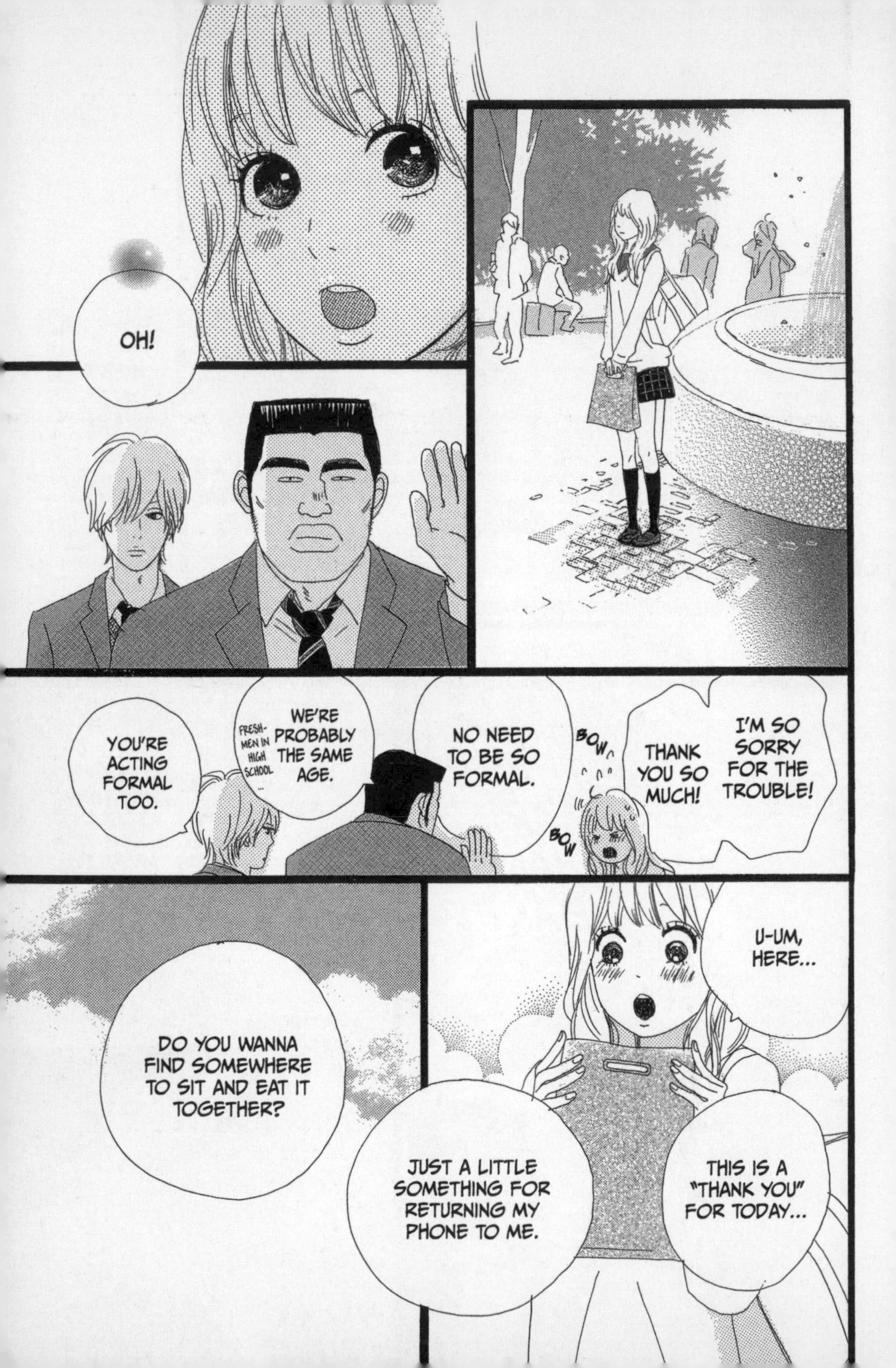
OH!
I'M SO SORRY FOR THE TROUBLE!
THANK YOU SO MUCH!
BOW BOW
NO NEED TO BE SO FORMAL.
WE'RE PROBABLY THE SAME AGE.
FRESHMEN IN HIGH SCHOOL...
YOU'RE ACTING FORMAL TOO.
U-UM, HERE...
THIS IS A "THANK YOU" FOR TODAY...
JUST A LITTLE SOMETHING FOR RETURNING MY PHONE TO ME.
DO YOU WANNA FIND SOMEWHERE TO SIT AND EAT IT TOGETHER?

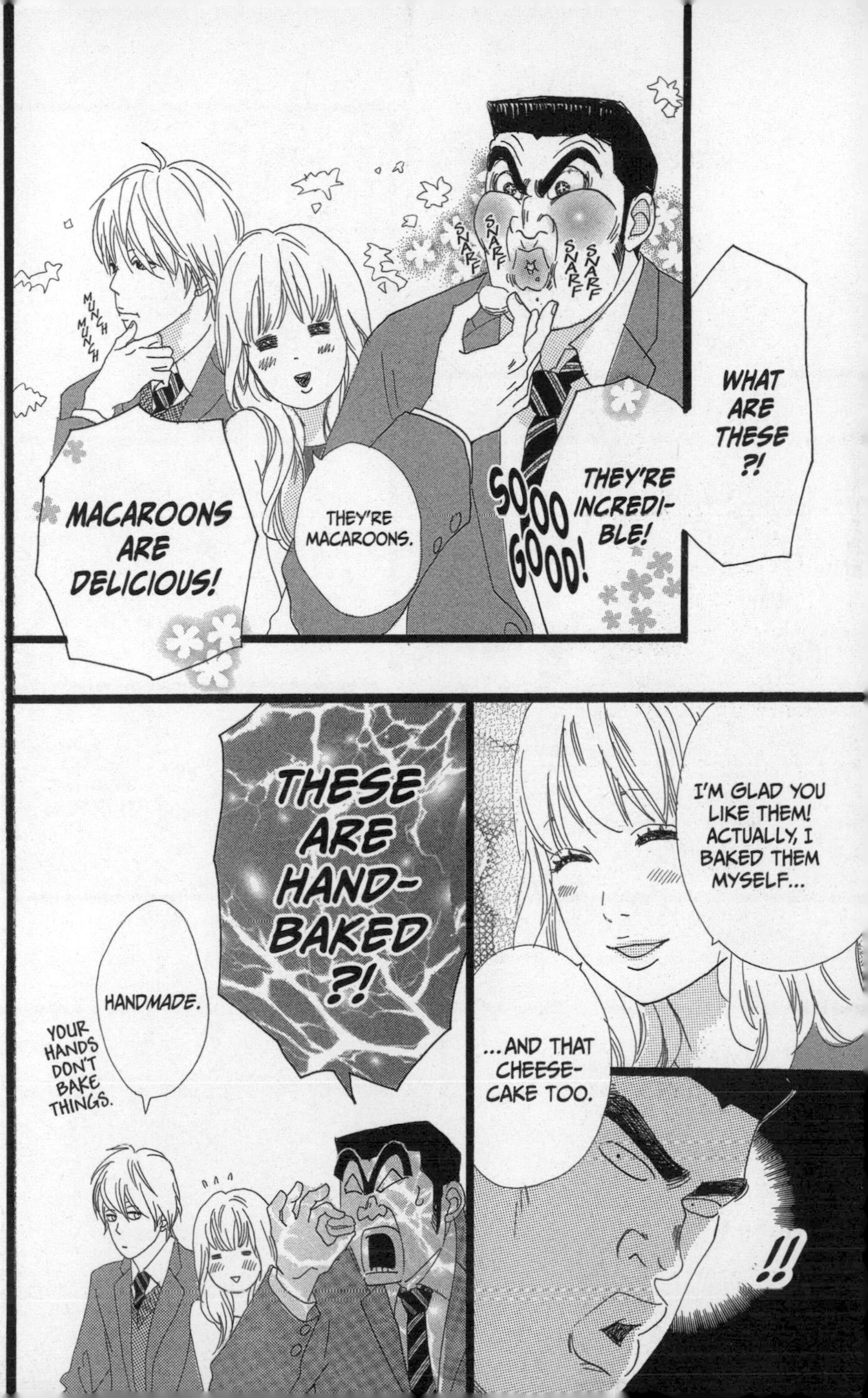
WHAT ARE THESE?!
THEY'RE INCREDIBLE!
SOOO GOOD!
SNARF SNARF SNARF SNARF
THEY'RE MACAROONS.
MUNCH MUNCH
MACAROONS ARE DELICIOUS!
I'M GLAD YOU LIKE THEM! ACTUALLY, I BAKED THEM MYSELF...
...AND THAT CHEESE-CAKE TOO.
!!
THESE ARE HAND-BAKED?!
HANDMADE.
YOUR HANDS DON'T BAKE THINGS.

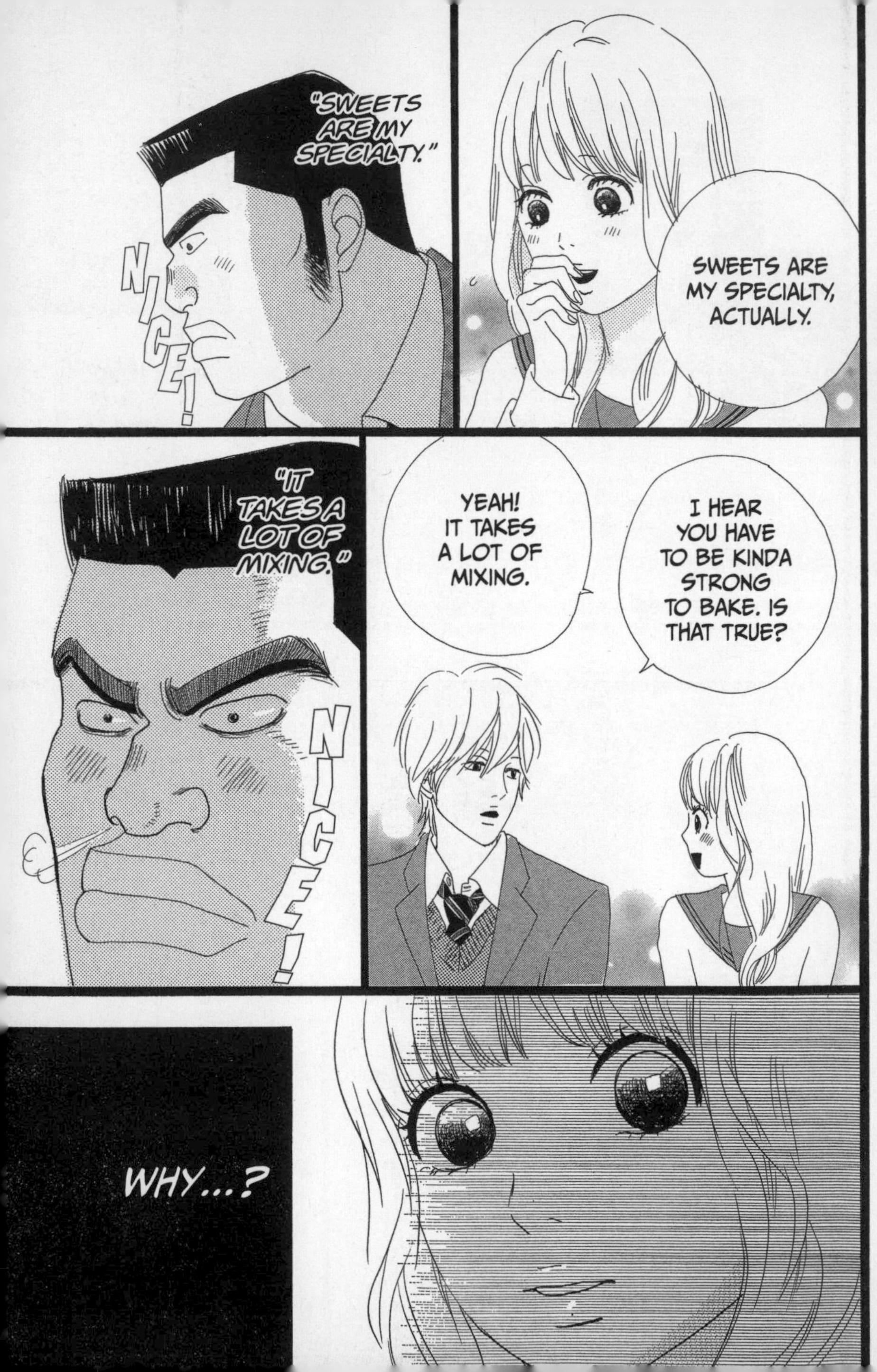
SWEETS ARE MY SPECIALTY, ACTUALLY.
"SWEETS ARE MY SPECIALTY."
NICE!
I HEAR YOU HAVE TO BE KINDA STRONG TO BAKE. IS THAT TRUE?
YEAH! IT TAKES A LOT OF MIXING.
"IT TAKES A LOT OF MIXING."
NICE!
WHY...?

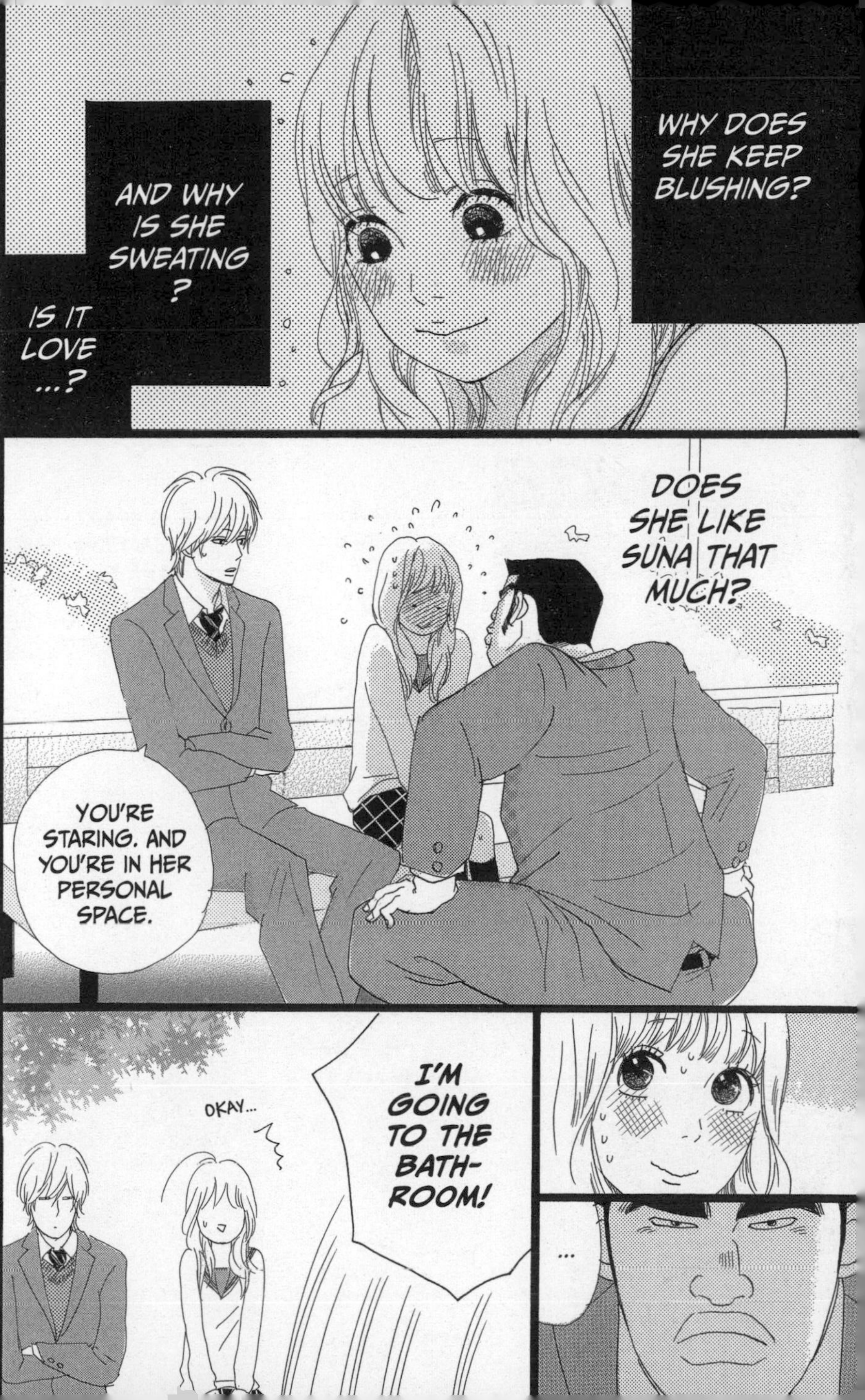
WHY DOES SHE KEEP BLUSHING?
AND WHY IS SHE SWEATING?
IS IT LOVE...?
DOES SHE LIKE SUNA THAT MUCH?
YOU'RE STARING. AND YOU'RE IN HER PERSONAL SPACE.
...
I'M GOING TO THE BATH-ROOM!
OKAY...

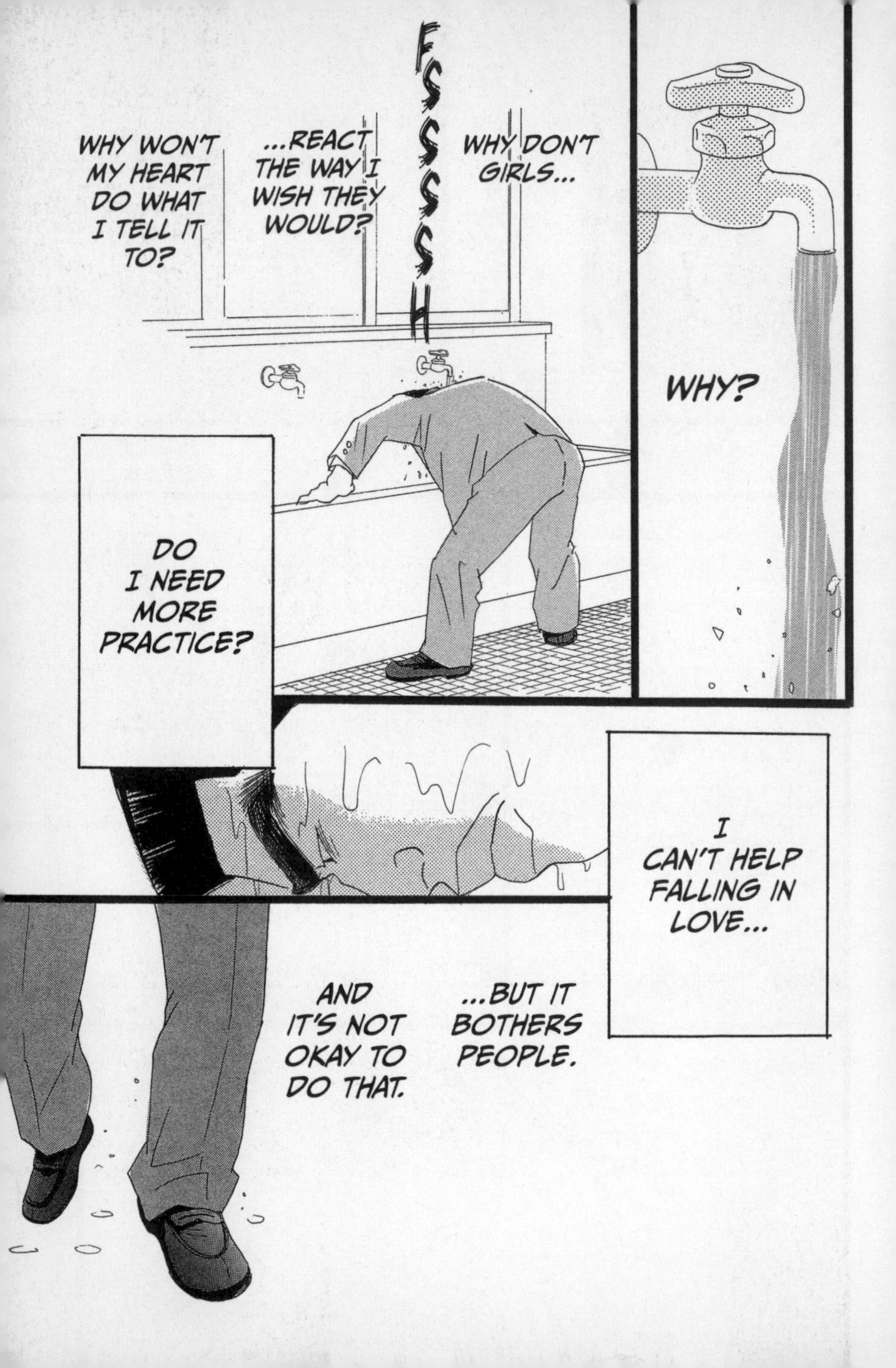
WHY?
WHY DON'T GIRLS...
FSSSSH
...REACT THE WAY I WISH THEY WOULD?
WHY WON'T MY HEART DO WHAT I TELL IT TO?
DO I NEED MORE PRACTICE?
I CAN'T HELP FALLING IN LOVE...
...BUT IT BOTHERS PEOPLE.
AND IT'S NOT OKAY TO DO THAT.

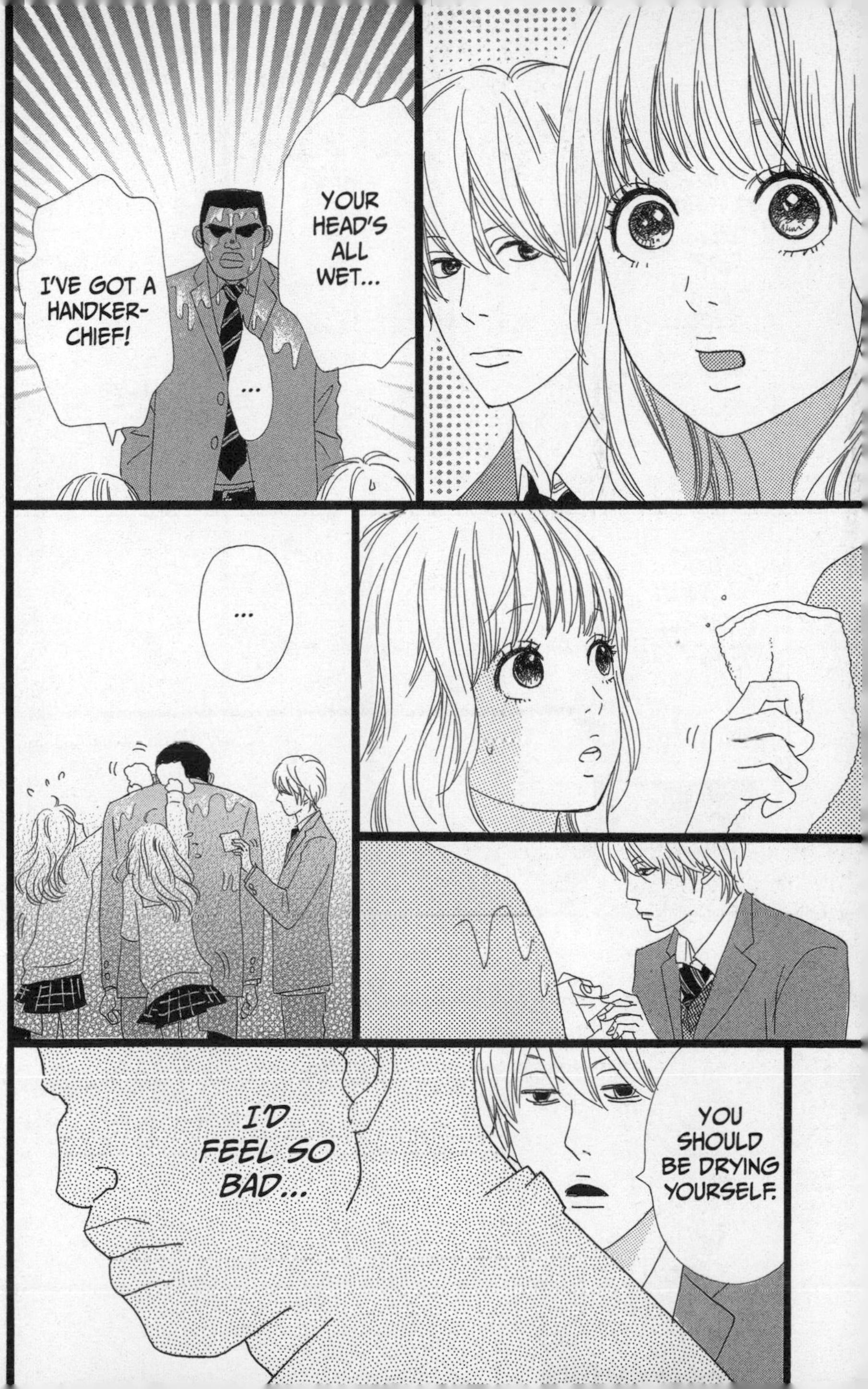
YOUR HEAD'S ALL WET...
I'VE GOT A HANDKER-CHIEF!
...
...
YOU SHOULD BE DRYING YOURSELF.
I'D FEEL SO BAD...

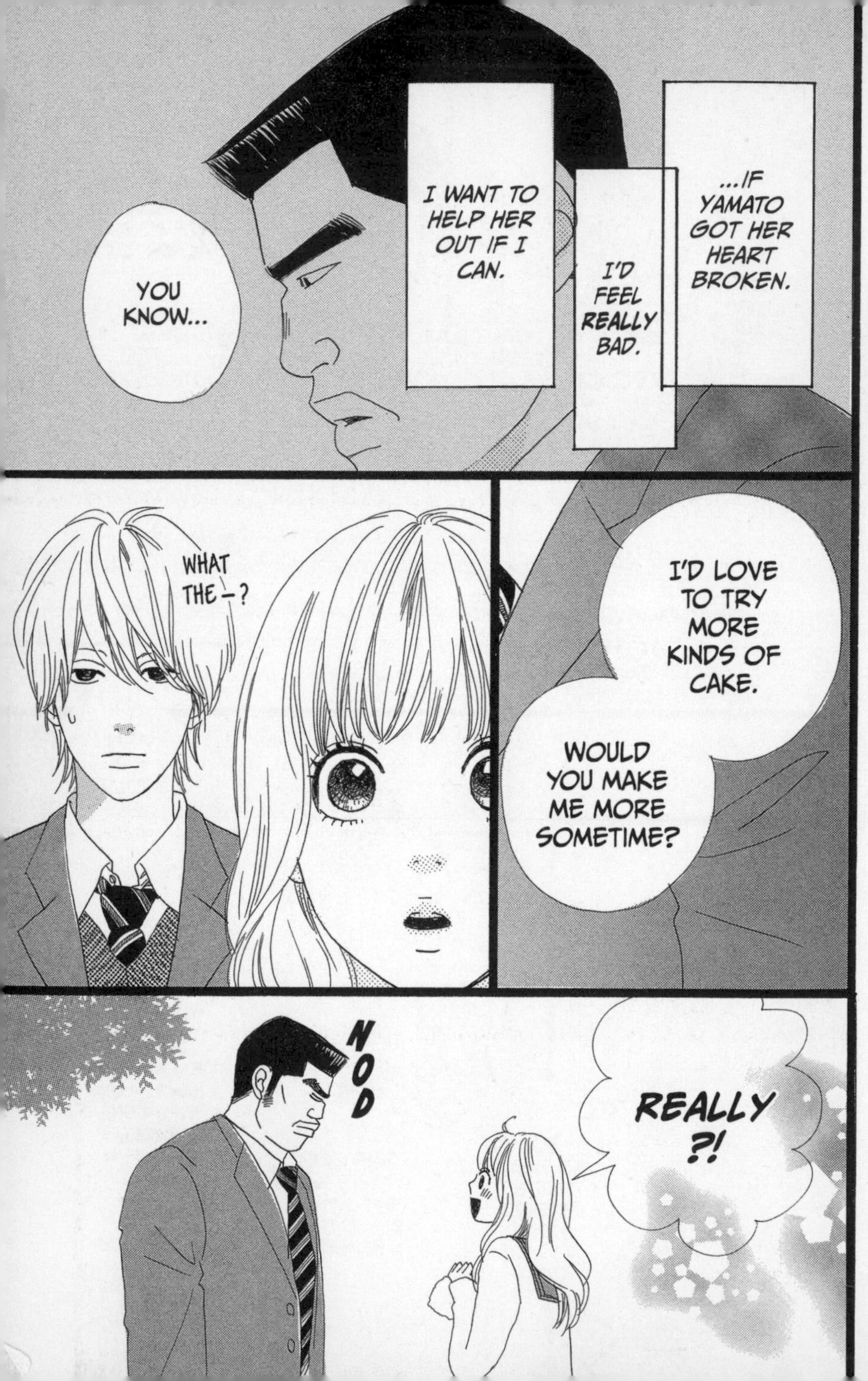
...IF YAMATO GOT HER HEART BROKEN.
I'D FEEL REALLY BAD.
I WANT TO HELP HER OUT IF I CAN.
YOU KNOW...
I'D LOVE TO TRY MORE KINDS OF CAKE.
WOULD YOU MAKE ME MORE SOMETIME?
WHAT THE—?
REALLY ?!
NOD

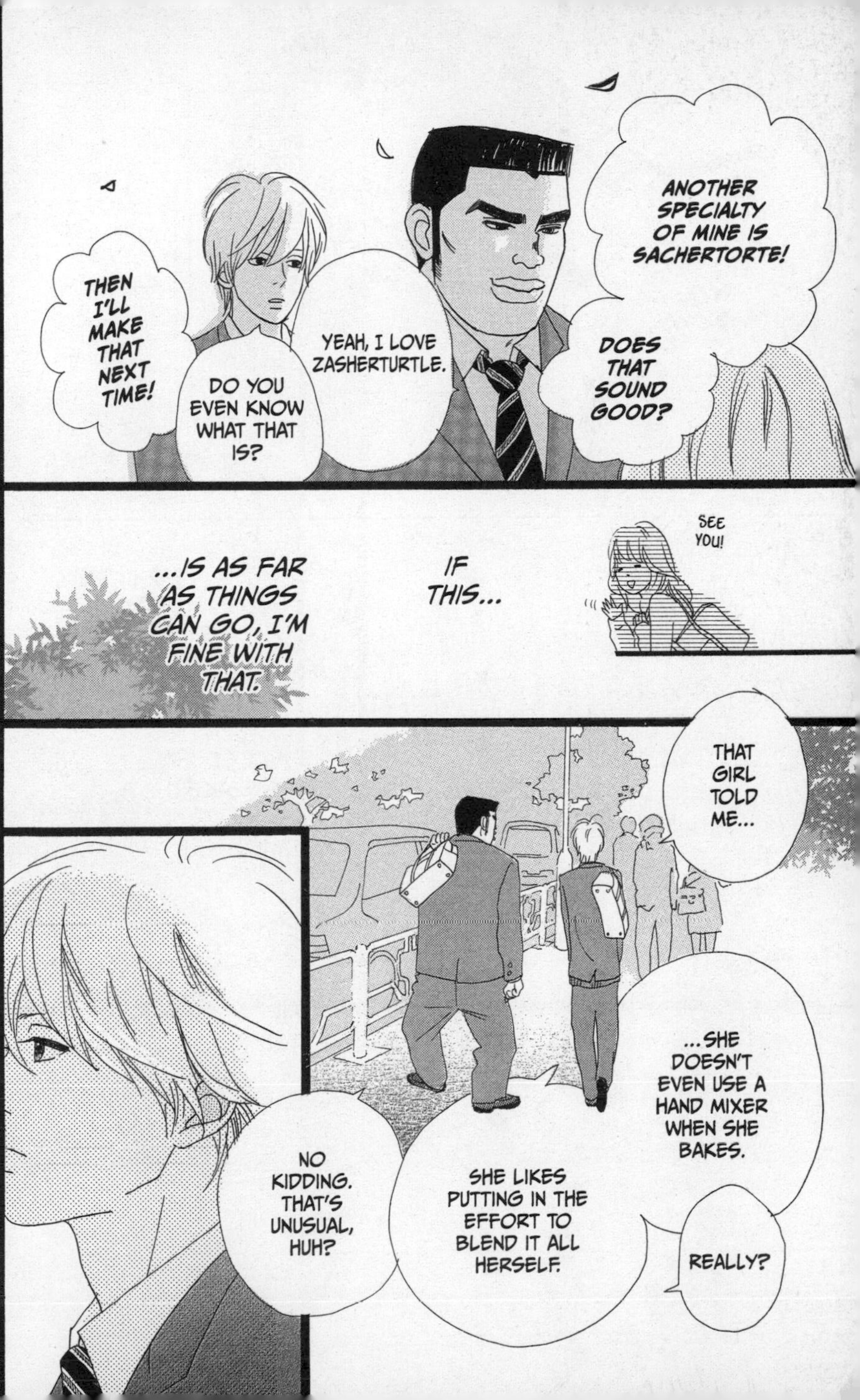
ANOTHER SPECIALTY OF MINE IS SACHERTORTE!
DOES THAT SOUND GOOD?
YEAH, I LOVE ZASHERTURTLE.
DO YOU EVEN KNOW WHAT THAT IS?
THEN I'LL MAKE THAT NEXT TIME!
SEE YOU!
IF THIS...
...IS AS FAR AS THINGS CAN GO, I'M FINE WITH THAT.
THAT GIRL TOLD ME...
...SHE DOESN'T EVEN USE A HAND MIXER WHEN SHE BAKES.
REALLY?
SHE LIKES PUTTING IN THE EFFORT TO BLEND IT ALL HERSELF.
NO KIDDING. THAT'S UNUSUAL, HUH?

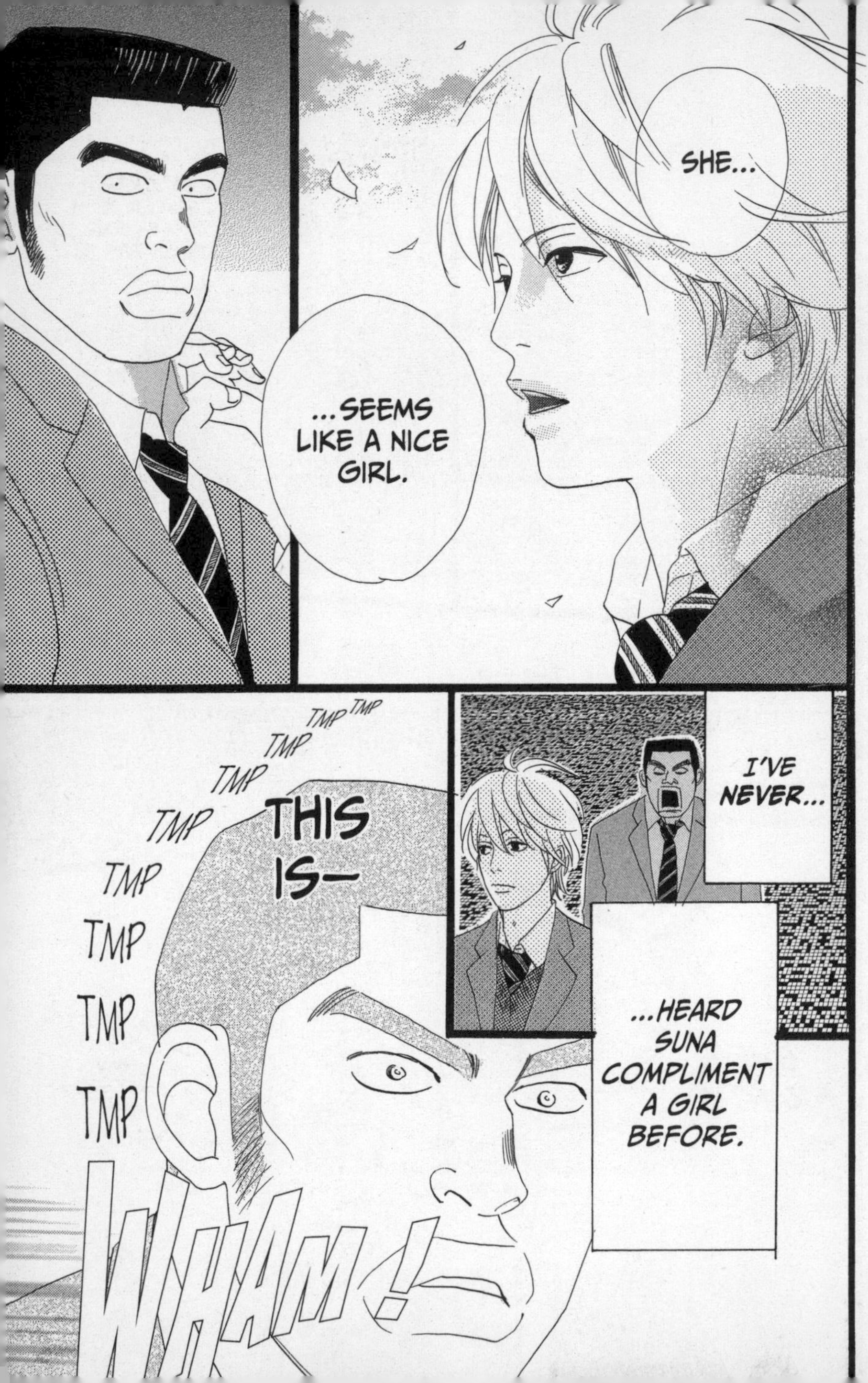
SHE...
...SEEMS LIKE A NICE GIRL.
I'VE NEVER...
...HEARD SUNA COMPLIMENT A GIRL BEFORE.
THIS IS—
TMP TMP TMP TMP TMP TMP TMP TMP TMP TMP
WHAM!

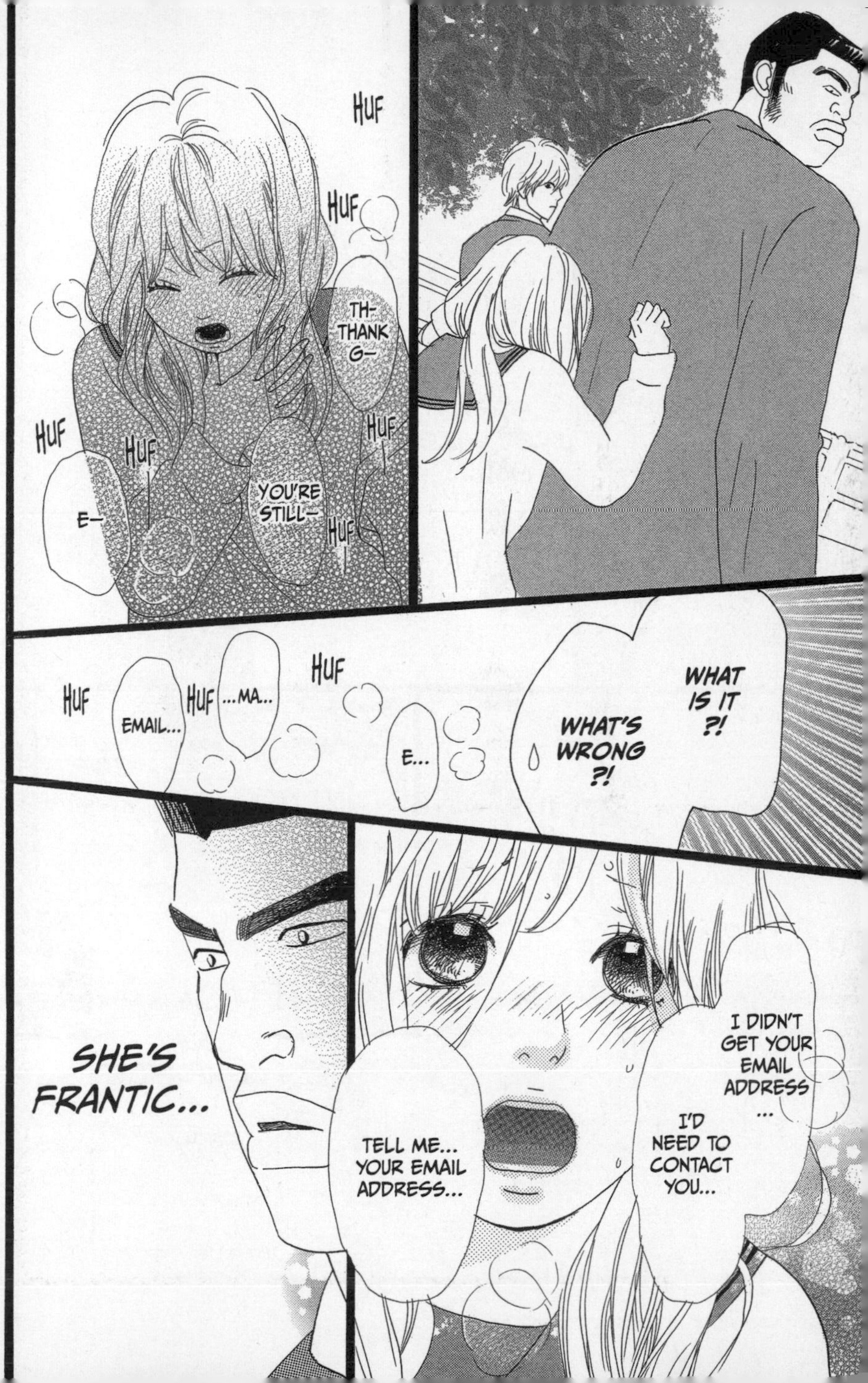
HUF
HUF
TH-THANK G—
HUF
HUF
YOU'RE STILL—
HUF
E—
HUF
WHAT IS IT ?!
WHAT'S WRONG ?!
E...
HUF
...MA...
HUF
EMAIL...
HUF
I DIDN'T GET YOUR EMAIL ADDRESS ...
I'D NEED TO CONTACT YOU...
TELL ME... YOUR EMAIL ADDRESS...
SHE'S FRANTIC...

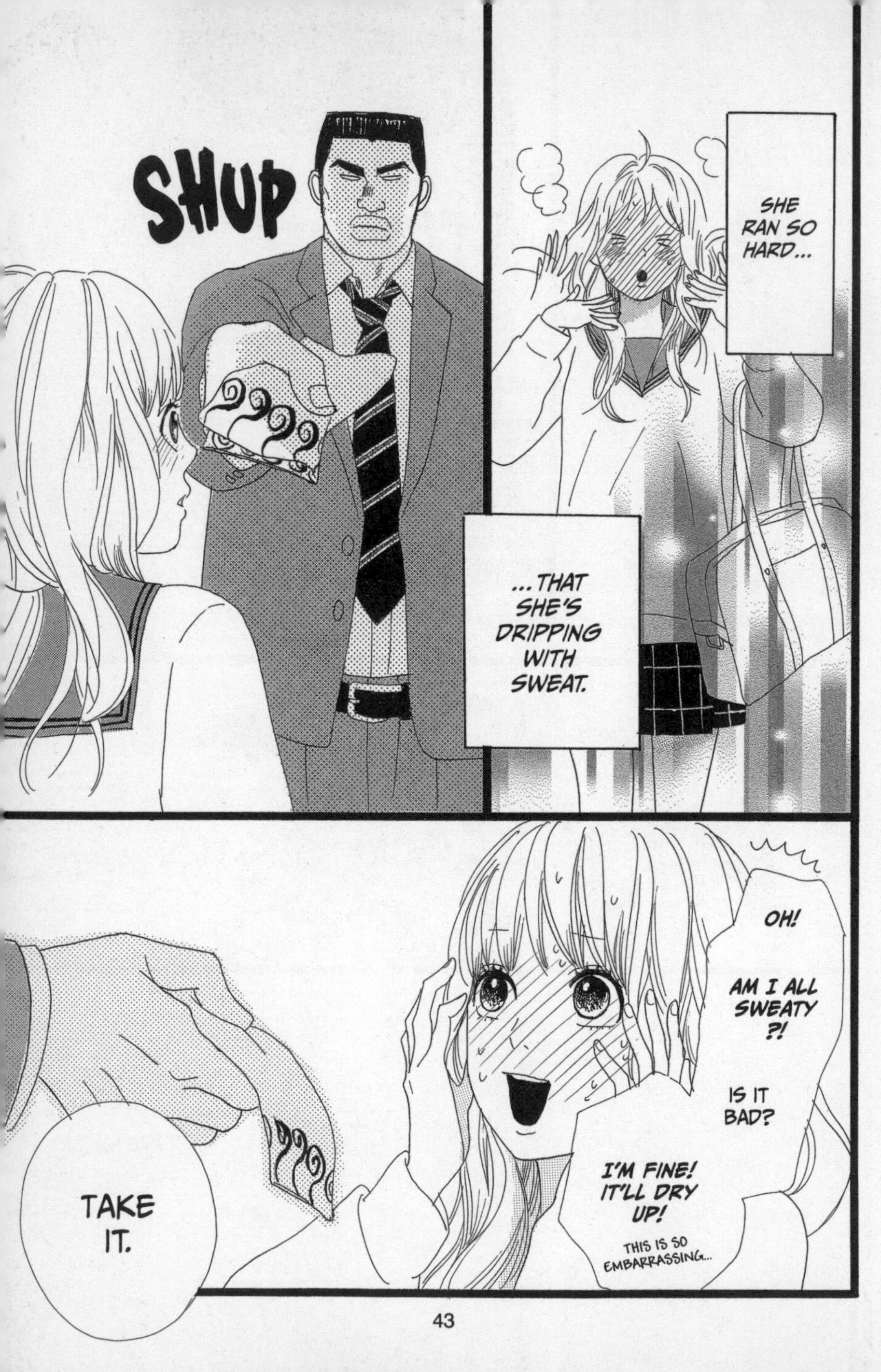
SHE RAN SO HARD...
...THAT SHE'S DRIPPING WITH SWEAT.
SHUP
OH!
AM I ALL SWEATY ?!
IS IT BAD?
I'M FINE! IT'LL DRY UP!
THIS IS SO EMBARRASSING...
TAKE IT.

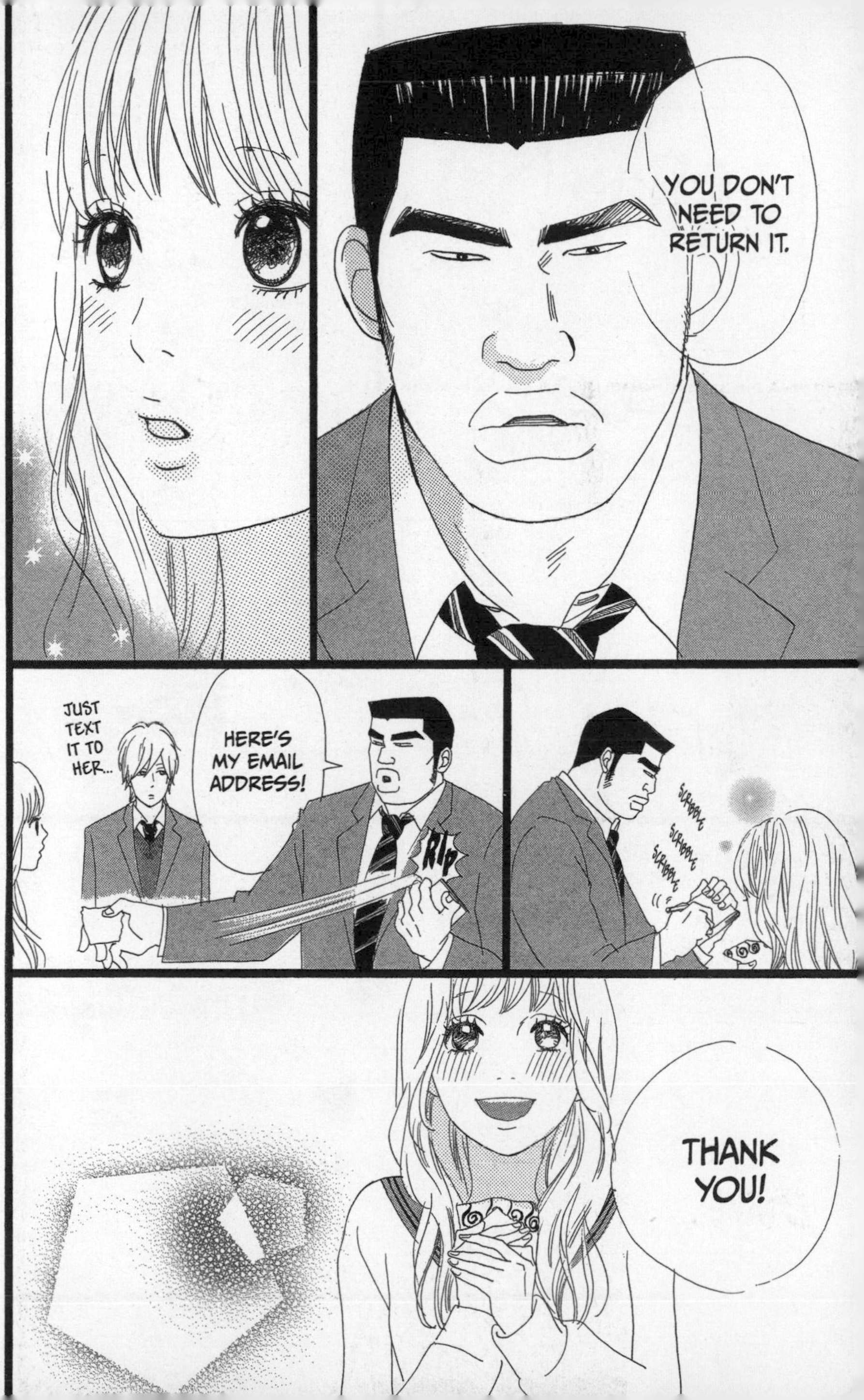
YOU DON'T NEED TO RETURN IT.
SCRIBBLE SCRIBBLE SCRIBBLE
HERE'S MY EMAIL ADDRESS!
JUST TEXT IT TO HER...
RIP
THANK YOU!

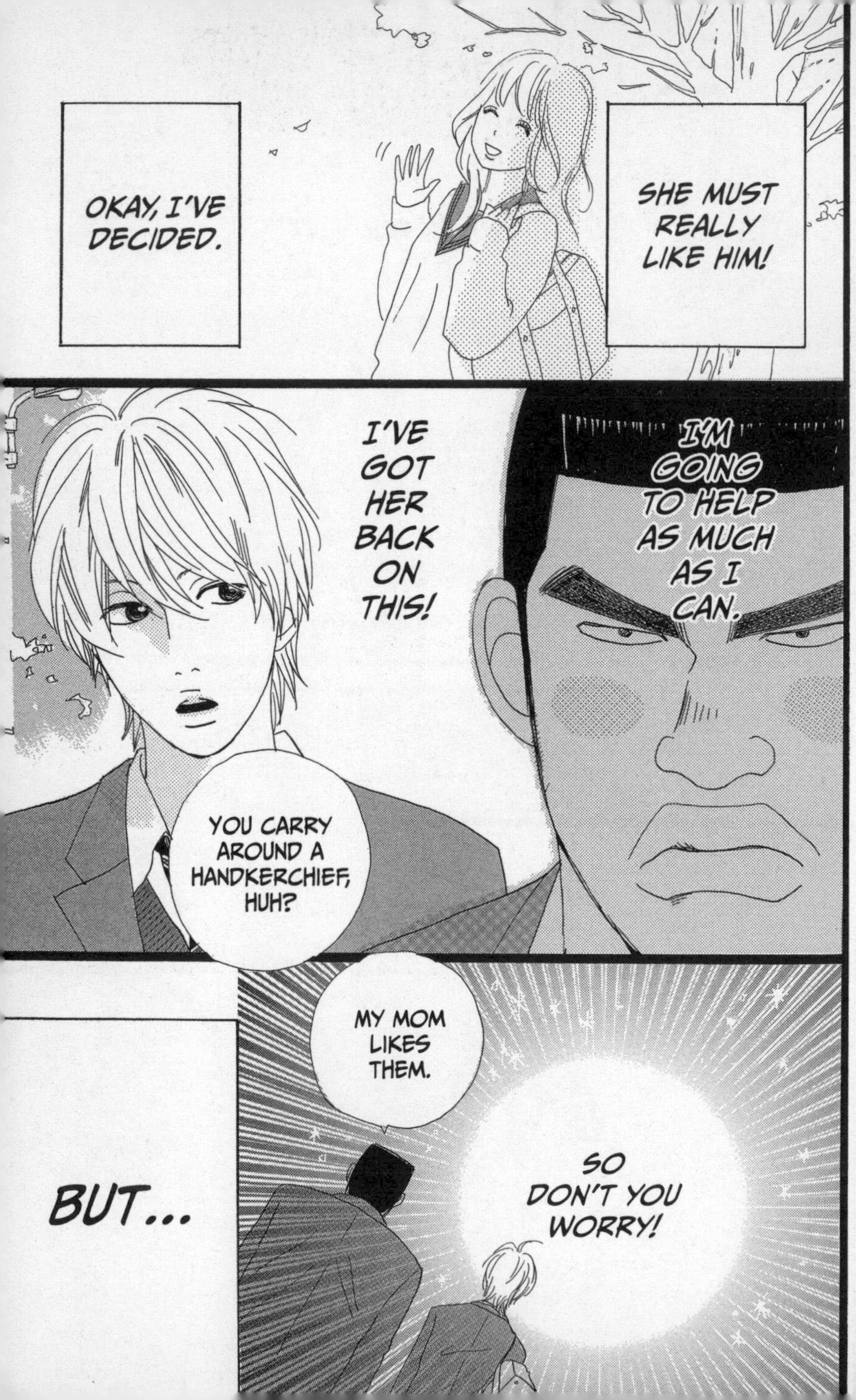
SHE MUST REALLY LIKE HIM!
OKAY, I'VE DECIDED.
I'M GOING TO HELP AS MUCH AS I CAN.
I'VE GOT HER BACK ON THIS!
YOU CARRY AROUND A HANDKERCHIEF, HUH?
MY MOM LIKES THEM.
SO DON'T YOU WORRY!
BUT...

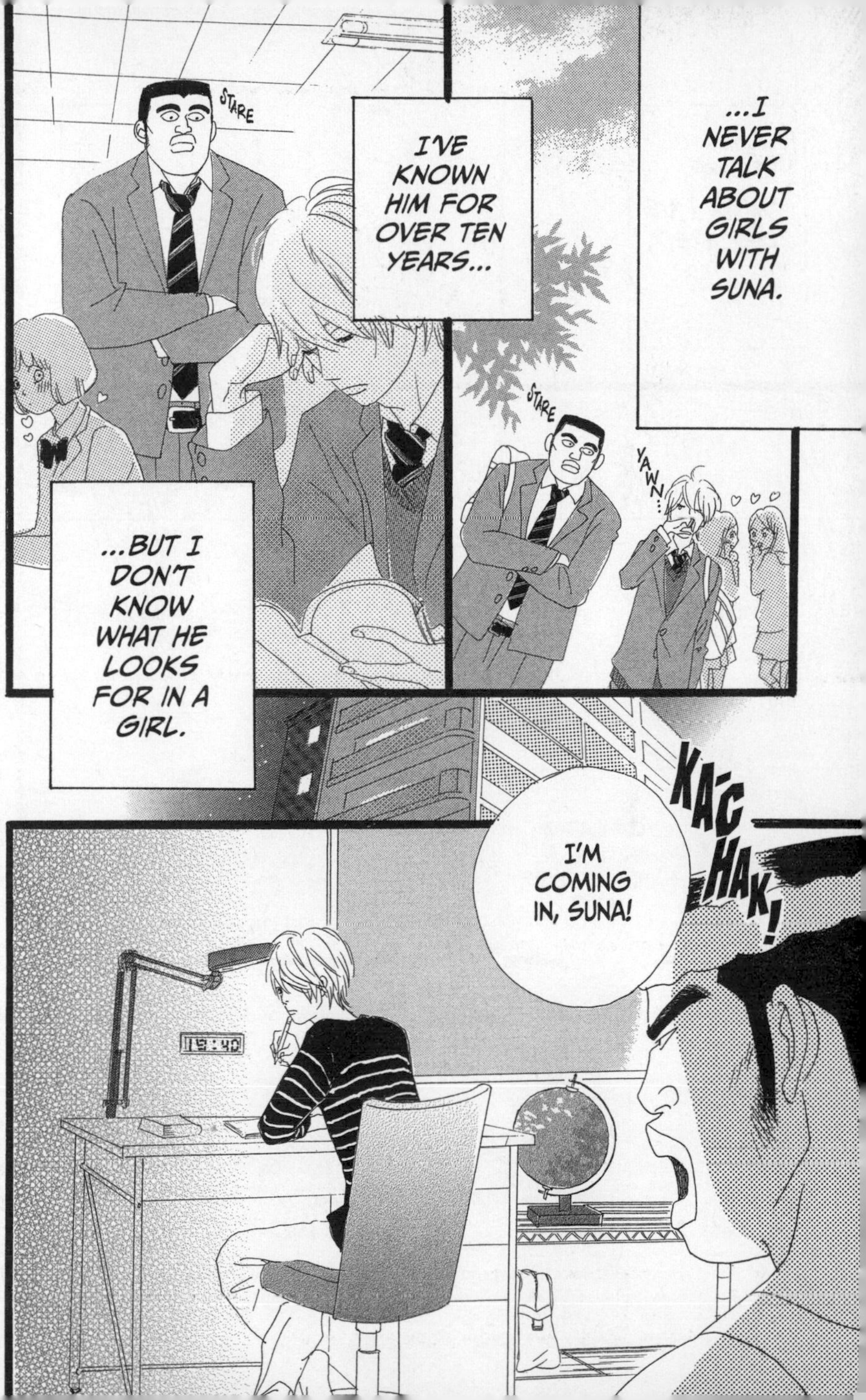
I'VE KNOWN HIM FOR OVER TEN YEARS...
STARE
...BUT I DON'T KNOW WHAT HE LOOKS FOR IN A GIRL.
...I NEVER TALK ABOUT GIRLS WITH SUNA.
STARE
YAWN...
KA-CHAK!
I'M COMING IN, SUNA!

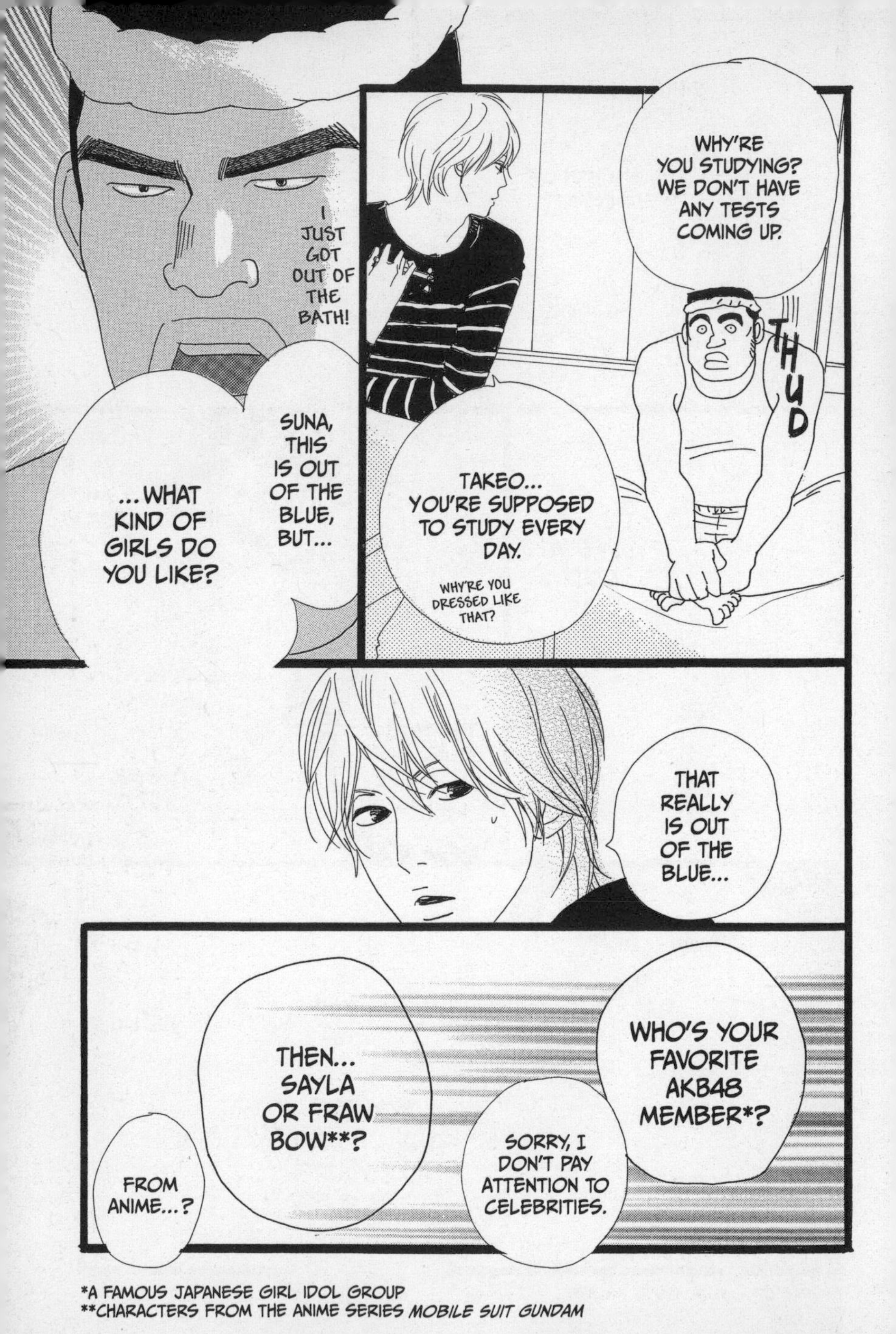
WHY'RE YOU STUDYING? WE DON'T HAVE ANY TESTS COMING UP.
THUD
TAKEO... YOU'RE SUPPOSED TO STUDY EVERY DAY.
WHY'RE YOU DRESSED LIKE THAT?
I JUST GOT OUT OF THE BATH!
SUNA, THIS IS OUT OF THE BLUE, BUT...
...WHAT KIND OF GIRLS DO YOU LIKE?
THAT REALLY IS OUT OF THE BLUE...
WHO'S YOUR FAVORITE AKB48 MEMBER*?
SORRY, I DON'T PAY ATTENTION TO CELEBRITIES.
THEN... SAYLA OR FRAW BOW**?
FROM ANIME...?

*A FAMOUS JAPANESE GIRL IDOL GROUP
**CHARACTERS FROM THE ANIME SERIES *MOBILE SUIT GUNDAM*

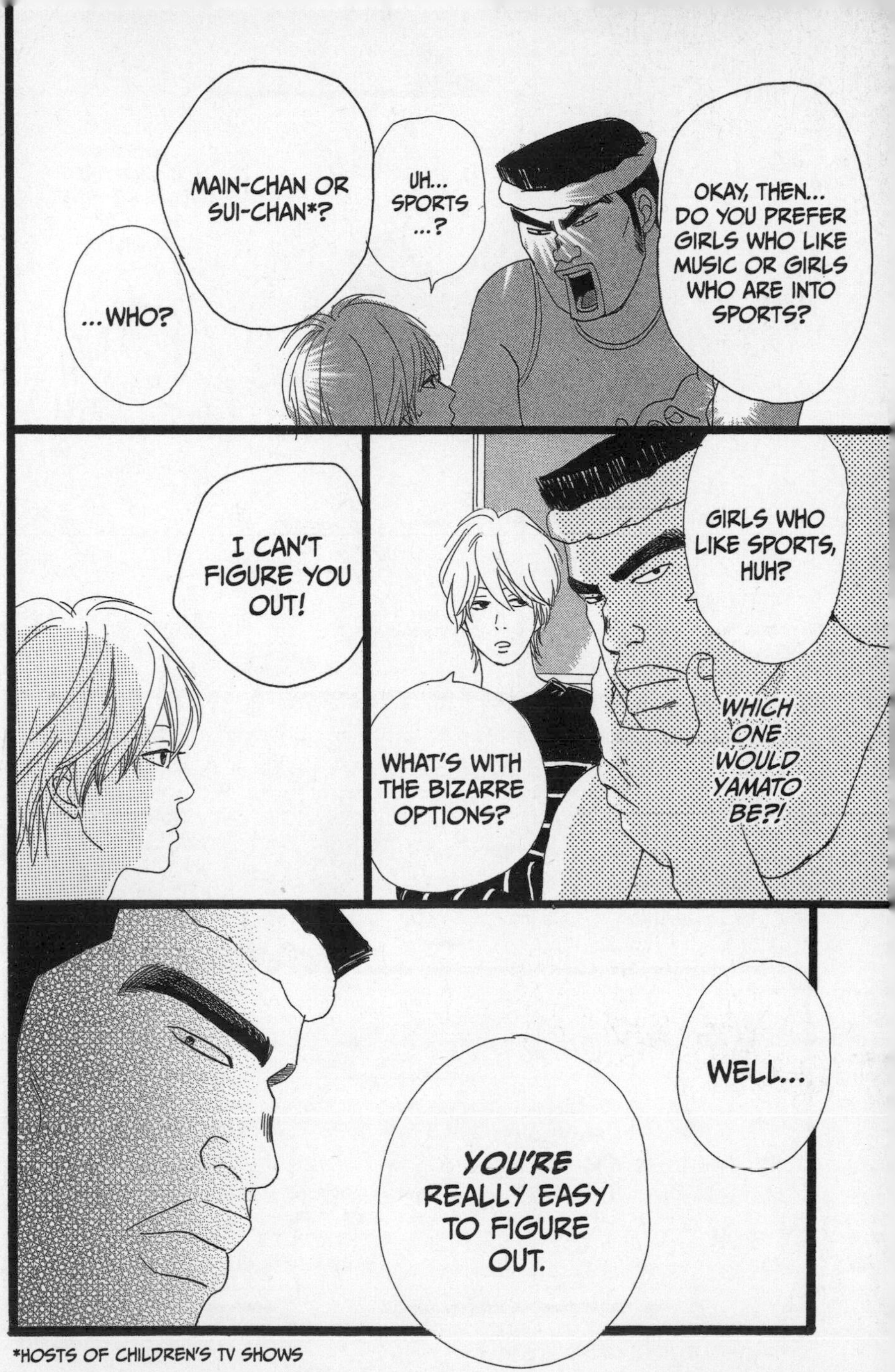
OKAY, THEN... DO YOU PREFER GIRLS WHO LIKE MUSIC OR GIRLS WHO ARE INTO SPORTS?
UH... SPORTS ...?
MAIN-CHAN OR SUI-CHAN*?
...WHO?
GIRLS WHO LIKE SPORTS, HUH?
WHICH ONE WOULD YAMATO BE?!
WHAT'S WITH THE BIZARRE OPTIONS?
I CAN'T FIGURE YOU OUT!
WELL...
YOU'RE REALLY EASY TO FIGURE OUT.

*HOSTS OF CHILDREN'S TV SHOWS

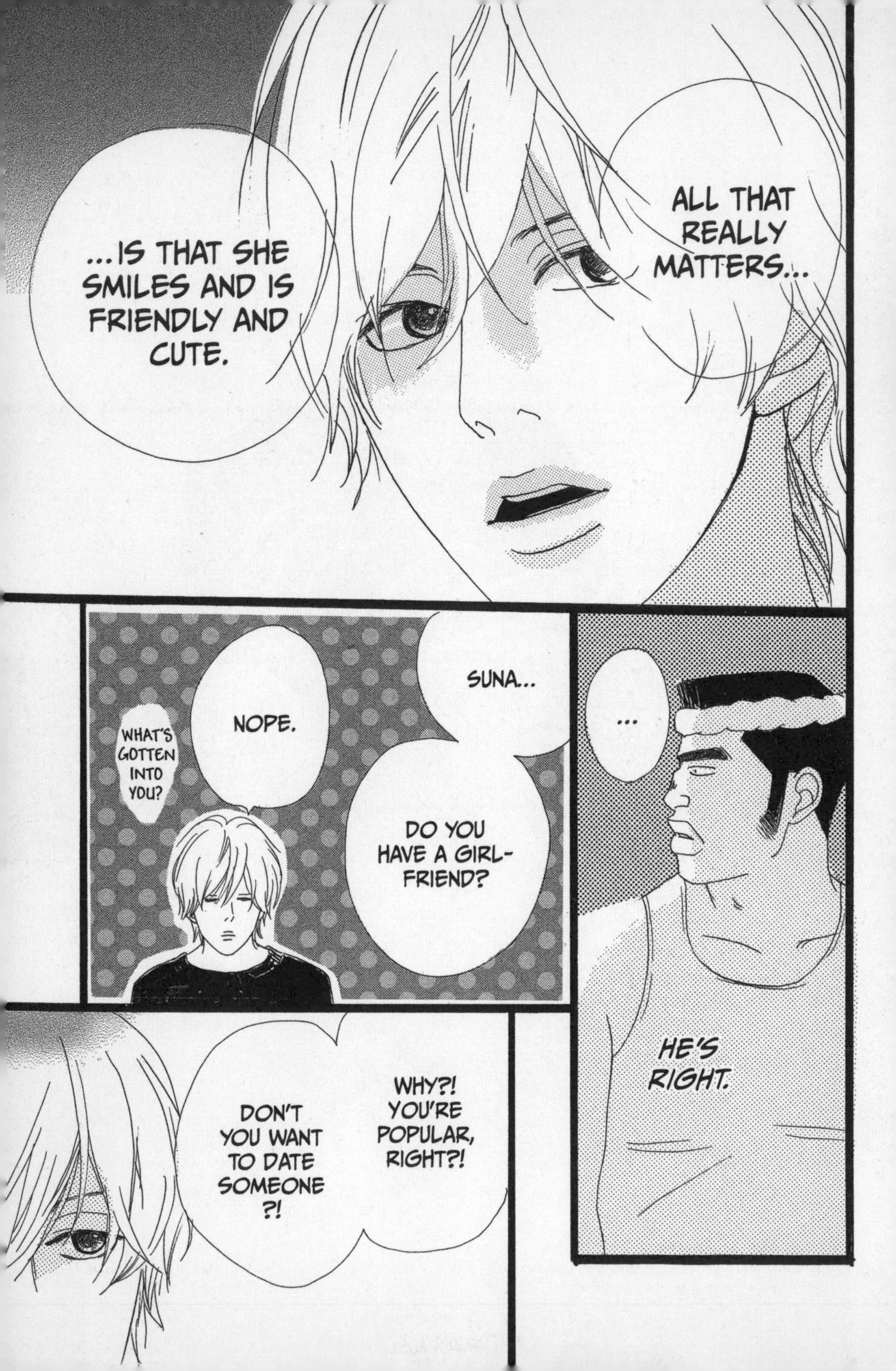
ALL THAT REALLY MATTERS...
...IS THAT SHE SMILES AND IS FRIENDLY AND CUTE.
...
HE'S RIGHT.
SUNA...
DO YOU HAVE A GIRL-FRIEND?
NOPE.
WHAT'S GOTTEN INTO YOU?
WHY?! YOU'RE POPULAR, RIGHT?!
DON'T YOU WANT TO DATE SOMEONE?!

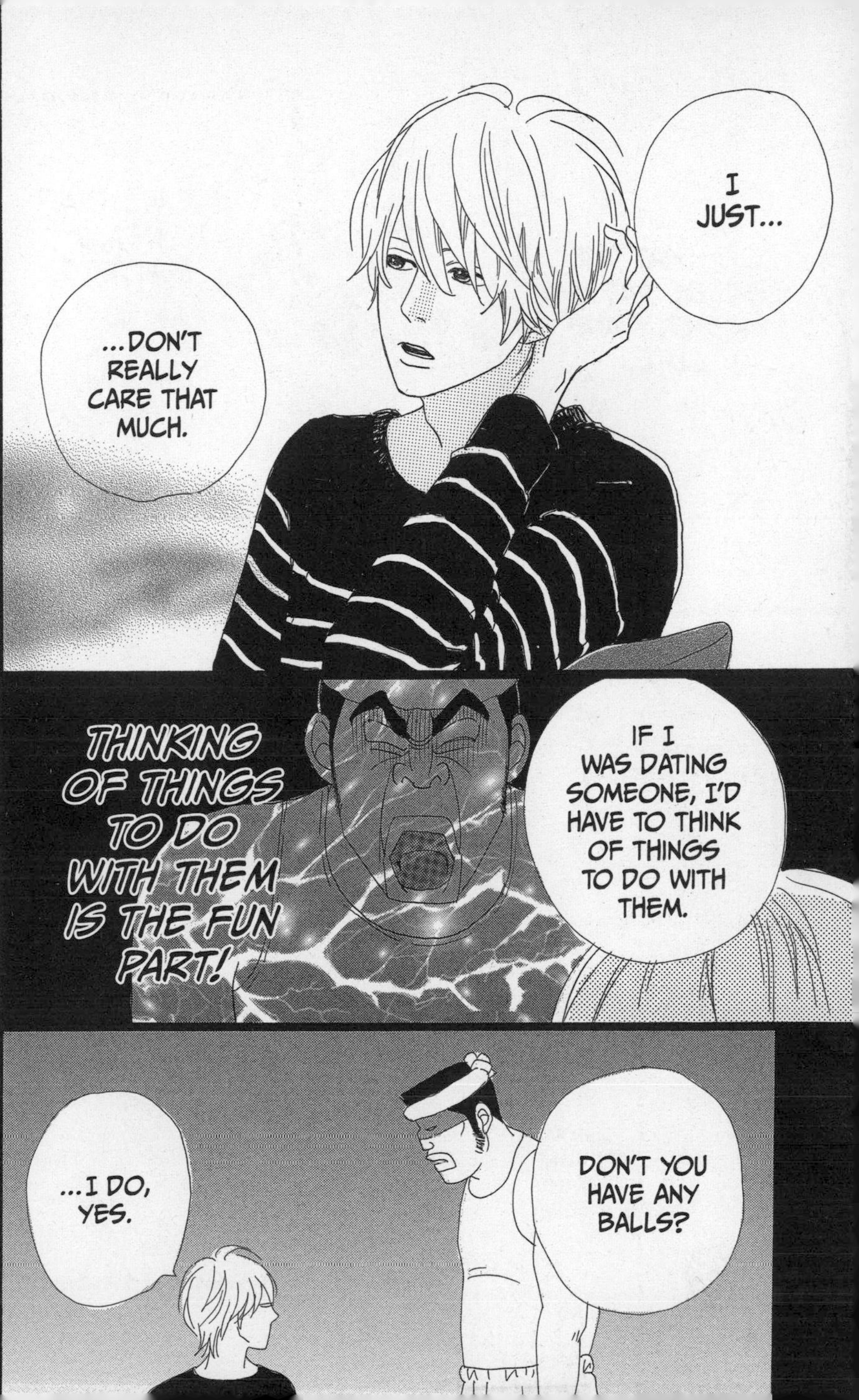
I JUST...
...DON'T REALLY CARE THAT MUCH.
IF I WAS DATING SOMEONE, I'D HAVE TO THINK OF THINGS TO DO WITH THEM.
THINKING OF THINGS TO DO WITH THEM IS THE FUN PART!
DON'T YOU HAVE ANY BALLS?
...I DO, YES.

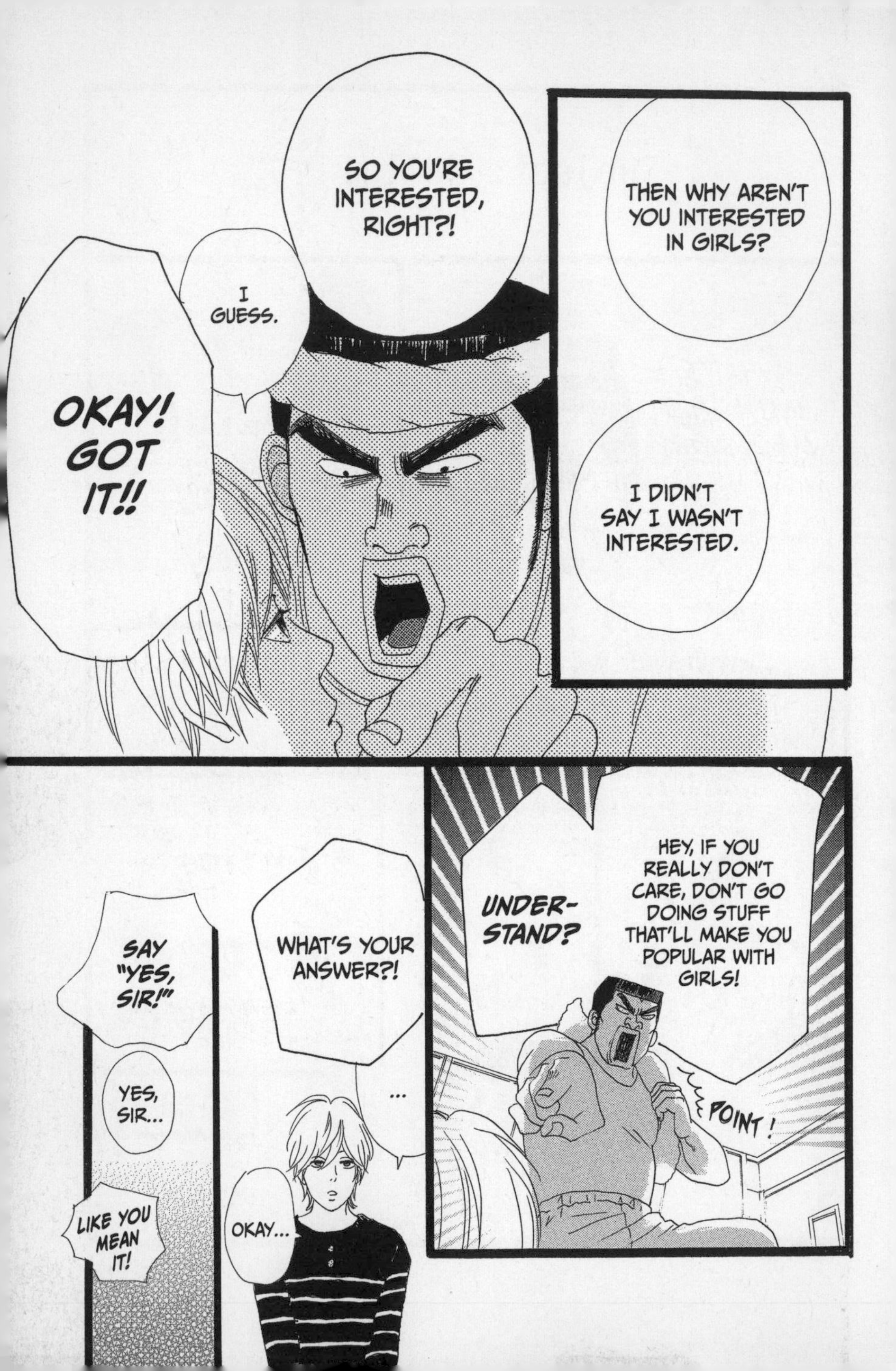
THEN WHY AREN'T YOU INTERESTED IN GIRLS?
I DIDN'T SAY I WASN'T INTERESTED.
SO YOU'RE INTERESTED, RIGHT?!
I GUESS.
OKAY! GOT IT!!
HEY, IF YOU REALLY DON'T CARE, DON'T GO DOING STUFF THAT'LL MAKE YOU POPULAR WITH GIRLS!
UNDER-STAND?
POINT!
WHAT'S YOUR ANSWER?!
...
OKAY...
SAY "YES, SIR!"
YES, SIR...
LIKE YOU MEAN IT!

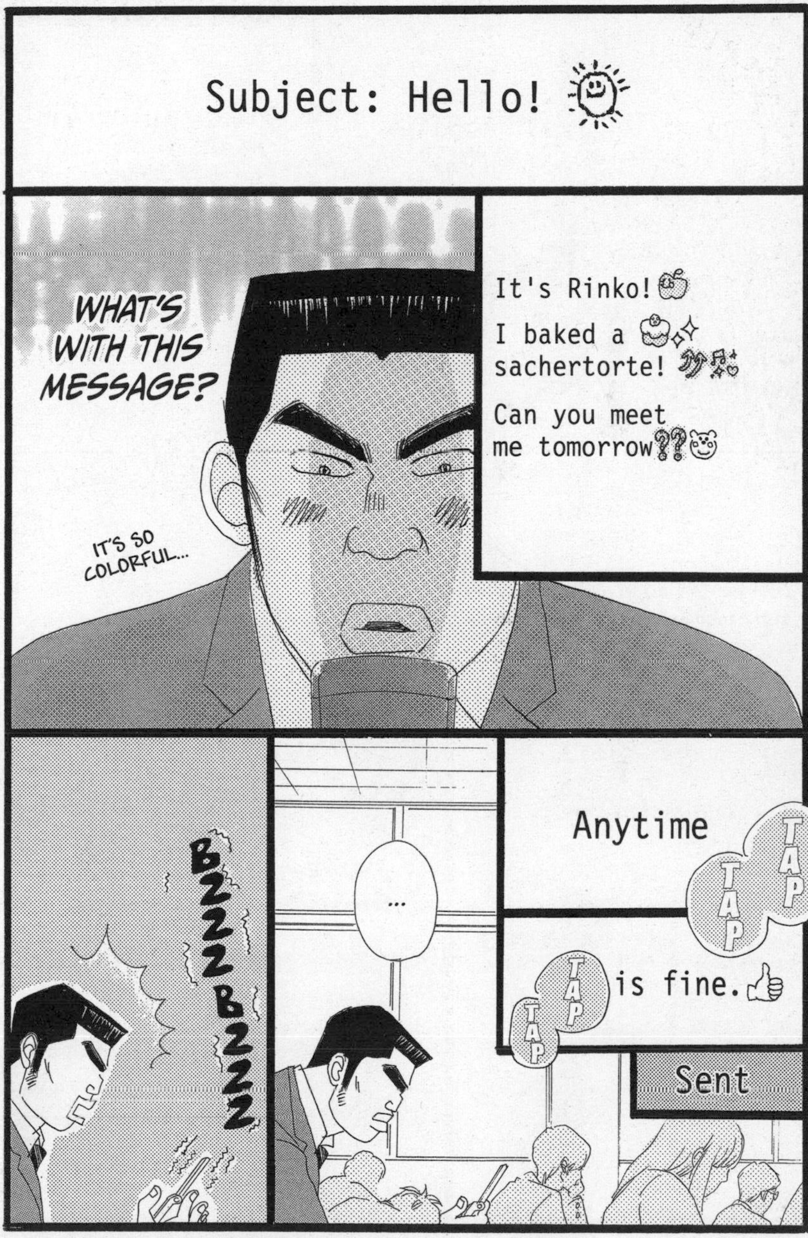

Subject: Hello!
It's Rinko!
I baked a sachertorte!
Can you meet me tomorrow??
WHAT'S WITH THIS MESSAGE?
IT'S SO COLORFUL...
Anytime
TAP TAP
is fine.
TAP TAP
Sent
...
BZZZ BZZZ

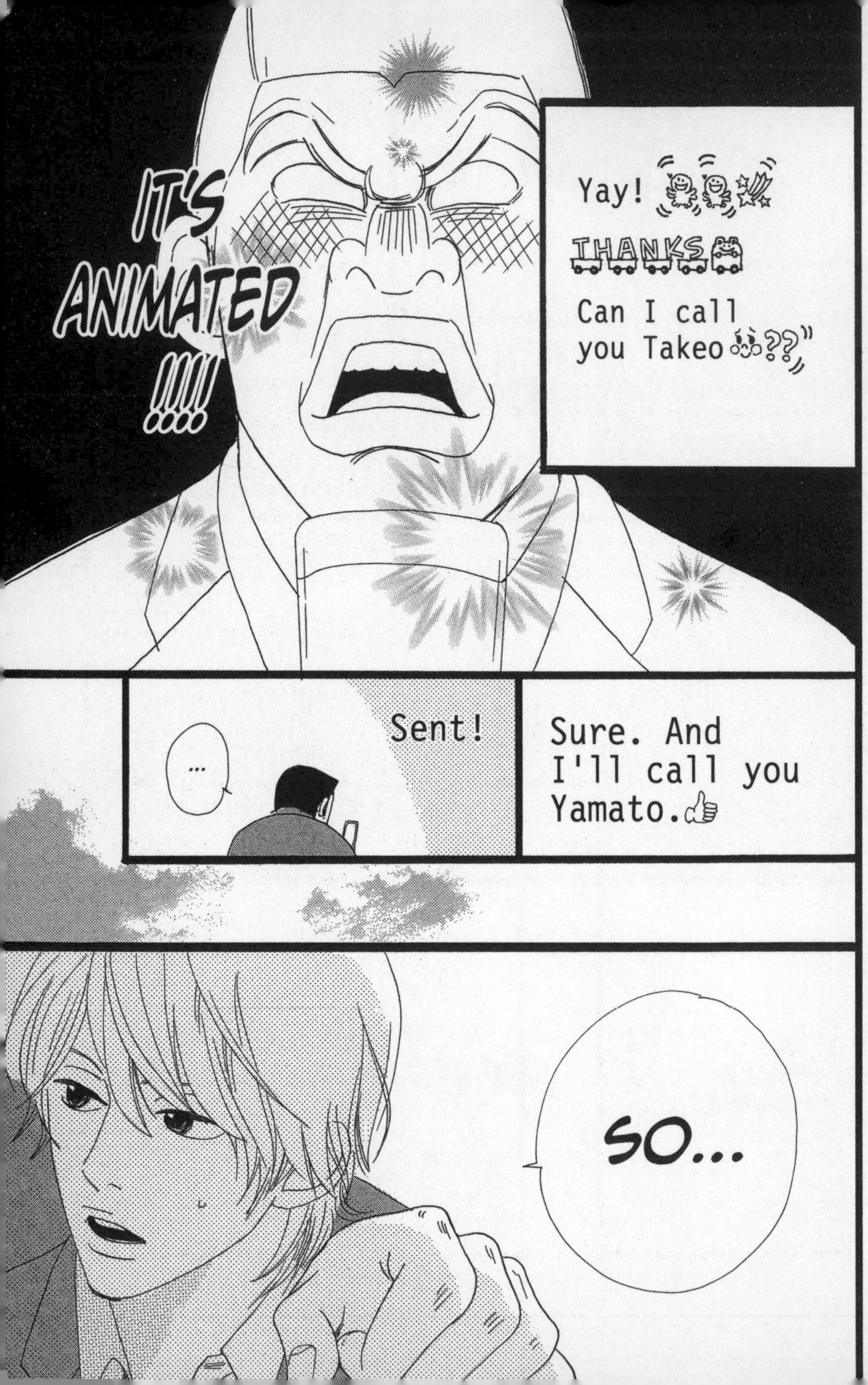
Yay!
THANKS
Can I call you Takeo??
IT'S ANIMATED!!!!
Sure. And I'll call you Yamato.
Sent!
...
SO...

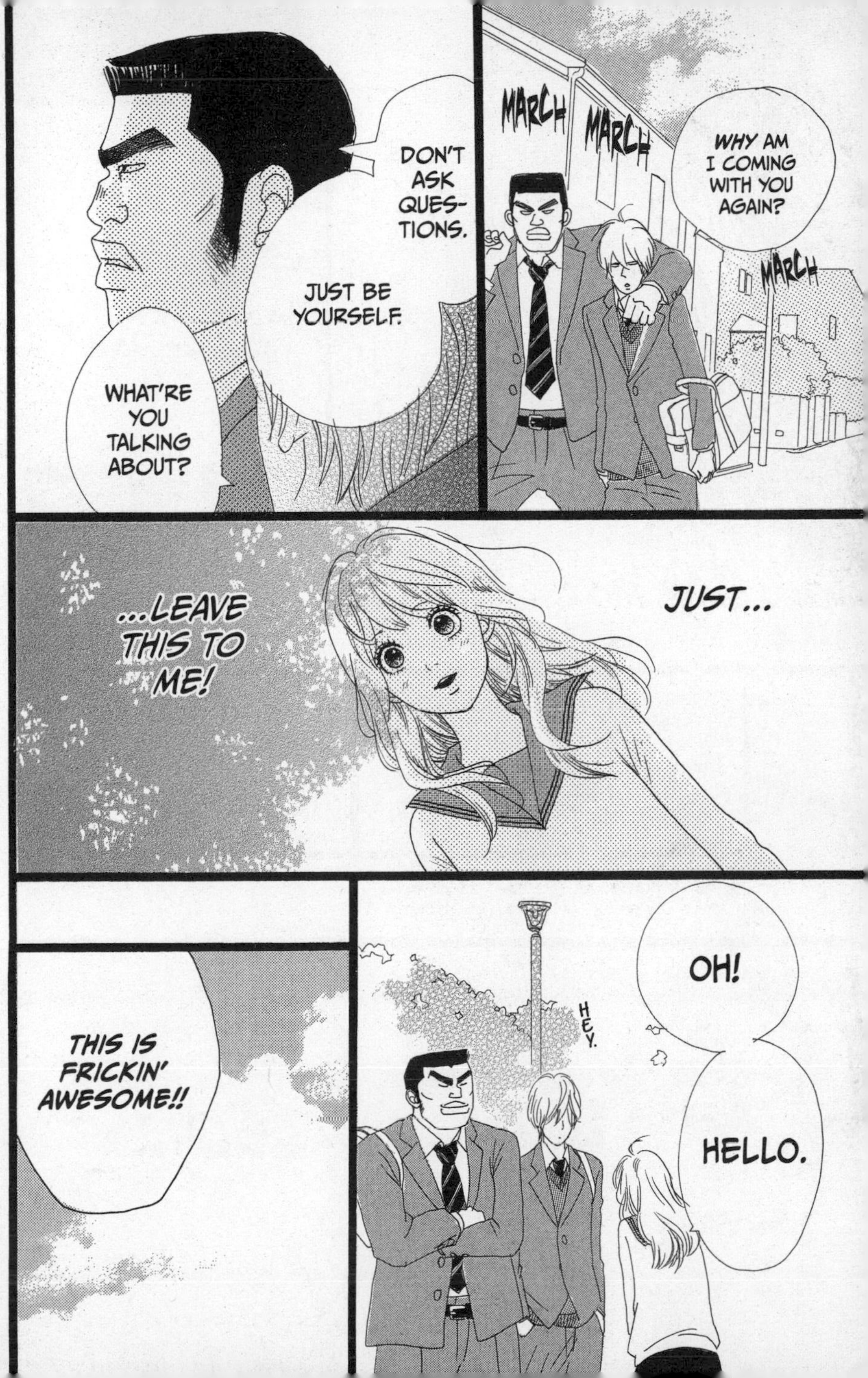
WHY AM I COMING WITH YOU AGAIN?
MARCH MARCH
MARCH
DON'T ASK QUES-TIONS.
JUST BE YOURSELF.
WHAT'RE YOU TALKING ABOUT?
JUST...
...LEAVE THIS TO ME!
OH!
HELLO.
HEY.
THIS IS FRICKIN' AWESOME!!

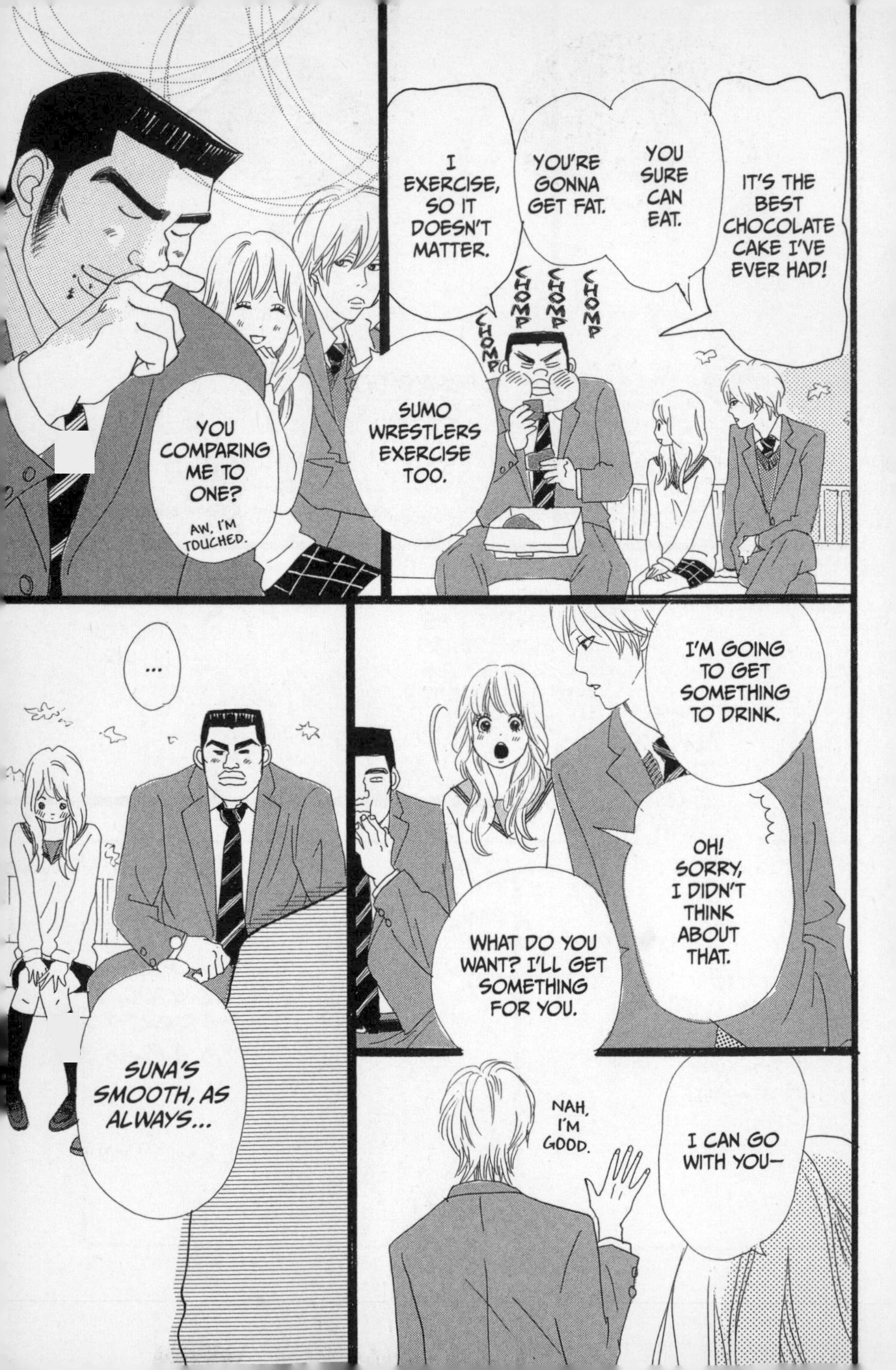
IT'S THE BEST CHOCOLATE CAKE I'VE EVER HAD!
YOU SURE CAN EAT.
YOU'RE GONNA GET FAT.
I EXERCISE, SO IT DOESN'T MATTER.
CHOMP CHOMP CHOMP CHOMP
SUMO WRESTLERS EXERCISE TOO.
YOU COMPARING ME TO ONE?
AW, I'M TOUCHED.
I'M GOING TO GET SOMETHING TO DRINK.
OH! SORRY, I DIDN'T THINK ABOUT THAT.
WHAT DO YOU WANT? I'LL GET SOMETHING FOR YOU.
I CAN GO WITH YOU—
NAH, I'M GOOD.
...
SUNA'S SMOOTH, AS ALWAYS...

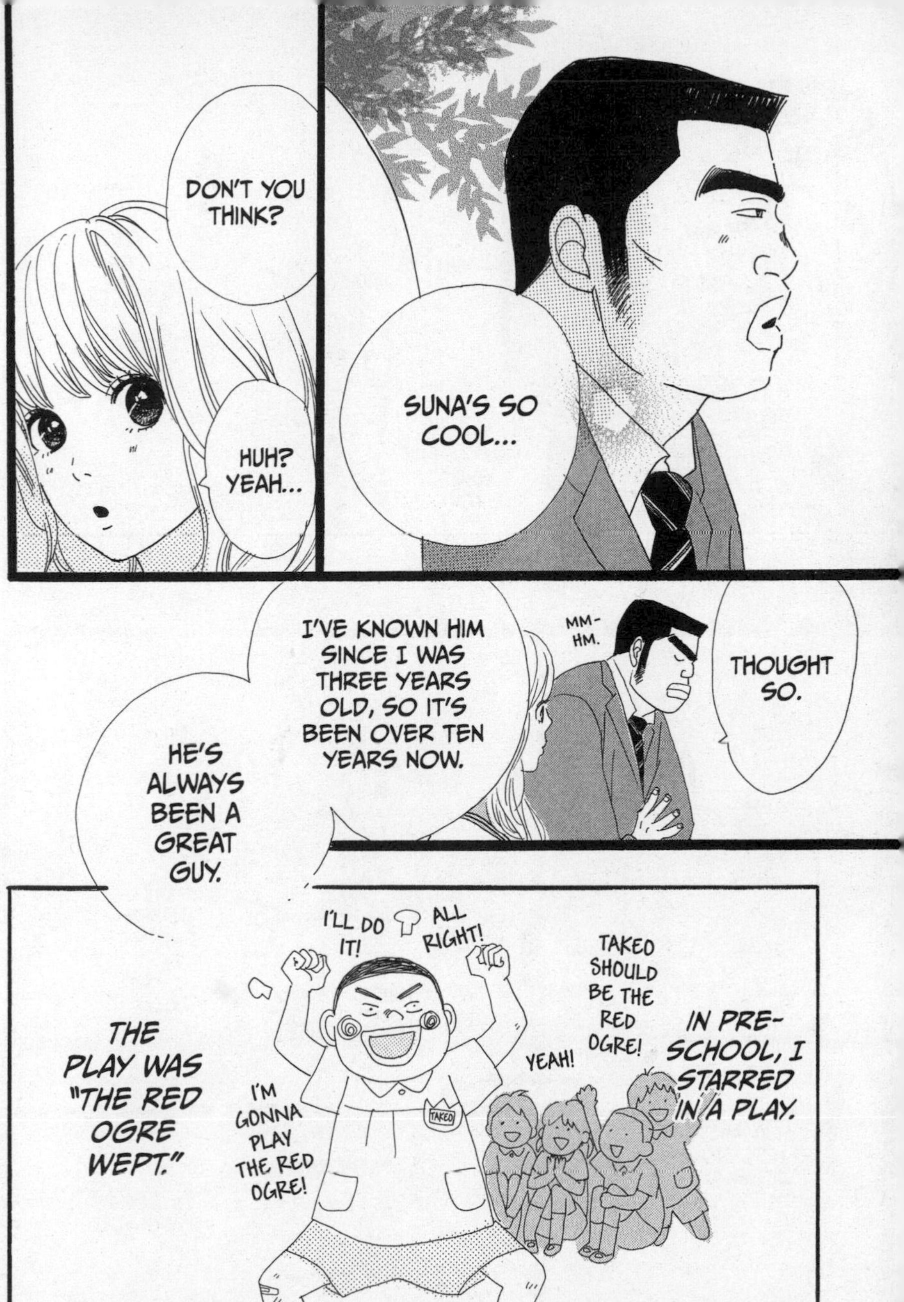
SUNA'S SO COOL...
DON'T YOU THINK?
HUH? YEAH...
THOUGHT SO.
MM-HM.
I'VE KNOWN HIM SINCE I WAS THREE YEARS OLD, SO IT'S BEEN OVER TEN YEARS NOW.
HE'S ALWAYS BEEN A GREAT GUY.
IN PRE-SCHOOL, I STARRED IN A PLAY.
TAKEO SHOULD BE THE RED OGRE!
YEAH!
ALL RIGHT!
I'LL DO IT!
TAKEO
I'M GONNA PLAY THE RED OGRE!
THE PLAY WAS "THE RED OGRE WEPT."

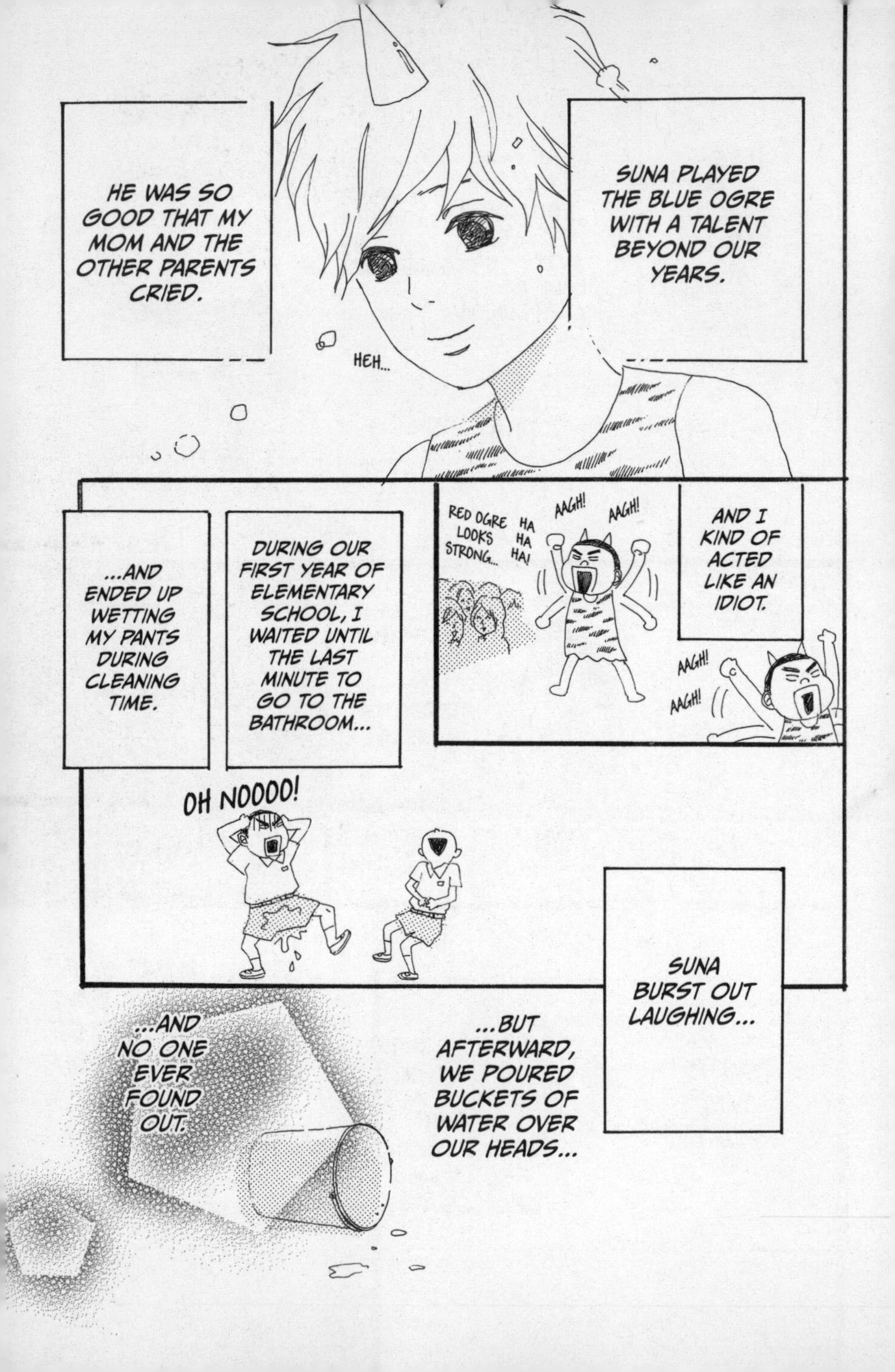
SUNA PLAYED THE BLUE OGRE WITH A TALENT BEYOND OUR YEARS.
HE WAS SO GOOD THAT MY MOM AND THE OTHER PARENTS CRIED.
HEH...
AND I KIND OF ACTED LIKE AN IDIOT.
AAGH!
AAGH!
HA HA HA!
RED OGRE LOOKS STRONG...
AAGH!
AAGH!
DURING OUR FIRST YEAR OF ELEMENTARY SCHOOL, I WAITED UNTIL THE LAST MINUTE TO GO TO THE BATHROOM...
...AND ENDED UP WETTING MY PANTS DURING CLEANING TIME.
OH NOOOO!
SUNA BURST OUT LAUGHING...
...BUT AFTERWARD, WE POURED BUCKETS OF WATER OVER OUR HEADS...
...AND NO ONE EVER FOUND OUT.

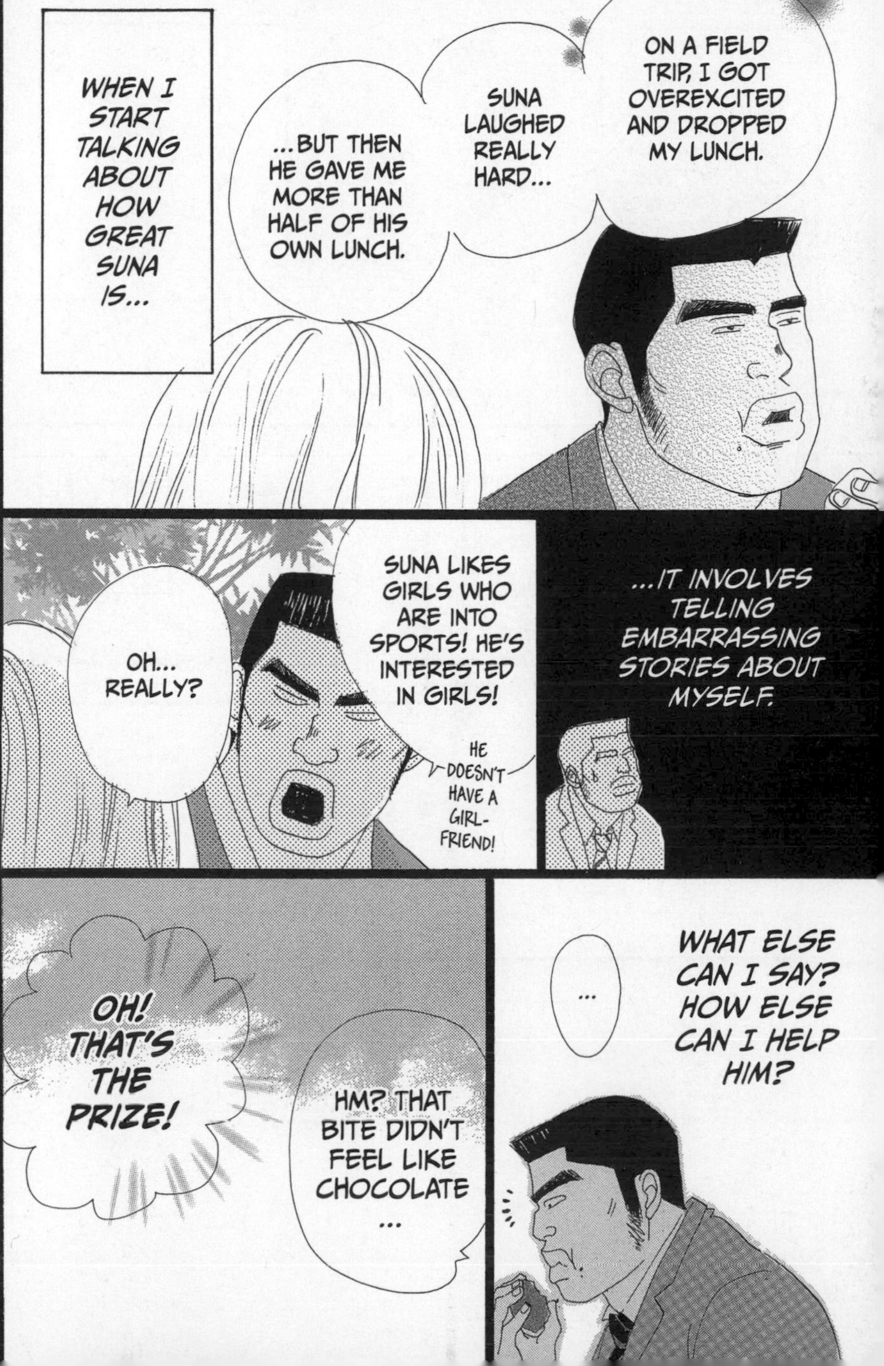
ON A FIELD TRIP, I GOT OVEREXCITED AND DROPPED MY LUNCH.
SUNA LAUGHED REALLY HARD...
...BUT THEN HE GAVE ME MORE THAN HALF OF HIS OWN LUNCH.
WHEN I START TALKING ABOUT HOW GREAT SUNA IS...
...IT INVOLVES TELLING EMBARRASSING STORIES ABOUT MYSELF.
SUNA LIKES GIRLS WHO ARE INTO SPORTS! HE'S INTERESTED IN GIRLS!
HE DOESN'T HAVE A GIRL-FRIEND!
OH... REALLY?
WHAT ELSE CAN I SAY? HOW ELSE CAN I HELP HIM?
...
HM? THAT BITE DIDN'T FEEL LIKE CHOCOLATE ...
OH! THAT'S THE PRIZE!

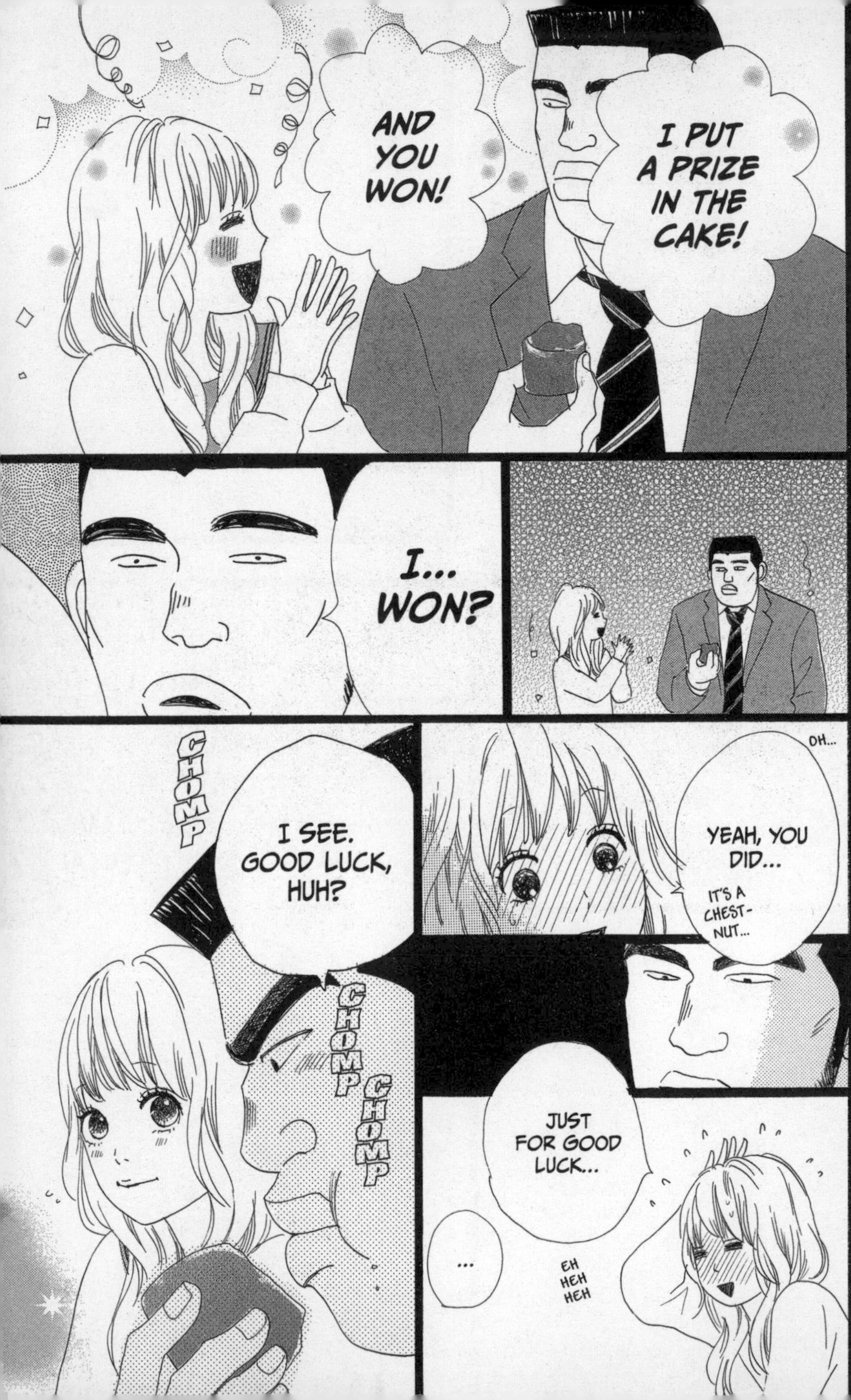
I PUT A PRIZE IN THE CAKE!
AND YOU WON!
I... WON?
OH...
YEAH, YOU DID...
IT'S A CHEST-NUT...
JUST FOR GOOD LUCK...
...
EH HEH HEH
CHOMP
I SEE. GOOD LUCK, HUH?
CHOMP
CHOMP

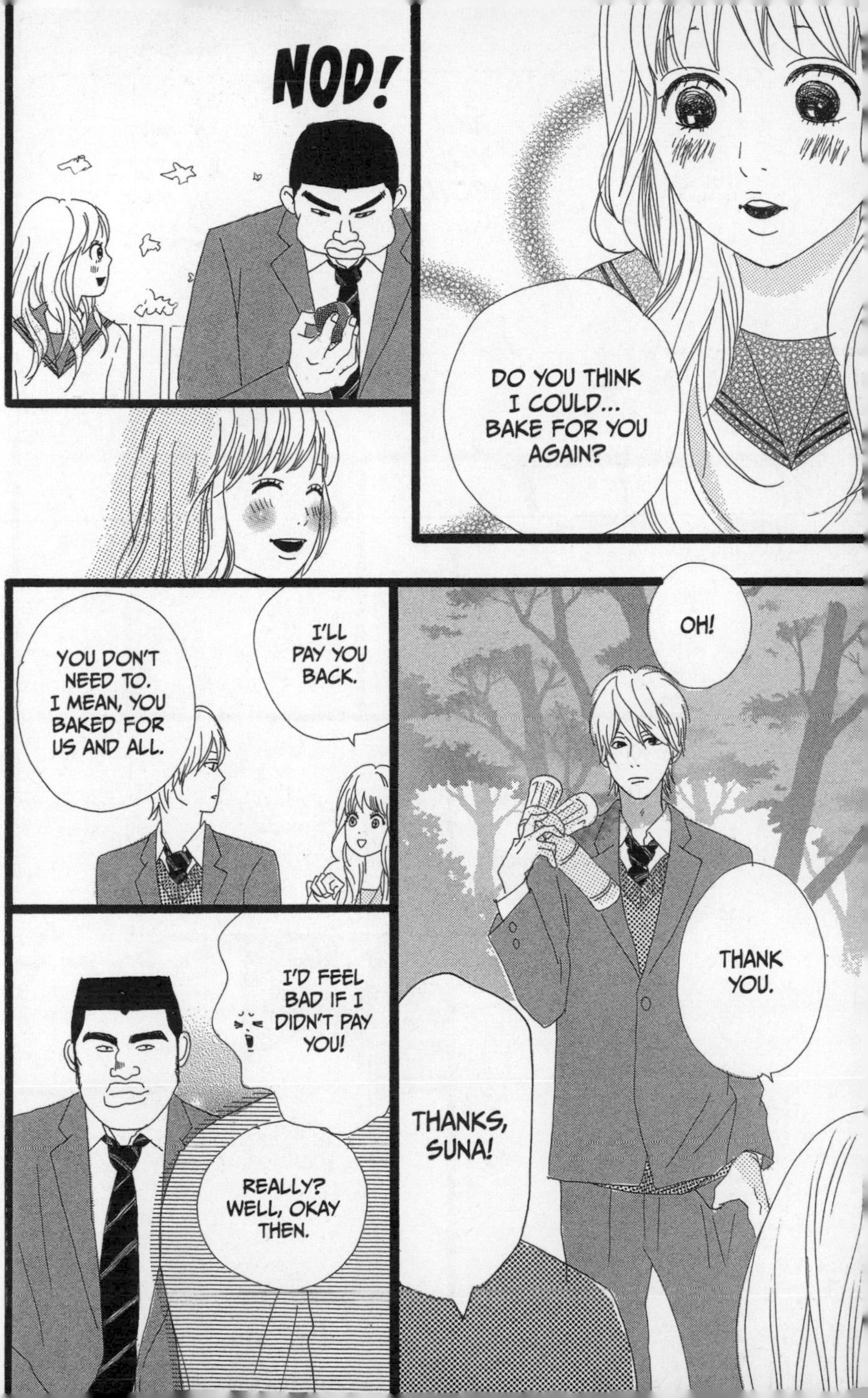
DO YOU THINK I COULD... BAKE FOR YOU AGAIN?
NOD!
OH!
THANK YOU.
THANKS, SUNA!
I'LL PAY YOU BACK.
YOU DON'T NEED TO. I MEAN, YOU BAKED FOR US AND ALL.
I'D FEEL BAD IF I DIDN'T PAY YOU!
REALLY? WELL, OKAY THEN.

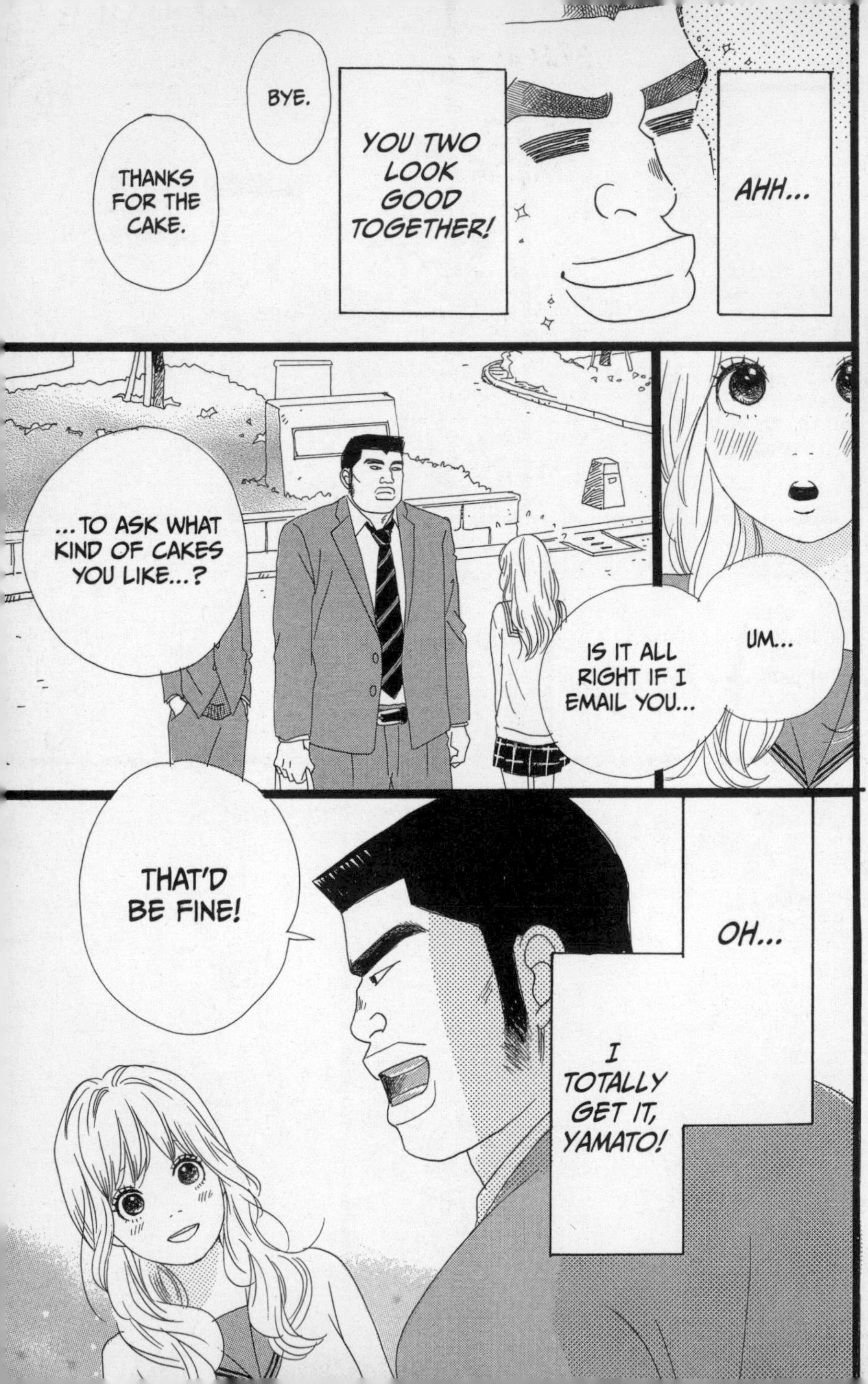
AHH...
YOU TWO LOOK GOOD TOGETHER!
BYE.
THANKS FOR THE CAKE.
UM...
IS IT ALL RIGHT IF I EMAIL YOU...
...TO ASK WHAT KIND OF CAKES YOU LIKE...?
THAT'D BE FINE!
OH...
I TOTALLY GET IT, YAMATO!

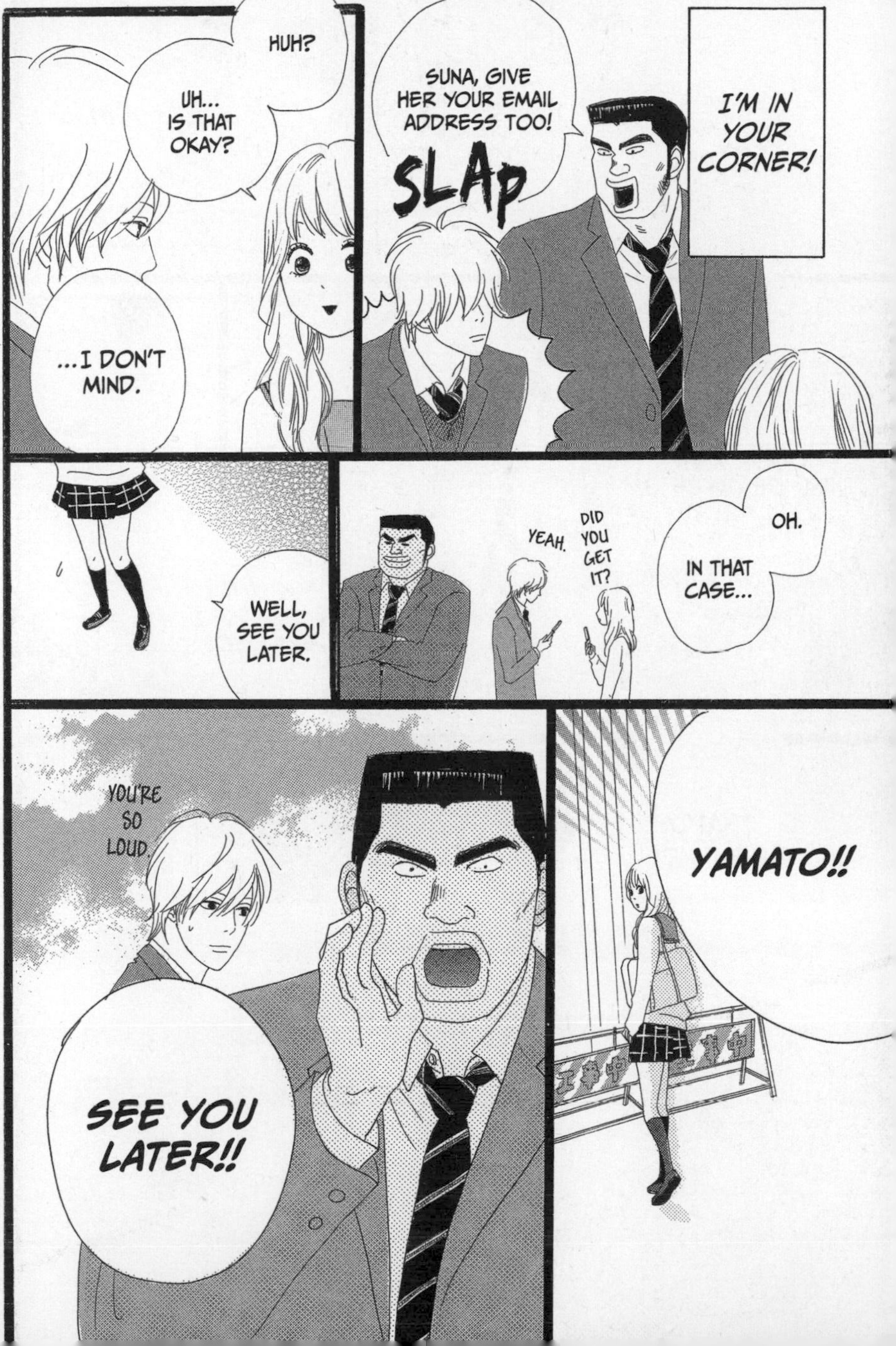
I'M IN YOUR CORNER!
SUNA, GIVE HER YOUR EMAIL ADDRESS TOO!
SLAP
HUH?
UH... IS THAT OKAY?
...I DON'T MIND.
OH.
IN THAT CASE...
DID YOU GET IT?
YEAH.
WELL, SEE YOU LATER.
YAMATO!!
SEE YOU LATER!!
YOU'RE SO LOUD.

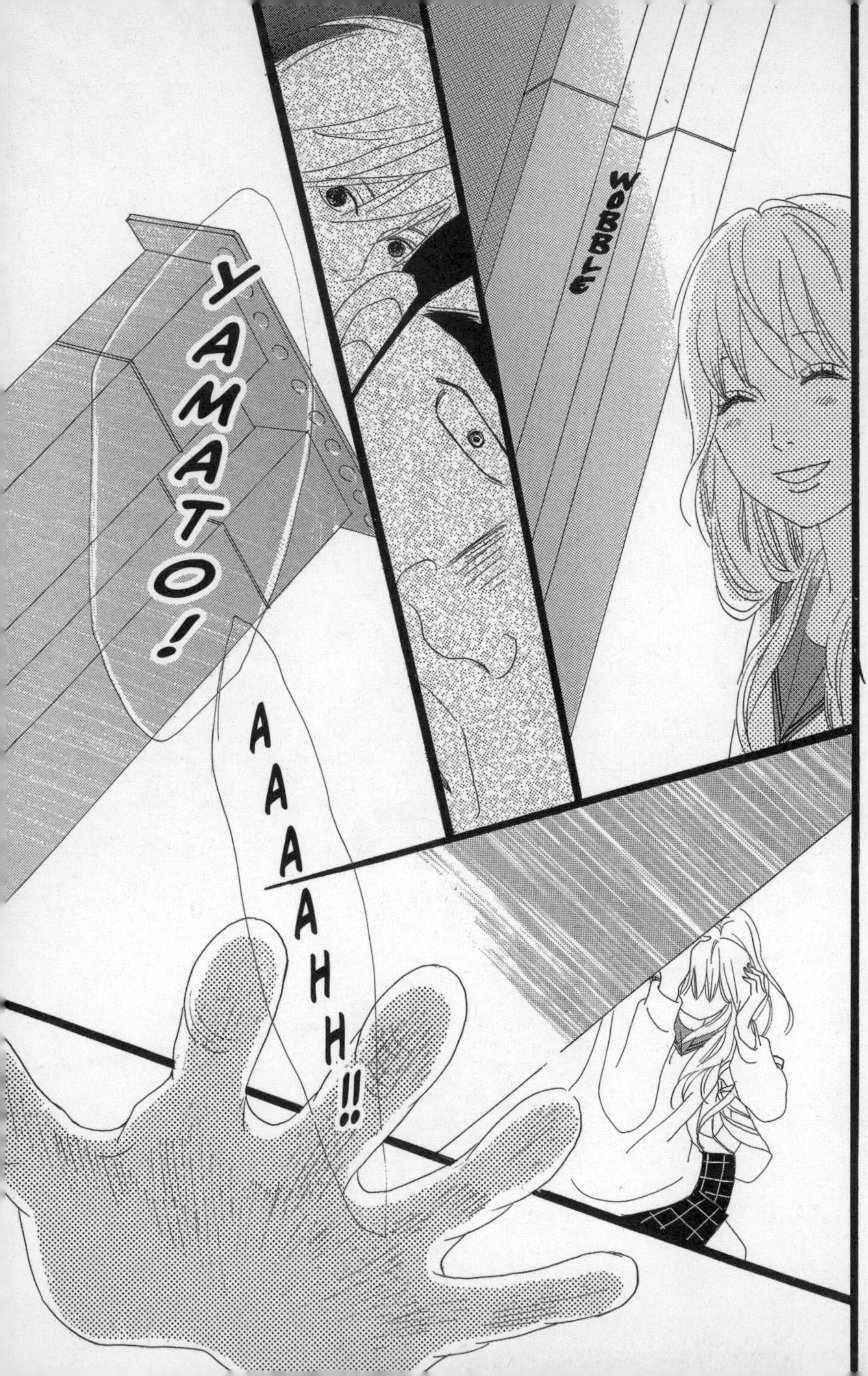
WOBBLE
YAMATO!
AAAAHH!!

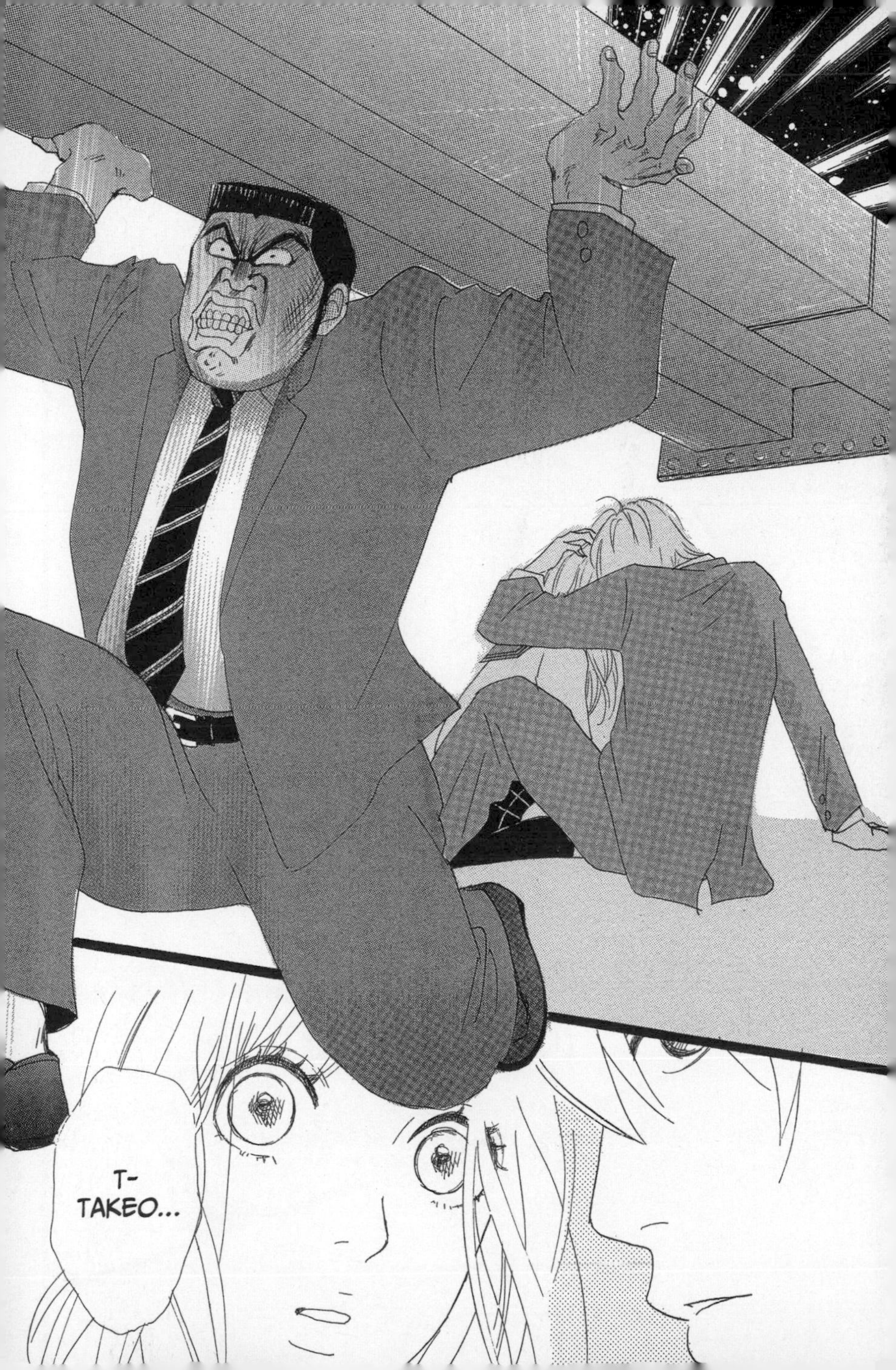
T-
TAKEO...

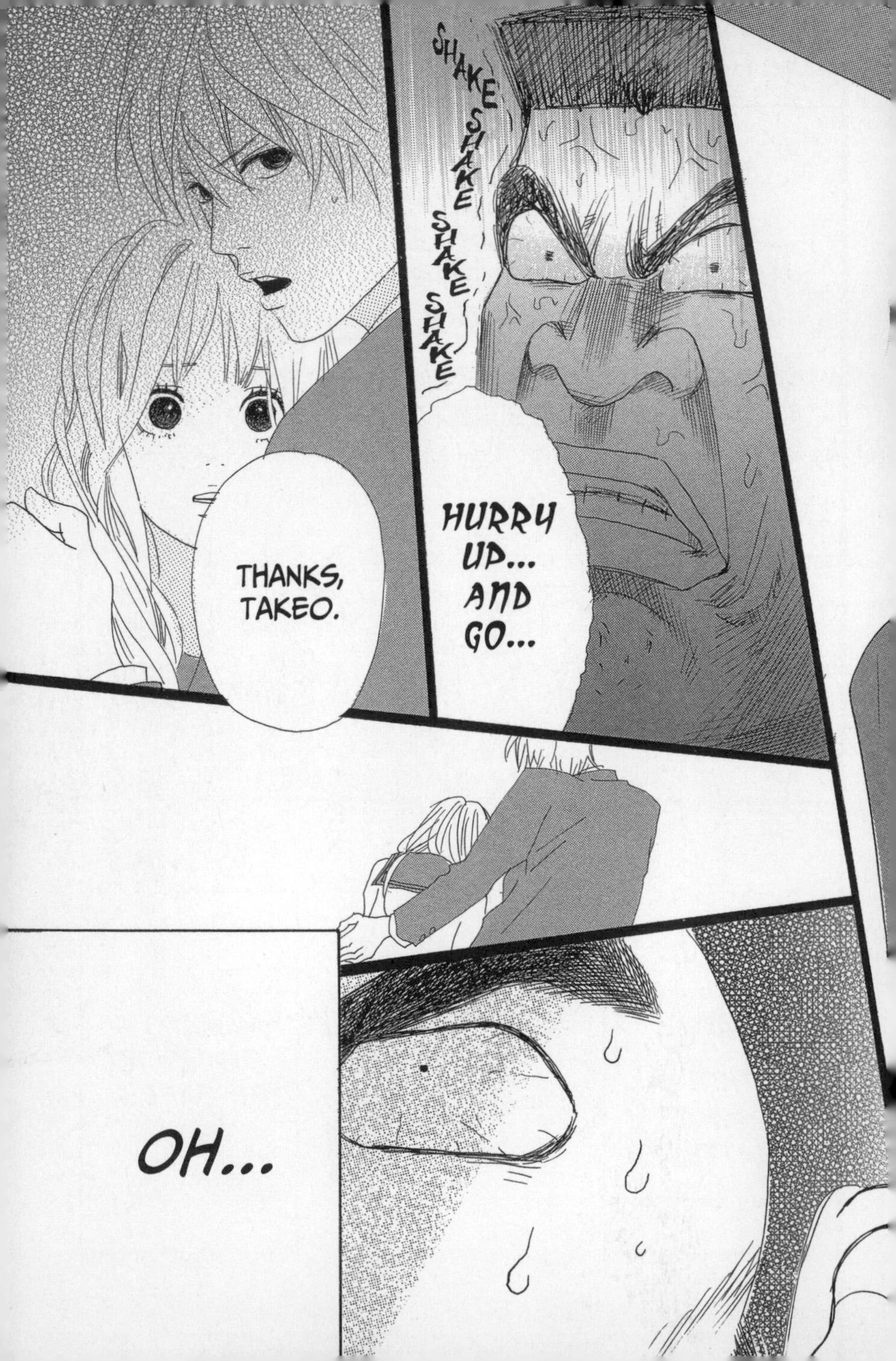
SHAKE SHAKE SHAKE SHAKE
HURRY UP... AND GO...
THANKS, TAKEO.
OH...

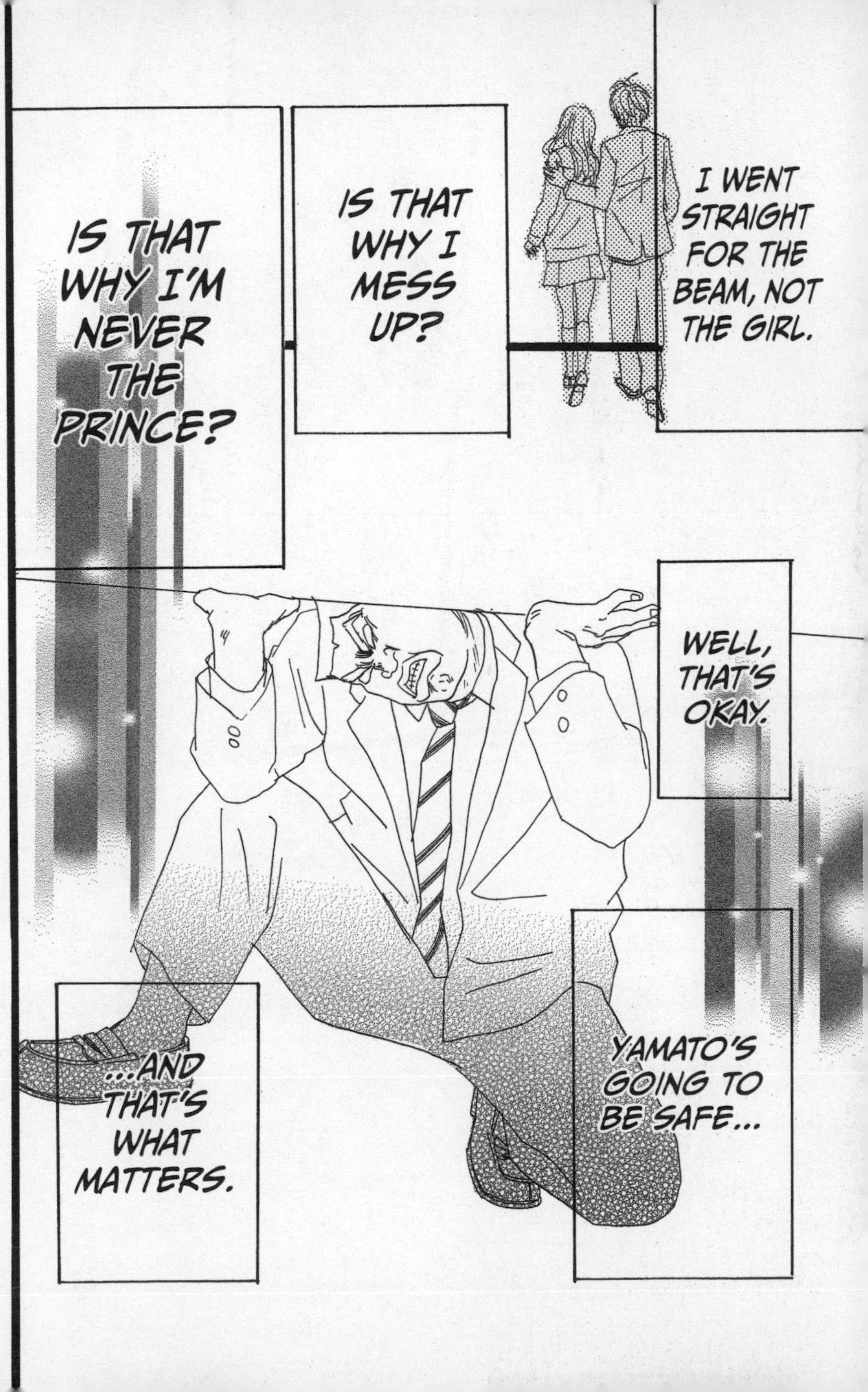
I WENT STRAIGHT FOR THE BEAM, NOT THE GIRL.
IS THAT WHY I MESS UP?
IS THAT WHY I'M NEVER THE PRINCE?
WELL, THAT'S OKAY.
YAMATO'S GOING TO BE SAFE...
...AND THAT'S WHAT MATTERS.

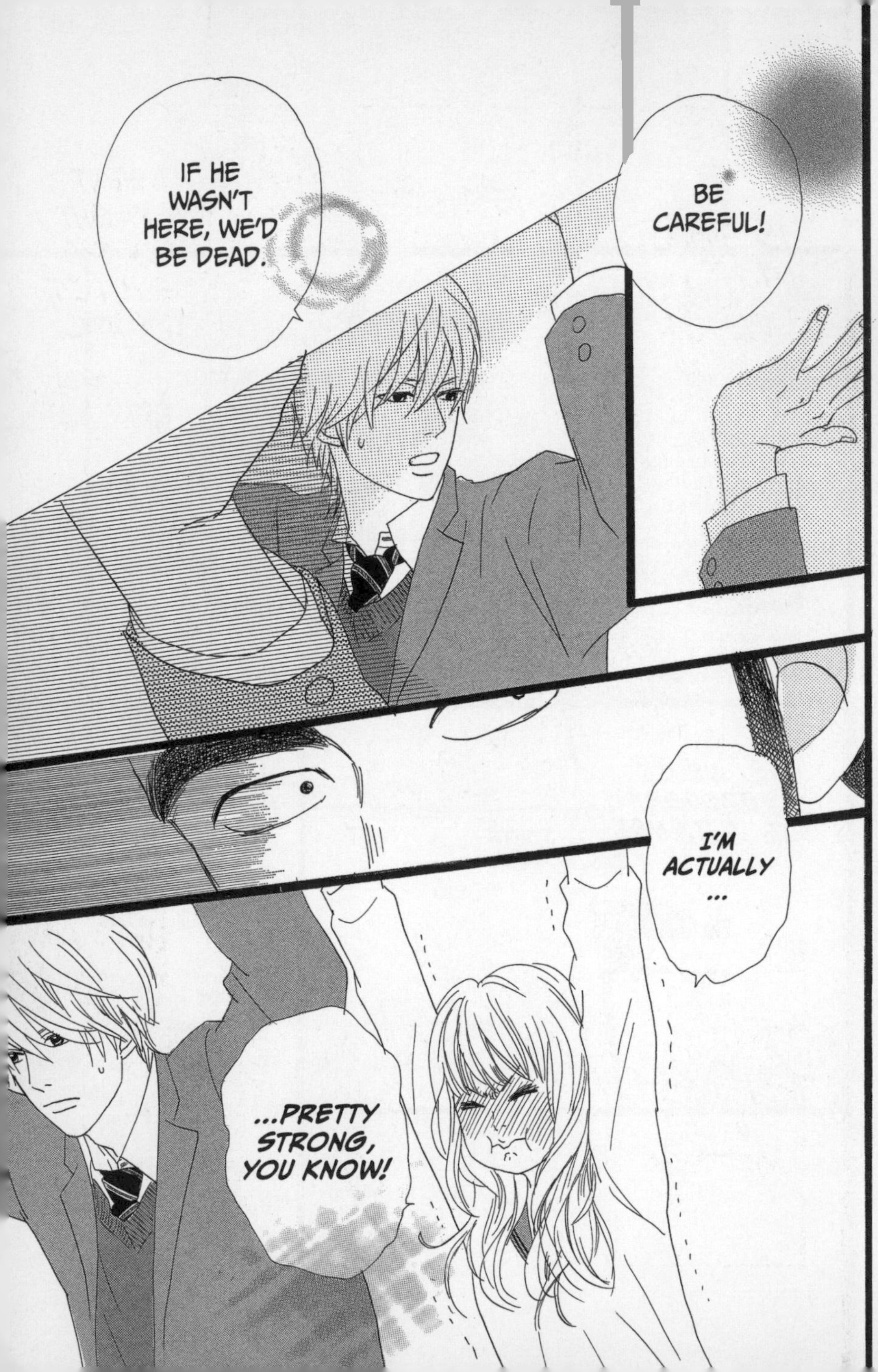
BE CAREFUL!
IF HE WASN'T HERE, WE'D BE DEAD.
I'M ACTUALLY ...
...PRETTY STRONG, YOU KNOW!

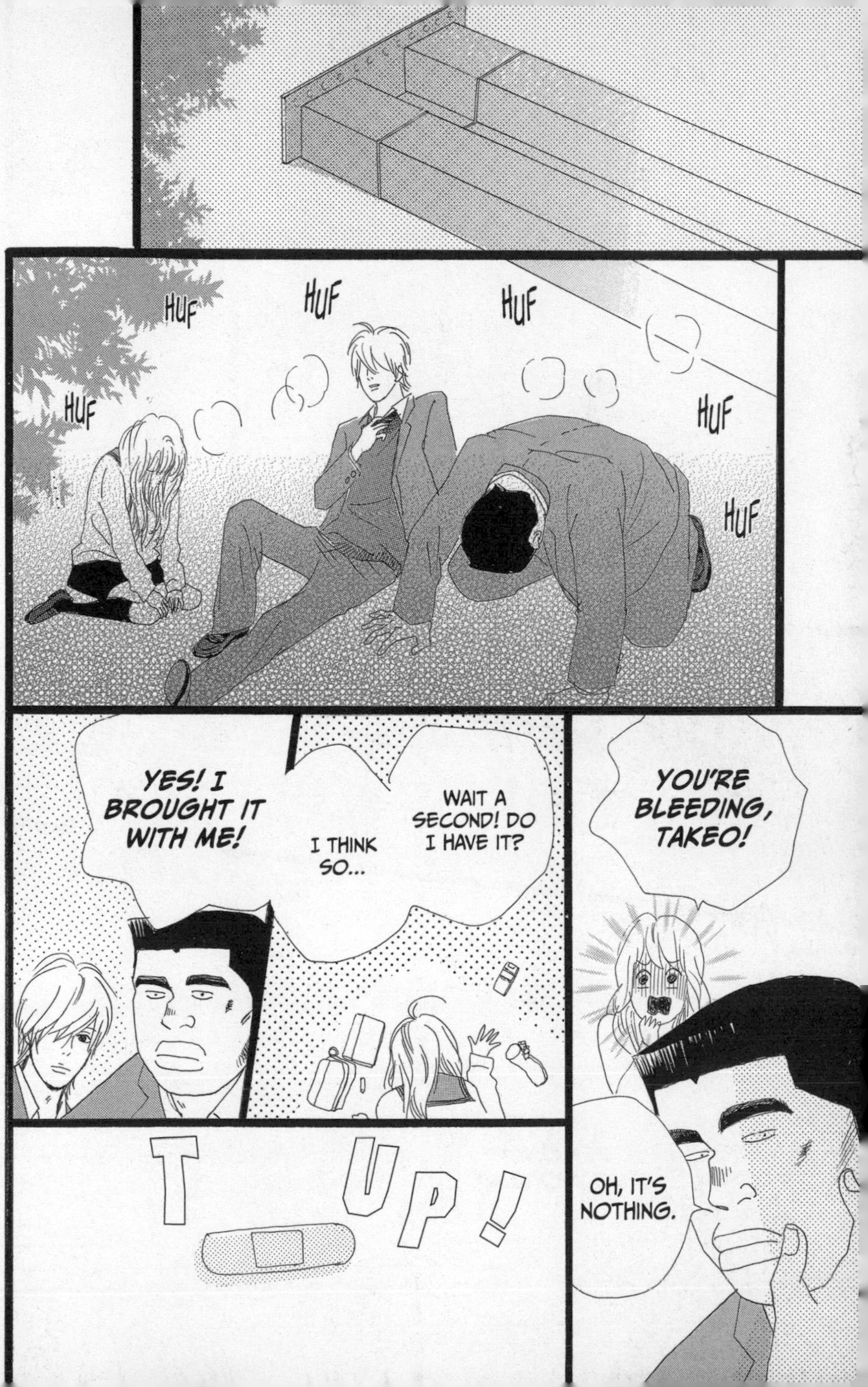
HUF
HUF
HUF
HUF
HUF
HUF
YOU'RE BLEEDING, TAKEO!
OH, IT'S NOTHING.
WAIT A SECOND! DO I HAVE IT?
I THINK SO...
YES! I BROUGHT IT WITH ME!
TUP!

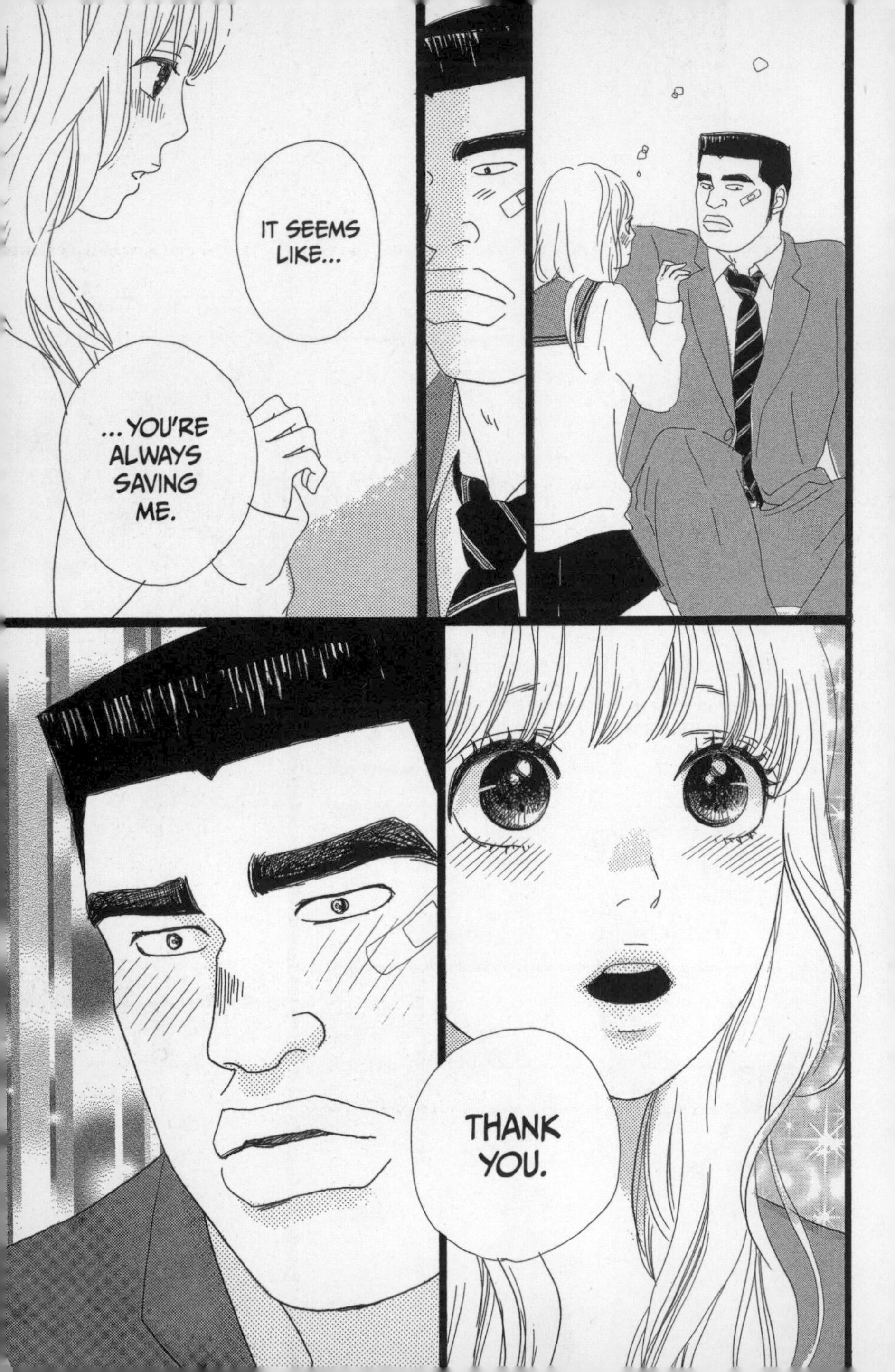
IT SEEMS LIKE...
...YOU'RE ALWAYS SAVING ME.
THANK YOU.

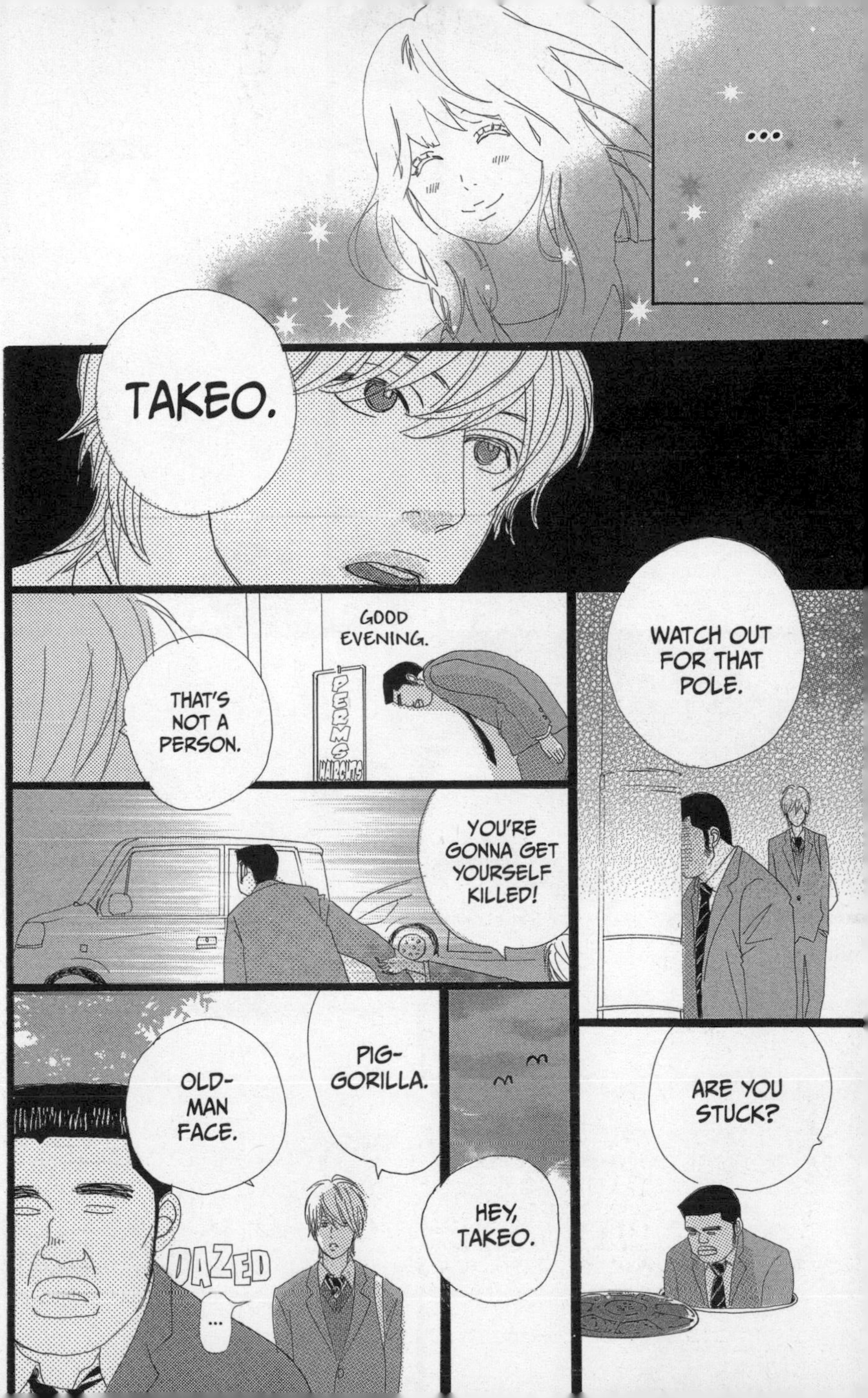
...
TAKEO.
WATCH OUT FOR THAT POLE.
GOOD EVENING.
THAT'S NOT A PERSON.
PERMS HAIRCUTS
YOU'RE GONNA GET YOURSELF KILLED!
ARE YOU STUCK?
HEY, TAKEO.
PIG-GORILLA.
OLD-MAN FACE.
DAZED
...

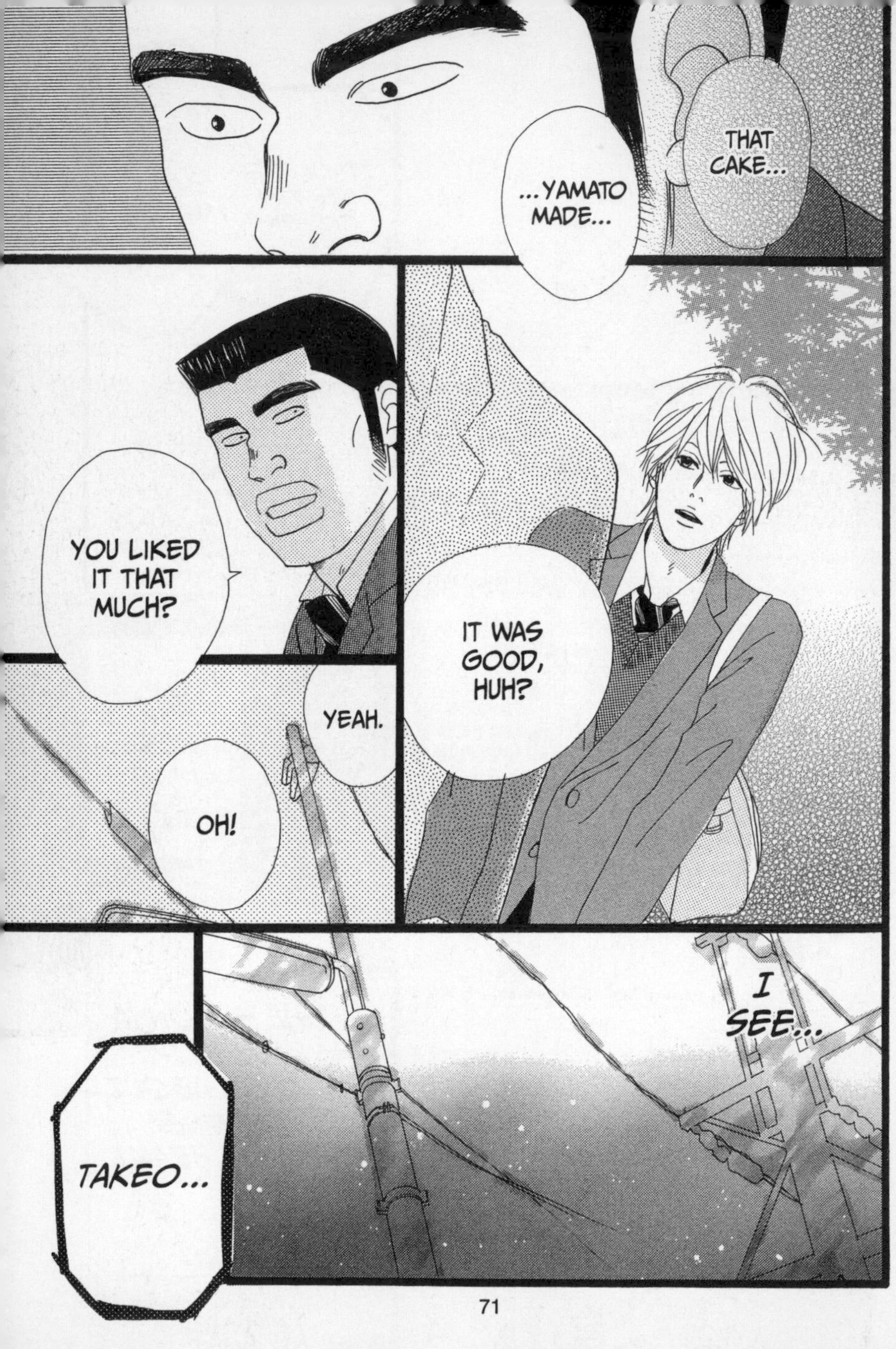
THAT CAKE...
...YAMATO MADE...
IT WAS GOOD, HUH?
YOU LIKED IT THAT MUCH?
YEAH.
OH!
I SEE...
TAKEO...

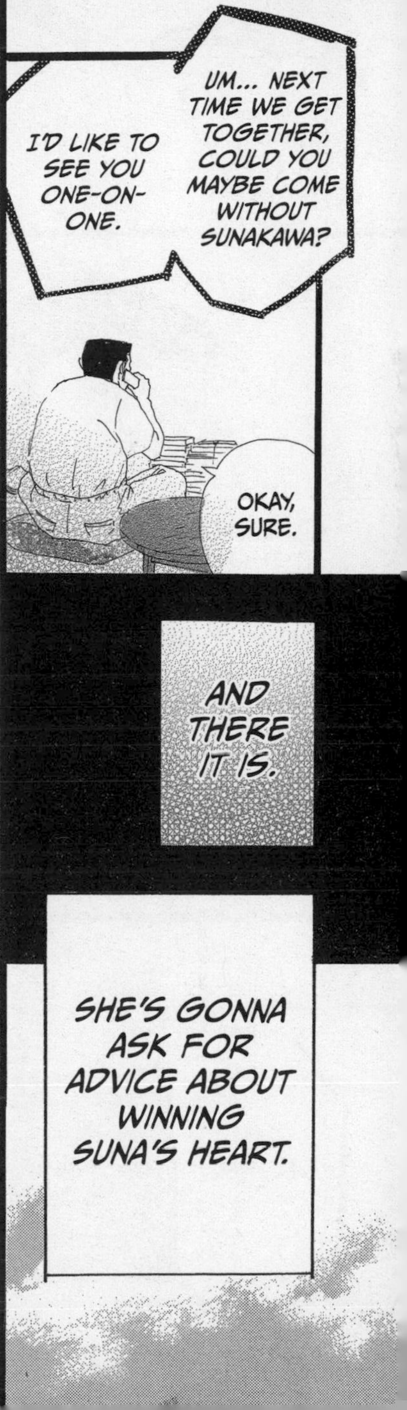
UM... NEXT TIME WE GET TOGETHER, COULD YOU MAYBE COME WITHOUT SUNAKAWA?
I'D LIKE TO SEE YOU ONE-ON-ONE.
OKAY, SURE.
AND THERE IT IS.
SHE'S GONNA ASK FOR ADVICE ABOUT WINNING SUNA'S HEART.

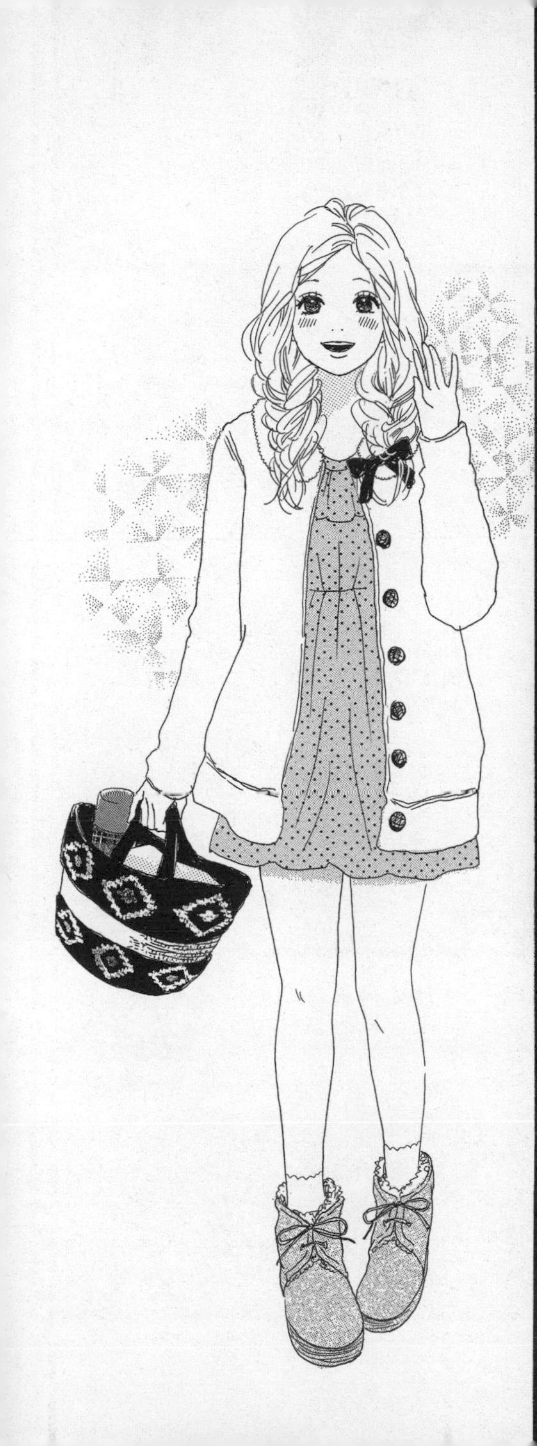

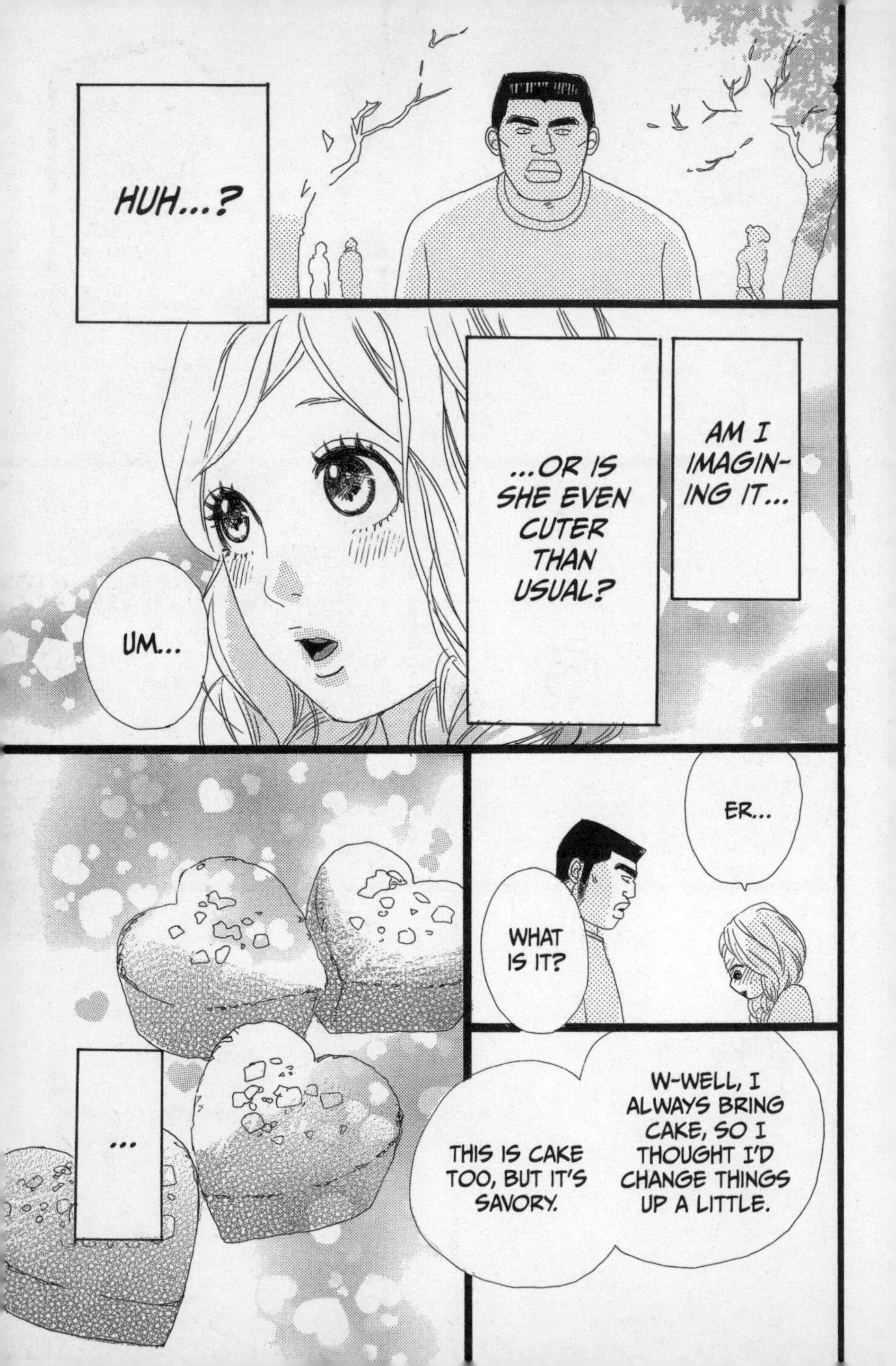
HUH...?
AM I IMAGINING IT...
...OR IS SHE EVEN CUTER THAN USUAL?
UM...
ER...
WHAT IS IT?
W-WELL, I ALWAYS BRING CAKE, SO I THOUGHT I'D CHANGE THINGS UP A LITTLE.
THIS IS CAKE TOO, BUT IT'S SAVORY.
...

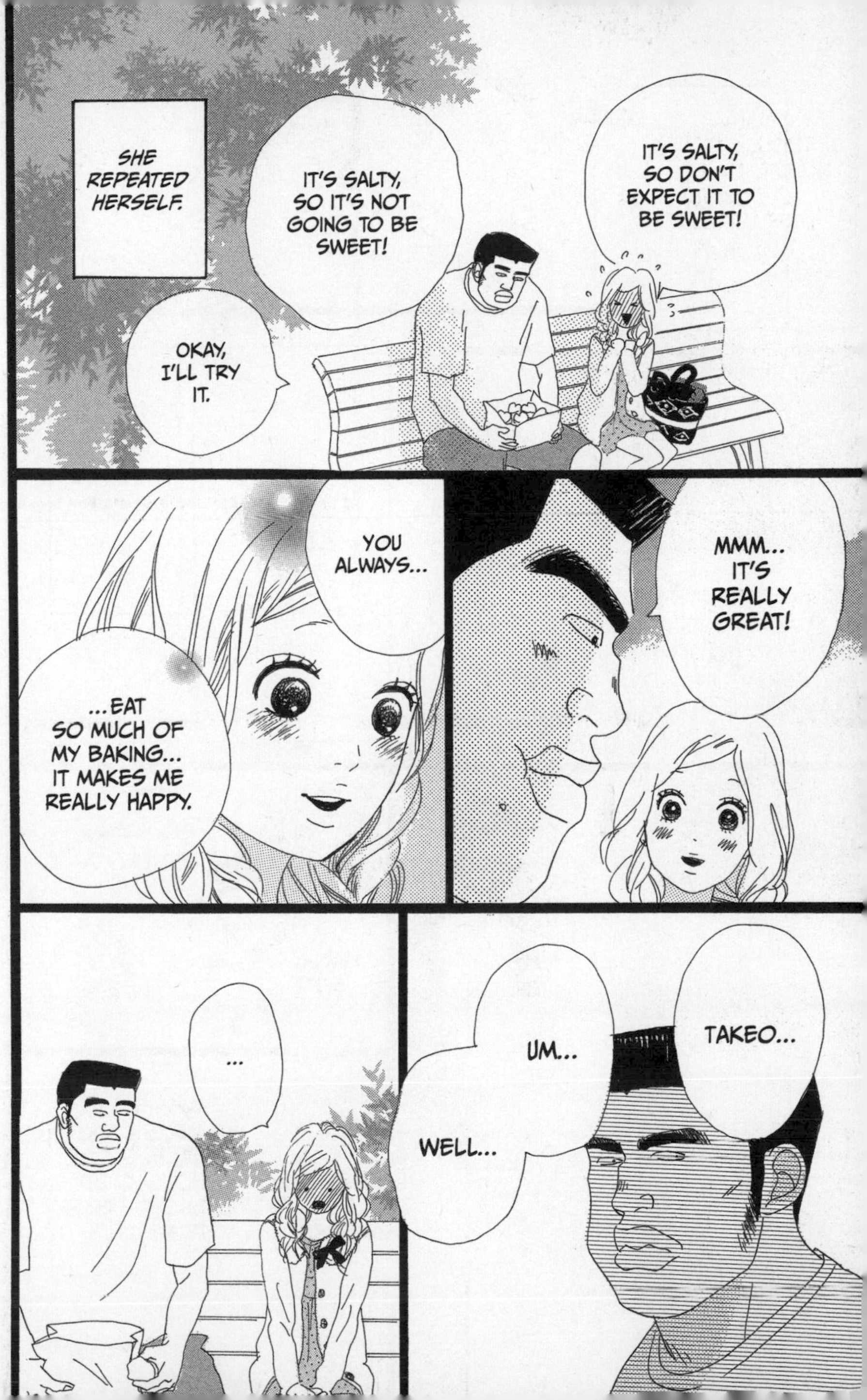
IT'S SALTY, SO DON'T EXPECT IT TO BE SWEET!
IT'S SALTY, SO IT'S NOT GOING TO BE SWEET!
SHE REPEATED HERSELF.
OKAY, I'LL TRY IT.
MMM... IT'S REALLY GREAT!
YOU ALWAYS...
...EAT SO MUCH OF MY BAKING... IT MAKES ME REALLY HAPPY.
TAKEO...
UM...
WELL...
...

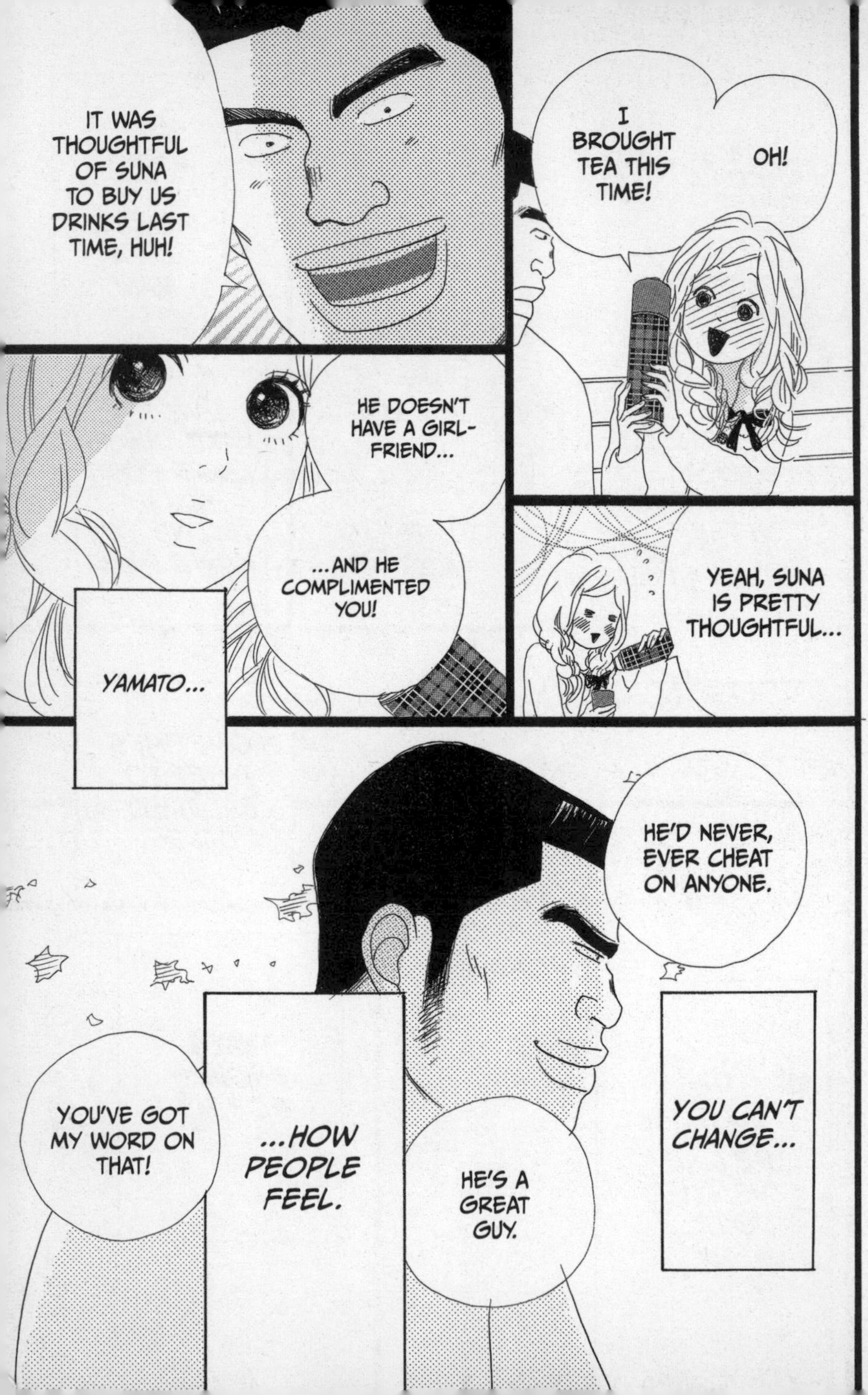
OH!
I BROUGHT TEA THIS TIME!
IT WAS THOUGHTFUL OF SUNA TO BUY US DRINKS LAST TIME, HUH!
YEAH, SUNA IS PRETTY THOUGHTFUL...
HE DOESN'T HAVE A GIRL-FRIEND...
...AND HE COMPLIMENTED YOU!
YAMATO...
HE'D NEVER, EVER CHEAT ON ANYONE.
YOU CAN'T CHANGE...
HE'S A GREAT GUY.
...HOW PEOPLE FEEL.
YOU'VE GOT MY WORD ON THAT!

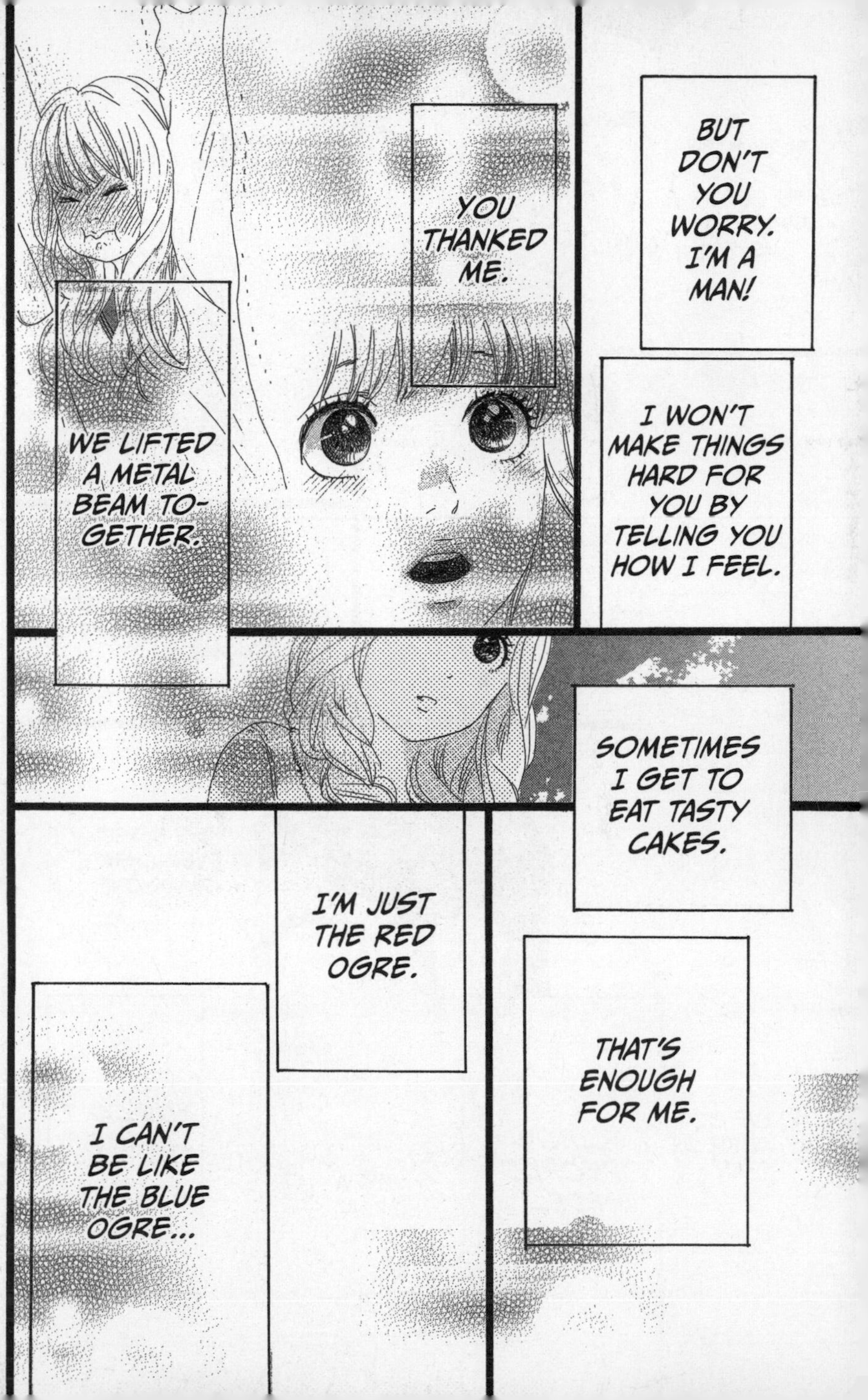
BUT DON'T YOU WORRY. I'M A MAN!
I WON'T MAKE THINGS HARD FOR YOU BY TELLING YOU HOW I FEEL.
YOU THANKED ME.
WE LIFTED A METAL BEAM TO-GETHER.
SOMETIMES I GET TO EAT TASTY CAKES.
THAT'S ENOUGH FOR ME.
I'M JUST THE RED OGRE.
I CAN'T BE LIKE THE BLUE OGRE...

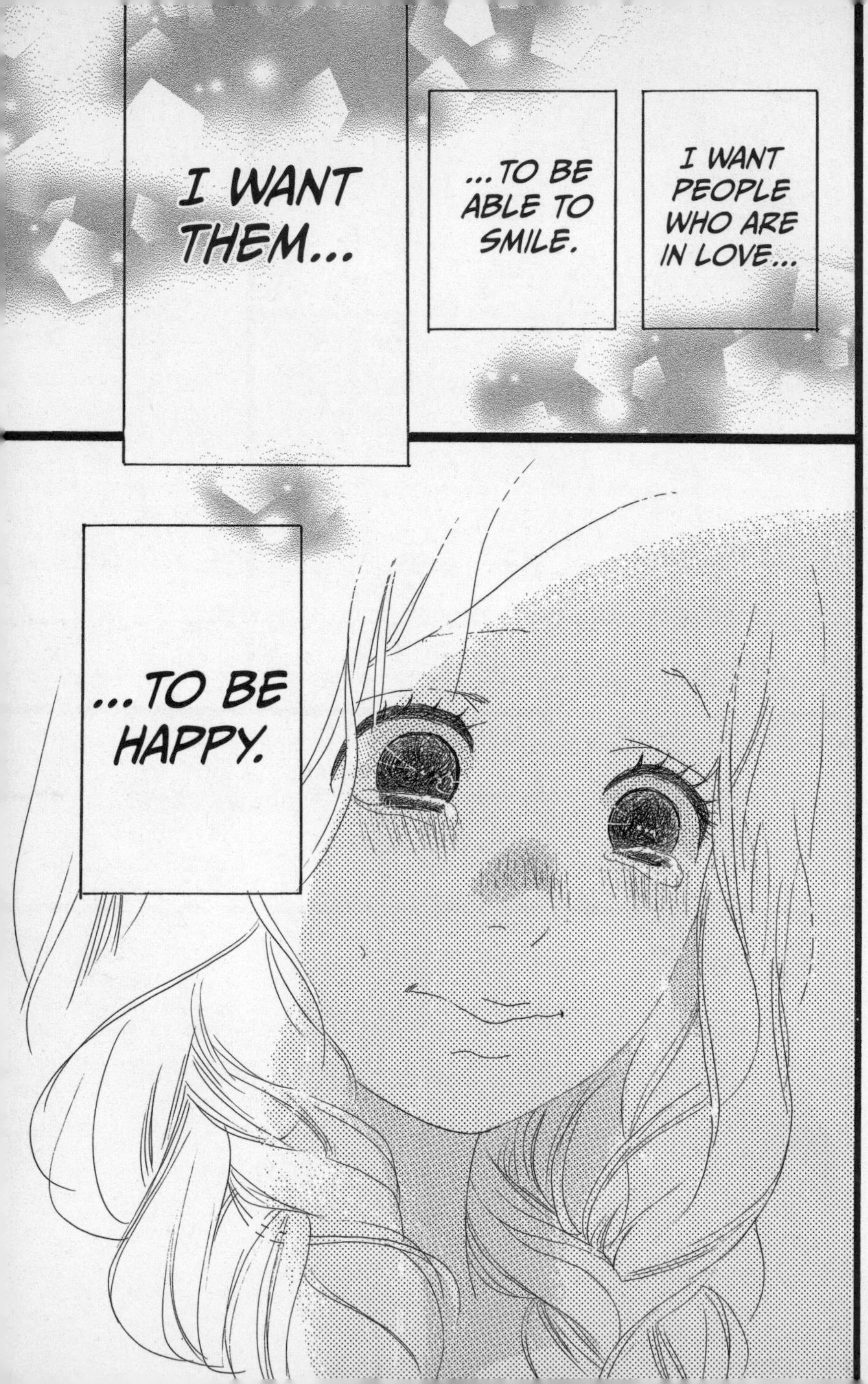
I WANT PEOPLE WHO ARE IN LOVE...
...TO BE ABLE TO SMILE.
I WANT THEM...
...TO BE HAPPY.

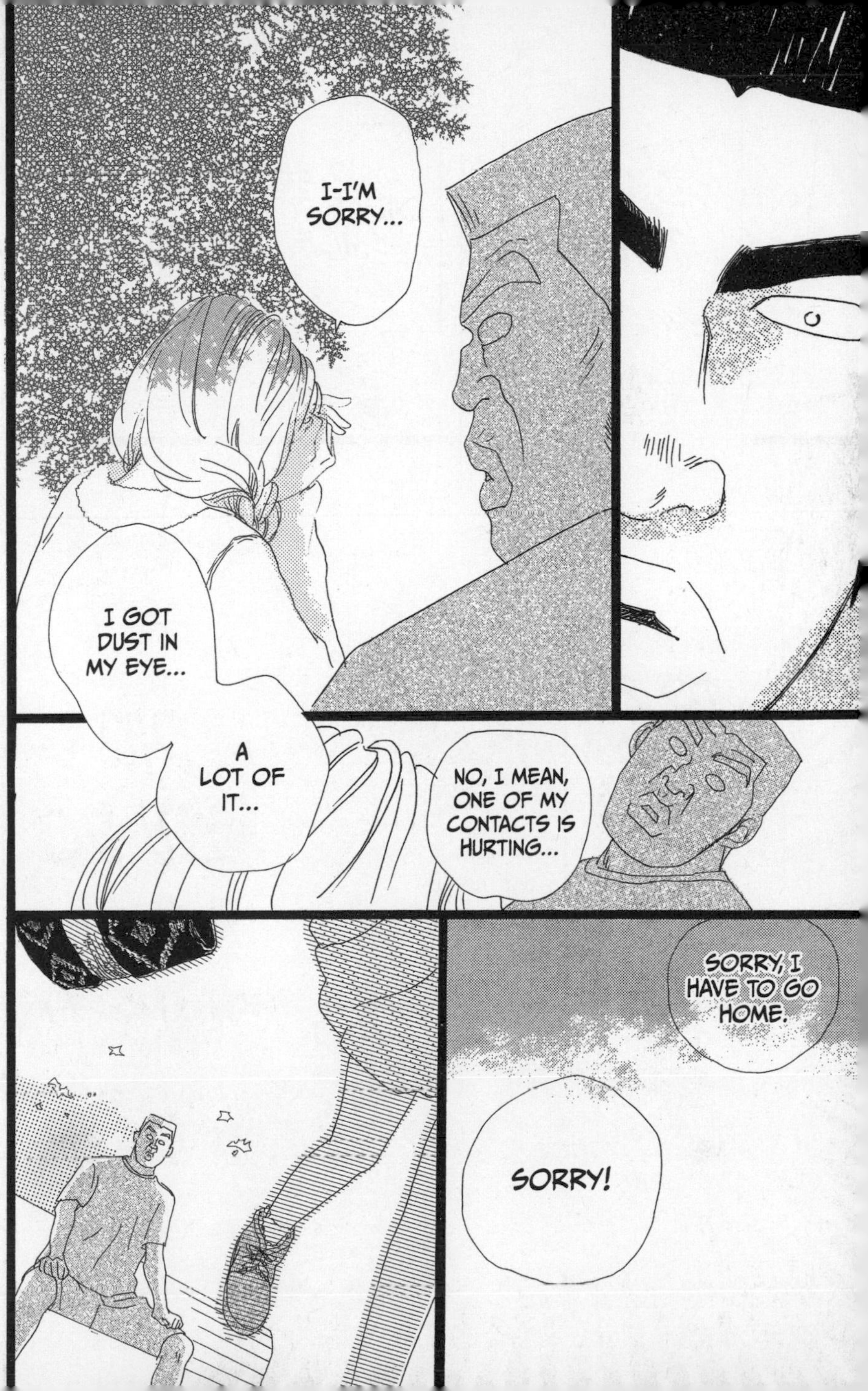
I-I'M SORRY...
I GOT DUST IN MY EYE...
A LOT OF IT...
NO, I MEAN, ONE OF MY CONTACTS IS HURTING...
SORRY, I HAVE TO GO HOME.
SORRY!

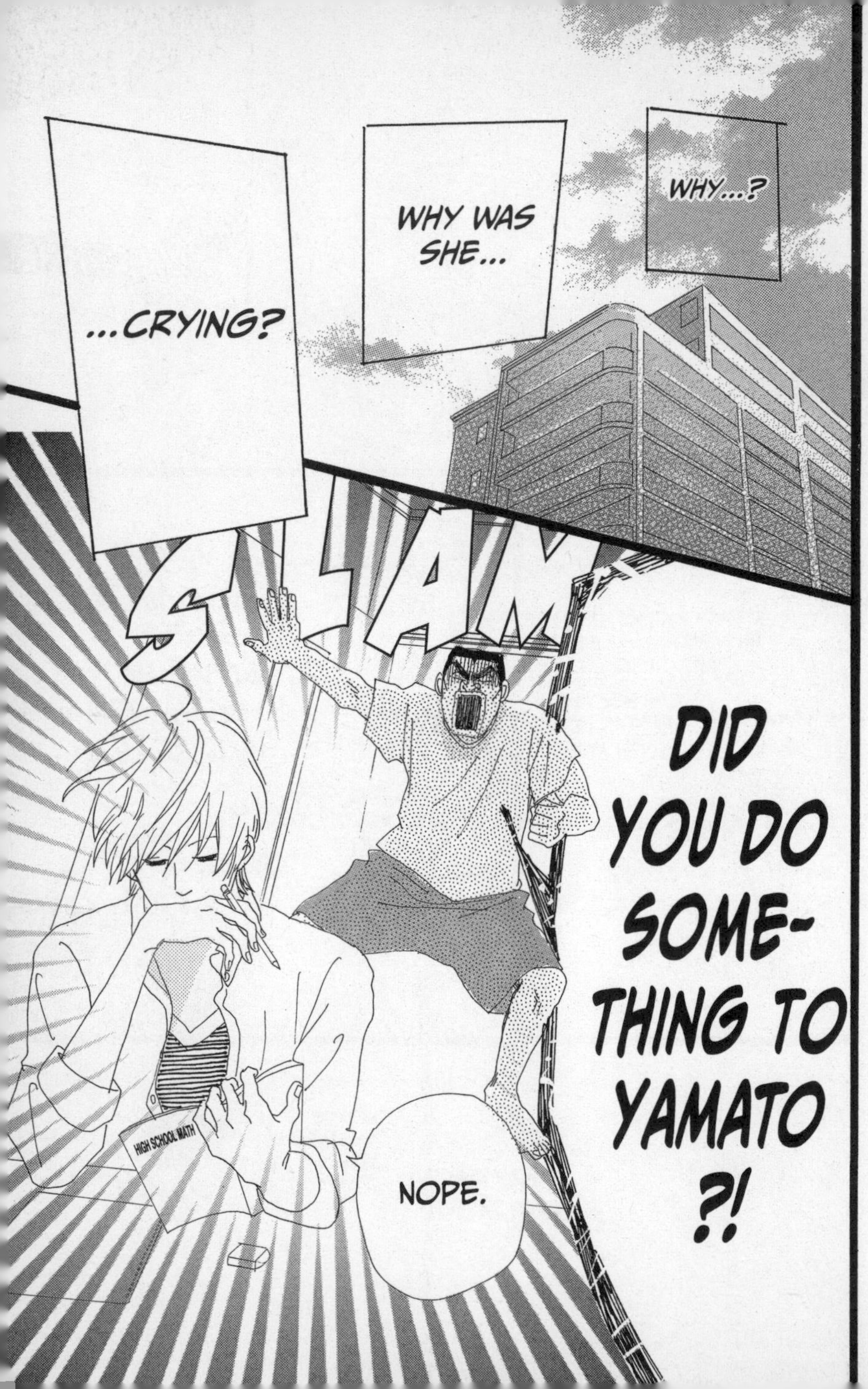
WHY...?
WHY WAS SHE...
...CRYING?
SLAM
DID YOU DO SOME-THING TO YAMATO ?!
NOPE.
HIGH SCHOOL MATH

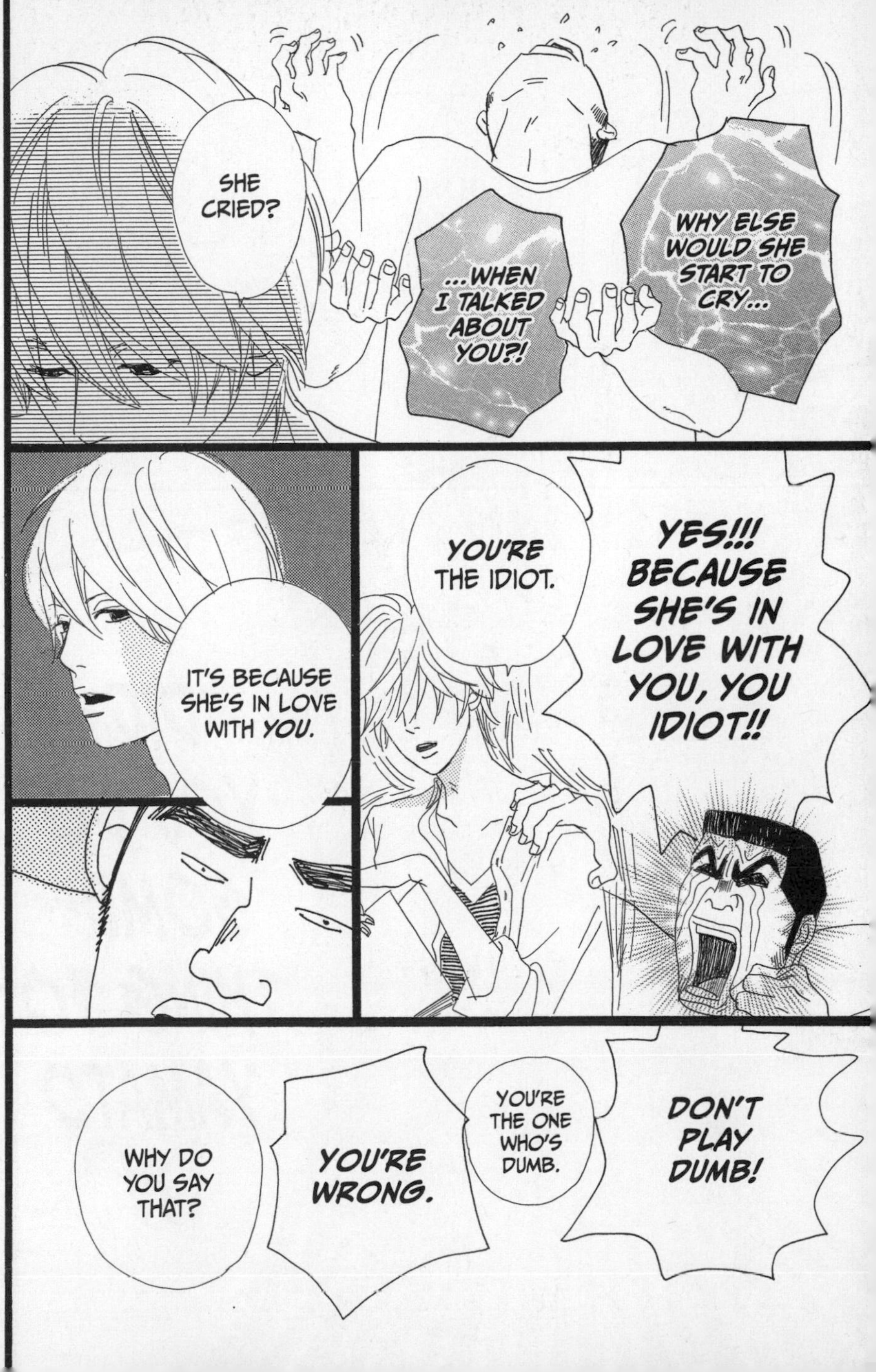
WHY ELSE WOULD SHE START TO CRY...
...WHEN I TALKED ABOUT YOU?!
SHE CRIED?
YES!!! BECAUSE SHE'S IN LOVE WITH YOU, YOU IDIOT!!
YOU'RE THE IDIOT.
IT'S BECAUSE SHE'S IN LOVE WITH YOU.
DON'T PLAY DUMB!
YOU'RE THE ONE WHO'S DUMB.
YOU'RE WRONG.
WHY DO YOU SAY THAT?

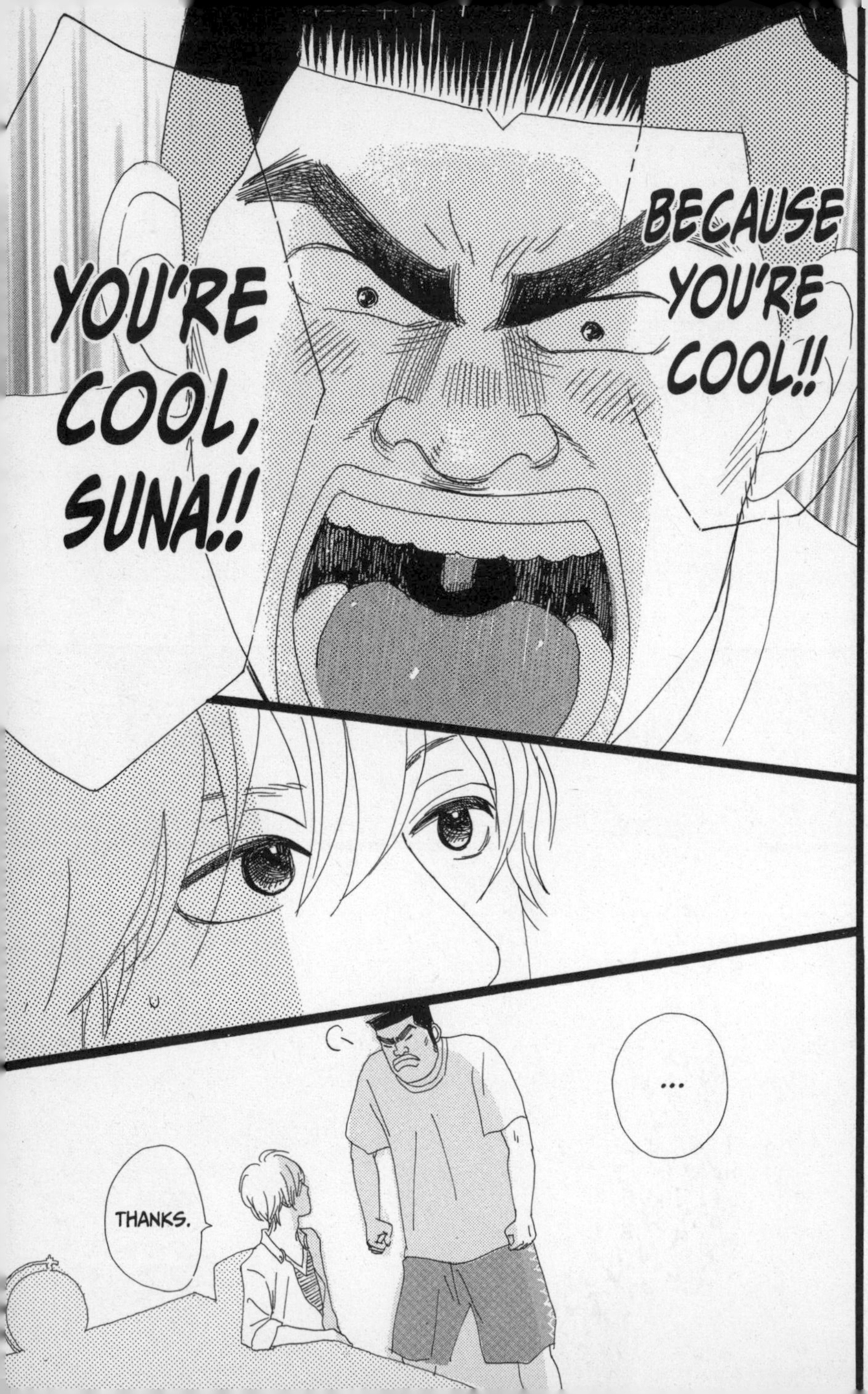
BECAUSE YOU'RE COOL!!
YOU'RE COOL, SUNA!!
...
THANKS.

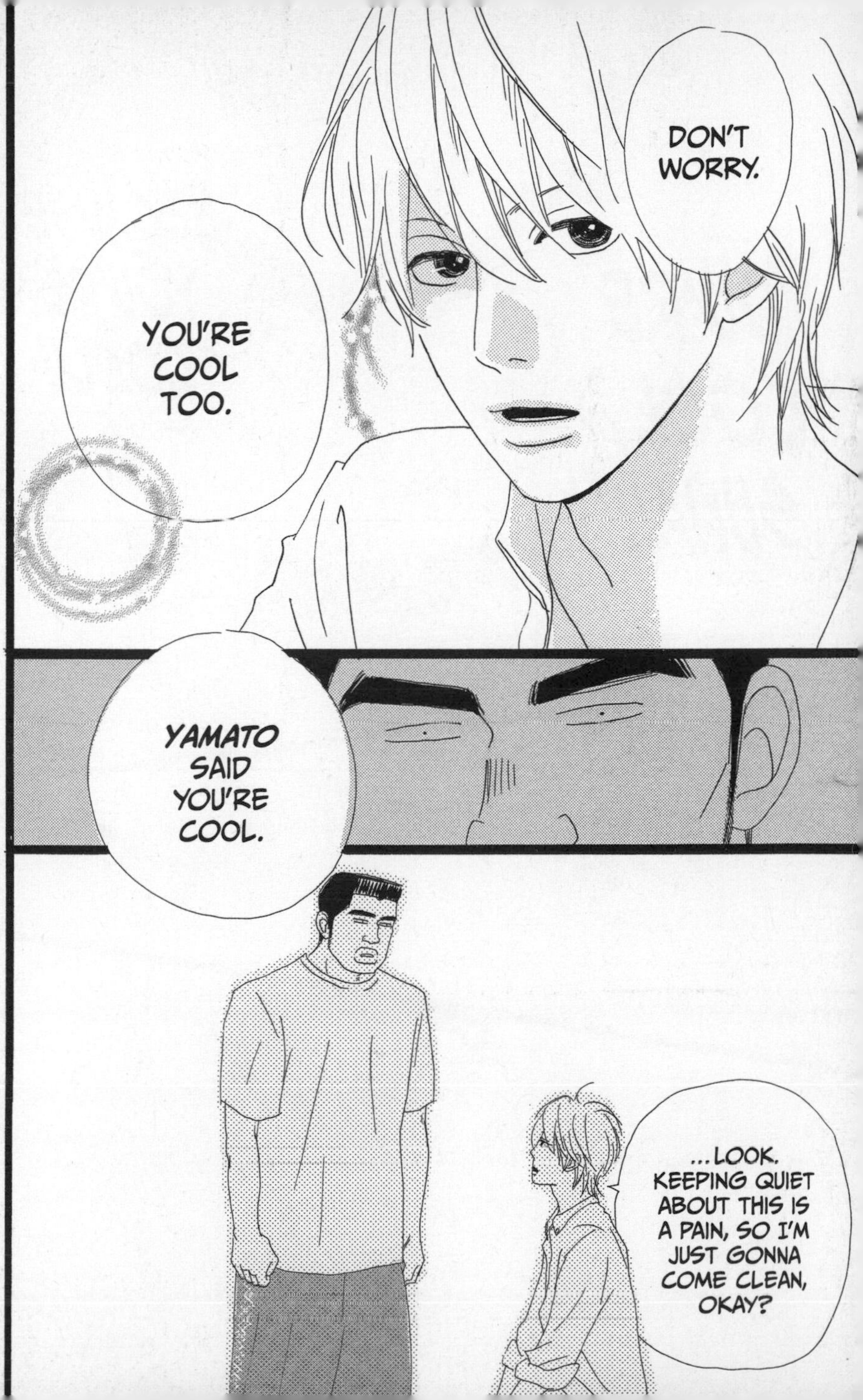
DON'T WORRY.
YOU'RE COOL TOO.
YAMATO SAID YOU'RE COOL.
...LOOK. KEEPING QUIET ABOUT THIS IS A PAIN, SO I'M JUST GONNA COME CLEAN, OKAY?

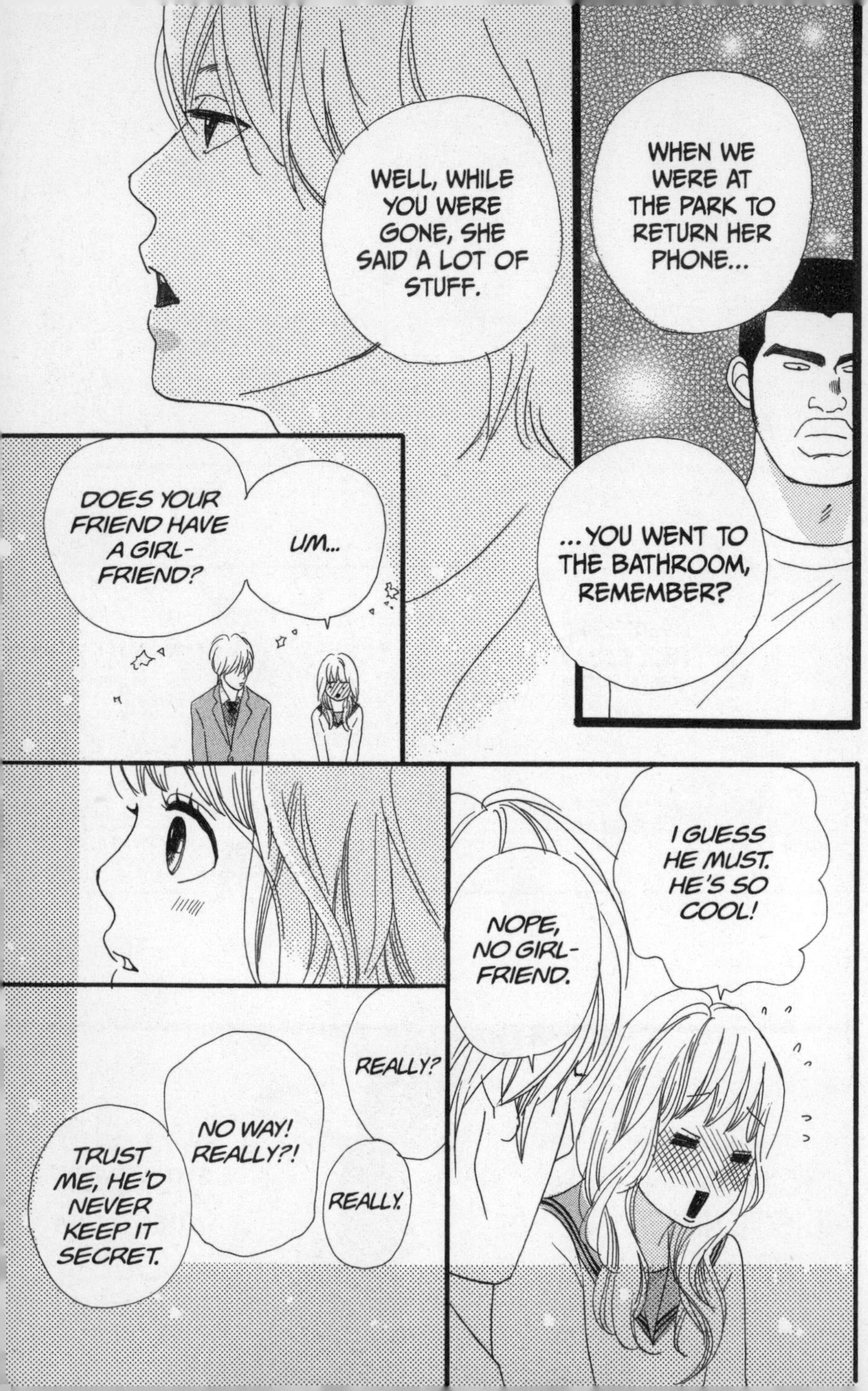
WHEN WE WERE AT THE PARK TO RETURN HER PHONE...
...YOU WENT TO THE BATHROOM, REMEMBER?
WELL, WHILE YOU WERE GONE, SHE SAID A LOT OF STUFF.
DOES YOUR FRIEND HAVE A GIRL-FRIEND?
UM...
I GUESS HE MUST. HE'S SO COOL!
NOPE, NO GIRL-FRIEND.
REALLY?
NO WAY! REALLY?!
REALLY.
TRUST ME, HE'D NEVER KEEP IT SECRET.

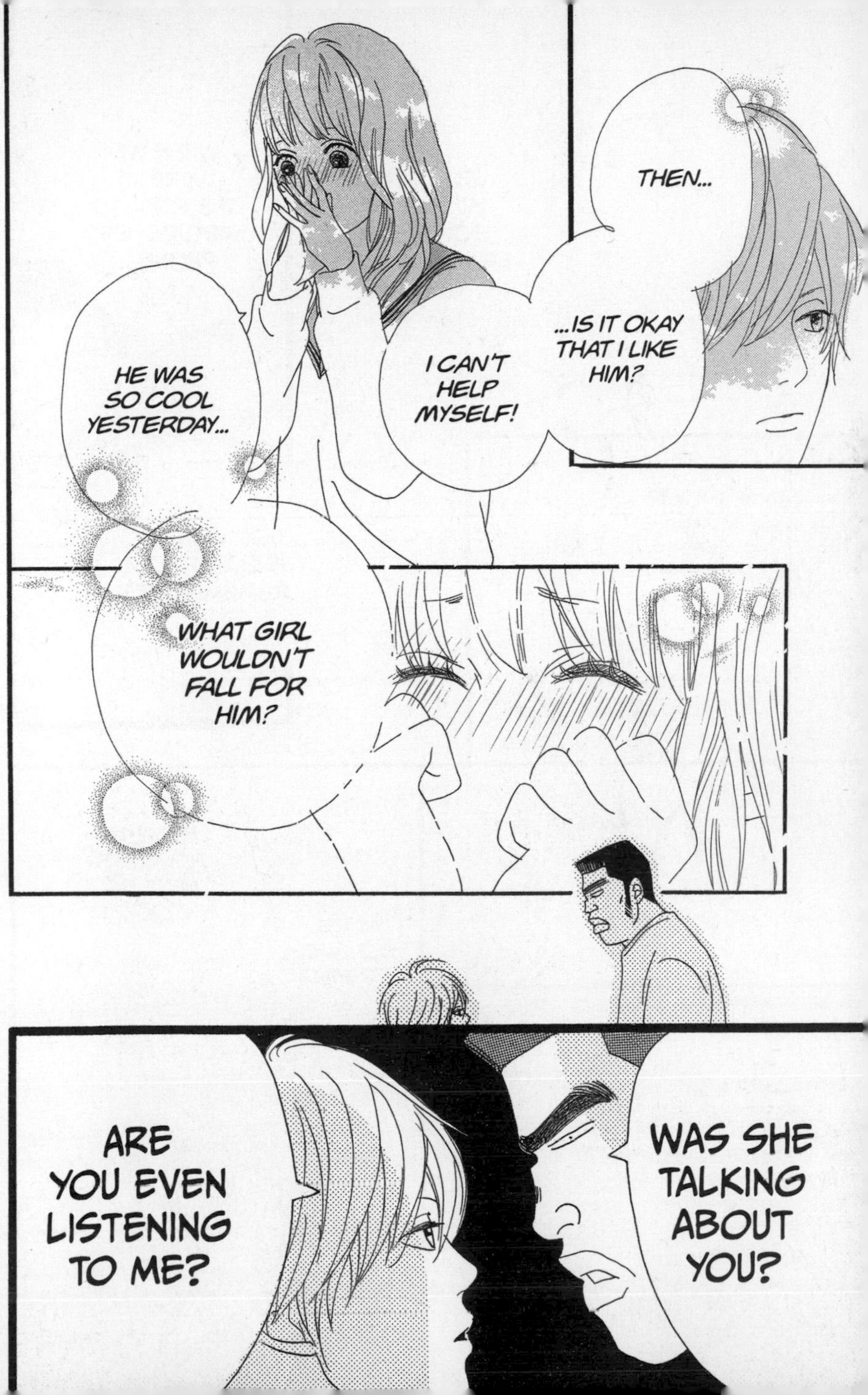
THEN...
...IS IT OKAY THAT I LIKE HIM?
I CAN'T HELP MYSELF!
HE WAS SO COOL YESTERDAY...
WHAT GIRL WOULDN'T FALL FOR HIM?
WAS SHE TALKING ABOUT YOU?
ARE YOU EVEN LISTENING TO ME?

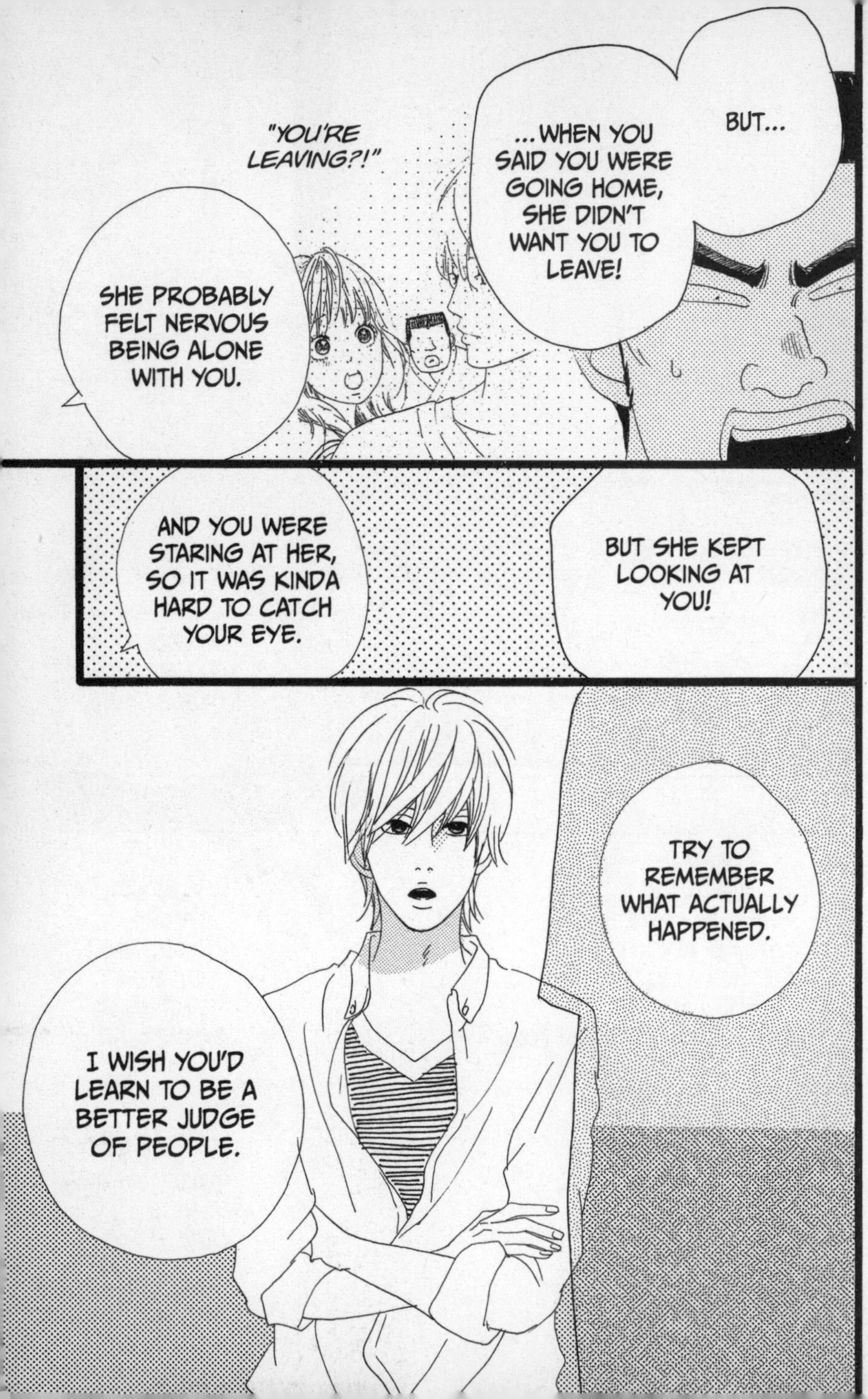
BUT...
...WHEN YOU SAID YOU WERE GOING HOME, SHE DIDN'T WANT YOU TO LEAVE!
"YOU'RE LEAVING?!"
SHE PROBABLY FELT NERVOUS BEING ALONE WITH YOU.
BUT SHE KEPT LOOKING AT YOU!
AND YOU WERE STARING AT HER, SO IT WAS KINDA HARD TO CATCH YOUR EYE.
TRY TO REMEMBER WHAT ACTUALLY HAPPENED.
I WISH YOU'D LEARN TO BE A BETTER JUDGE OF PEOPLE.

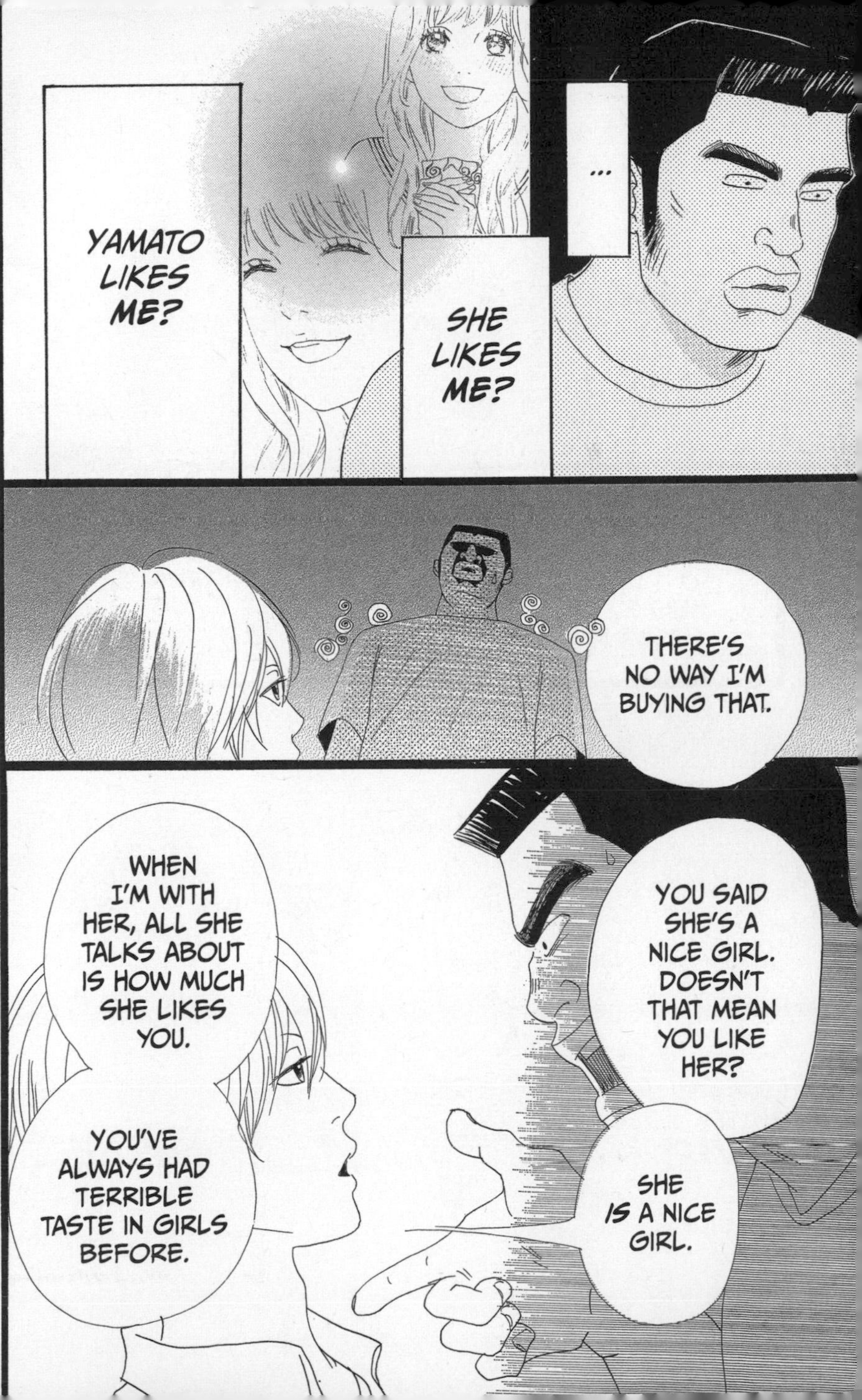
...
SHE LIKES ME?
YAMATO LIKES ME?
THERE'S NO WAY I'M BUYING THAT.
YOU SAID SHE'S A NICE GIRL. DOESN'T THAT MEAN YOU LIKE HER?
SHE *IS* A NICE GIRL.
WHEN I'M WITH HER, ALL SHE TALKS ABOUT IS HOW MUCH SHE LIKES YOU.
YOU'VE ALWAYS HAD TERRIBLE TASTE IN GIRLS BEFORE.

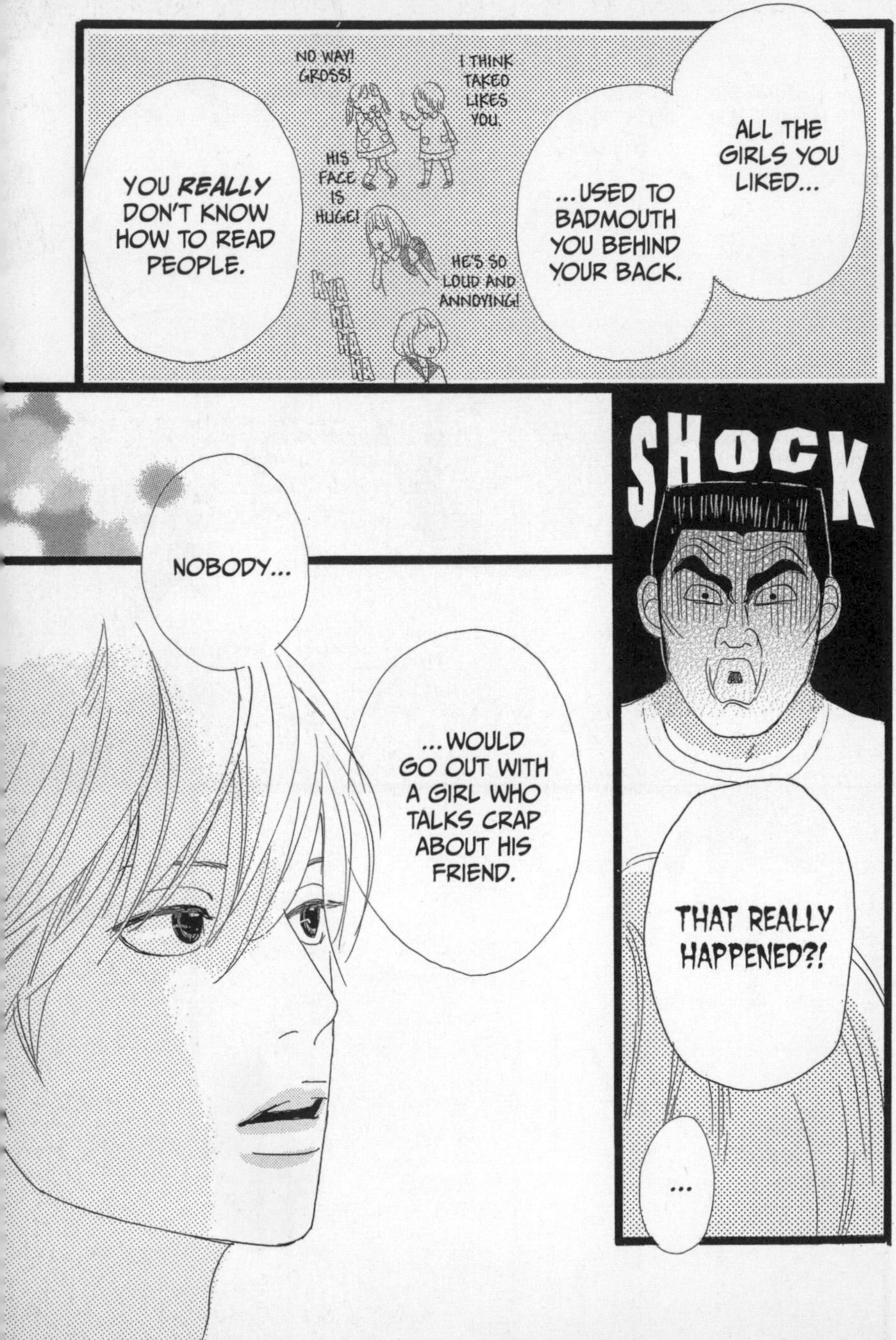
ALL THE GIRLS YOU LIKED...
...USED TO BADMOUTH YOU BEHIND YOUR BACK.
I THINK TAKEO LIKES YOU.
NO WAY! GROSS!
HIS FACE IS HUGE!
HE'S SO LOUD AND ANNOYING!
YOU REALLY DON'T KNOW HOW TO READ PEOPLE.
SHOCK
THAT REALLY HAPPENED?!
...
NOBODY...
...WOULD GO OUT WITH A GIRL WHO TALKS CRAP ABOUT HIS FRIEND.

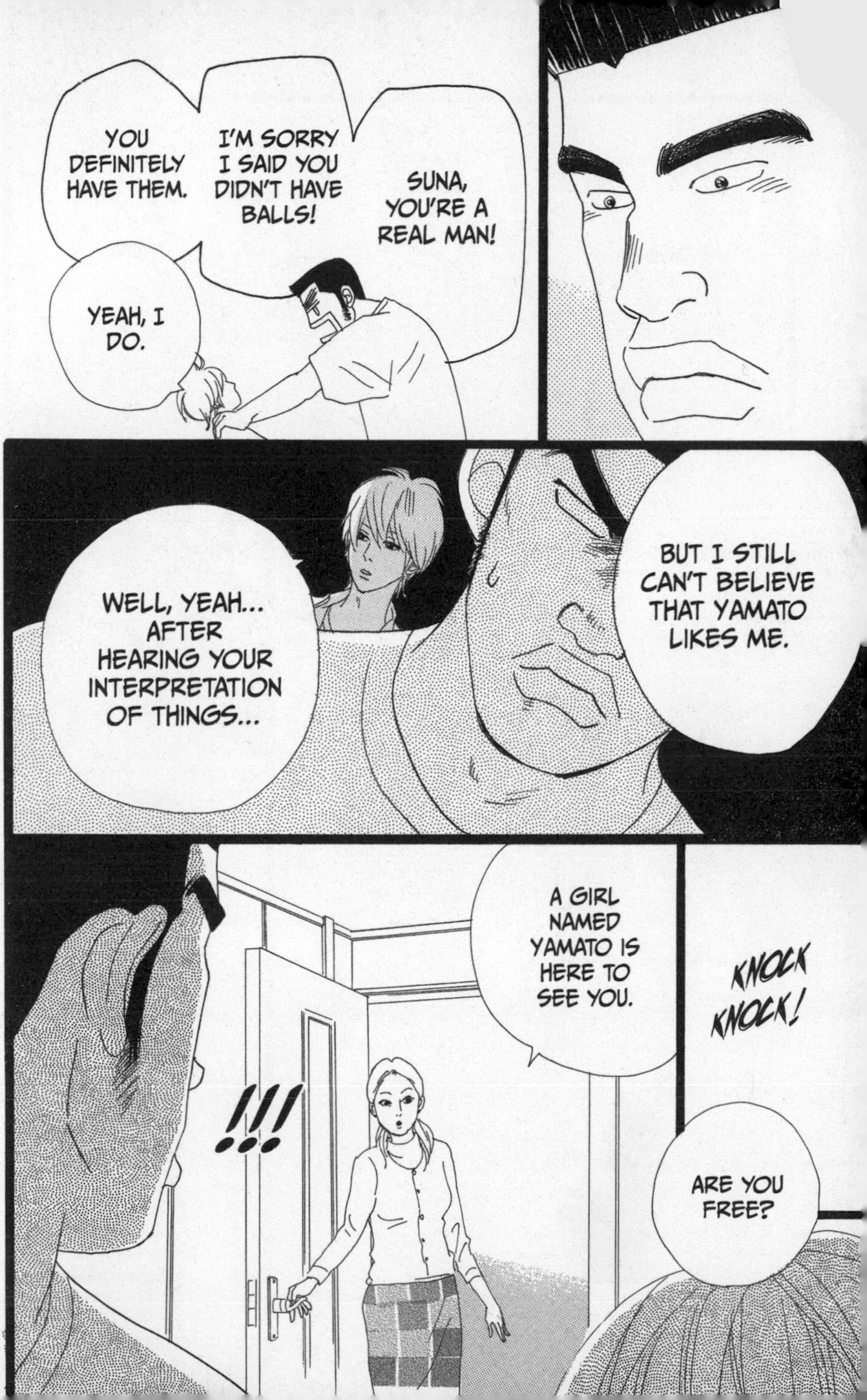
SUNA, YOU'RE A REAL MAN!
I'M SORRY I SAID YOU DIDN'T HAVE BALLS!
YOU DEFINITELY HAVE THEM.
YEAH, I DO.
BUT I STILL CAN'T BELIEVE THAT YAMATO LIKES ME.
WELL, YEAH... AFTER HEARING YOUR INTERPRETATION OF THINGS...
KNOCK KNOCK!
ARE YOU FREE?
A GIRL NAMED YAMATO IS HERE TO SEE YOU.
!!!

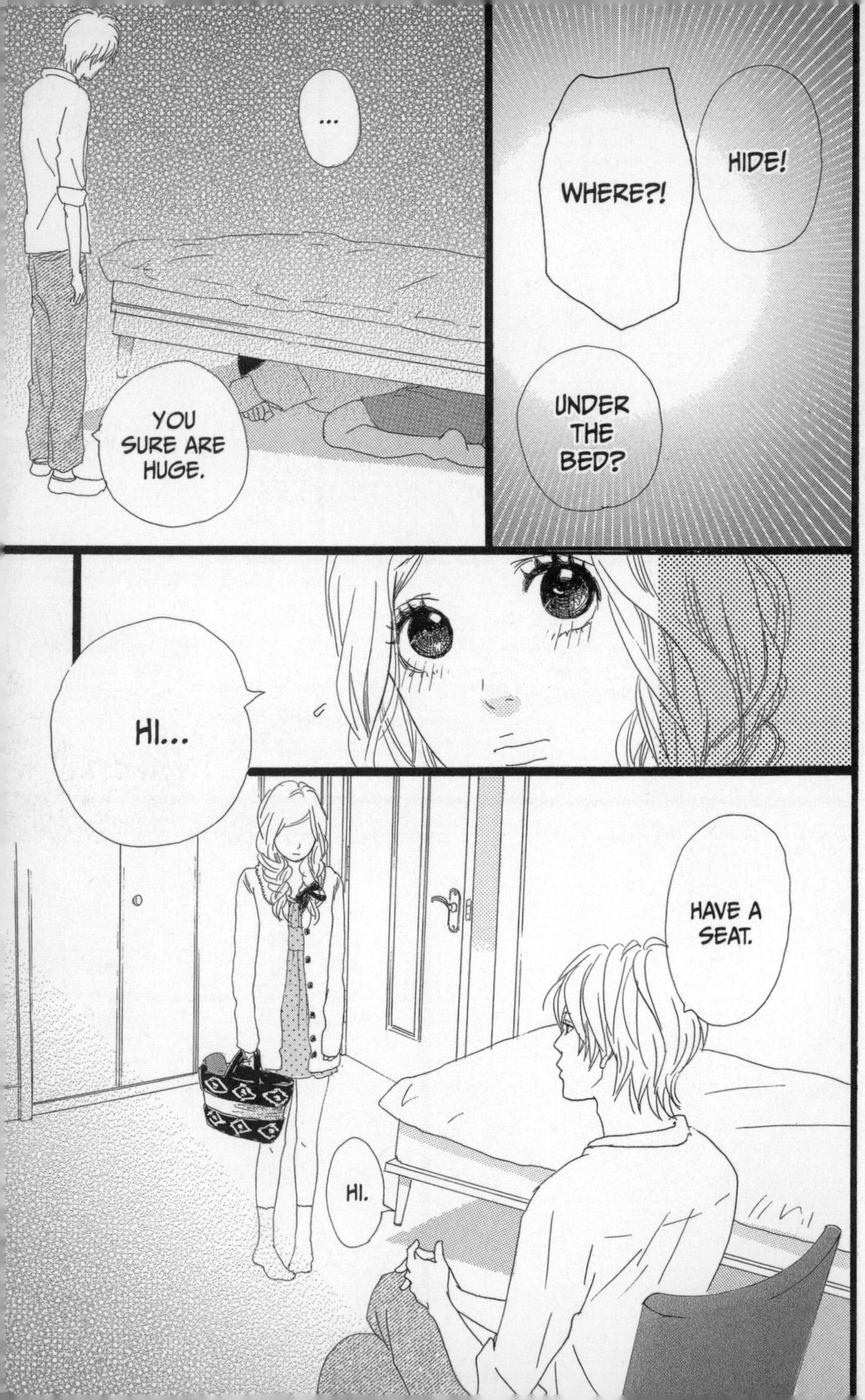
HIDE!
WHERE?!
UNDER THE BED?
...
YOU SURE ARE HUGE.
HI...
HAVE A SEAT.
HI.

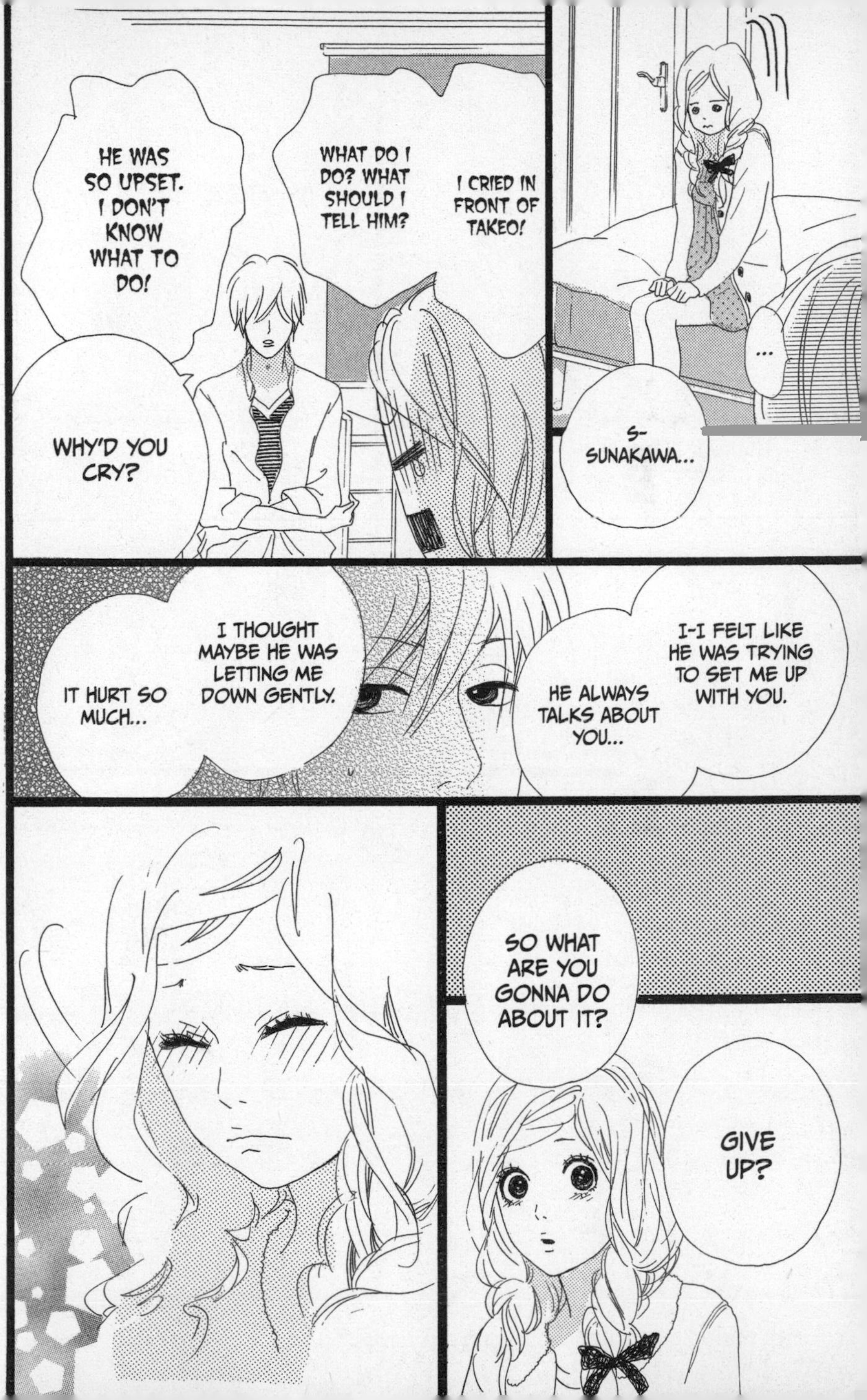

...
S-SUNAKAWA...
I CRIED IN FRONT OF TAKEO!
WHAT DO I DO? WHAT SHOULD I TELL HIM?
HE WAS SO UPSET. I DON'T KNOW WHAT TO DO!
WHY'D YOU CRY?
I-I FELT LIKE HE WAS TRYING TO SET ME UP WITH YOU.
HE ALWAYS TALKS ABOUT YOU...
I THOUGHT MAYBE HE WAS LETTING ME DOWN GENTLY.
IT HURT SO MUCH...
SO WHAT ARE YOU GONNA DO ABOUT IT?
GIVE UP?

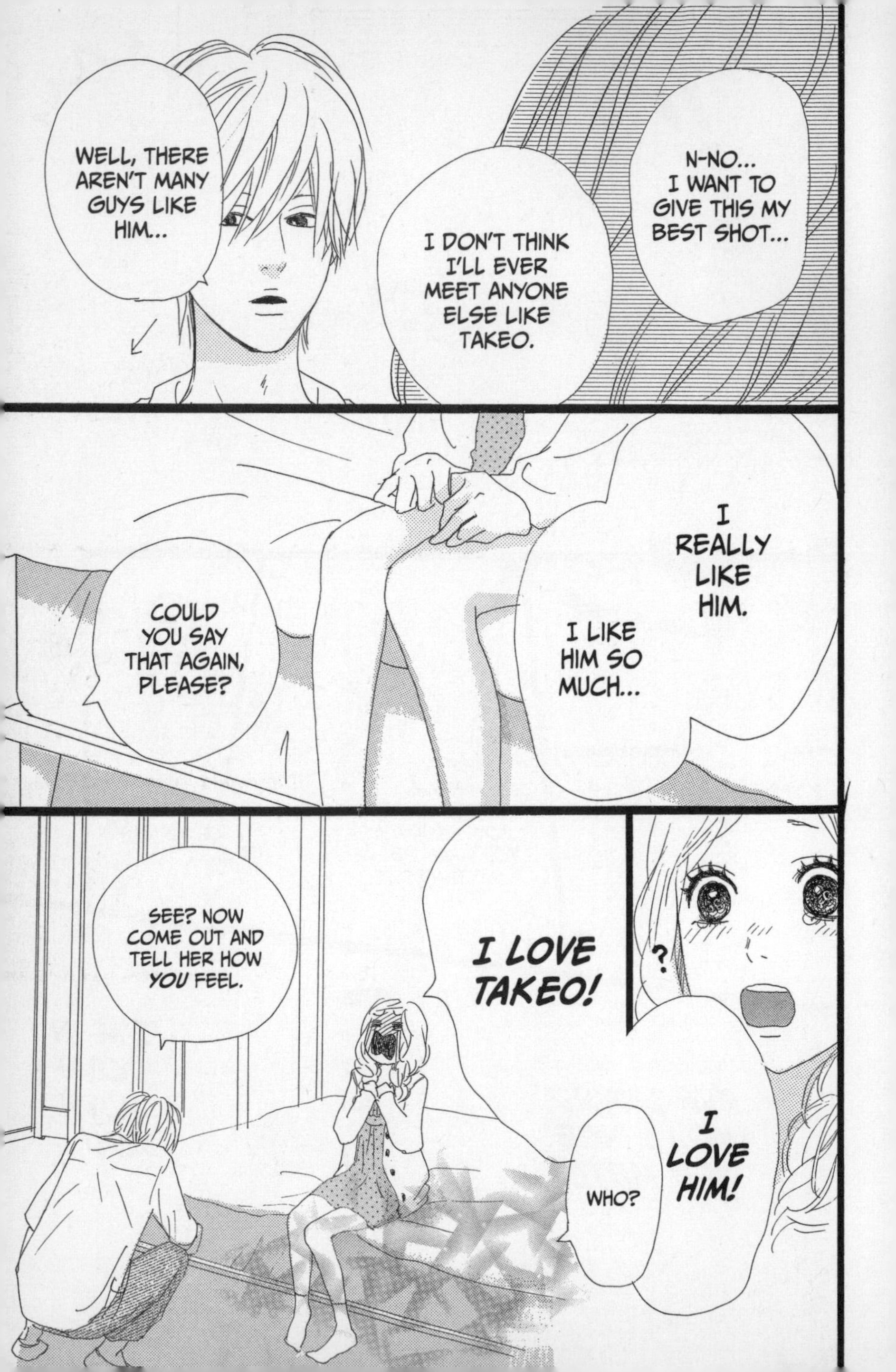
N-NO... I WANT TO GIVE THIS MY BEST SHOT...
I DON'T THINK I'LL EVER MEET ANYONE ELSE LIKE TAKEO.
WELL, THERE AREN'T MANY GUYS LIKE HIM...
I REALLY LIKE HIM.
I LIKE HIM SO MUCH...
COULD YOU SAY THAT AGAIN, PLEASE?
?
I LOVE HIM!
WHO?
I LOVE TAKEO!
SEE? NOW COME OUT AND TELL HER HOW *YOU* FEEL.

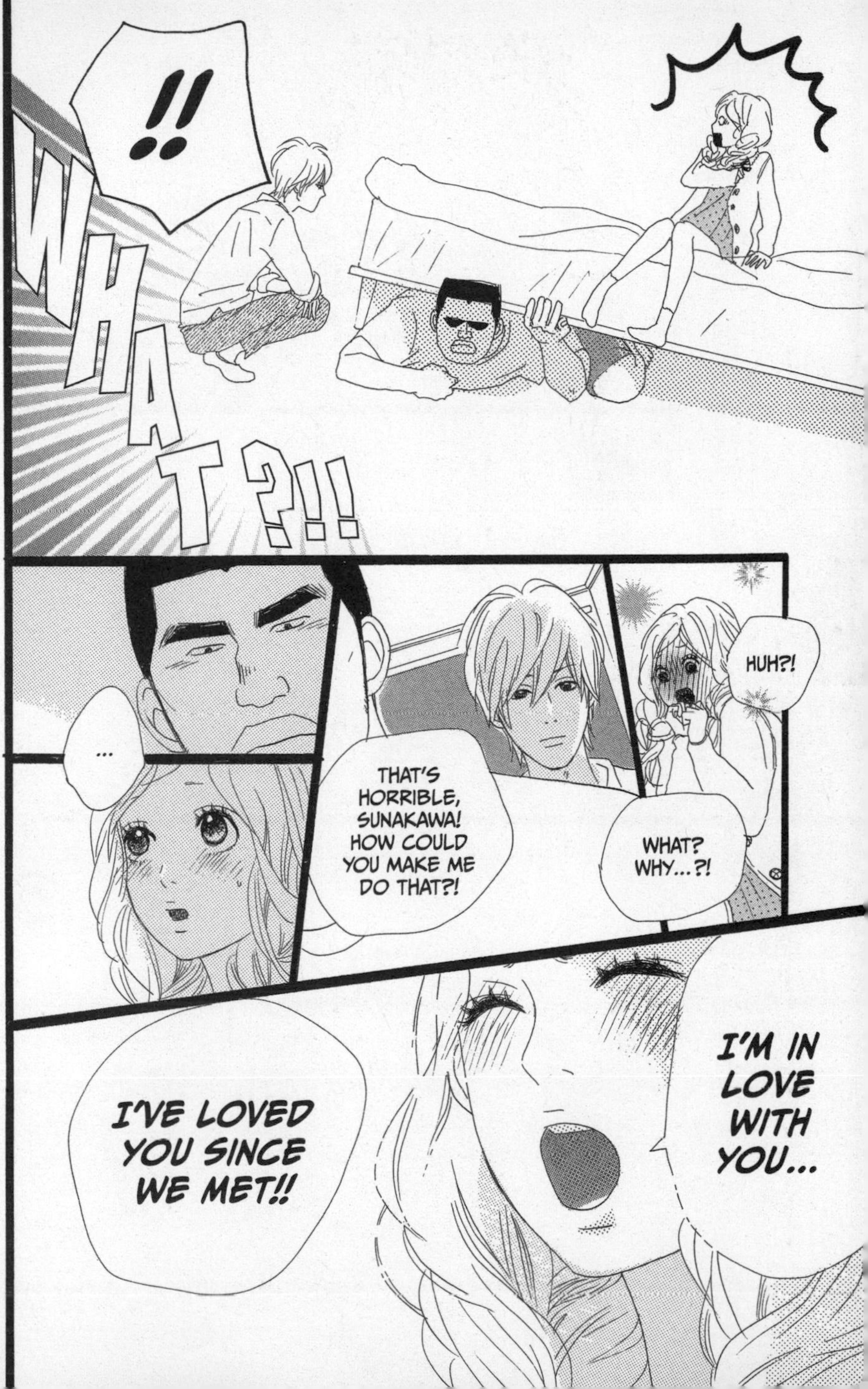
!!
WHAT?!!
HUH?!
WHAT? WHY...?!
THAT'S HORRIBLE, SUNAKAWA! HOW COULD YOU MAKE ME DO THAT?!
...
I'M IN LOVE WITH YOU...
I'VE LOVED YOU SINCE WE MET!!

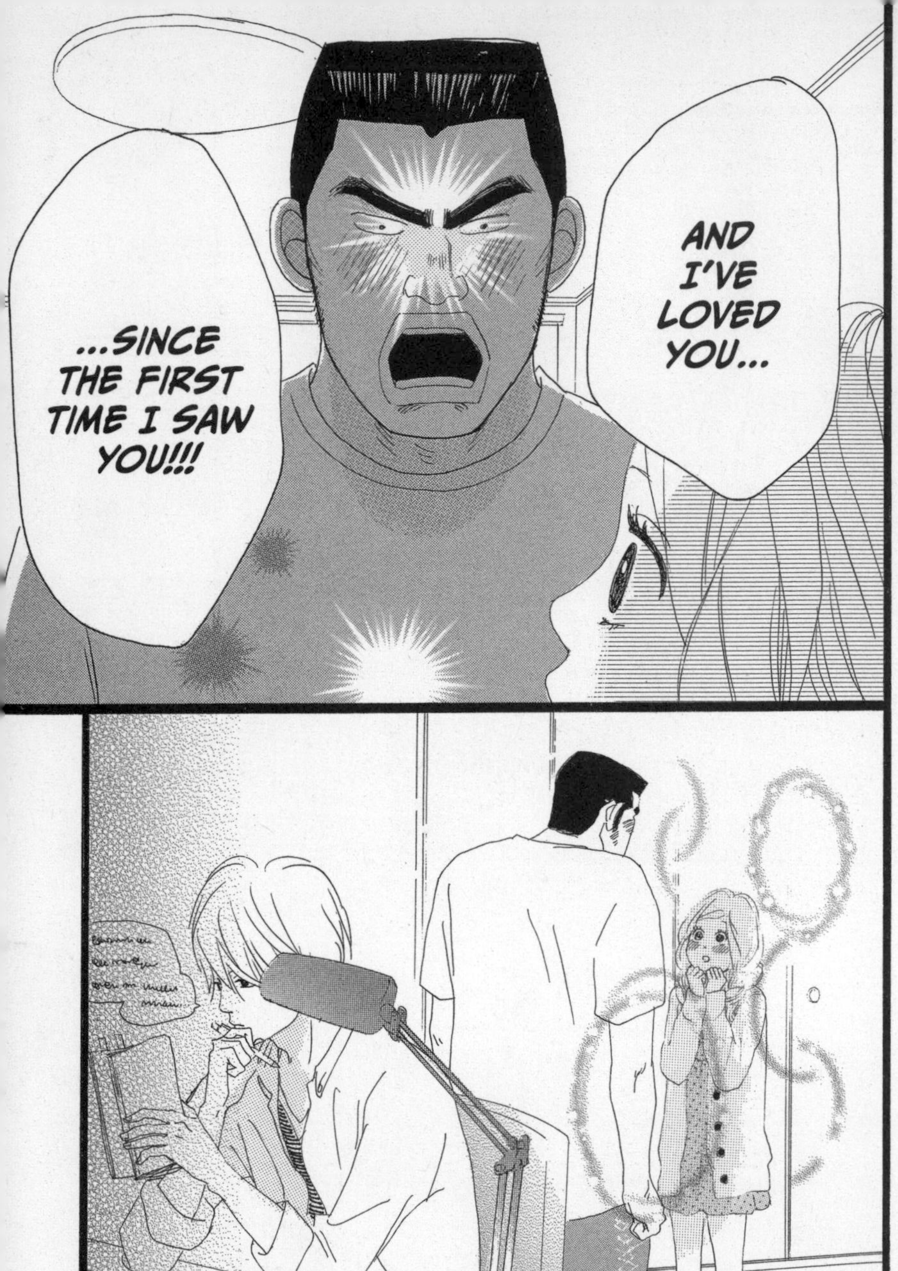
AND I'VE LOVED YOU...
...SINCE THE FIRST TIME I SAW YOU!!!

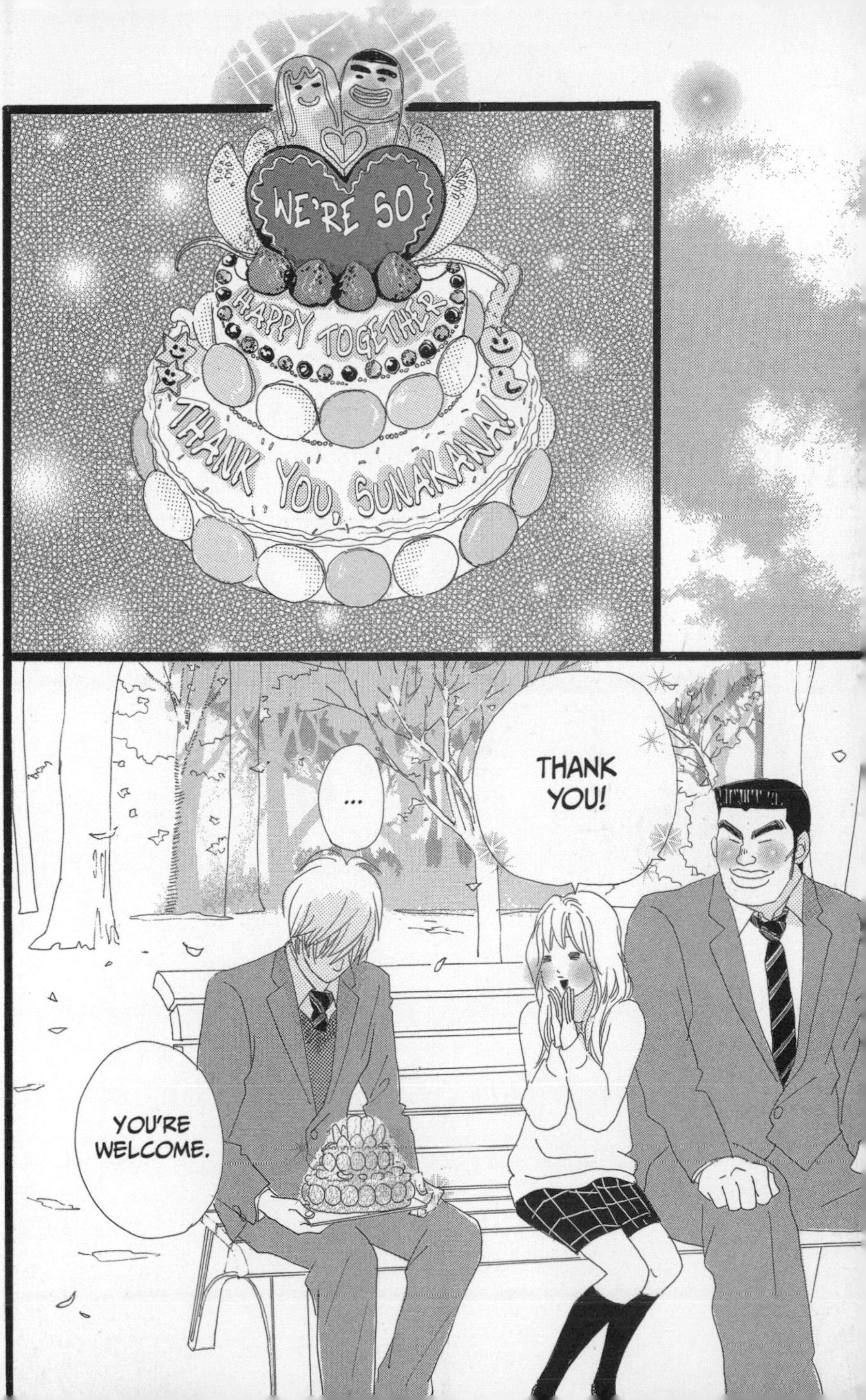
WE'RE SO
HAPPY TOGETHER
THANK YOU, SUNAKAWA!
THANK YOU!
...
YOU'RE WELCOME.

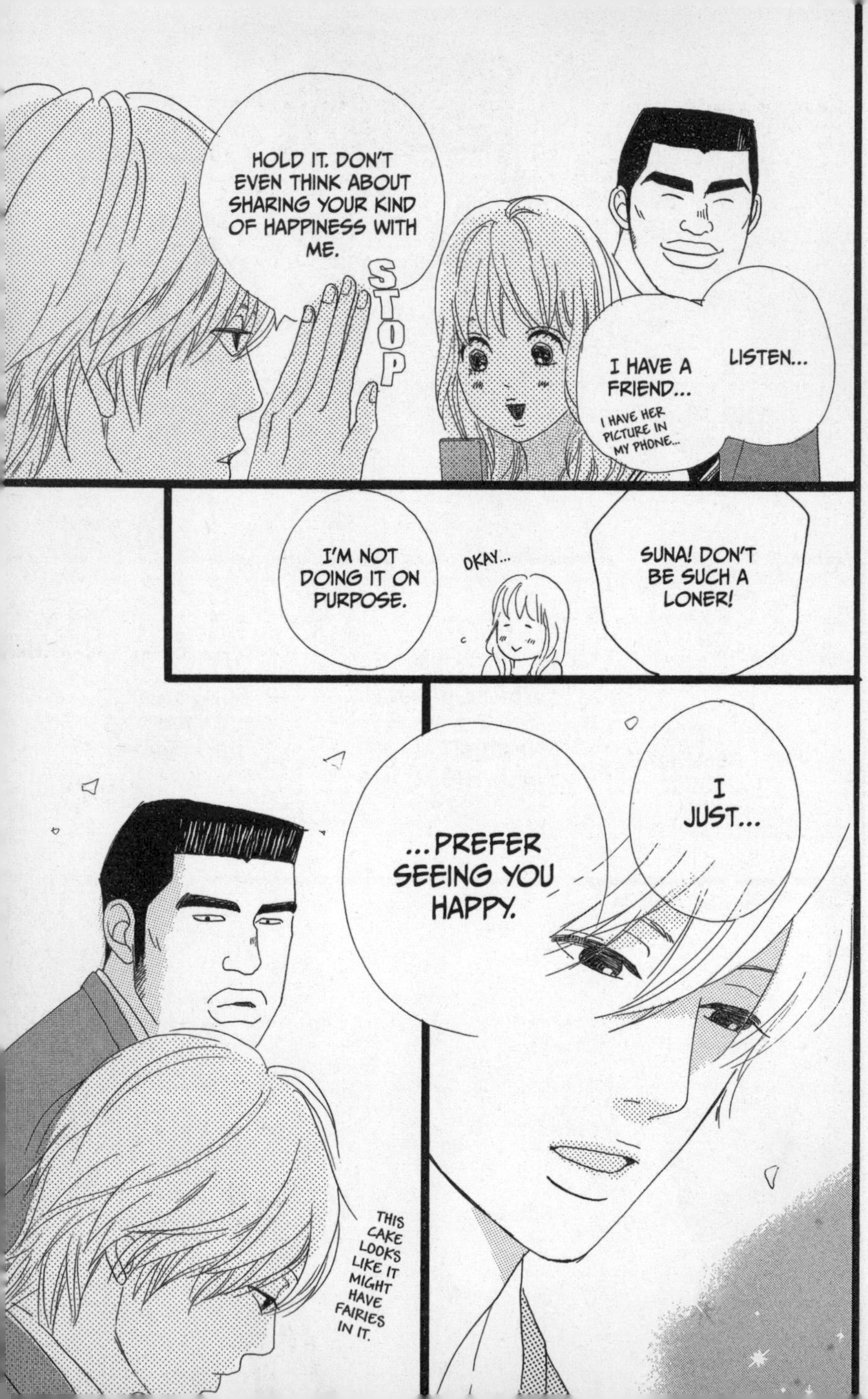
LISTEN...
I HAVE A FRIEND...
I HAVE HER PICTURE IN MY PHONE...
HOLD IT. DON'T EVEN THINK ABOUT SHARING YOUR KIND OF HAPPINESS WITH ME.
STOP
SUNA! DON'T BE SUCH A LONER!
OKAY...
I'M NOT DOING IT ON PURPOSE.
I JUST...
...PREFER SEEING YOU HAPPY.
THIS CAKE LOOKS LIKE IT MIGHT HAVE FAIRIES IN IT.

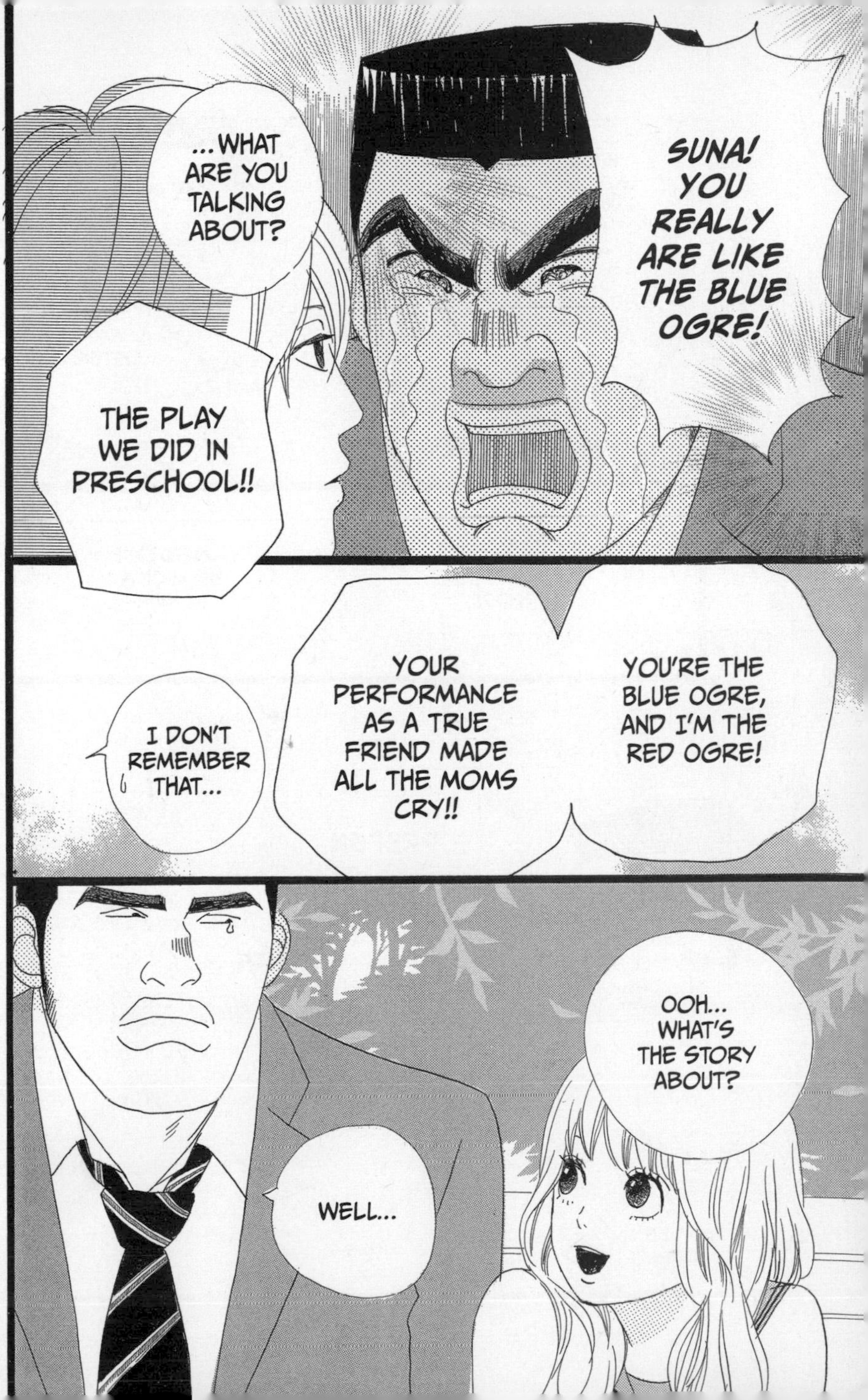
SUNA! YOU REALLY ARE LIKE THE BLUE OGRE!
...WHAT ARE YOU TALKING ABOUT?
THE PLAY WE DID IN PRESCHOOL!!
YOU'RE THE BLUE OGRE, AND I'M THE RED OGRE!
YOUR PERFORMANCE AS A TRUE FRIEND MADE ALL THE MOMS CRY!!
I DON'T REMEMBER THAT...
OOH... WHAT'S THE STORY ABOUT?
WELL...

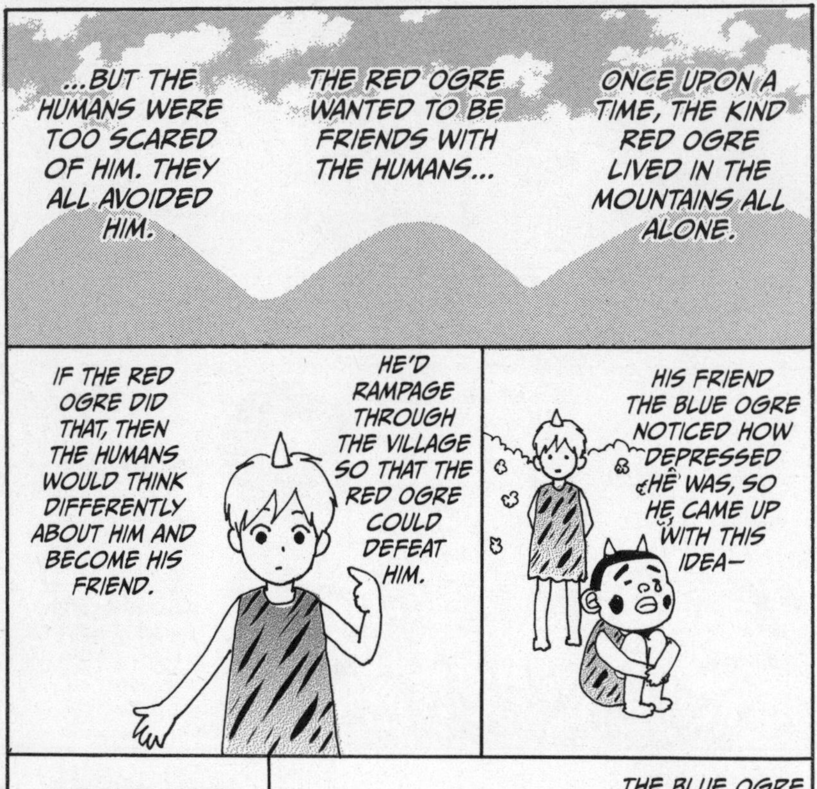

ONCE UPON A TIME, THE KIND RED OGRE LIVED IN THE MOUNTAINS ALL ALONE.
THE RED OGRE WANTED TO BE FRIENDS WITH THE HUMANS...
...BUT THE HUMANS WERE TOO SCARED OF HIM. THEY ALL AVOIDED HIM.
HIS FRIEND THE BLUE OGRE NOTICED HOW DEPRESSED HE WAS, SO HE CAME UP WITH THIS IDEA—
HE'D RAMPAGE THROUGH THE VILLAGE SO THAT THE RED OGRE COULD DEFEAT HIM.
IF THE RED OGRE DID THAT, THEN THE HUMANS WOULD THINK DIFFERENTLY ABOUT HIM AND BECOME HIS FRIEND.
THE BLUE OGRE WENT TO THE VILLAGE AND RAN WILD, ALL WHILE TRYING NOT TO HURT THE HUMANS. THE RED OGRE PRETENDED TO DEFEAT HIM.
THE BLUE OGRE PRETENDED TO BE DEFEATED AND RAN AWAY.

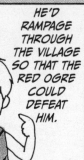

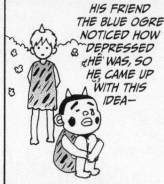

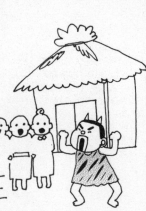

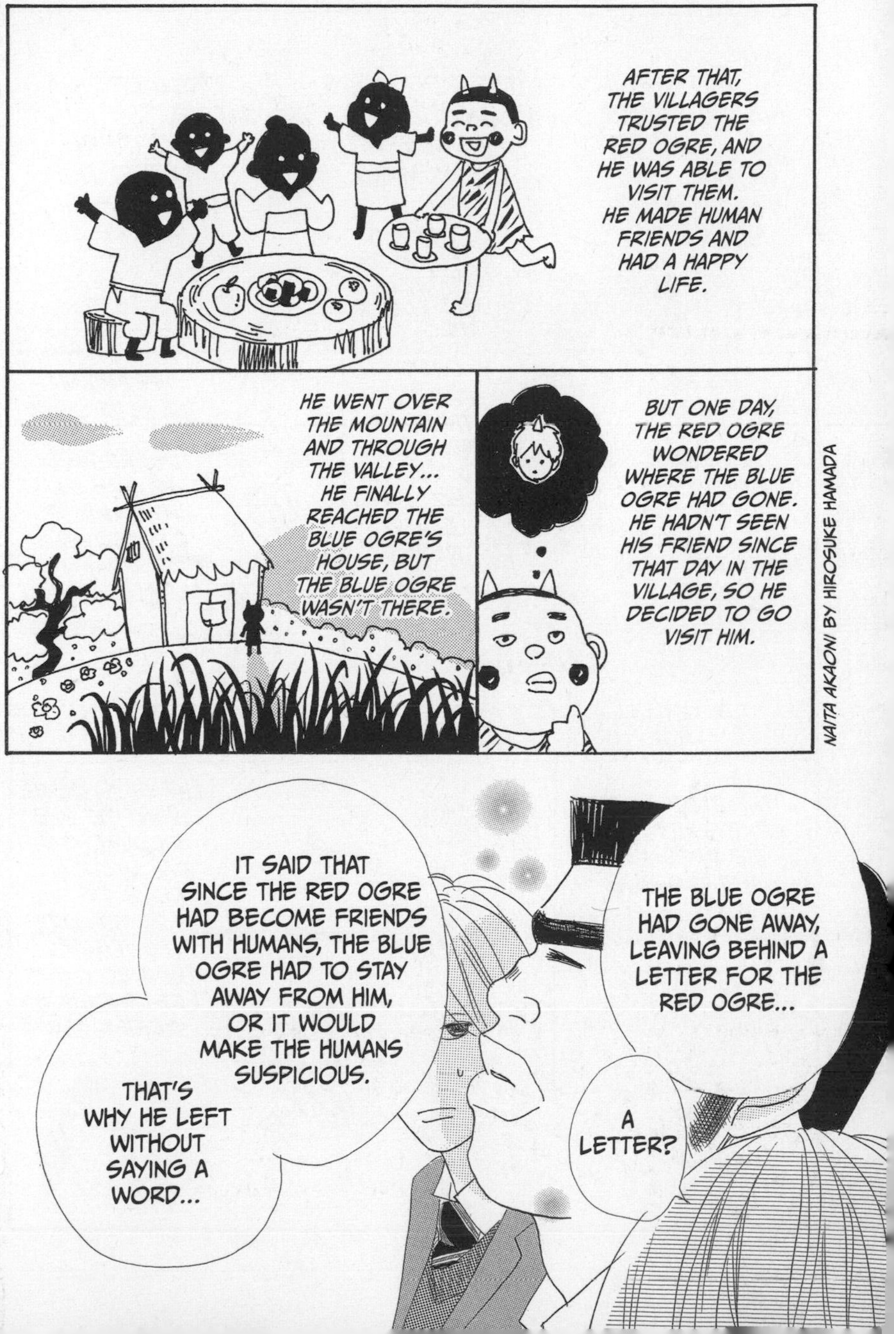
AFTER THAT, THE VILLAGERS TRUSTED THE RED OGRE, AND HE WAS ABLE TO VISIT THEM. HE MADE HUMAN FRIENDS AND HAD A HAPPY LIFE.
BUT ONE DAY, THE RED OGRE WONDERED WHERE THE BLUE OGRE HAD GONE. HE HADN'T SEEN HIS FRIEND SINCE THAT DAY IN THE VILLAGE, SO HE DECIDED TO GO VISIT HIM.
HE WENT OVER THE MOUNTAIN AND THROUGH THE VALLEY... HE FINALLY REACHED THE BLUE OGRE'S HOUSE, BUT THE BLUE OGRE WASN'T THERE.
THE BLUE OGRE HAD GONE AWAY, LEAVING BEHIND A LETTER FOR THE RED OGRE...
A LETTER?
IT SAID THAT SINCE THE RED OGRE HAD BECOME FRIENDS WITH HUMANS, THE BLUE OGRE HAD TO STAY AWAY FROM HIM, OR IT WOULD MAKE THE HUMANS SUSPICIOUS.
THAT'S WHY HE LEFT WITHOUT SAYING A WORD...

NAITA AKAONI BY HIROSUKE HAMADA

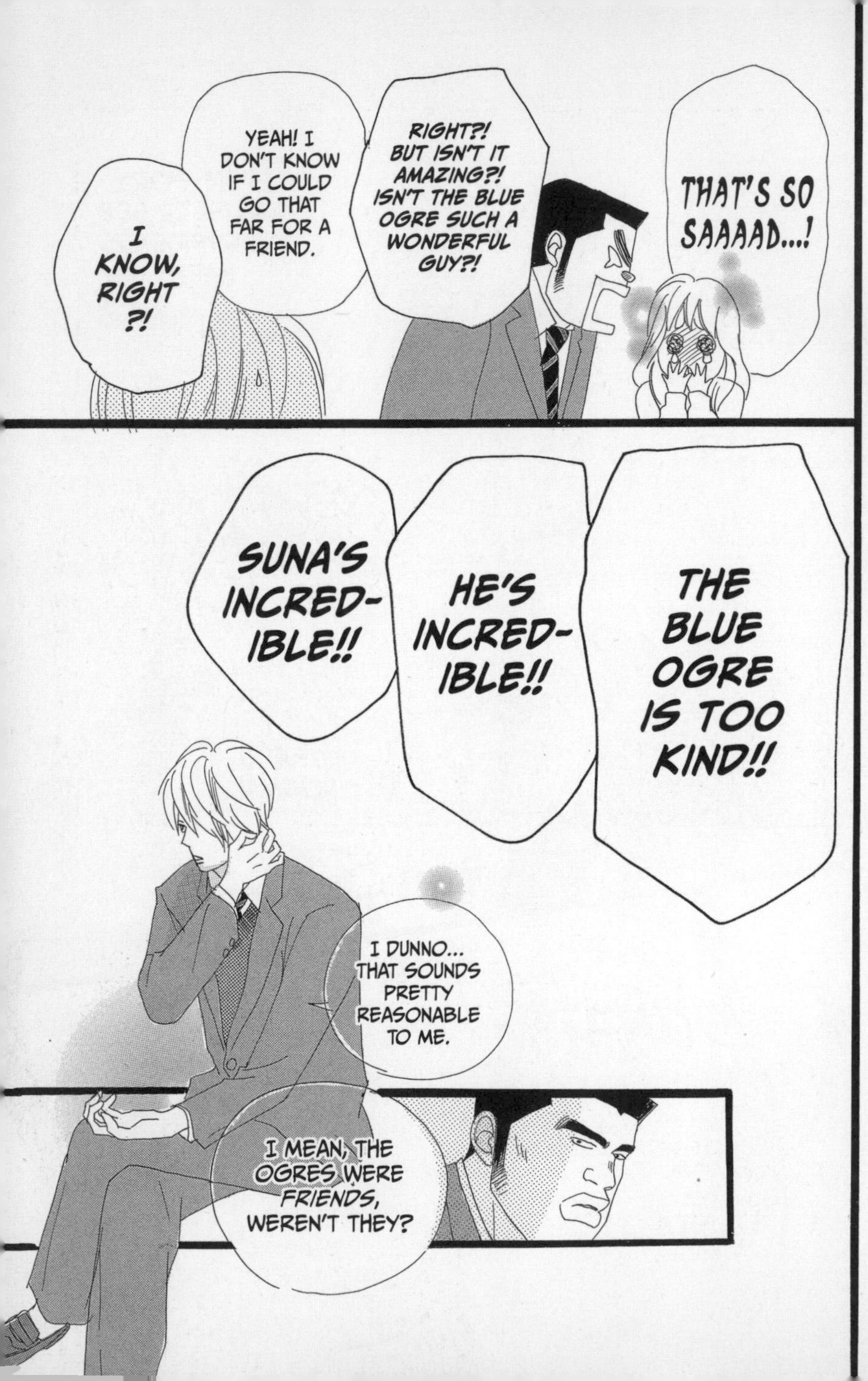
THAT'S SO SAAAAD...!
RIGHT?! BUT ISN'T IT AMAZING?! ISN'T THE BLUE OGRE SUCH A WONDERFUL GUY?!
YEAH! I DON'T KNOW IF I COULD GO THAT FAR FOR A FRIEND.
I KNOW, RIGHT?!
THE BLUE OGRE IS TOO KIND!!
HE'S INCRED-IBLE!!
SUNA'S INCRED-IBLE!!
I DUNNO... THAT SOUNDS PRETTY REASONABLE TO ME.
I MEAN, THE OGRES WERE FRIENDS, WEREN'T THEY?

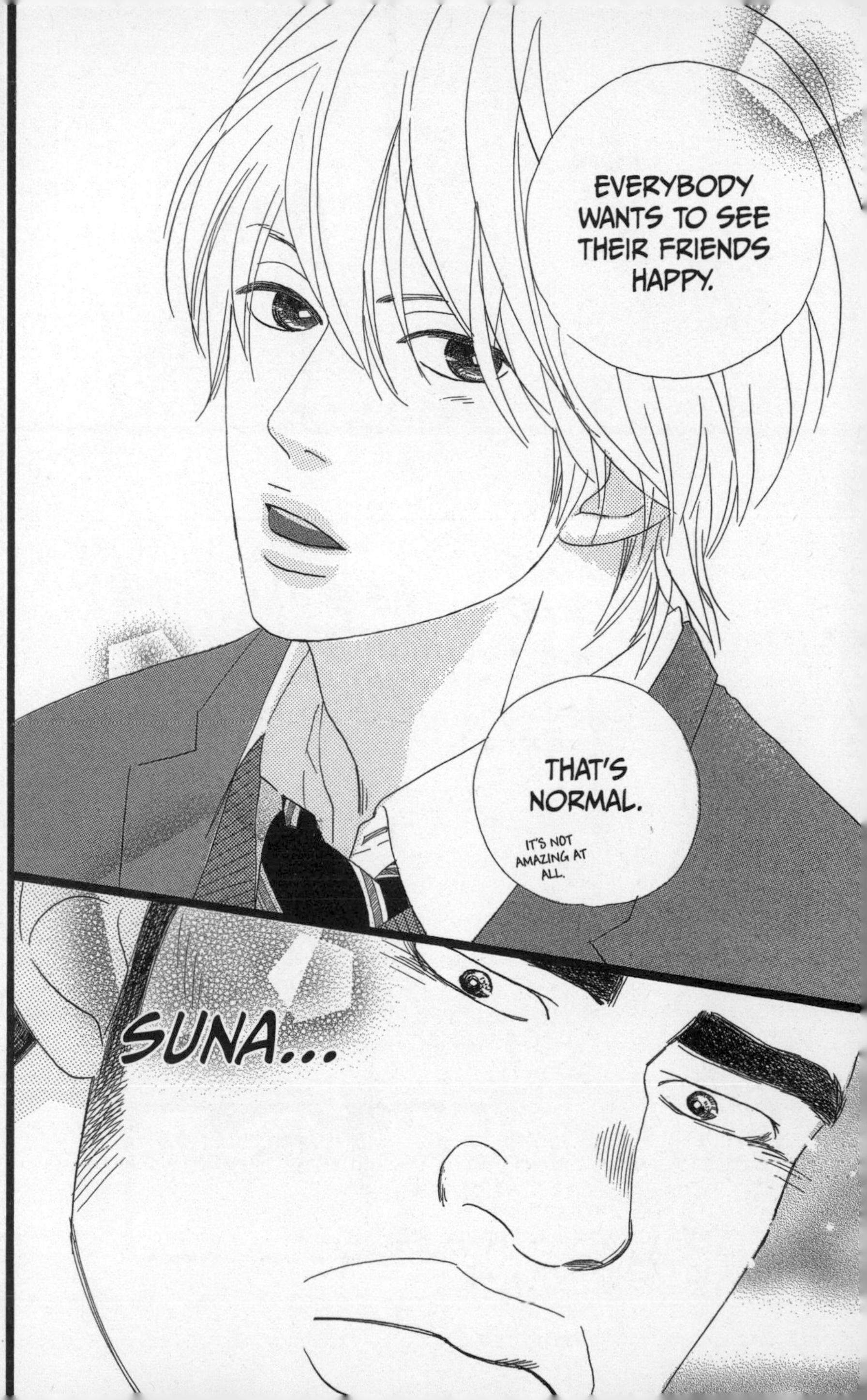
EVERYBODY WANTS TO SEE THEIR FRIENDS HAPPY.
THAT'S NORMAL.
IT'S NOT AMAZING AT ALL.
SUNA...

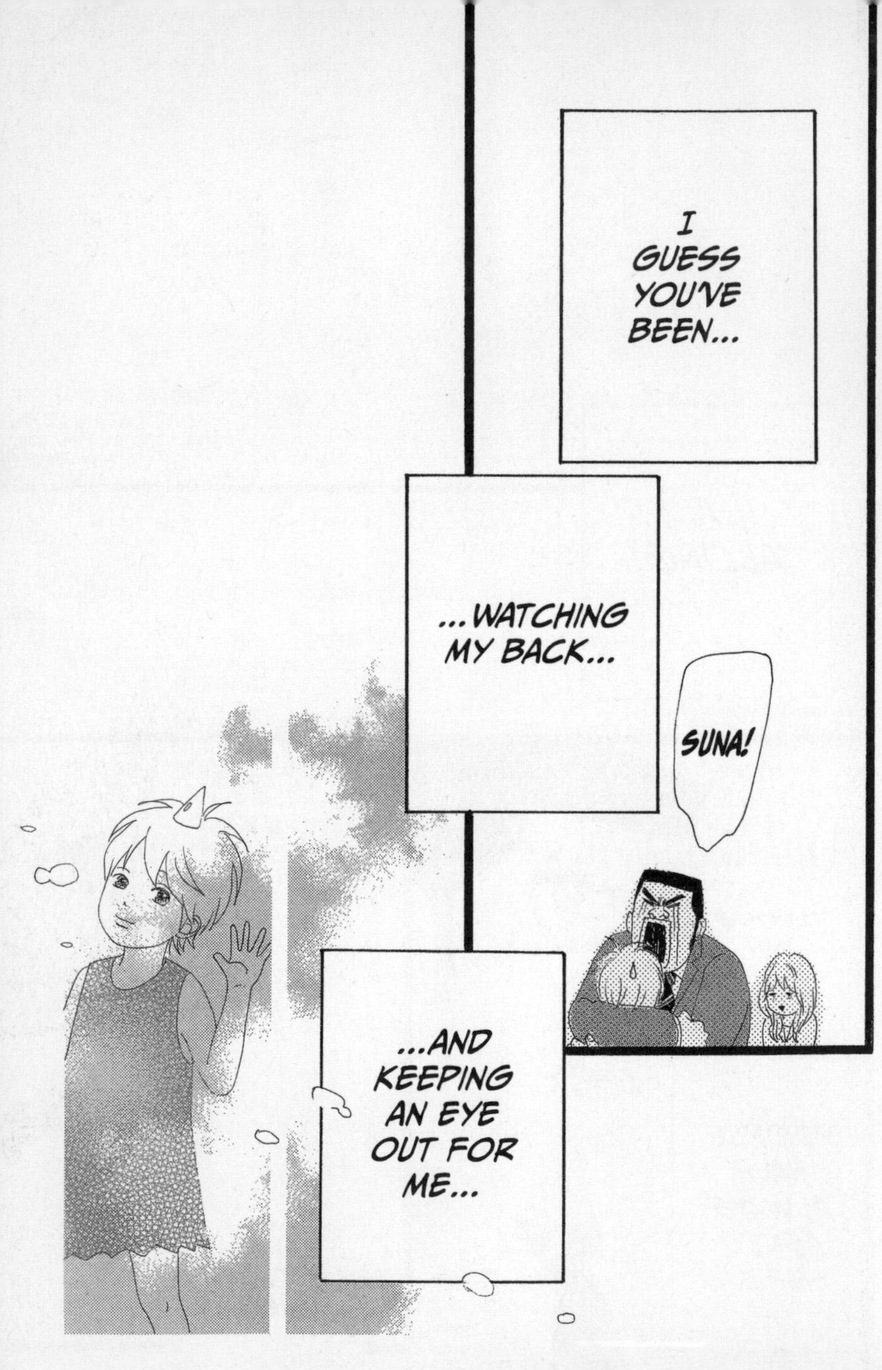
I GUESS YOU'VE BEEN...
...WATCHING MY BACK...
SUNA!
...AND KEEPING AN EYE OUT FOR ME...

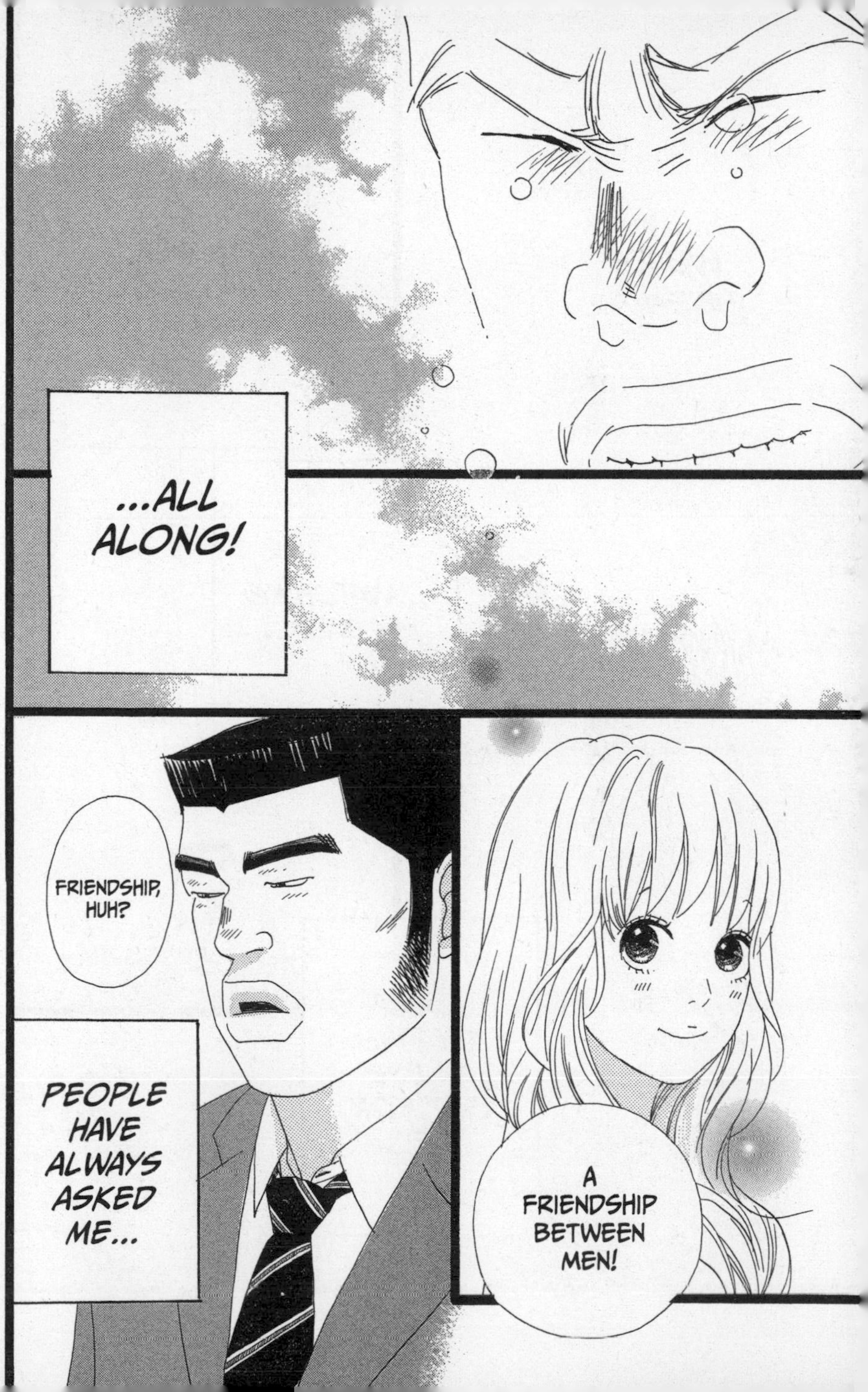
...ALL ALONG!
A FRIENDSHIP BETWEEN MEN!
FRIENDSHIP, HUH?
PEOPLE HAVE ALWAYS ASKED ME...

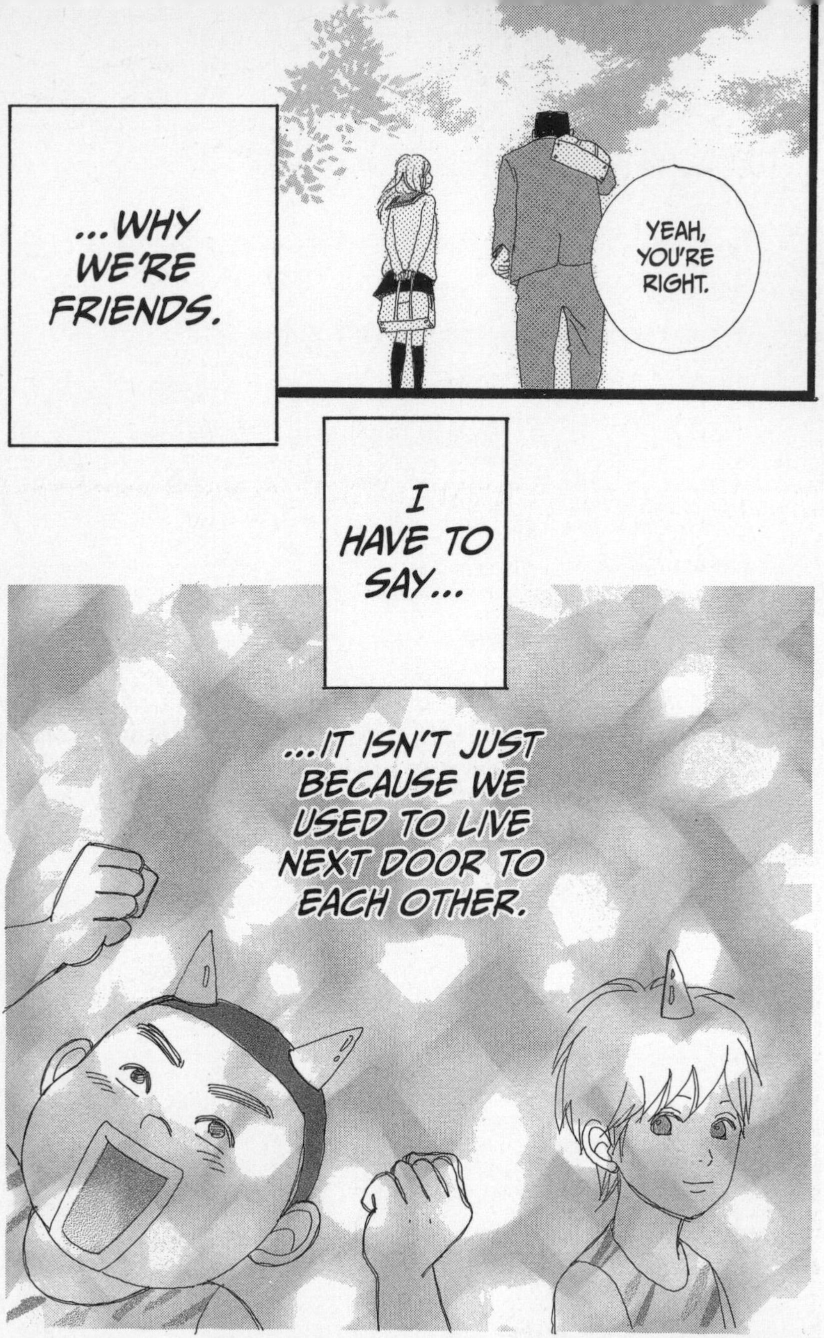
YEAH, YOU'RE RIGHT.
...WHY WE'RE FRIENDS.
I HAVE TO SAY...
...IT ISN'T JUST BECAUSE WE USED TO LIVE NEXT DOOR TO EACH OTHER.

HELLO, THIS IS ARUKO!

I'm illustrating a story by Kazune Kawahara, whom I admire tremendously. Yay! ♫♪
After taking a closer look, the art in the first chapter seems overdone. I was like, "What?!"
I was trying to portray a wonderful story... I had a lot of fun doing it! The fun part about it was drawing macho men. When I draw a manly guy's face, I make the same expression myself.
How strange!

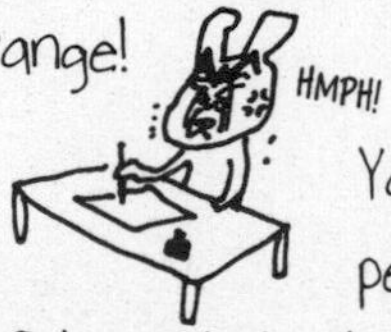
HMPH!

Yamato and Sunakawa are good people. And if I had a macho guy for a boyfriend, I'd be totally happy. Or a macho son would be fine too... And if I had a macho dad, that would be amazing! Kawahara Sensei is soooo macho for creating a character like that! ✧✧
Those are the things that went through my head as I drew. Kawahara Sensei, thank you for giving me free rein to draw these guys. And to my editor, TSGWR, thank you for letting me collaborate on this story. And to all of the readers, thank you so much!
Volume 2 is coming out soon!
Look forward to it! (I know I am.)

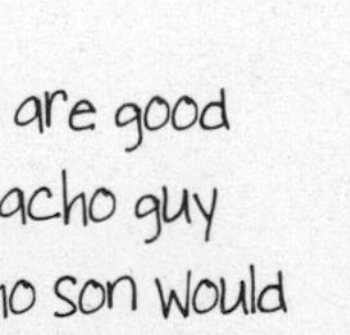

Grateful dance!

Aruko

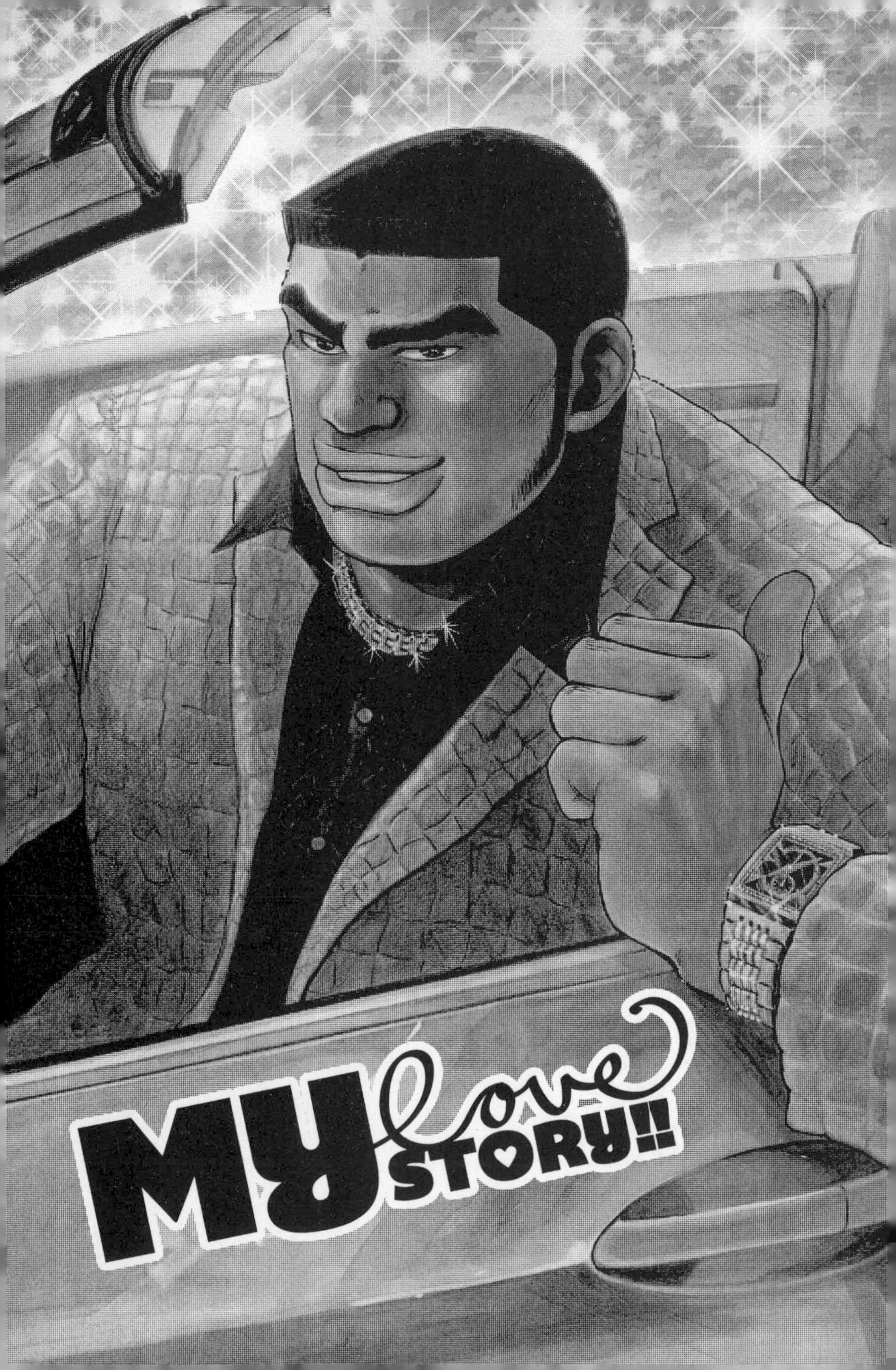
MY love STORY!!

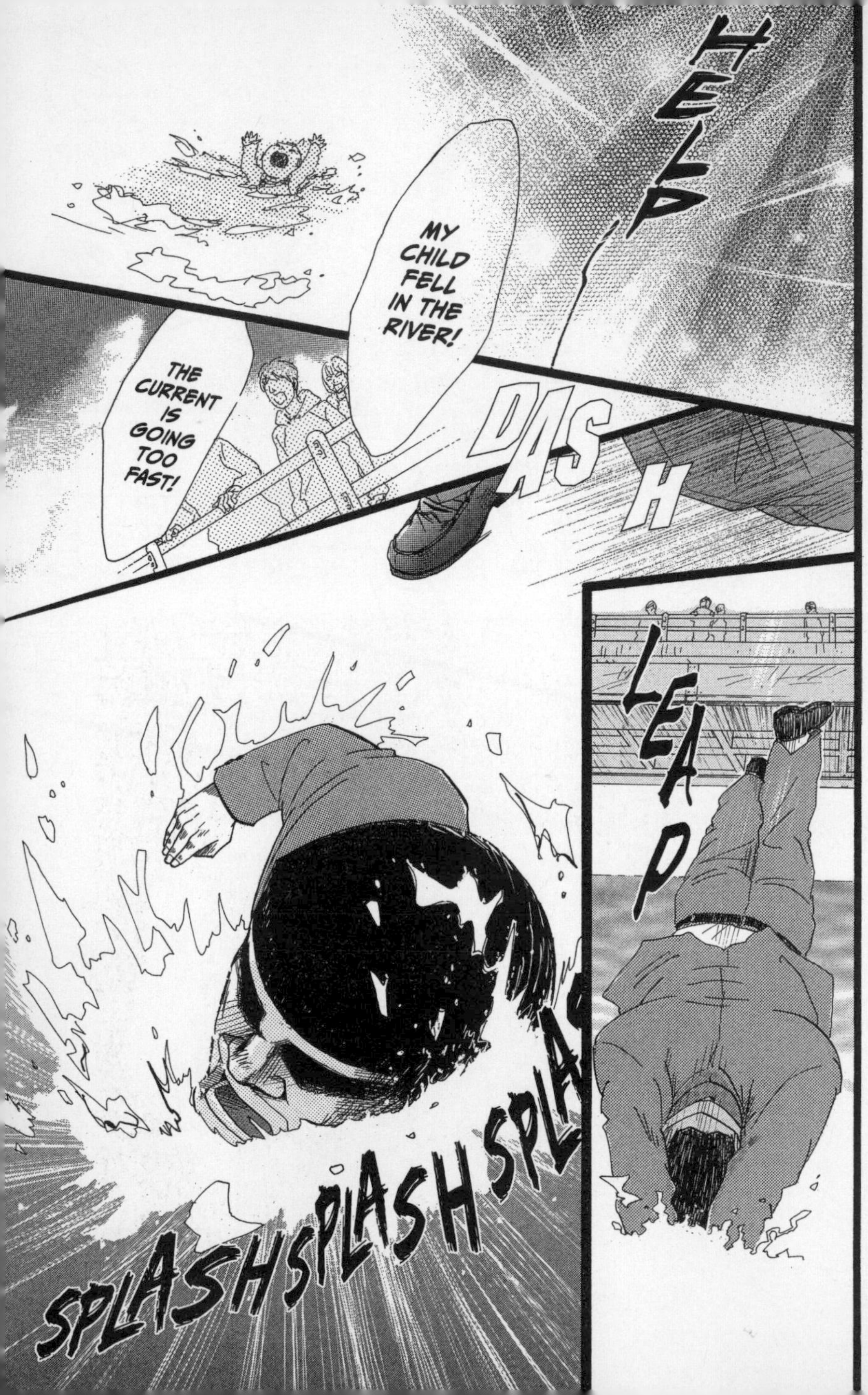
HELP
MY CHILD FELL IN THE RIVER!
THE CURRENT IS GOING TOO FAST!
DASH
LEAP
SPLASH SPLASH SPLAS

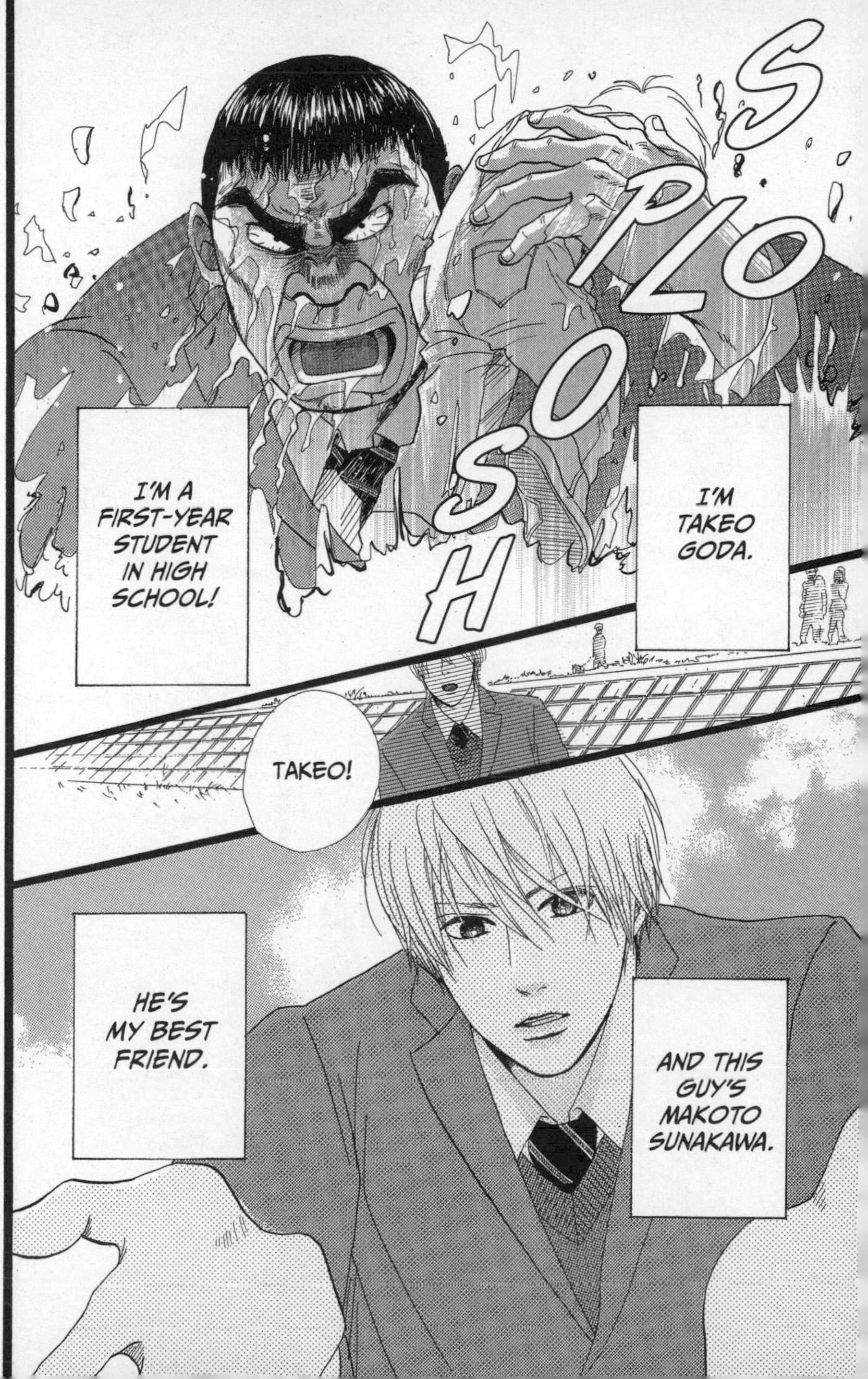
SPLOOSH
I'M TAKEO GODA.
I'M A FIRST-YEAR STUDENT IN HIGH SCHOOL!
TAKEO!
AND THIS GUY'S MAKOTO SUNAKAWA.
HE'S MY BEST FRIEND.

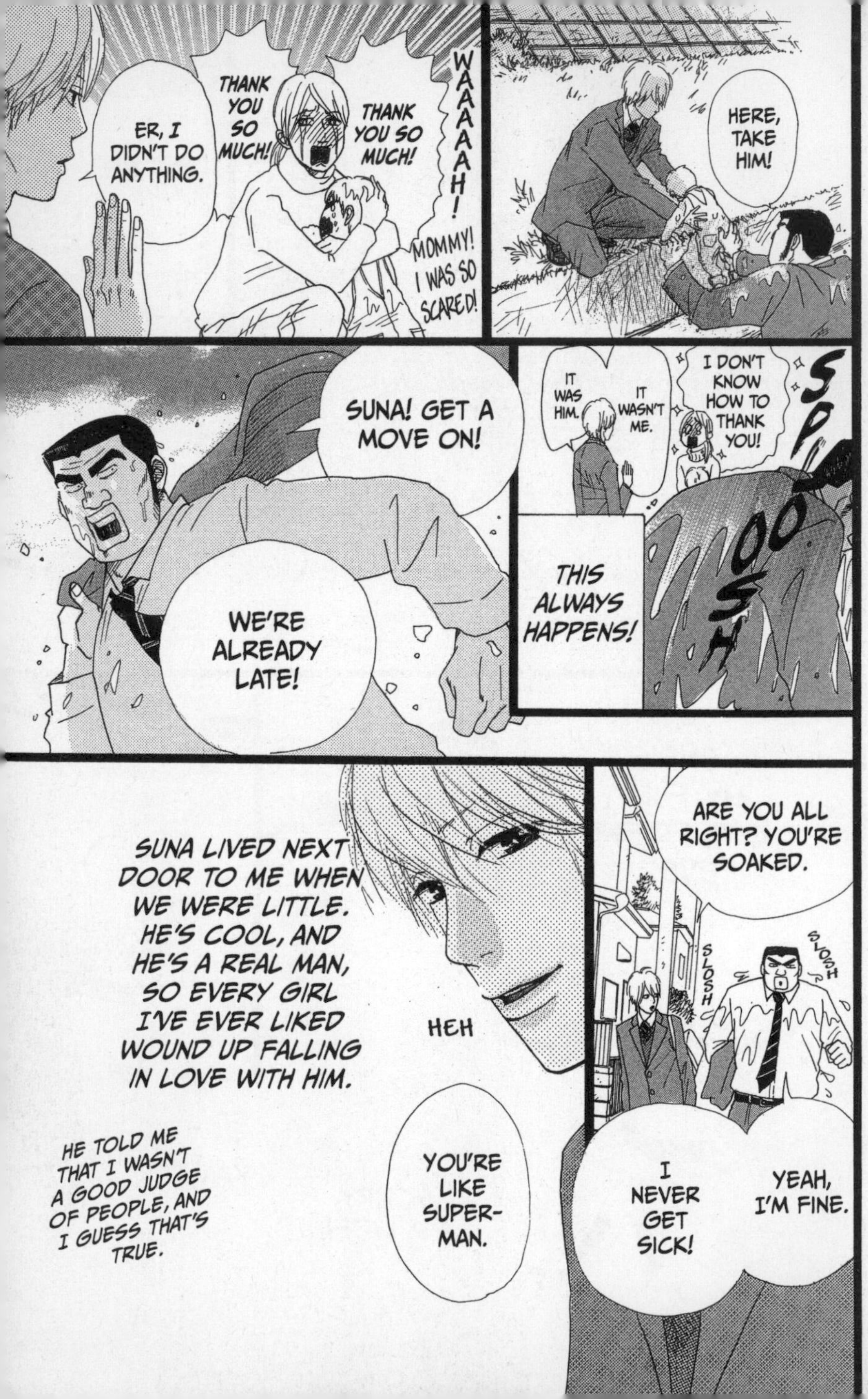
HERE, TAKE HIM!
WAAAAAAH!
MOMMY! I WAS SO SCARED!
THANK YOU SO MUCH!
THANK YOU SO MUCH!
ER, I DIDN'T DO ANYTHING.
I DON'T KNOW HOW TO THANK YOU!
IT WASN'T ME.
IT WAS HIM.
THIS ALWAYS HAPPENS!
SUNA! GET A MOVE ON!
WE'RE ALREADY LATE!
ARE YOU ALL RIGHT? YOU'RE SOAKED.
SLOSH
SLOSH
YEAH, I'M FINE.
I NEVER GET SICK!
HEH
SUNA LIVED NEXT DOOR TO ME WHEN WE WERE LITTLE. HE'S COOL, AND HE'S A REAL MAN, SO EVERY GIRL I'VE EVER LIKED WOUND UP FALLING IN LOVE WITH HIM.
YOU'RE LIKE SUPER-MAN.
HE TOLD ME THAT I WASN'T A GOOD JUDGE OF PEOPLE, AND I GUESS THAT'S TRUE.

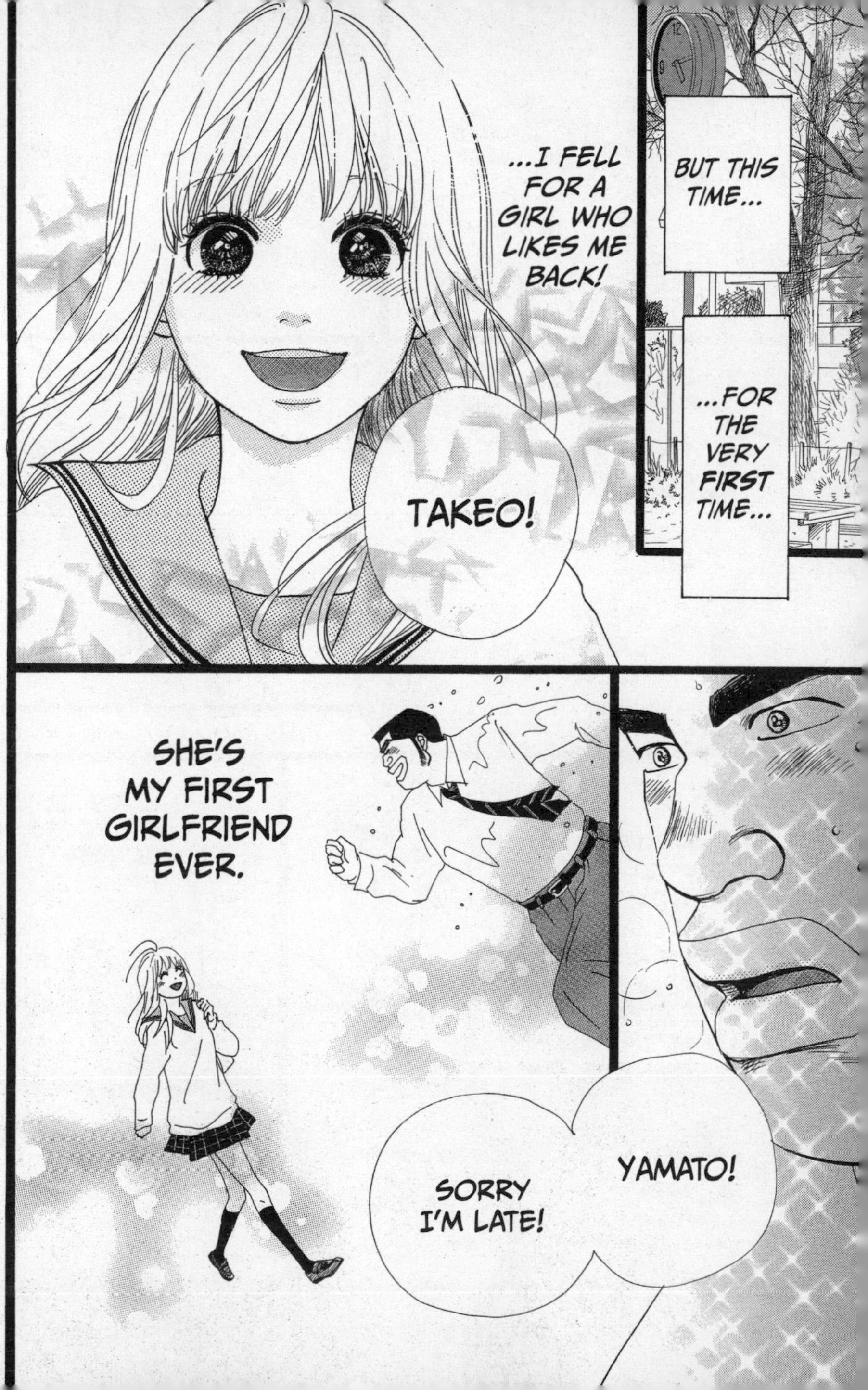
BUT THIS TIME...
...FOR THE VERY FIRST TIME...
...I FELL FOR A GIRL WHO LIKES ME BACK!
TAKEO!
SHE'S MY FIRST GIRLFRIEND EVER.
YAMATO!
SORRY I'M LATE!

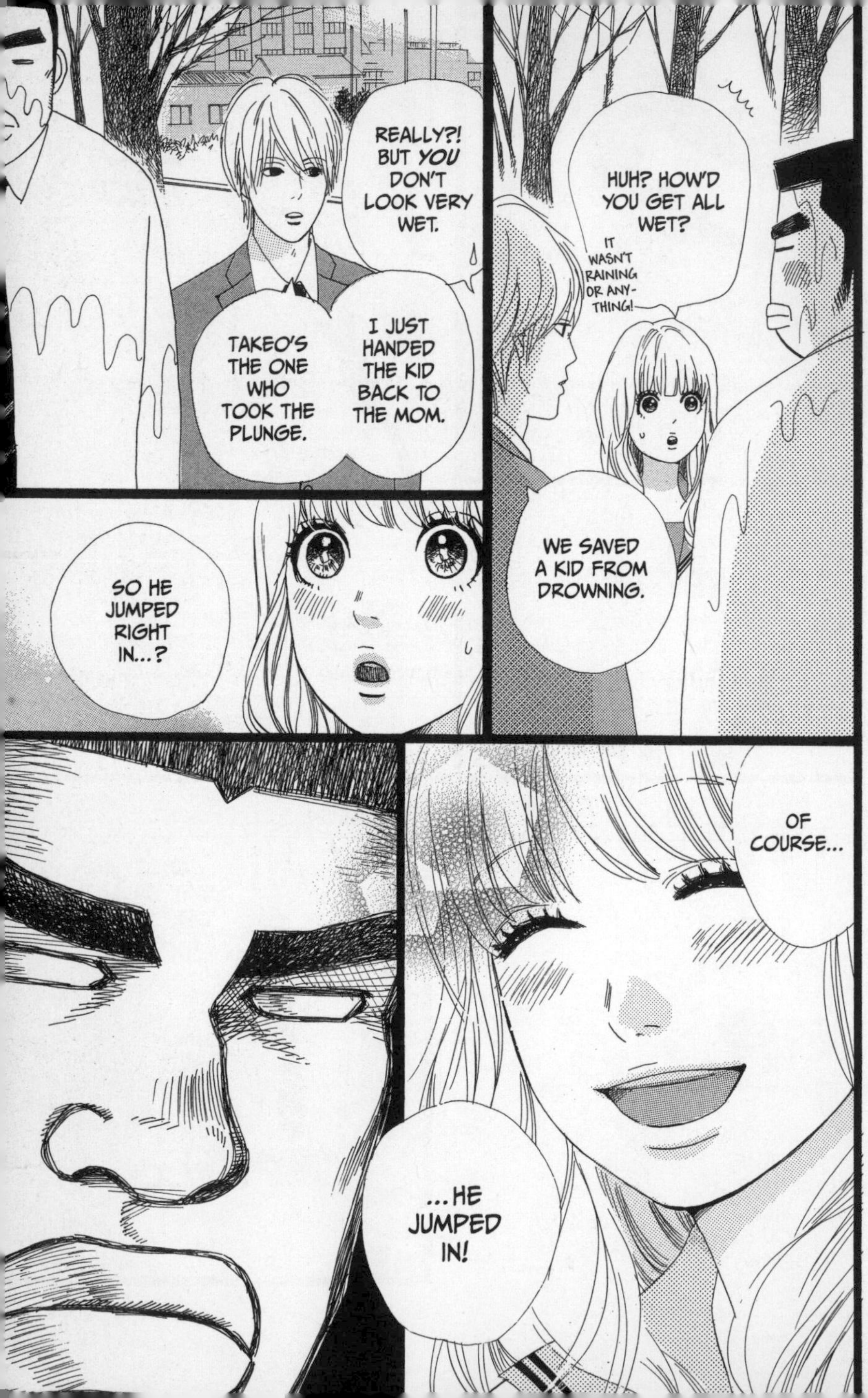
HUH? HOW'D YOU GET ALL WET?
IT WASN'T RAINING OR ANYTHING!
WE SAVED A KID FROM DROWNING.
REALLY?! BUT *YOU* DON'T LOOK VERY WET.
I JUST HANDED THE KID BACK TO THE MOM.
TAKEO'S THE ONE WHO TOOK THE PLUNGE.
SO HE JUMPED RIGHT IN...?
OF COURSE...
...HE JUMPED IN!

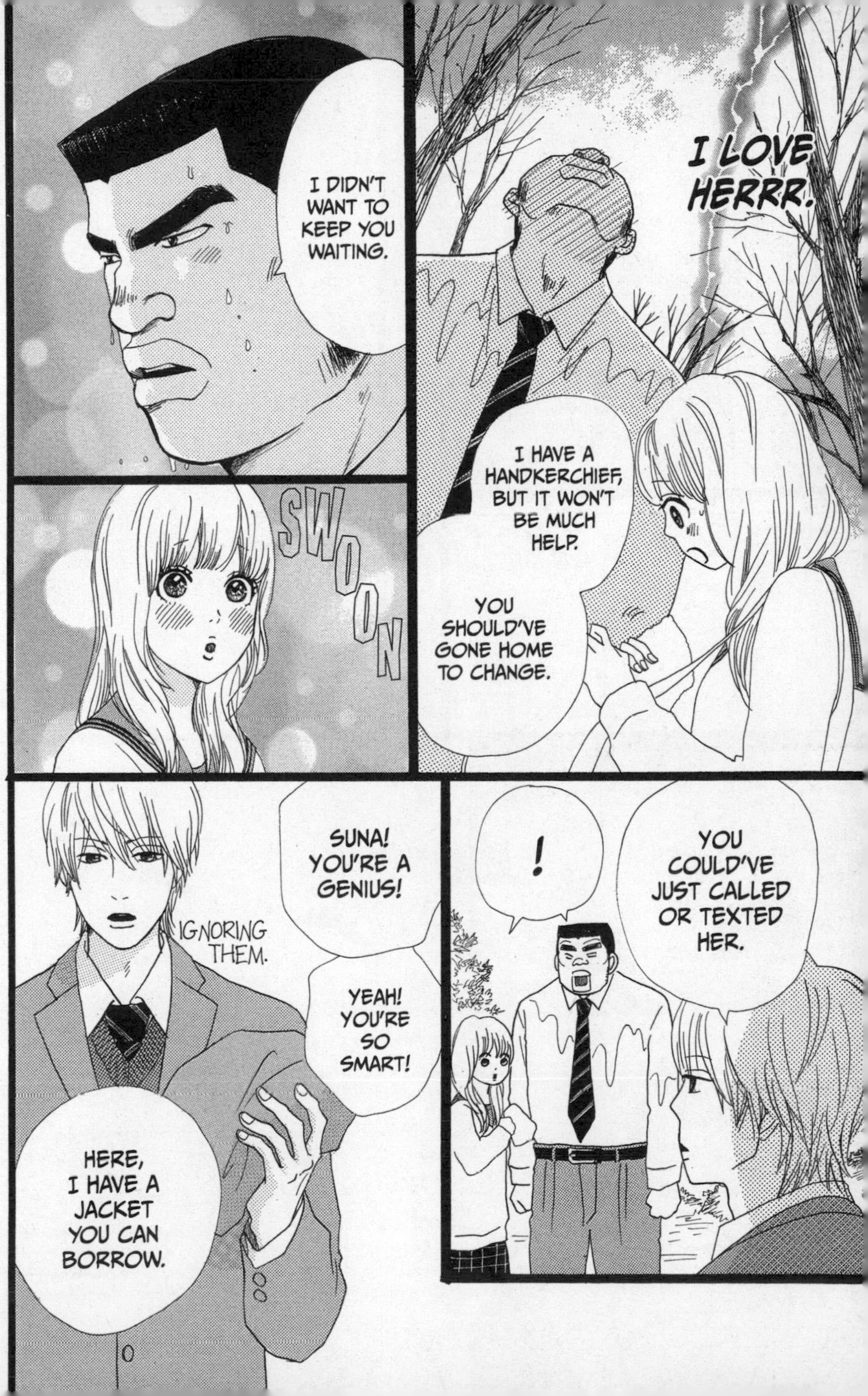
I LOVE HERRR.
I HAVE A HANDKERCHIEF, BUT IT WON'T BE MUCH HELP.
YOU SHOULD'VE GONE HOME TO CHANGE.
I DIDN'T WANT TO KEEP YOU WAITING.
SWOON
YOU COULD'VE JUST CALLED OR TEXTED HER.
!
SUNA! YOU'RE A GENIUS!
IGNORING THEM.
YEAH! YOU'RE SO SMART!
HERE, I HAVE A JACKET YOU CAN BORROW.

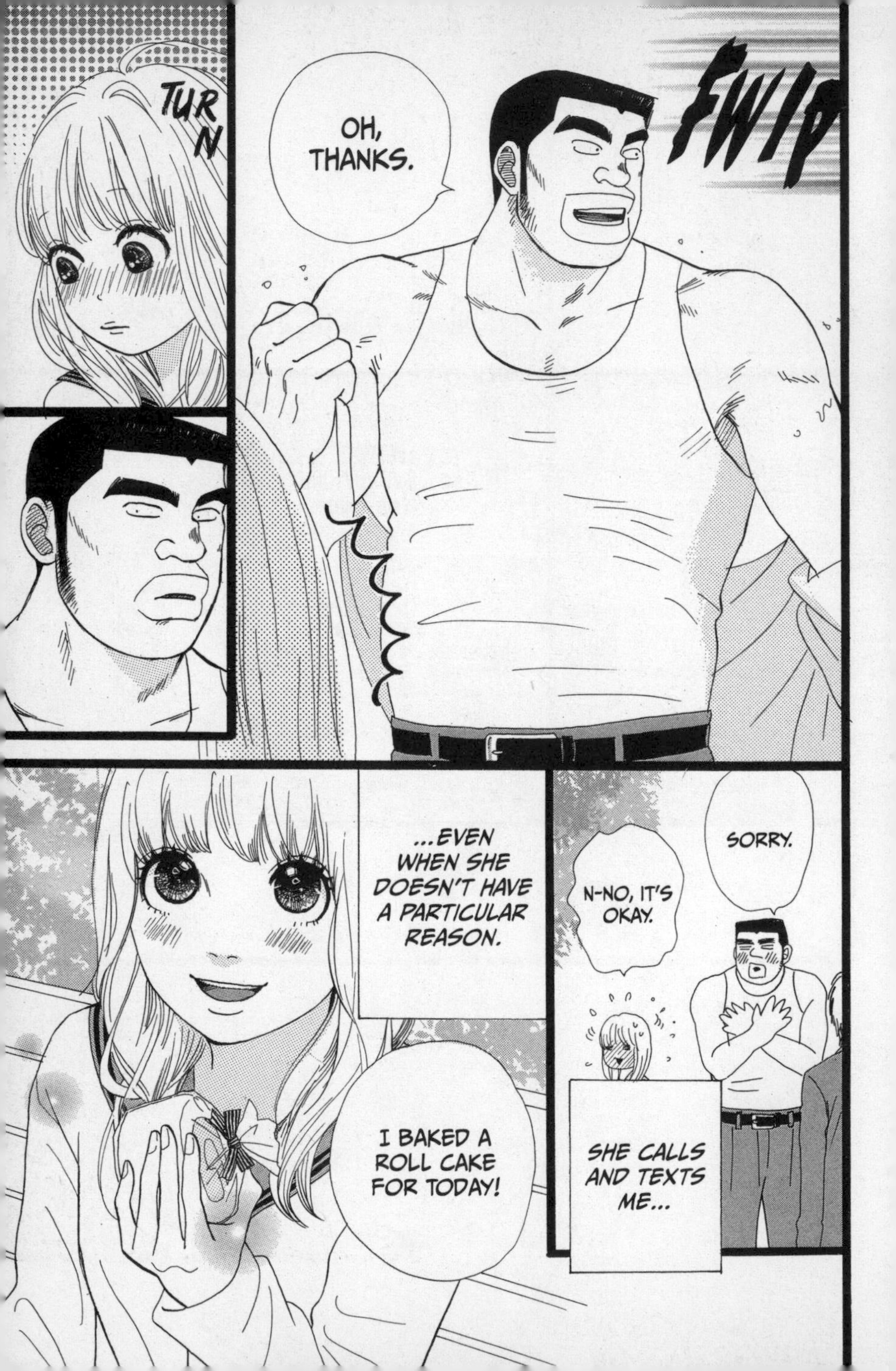
FWIP
OH, THANKS.
TURN
SORRY.
N-NO, IT'S OKAY.
SHE CALLS AND TEXTS ME...
...EVEN WHEN SHE DOESN'T HAVE A PARTICULAR REASON.
I BAKED A ROLL CAKE FOR TODAY!

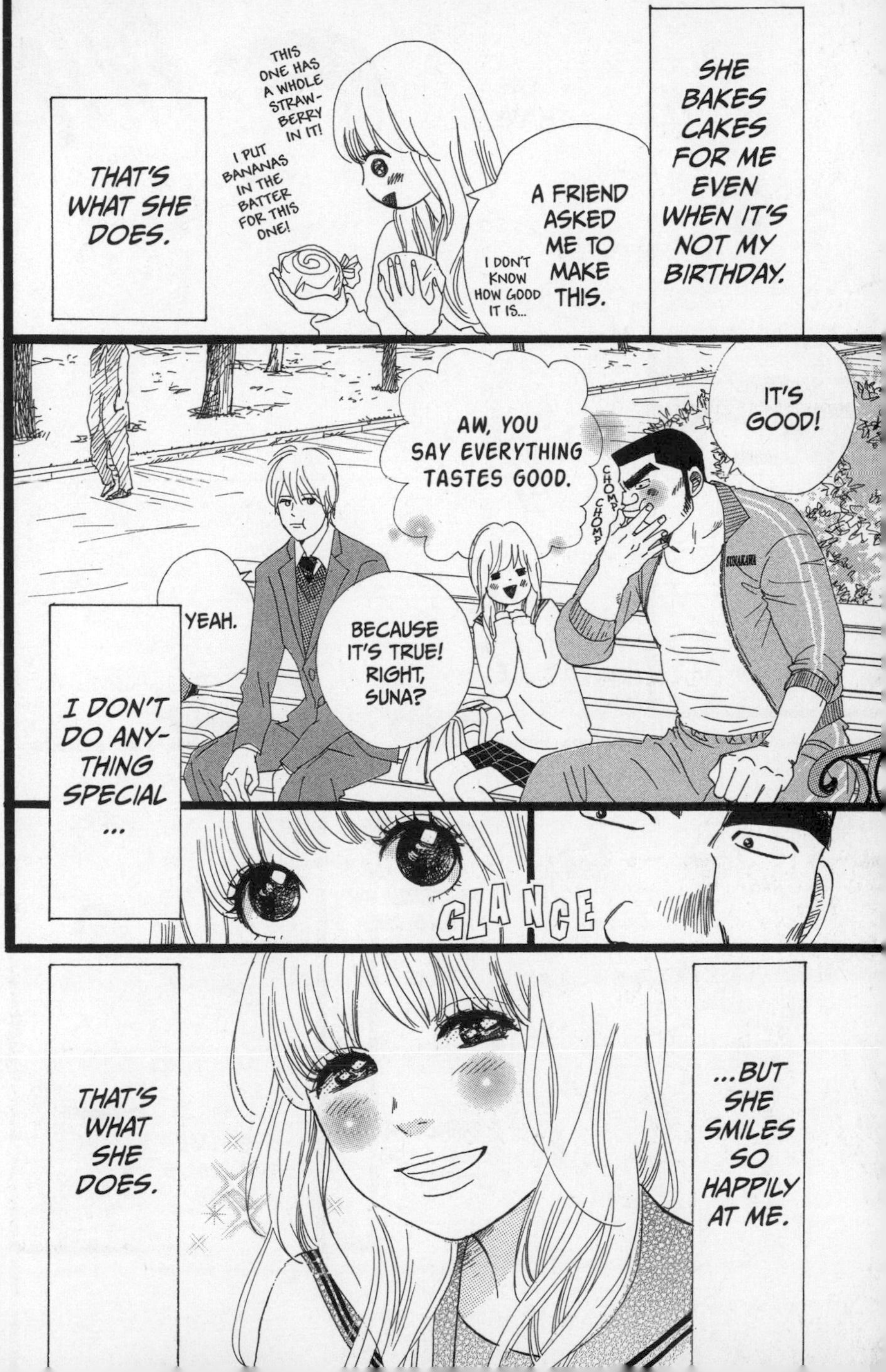

SHE BAKES CAKES FOR ME EVEN WHEN IT'S NOT MY BIRTHDAY.
A FRIEND ASKED ME TO MAKE THIS.
I DON'T KNOW HOW GOOD IT IS...
THIS ONE HAS A WHOLE STRAW-BERRY IN IT!
I PUT BANANAS IN THE BATTER FOR THIS ONE!
THAT'S WHAT SHE DOES.
IT'S GOOD!
CHOMP CHOMP
AW, YOU SAY EVERYTHING TASTES GOOD.
BECAUSE IT'S TRUE! RIGHT, SUNA?
YEAH.
I DON'T DO ANY-THING SPECIAL...
GLANCE
...BUT SHE SMILES SO HAPPILY AT ME.
THAT'S WHAT SHE DOES.

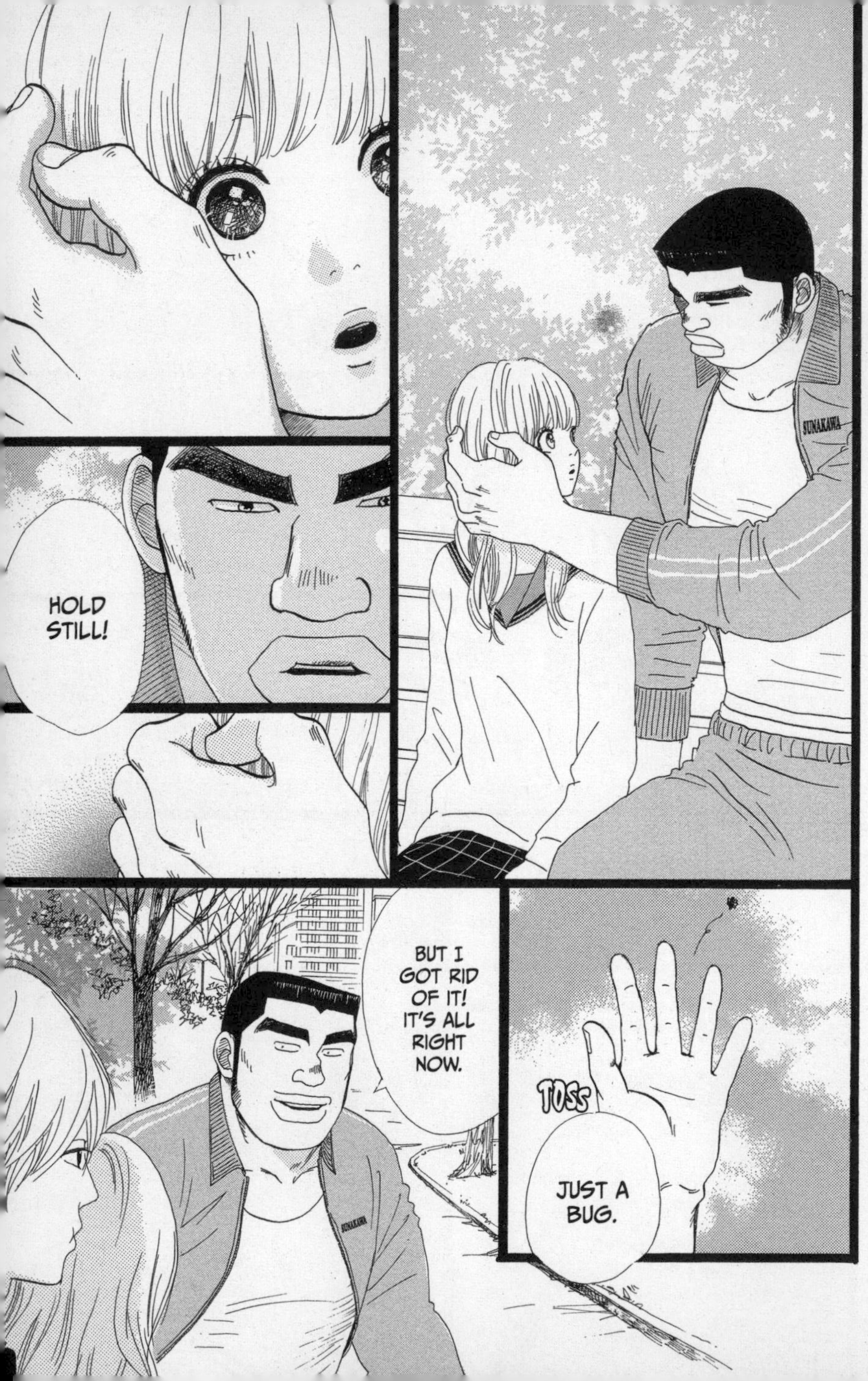
SUNAKAWA
HOLD STILL!
TOSS
JUST A BUG.
BUT I GOT RID OF IT! IT'S ALL RIGHT NOW.
SUNAKAWA

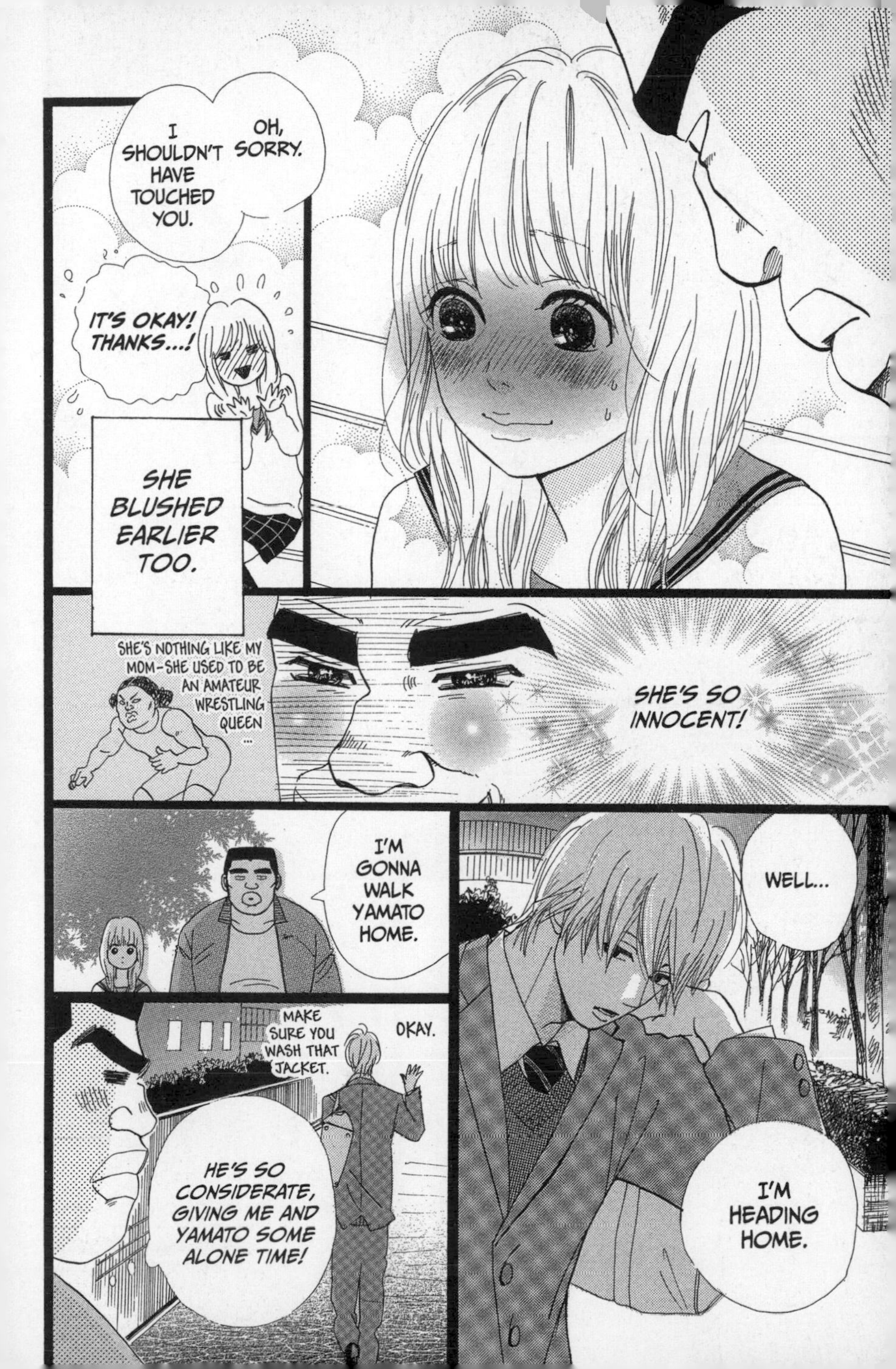
OH, SORRY. I SHOULDN'T HAVE TOUCHED YOU.
IT'S OKAY! THANKS...!
SHE BLUSHED EARLIER TOO.
SHE'S SO INNOCENT!
SHE'S NOTHING LIKE MY MOM—SHE USED TO BE AN AMATEUR WRESTLING QUEEN...
WELL...
I'M HEADING HOME.
I'M GONNA WALK YAMATO HOME.
OKAY.
MAKE SURE YOU WASH THAT JACKET.
HE'S SO CONSIDERATE, GIVING ME AND YAMATO SOME ALONE TIME!

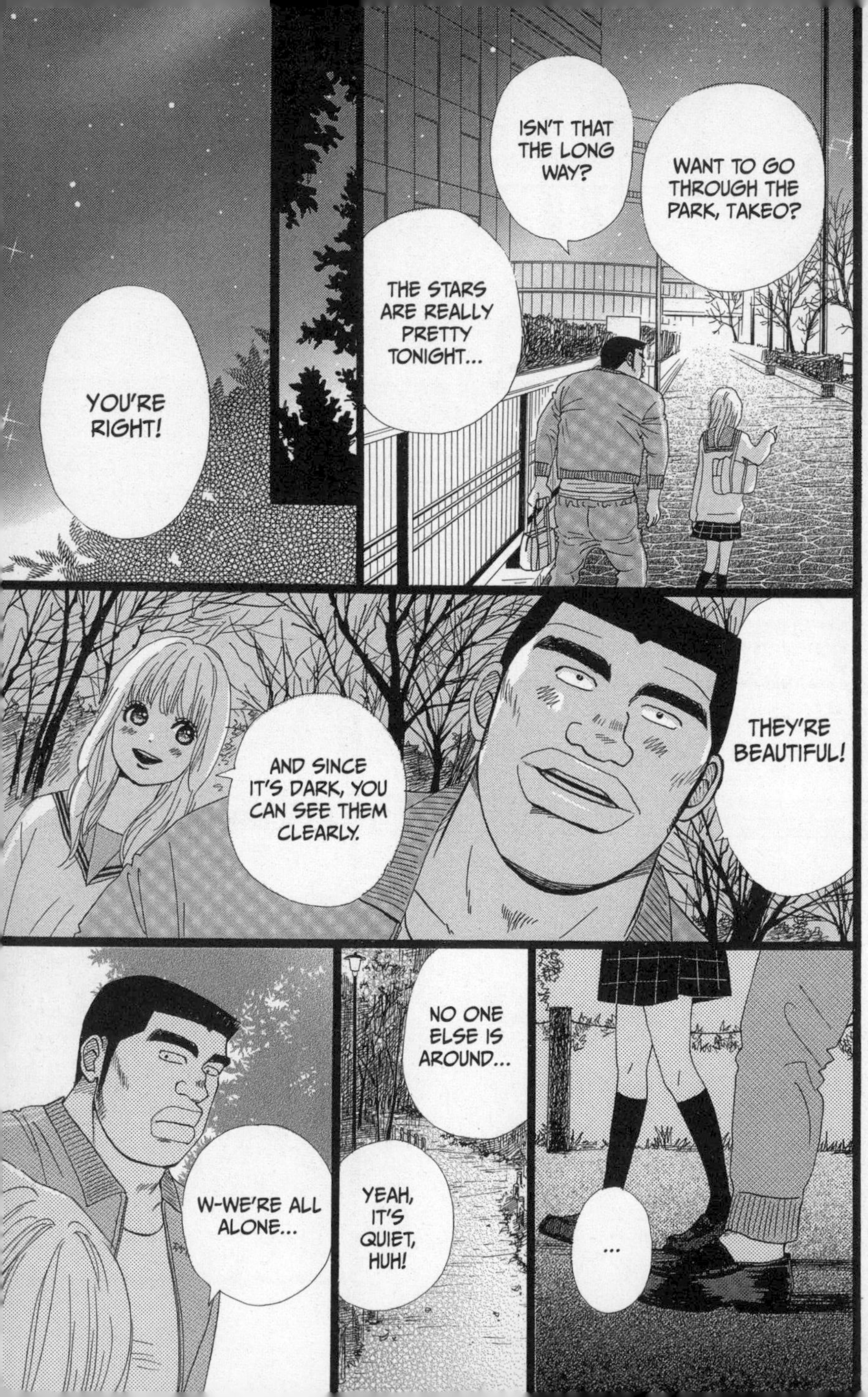
WANT TO GO THROUGH THE PARK, TAKEO?
ISN'T THAT THE LONG WAY?
THE STARS ARE REALLY PRETTY TONIGHT...
YOU'RE RIGHT!
THEY'RE BEAUTIFUL!
AND SINCE IT'S DARK, YOU CAN SEE THEM CLEARLY.
...
NO ONE ELSE IS AROUND...
YEAH, IT'S QUIET, HUH!
W-WE'RE ALL ALONE...

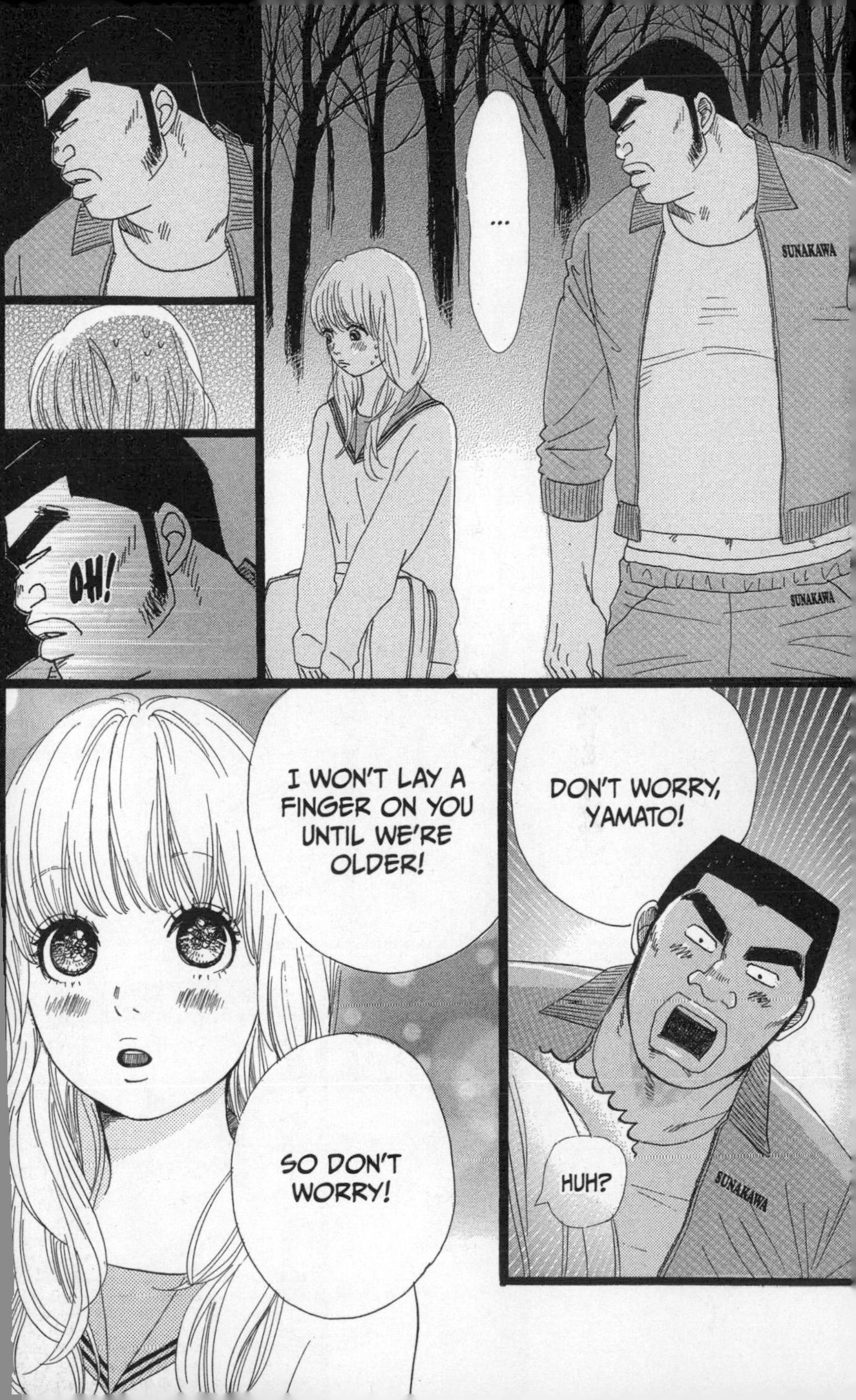
...
SUNAKAWA
SUNAKAWA
OH!
DON'T WORRY, YAMATO!
SUNAKAWA
HUH?
I WON'T LAY A FINGER ON YOU UNTIL WE'RE OLDER!
SO DON'T WORRY!

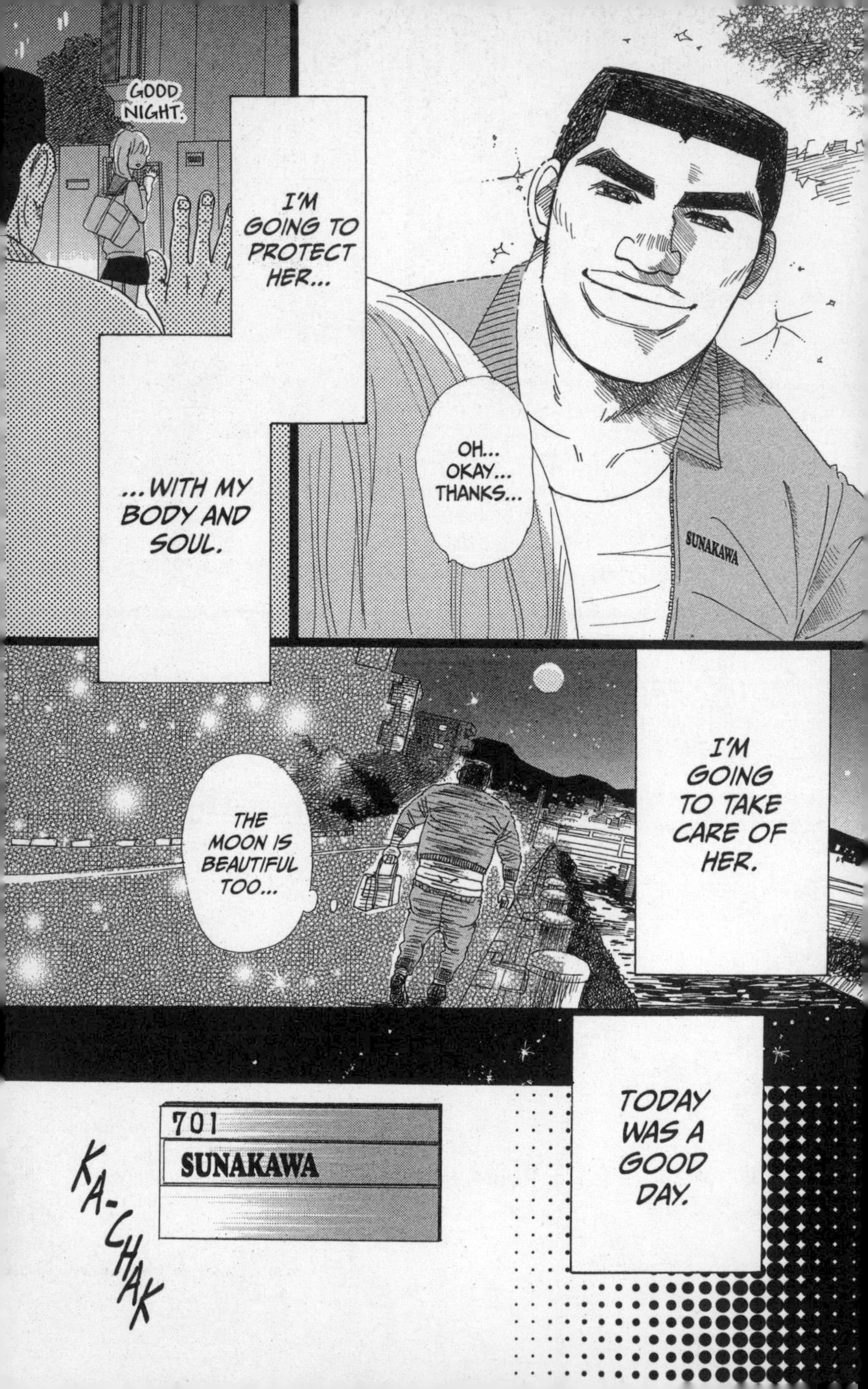
OH... OKAY... THANKS...
I'M GOING TO PROTECT HER...
GOOD NIGHT.
...WITH MY BODY AND SOUL.
I'M GOING TO TAKE CARE OF HER.
THE MOON IS BEAUTIFUL TOO...
TODAY WAS A GOOD DAY.
701
SUNAKAWA
KA-CHAK

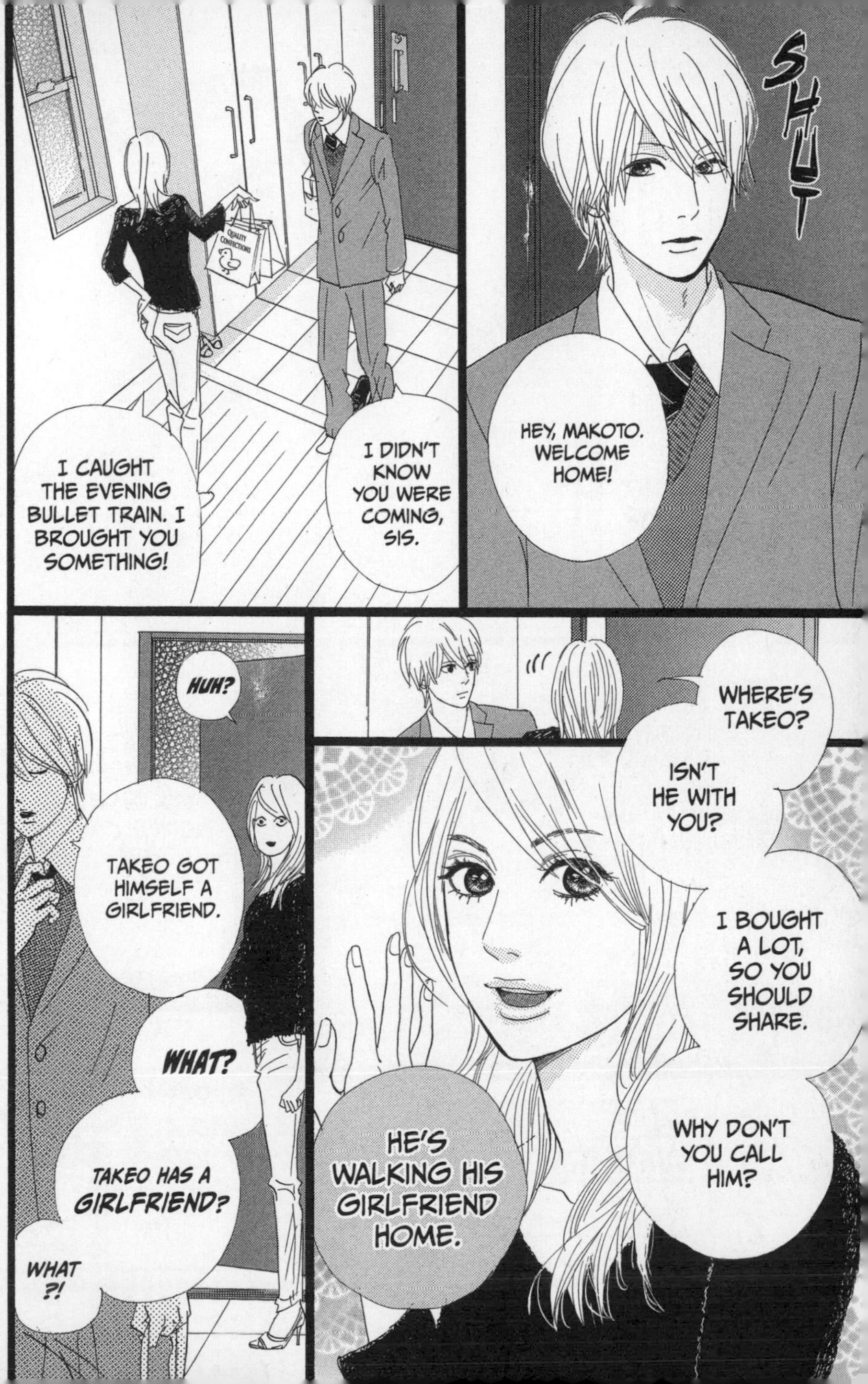
SHUT
HEY, MAKOTO. WELCOME HOME!
I DIDN'T KNOW YOU WERE COMING, SIS.
I CAUGHT THE EVENING BULLET TRAIN. I BROUGHT YOU SOMETHING!
QUALITY CONFECTIONS
WHERE'S TAKEO?
ISN'T HE WITH YOU?
I BOUGHT A LOT, SO YOU SHOULD SHARE.
WHY DON'T YOU CALL HIM?
HE'S WALKING HIS GIRLFRIEND HOME.
HUH?
TAKEO GOT HIMSELF A GIRLFRIEND.
WHAT?
TAKEO HAS A GIRLFRIEND?
WHAT ?!

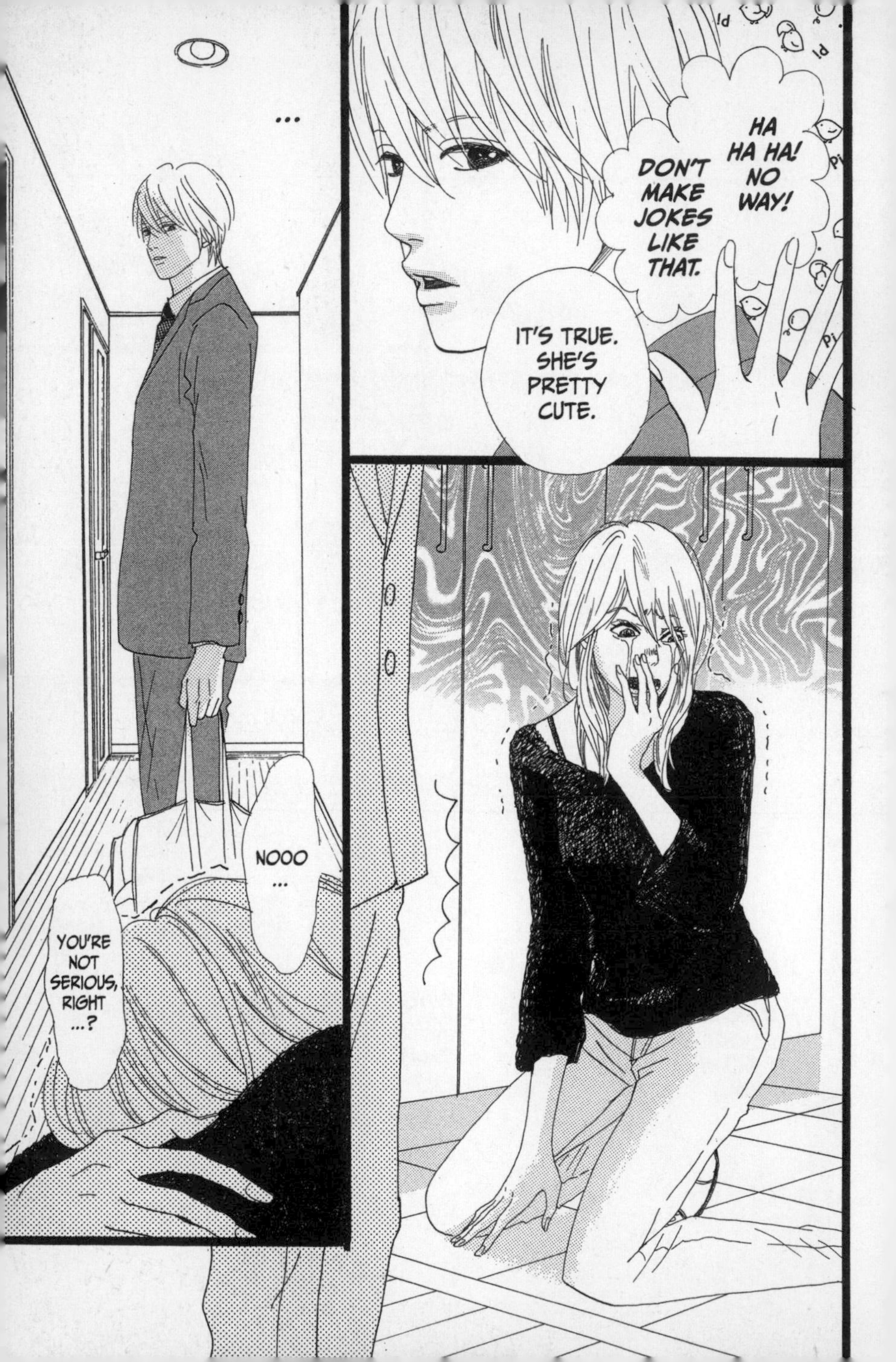
HA HA HA! NO WAY!
DON'T MAKE JOKES LIKE THAT.
IT'S TRUE. SHE'S PRETTY CUTE.
...
NOOO ...
YOU'RE NOT SERIOUS, RIGHT ...?

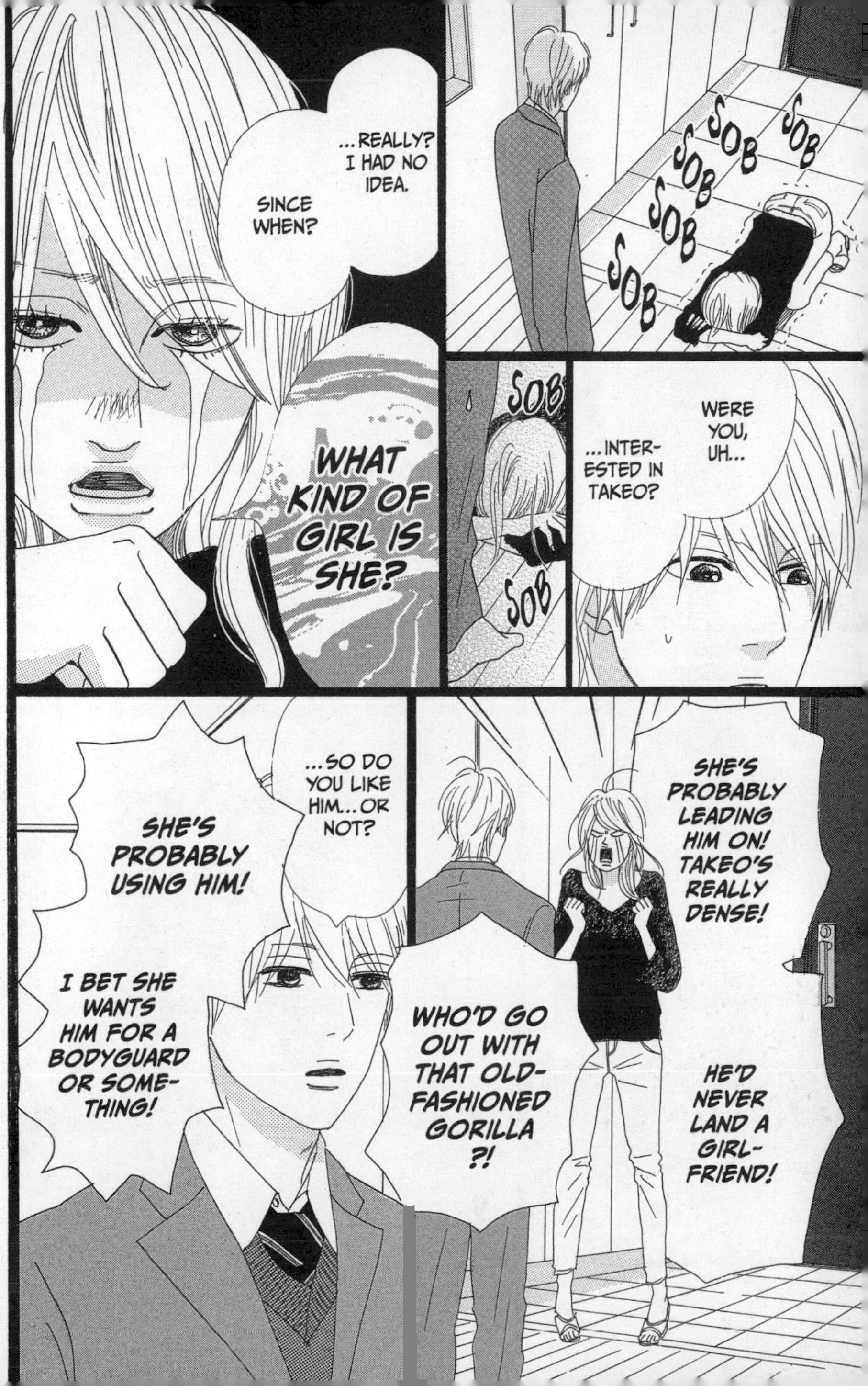
SOB SOB SOB SOB SOB SOB
WERE YOU, UH...
...INTER-ESTED IN TAKEO?
SOB SOB
...REALLY? I HAD NO IDEA.
SINCE WHEN?
WHAT KIND OF GIRL IS SHE?
SHE'S PROBABLY LEADING HIM ON! TAKEO'S REALLY DENSE!
HE'D NEVER LAND A GIRL-FRIEND!
WHO'D GO OUT WITH THAT OLD-FASHIONED GORILLA ?!
...SO DO YOU LIKE HIM...OR NOT?
SHE'S PROBABLY USING HIM!
I BET SHE WANTS HIM FOR A BODYGUARD OR SOME-THING!

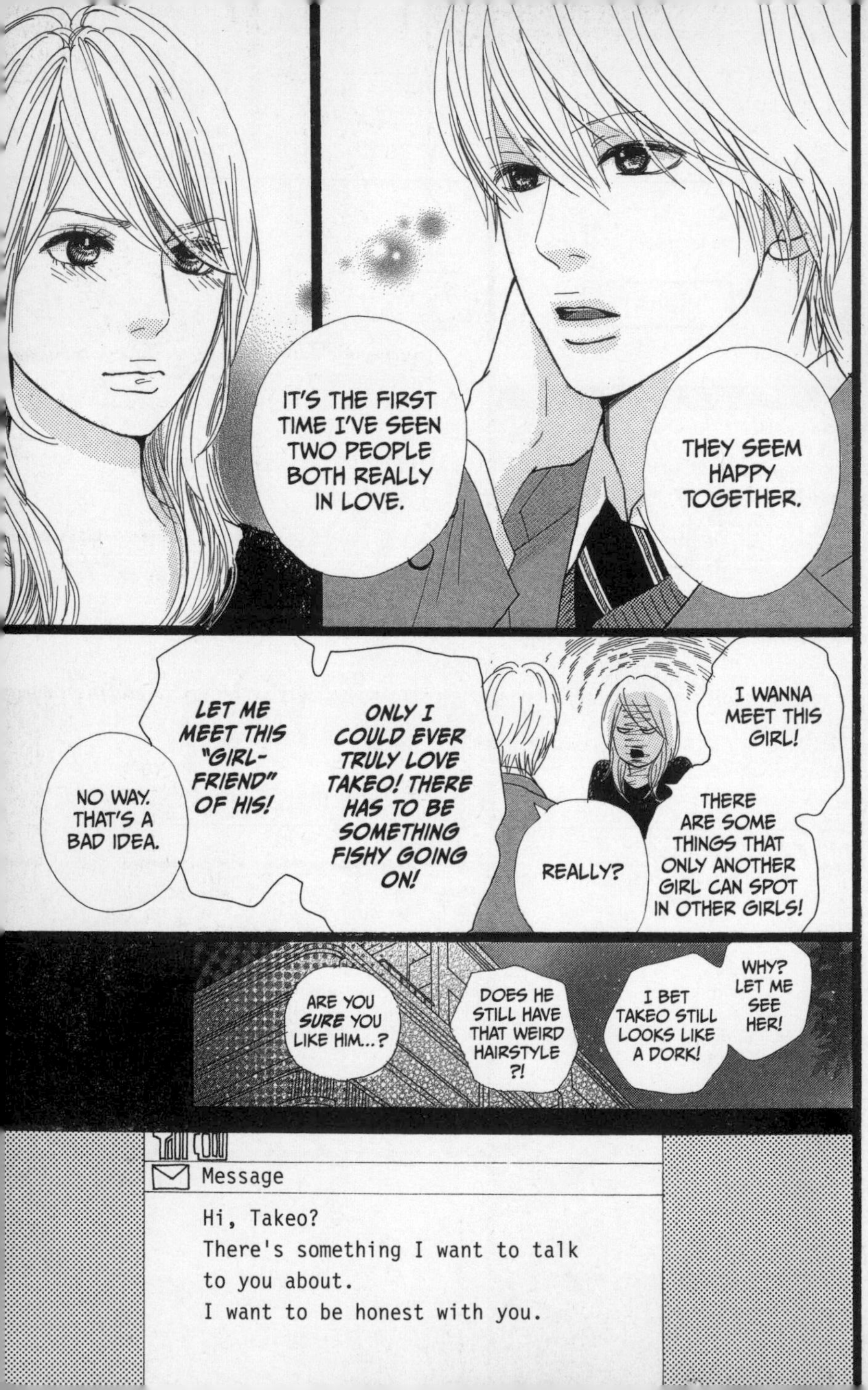
THEY SEEM HAPPY TOGETHER.
IT'S THE FIRST TIME I'VE SEEN TWO PEOPLE BOTH REALLY IN LOVE.
I WANNA MEET THIS GIRL!
THERE ARE SOME THINGS THAT ONLY ANOTHER GIRL CAN SPOT IN OTHER GIRLS!
REALLY?
ONLY I COULD EVER TRULY LOVE TAKEO! THERE HAS TO BE SOMETHING FISHY GOING ON!
LET ME MEET THIS "GIRL-FRIEND" OF HIS!
NO WAY. THAT'S A BAD IDEA.
WHY? LET ME SEE HER!
I BET TAKEO STILL LOOKS LIKE A DORK!
DOES HE STILL HAVE THAT WEIRD HAIRSTYLE ?!
ARE YOU SURE YOU LIKE HIM...?
Message
Hi, Takeo?
There's something I want to talk to you about.
I want to be honest with you.

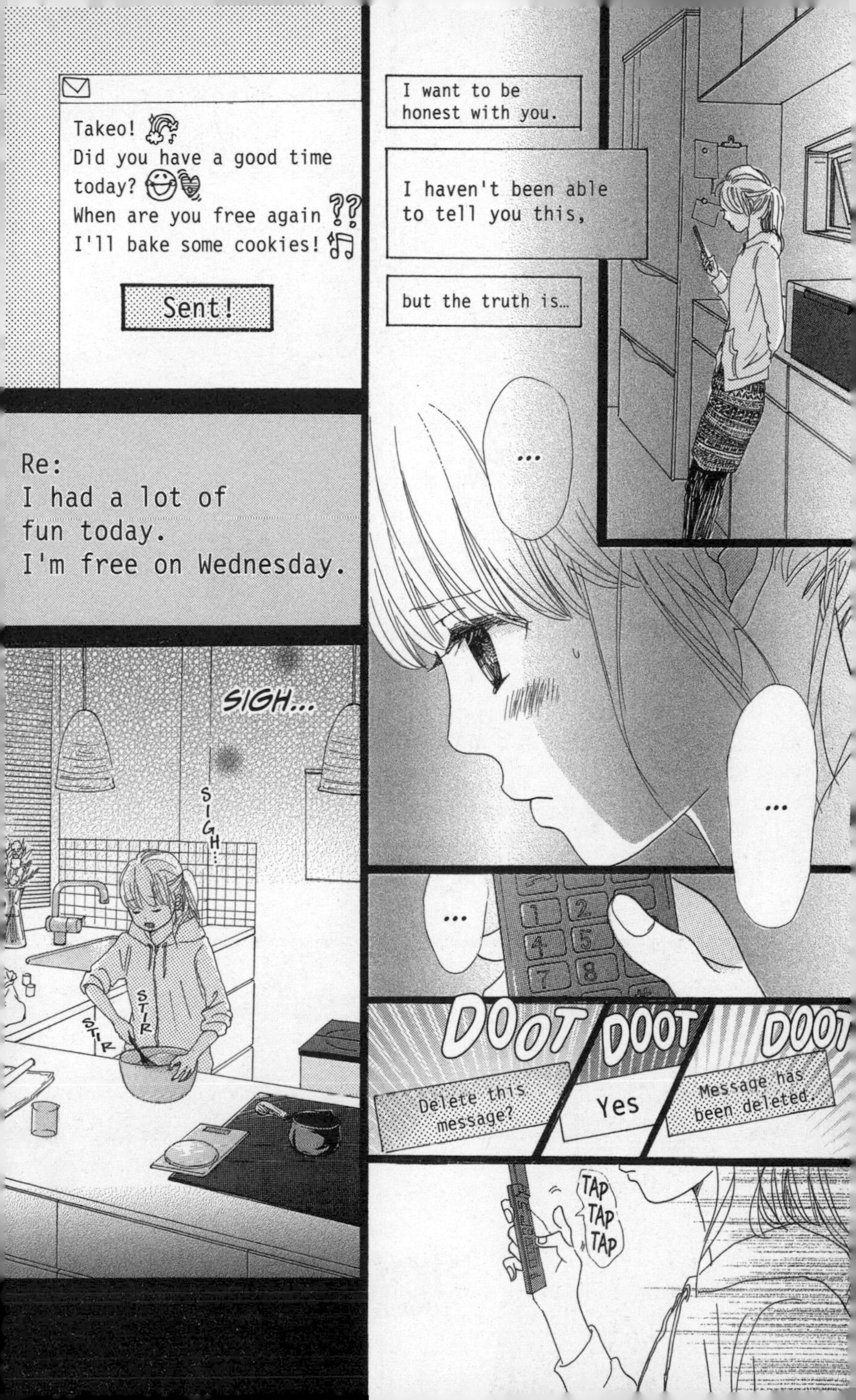
Takeo!
Did you have a good time today?
When are you free again ??
I'll bake some cookies!
Sent!
Re:
I had a lot of fun today.
I'm free on Wednesday.
SIGH...
SIGH...
STIR
STIR
I want to be honest with you.
I haven't been able to tell you this,
but the truth is...
...
...
...
DOOT
DOOT
DOOT
Delete this message?
Yes
Message has been deleted.
TAP TAP TAP

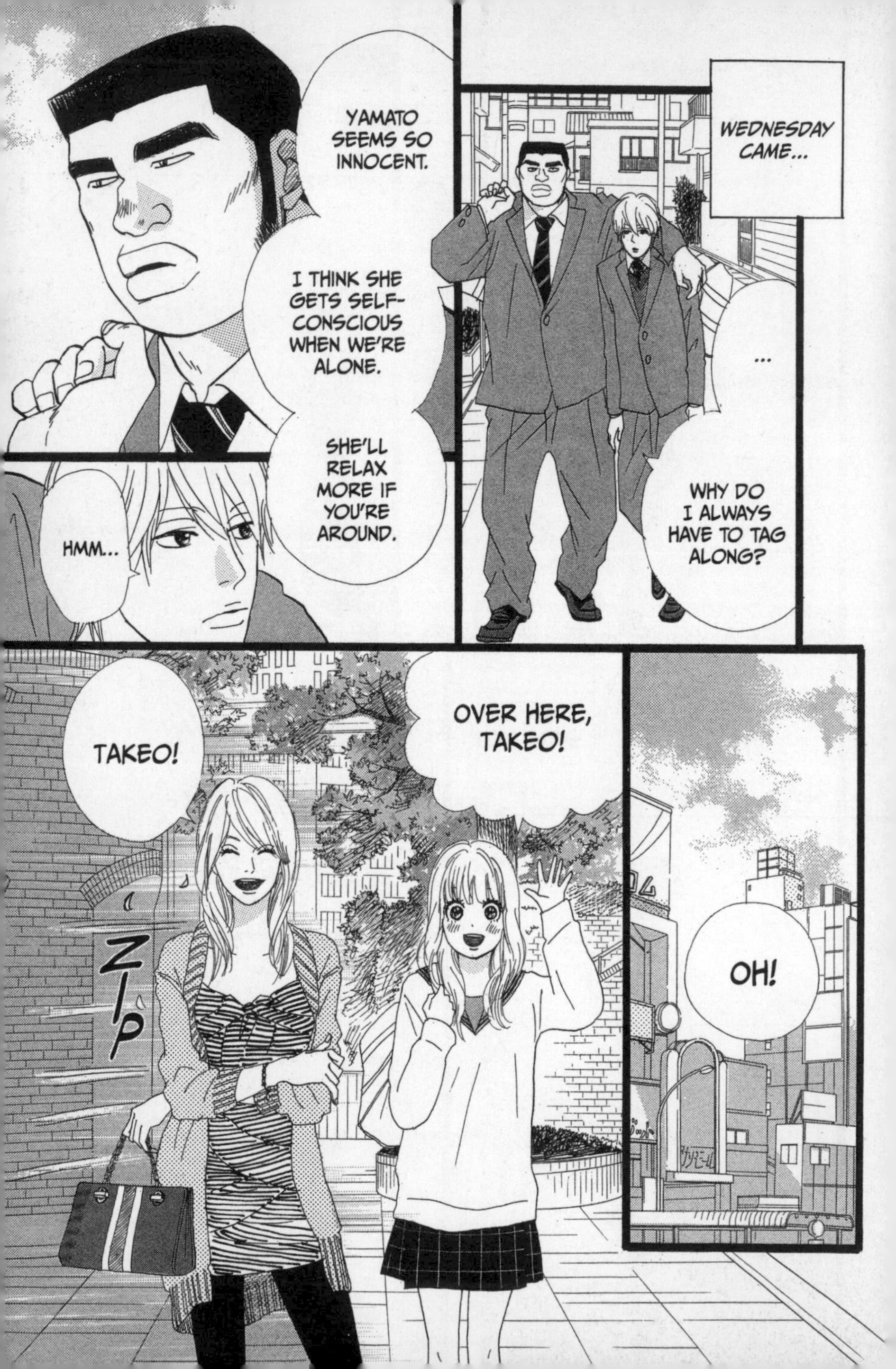
WEDNESDAY CAME...
...
WHY DO I ALWAYS HAVE TO TAG ALONG?
YAMATO SEEMS SO INNOCENT.
I THINK SHE GETS SELF-CONSCIOUS WHEN WE'RE ALONE.
SHE'LL RELAX MORE IF YOU'RE AROUND.
HMM...
OH!
OVER HERE, TAKEO!
TAKEO!
ZIP

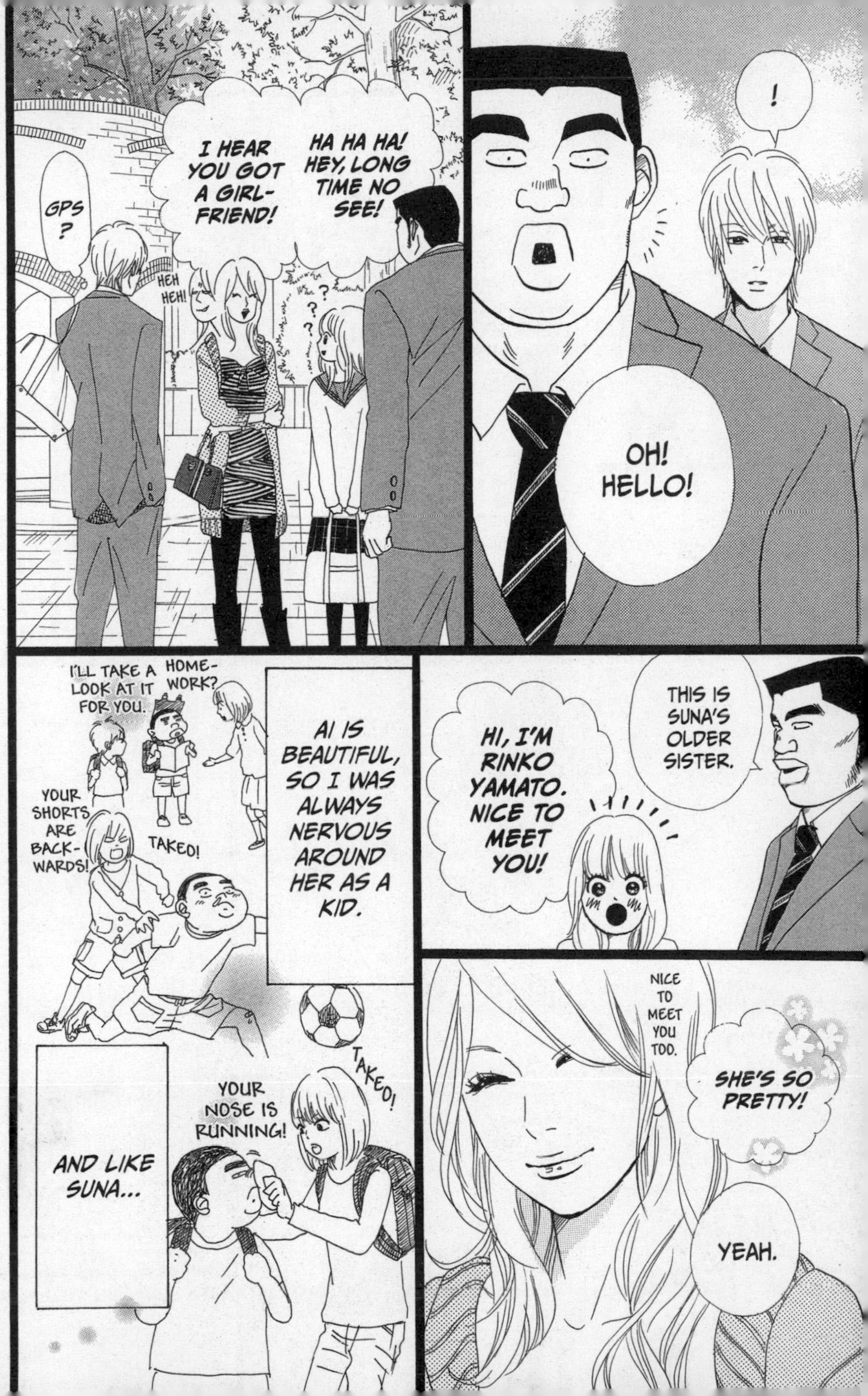
!
OH! HELLO!
HA HA HA! HEY, LONG TIME NO SEE!
I HEAR YOU GOT A GIRL-FRIEND!
?
HEH HEH!
GPS?
THIS IS SUNA'S OLDER SISTER.
HI, I'M RINKO YAMATO. NICE TO MEET YOU!
NICE TO MEET YOU TOO.
SHE'S SO PRETTY!
YEAH.
AI IS BEAUTIFUL, SO I WAS ALWAYS NERVOUS AROUND HER AS A KID.
HOME-WORK?
I'LL TAKE A LOOK AT IT FOR YOU.
TAKEO!
YOUR SHORTS ARE BACK-WARDS!
TAKEO!
YOUR NOSE IS RUNNING!
AND LIKE SUNA...

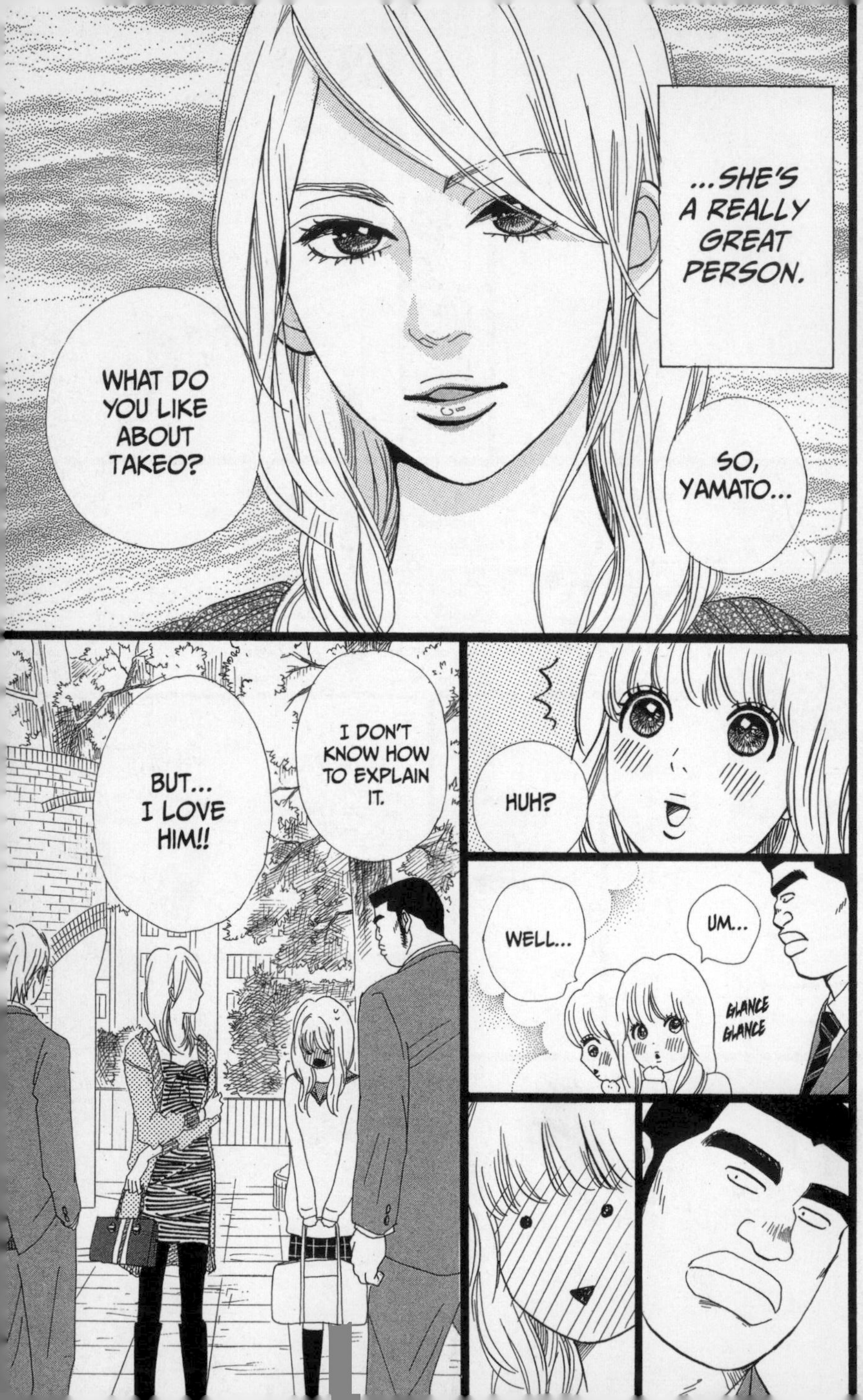
...SHE'S A REALLY GREAT PERSON.
SO, YAMATO...
WHAT DO YOU LIKE ABOUT TAKEO?
HUH?
UM...
WELL...
GLANCE GLANCE
I DON'T KNOW HOW TO EXPLAIN IT.
BUT... I LOVE HIM!!

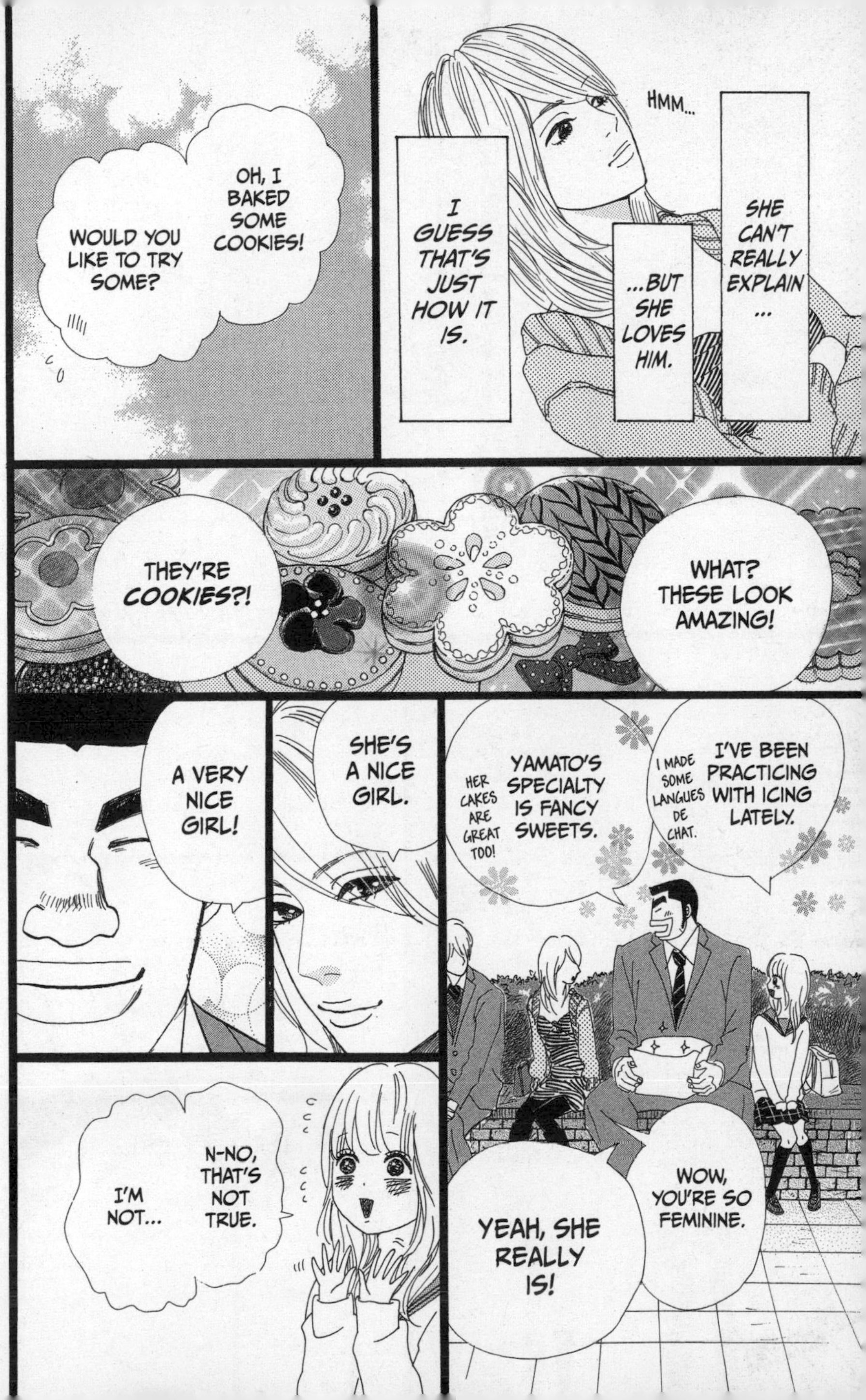
HMM...
SHE CAN'T REALLY EXPLAIN...
...BUT SHE LOVES HIM.
I GUESS THAT'S JUST HOW IT IS.
OH, I BAKED SOME COOKIES!
WOULD YOU LIKE TO TRY SOME?
WHAT? THESE LOOK AMAZING!
THEY'RE COOKIES?!
I'VE BEEN PRACTICING WITH ICING LATELY.
I MADE SOME LANGUES DE CHAT.
YAMATO'S SPECIALTY IS FANCY SWEETS.
HER CAKES ARE GREAT TOO!
WOW, YOU'RE SO FEMININE.
YEAH, SHE REALLY IS!
SHE'S A NICE GIRL.
A VERY NICE GIRL!
N-NO, THAT'S NOT TRUE.
I'M NOT...

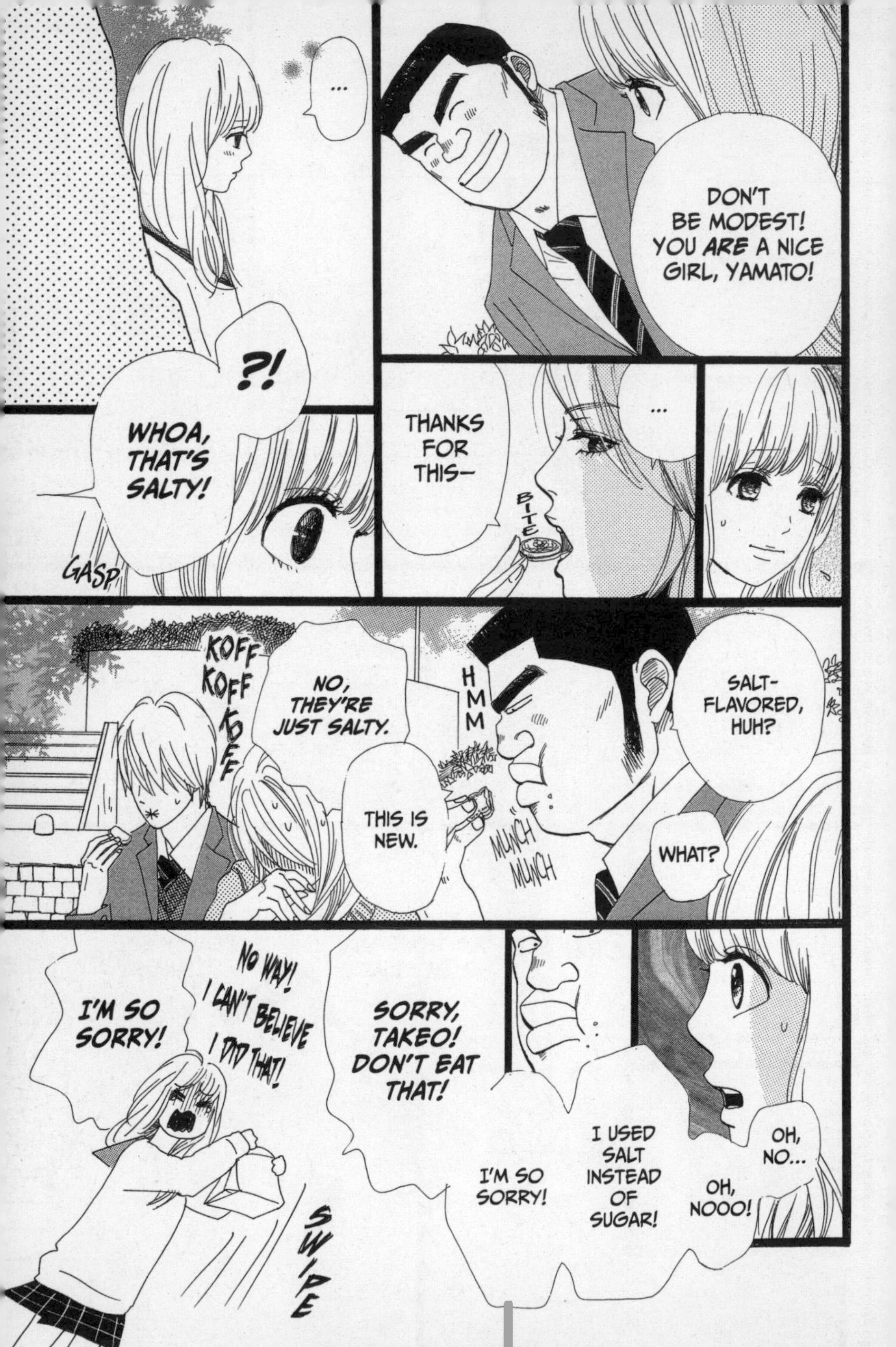
DON'T BE MODEST! YOU *ARE* A NICE GIRL, YAMATO!
...
...
THANKS FOR THIS—
BITE
?!
WHOA, THAT'S SALTY!
GASP
SALT-FLAVORED, HUH?
WHAT?
HMM
MUNCH MUNCH
THIS IS NEW.
NO, THEY'RE JUST SALTY.
KOFF KOFF KOFF KOFF
OH, NO...
OH, NOOO!
I USED SALT INSTEAD OF SUGAR!
I'M SO SORRY!
SORRY, TAKEO! DON'T EAT THAT!
NO WAY! I CAN'T BELIEVE I DID THAT!
I'M SO SORRY!
SWIPE

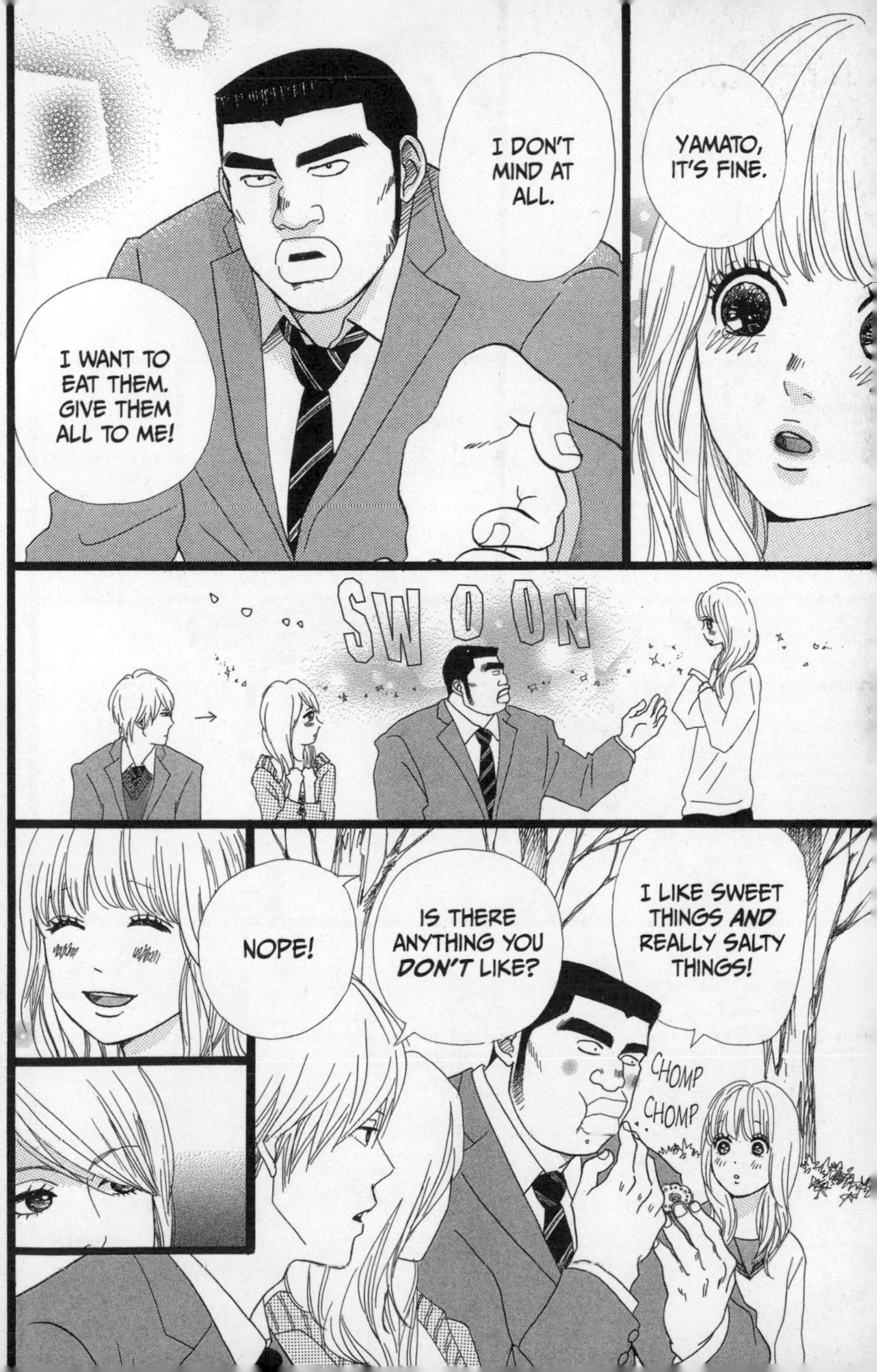
YAMATO, IT'S FINE.
I DON'T MIND AT ALL.
I WANT TO EAT THEM. GIVE THEM ALL TO ME!
SWOON
I LIKE SWEET THINGS *AND* REALLY SALTY THINGS!
IS THERE ANYTHING YOU *DON'T* LIKE?
CHOMP CHOMP
NOPE!

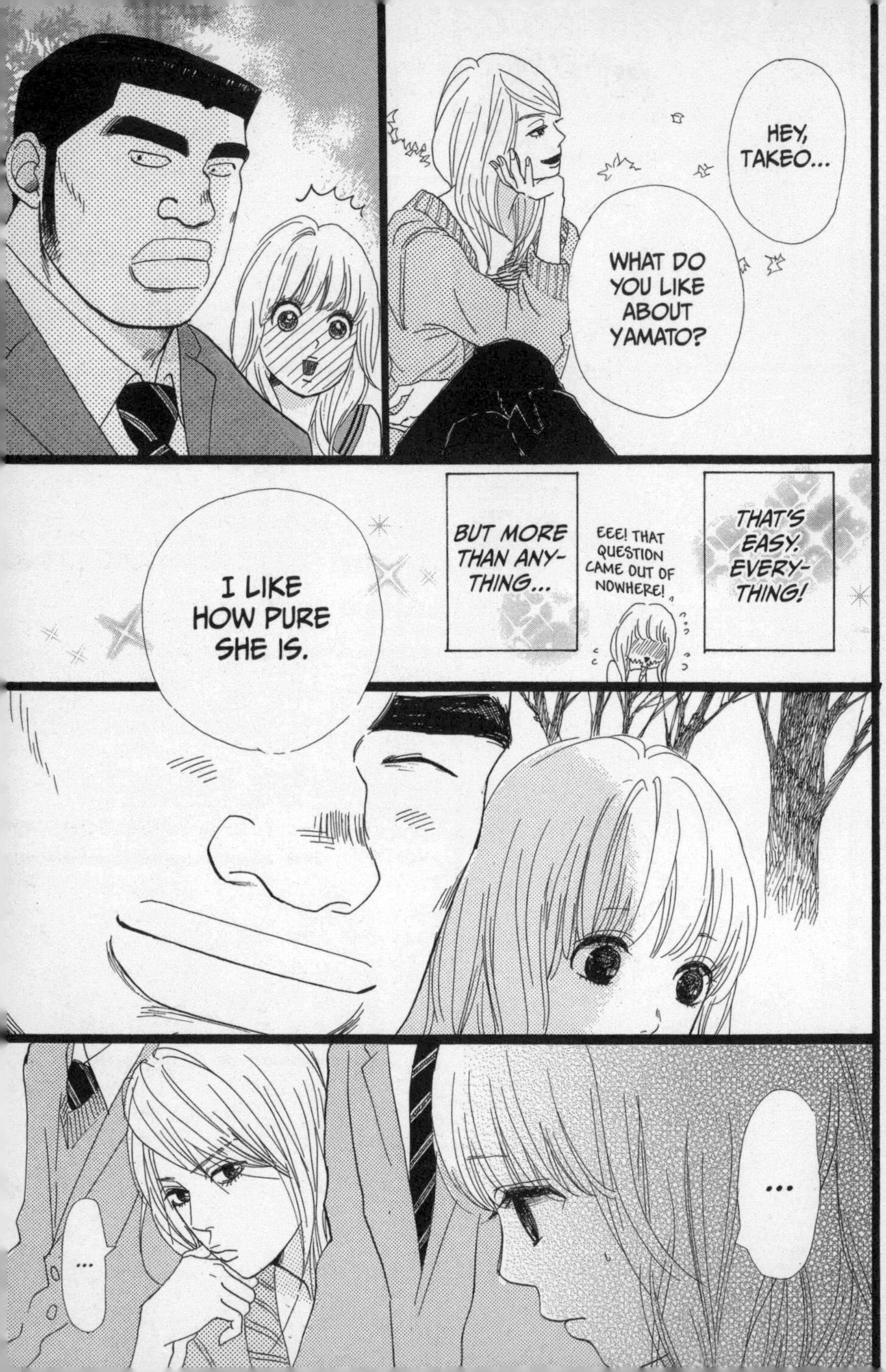
HEY, TAKEO...
WHAT DO YOU LIKE ABOUT YAMATO?
THAT'S EASY. EVERYTHING!
EEE! THAT QUESTION CAME OUT OF NOWHERE!
BUT MORE THAN ANYTHING...
I LIKE HOW PURE SHE IS.
...
...

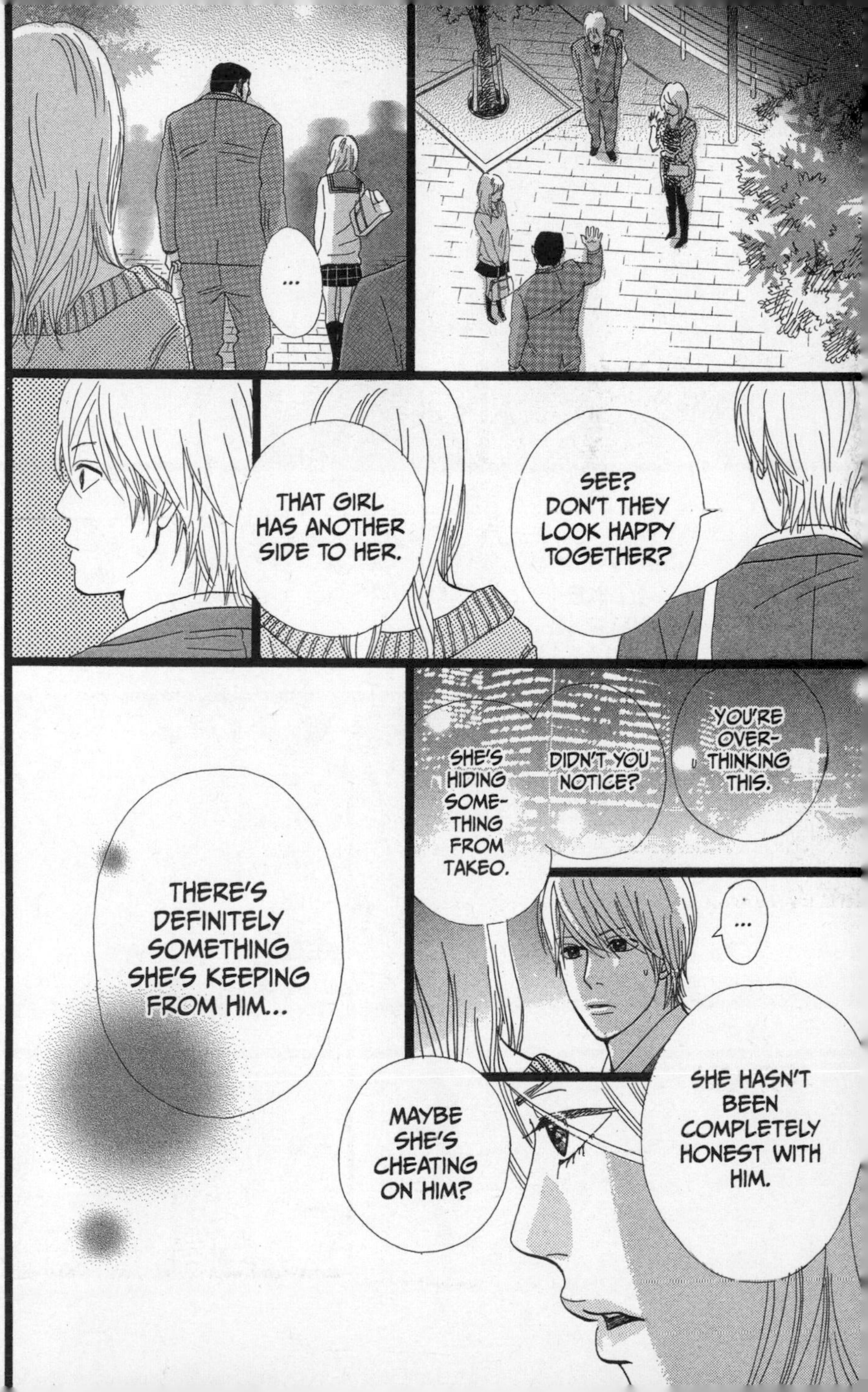
...
SEE? DON'T THEY LOOK HAPPY TOGETHER?
THAT GIRL HAS ANOTHER SIDE TO HER.
YOU'RE OVER-THINKING THIS.
DIDN'T YOU NOTICE?
SHE'S HIDING SOME-THING FROM TAKEO.
...
SHE HASN'T BEEN COMPLETELY HONEST WITH HIM.
MAYBE SHE'S CHEATING ON HIM?
THERE'S DEFINITELY SOMETHING SHE'S KEEPING FROM HIM...

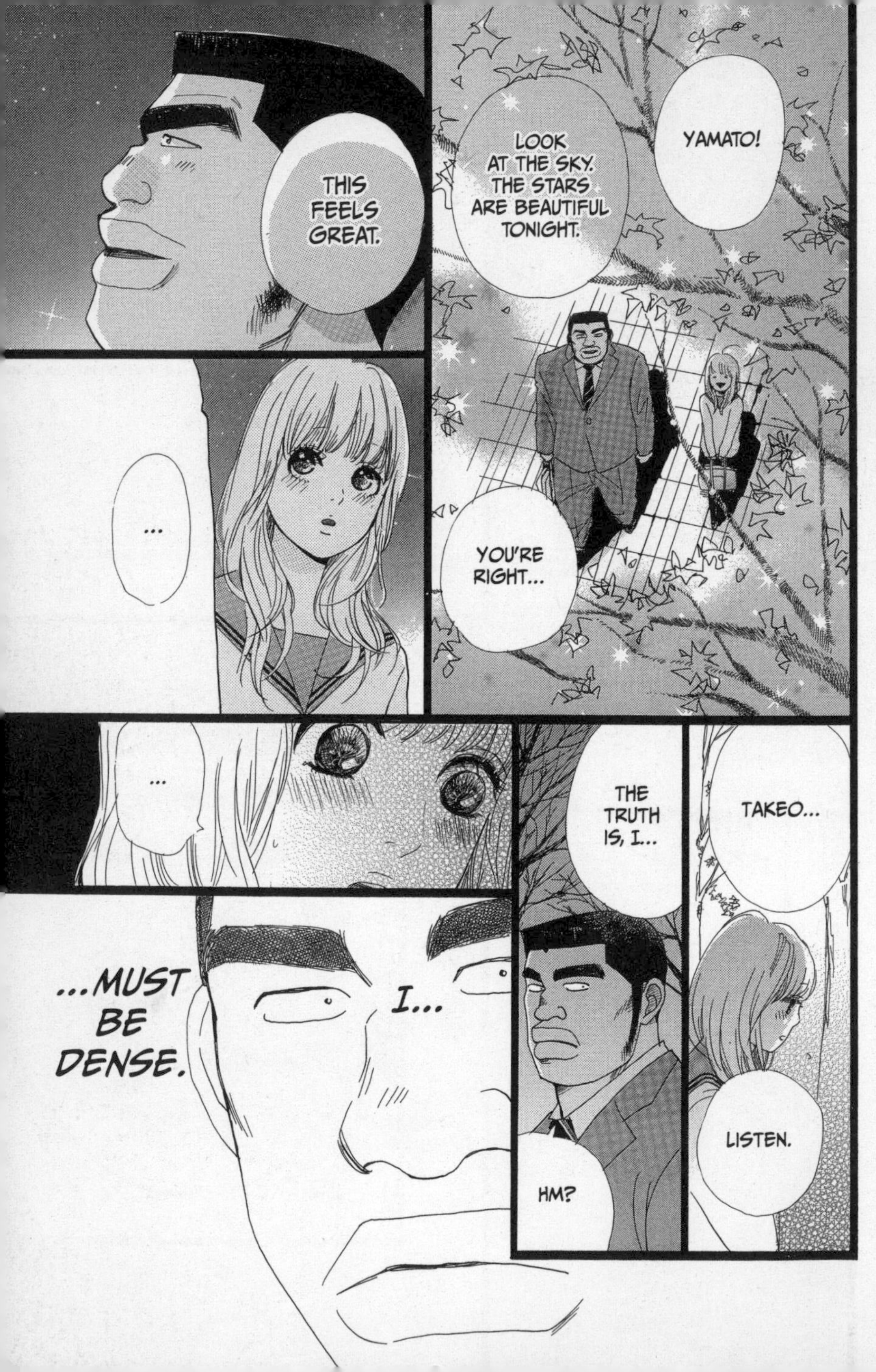
YAMATO!
LOOK AT THE SKY. THE STARS ARE BEAUTIFUL TONIGHT.
YOU'RE RIGHT...
THIS FEELS GREAT.
...
TAKEO...
LISTEN.
THE TRUTH IS, I...
HM?
...
I...
...MUST BE DENSE.

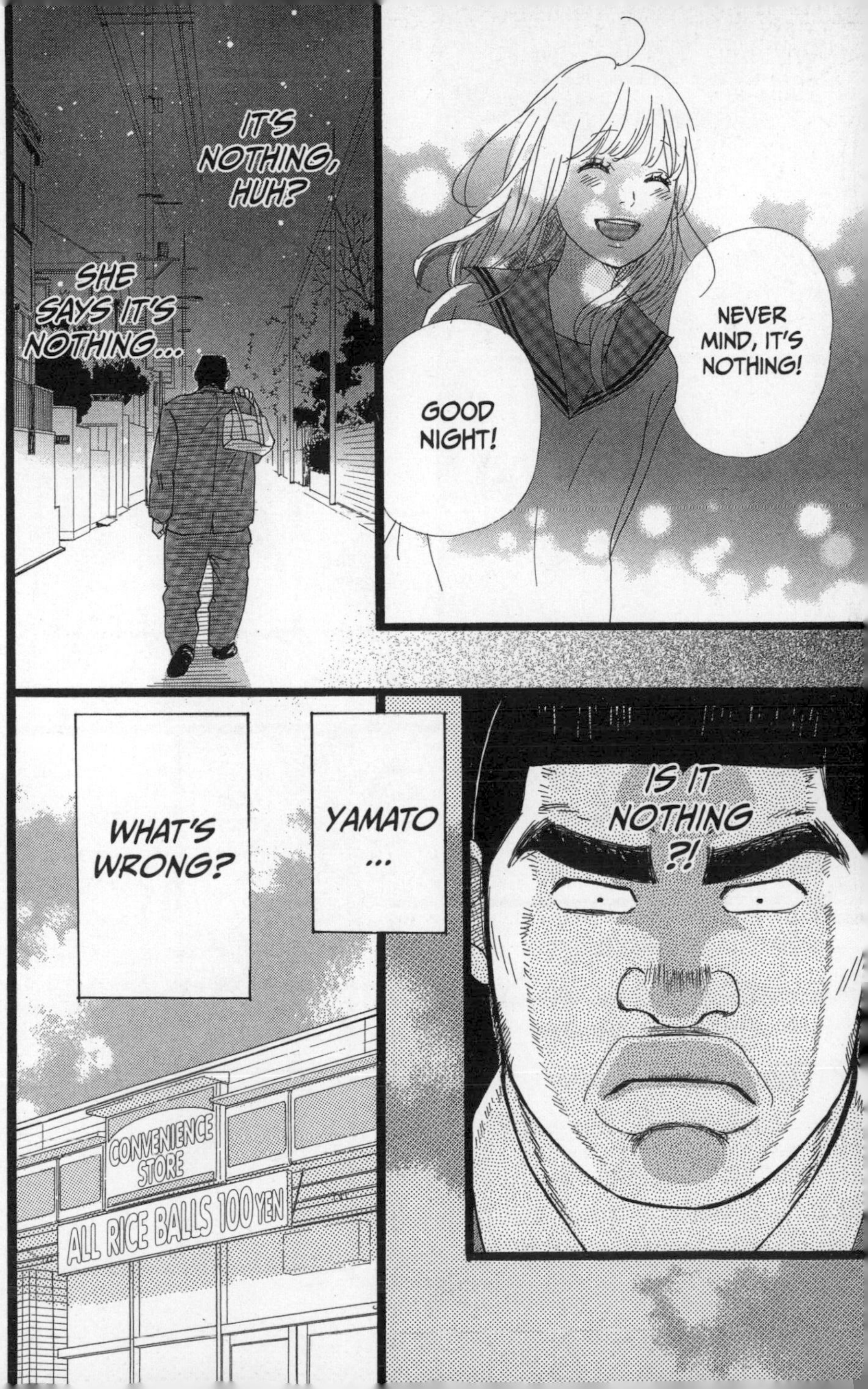
NEVER MIND, IT'S NOTHING!
GOOD NIGHT!
IT'S NOTHING, HUH?
SHE SAYS IT'S NOTHING...
IS IT NOTHING ?!
YAMATO ...
WHAT'S WRONG?
CONVENIENCE STORE
ALL RICE BALLS 100 YEN

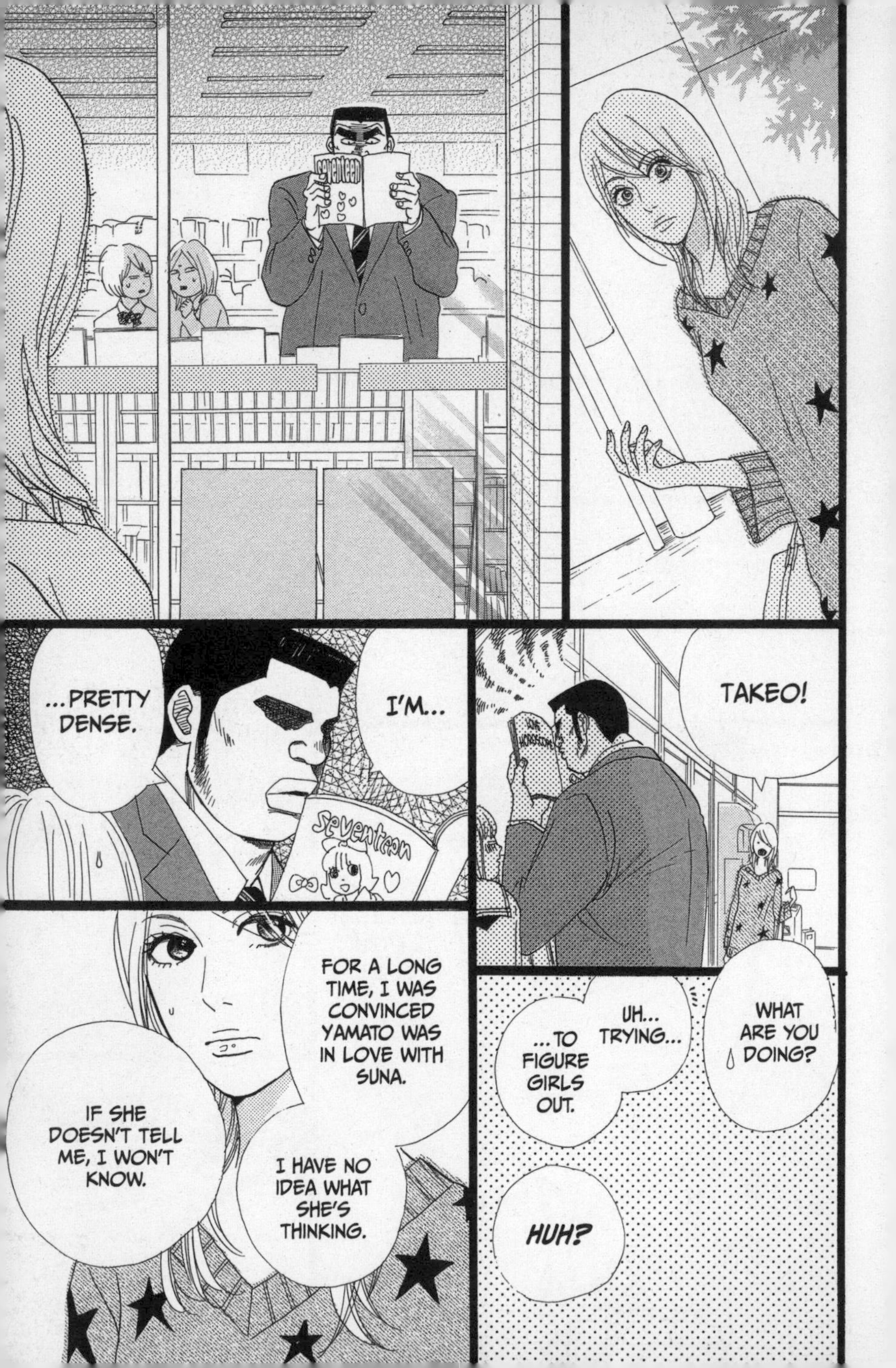
Seventeen
TAKEO!
I'M...
...PRETTY DENSE.
Seventeen
WHAT ARE YOU DOING?
UH... TRYING...
...TO FIGURE GIRLS OUT.
HUH?
FOR A LONG TIME, I WAS CONVINCED YAMATO WAS IN LOVE WITH SUNA.
IF SHE DOESN'T TELL ME, I WON'T KNOW.
I HAVE NO IDEA WHAT SHE'S THINKING.

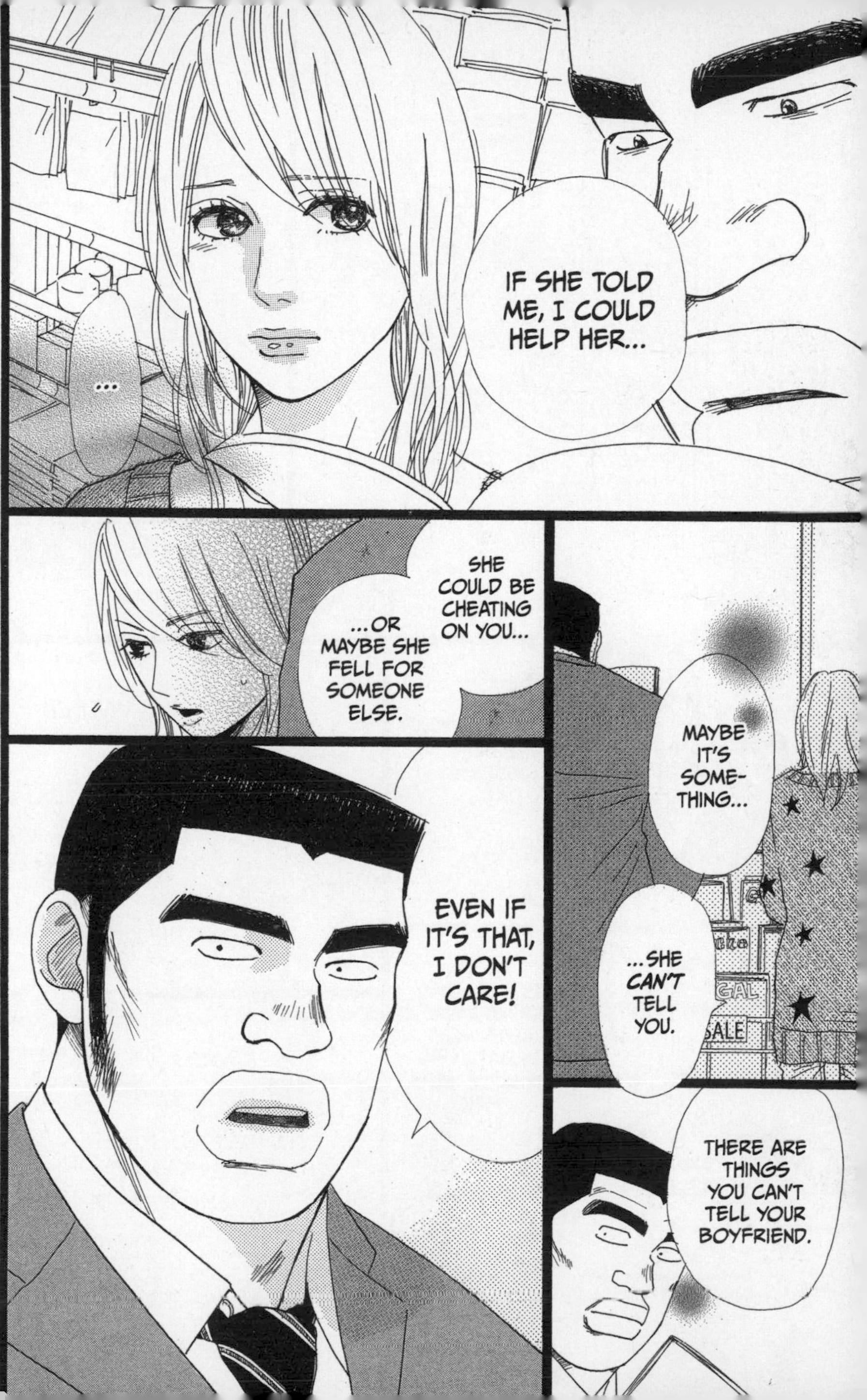
IF SHE TOLD ME, I COULD HELP HER...
...
MAYBE IT'S SOME-THING...
...SHE CAN'T TELL YOU.
THERE ARE THINGS YOU CAN'T TELL YOUR BOYFRIEND.
SHE COULD BE CHEATING ON YOU...
...OR MAYBE SHE FELL FOR SOMEONE ELSE.
EVEN IF IT'S THAT, I DON'T CARE!

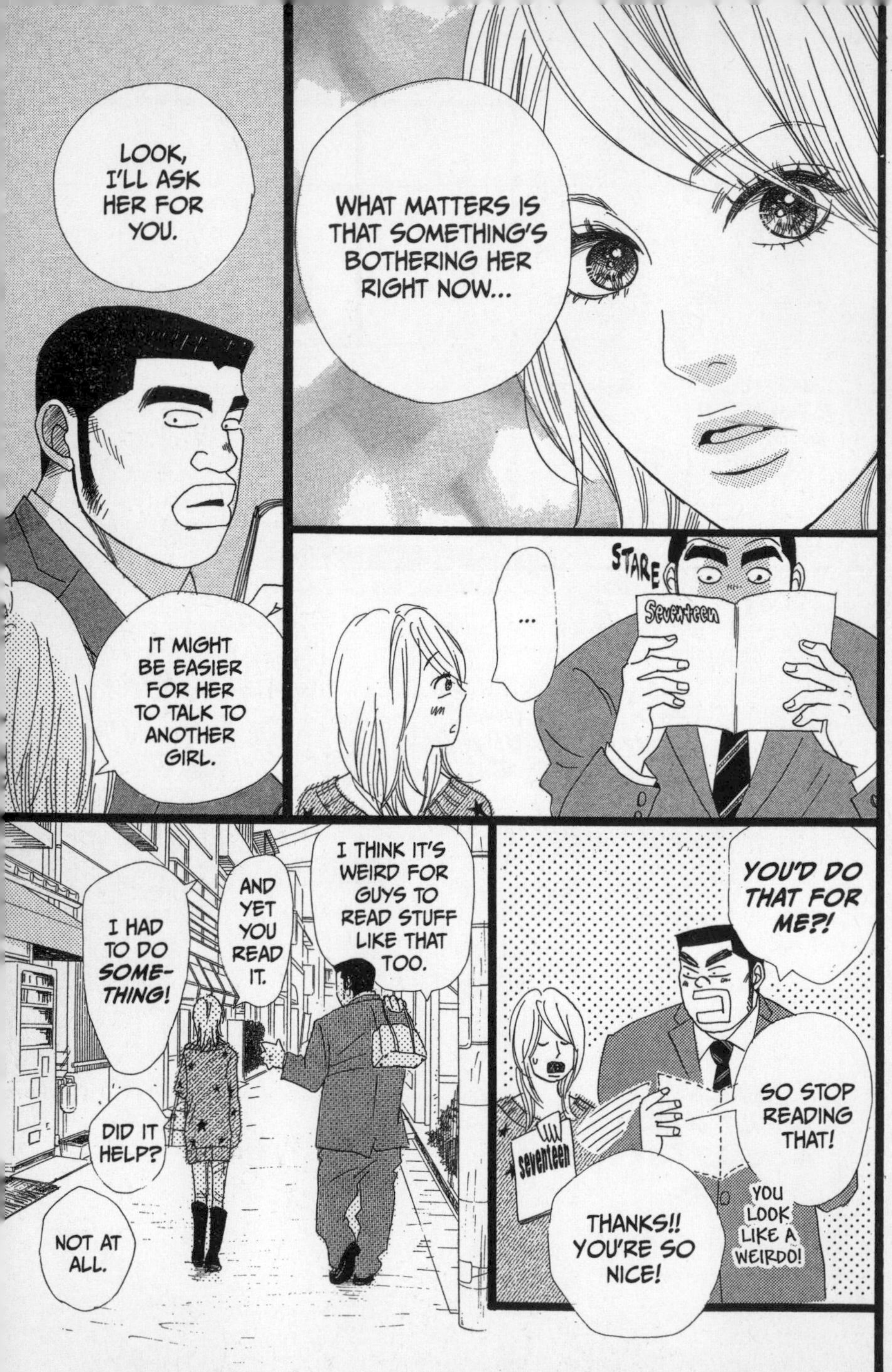
WHAT MATTERS IS THAT SOMETHING'S BOTHERING HER RIGHT NOW...
STARE
...
Seventeen
LOOK, I'LL ASK HER FOR YOU.
IT MIGHT BE EASIER FOR HER TO TALK TO ANOTHER GIRL.
YOU'D DO THAT FOR ME?!
SO STOP READING THAT!
THANKS!! YOU'RE SO NICE!
YOU LOOK LIKE A WEIRDO!
Seventeen
I THINK IT'S WEIRD FOR GUYS TO READ STUFF LIKE THAT TOO.
AND YET YOU READ IT.
I HAD TO DO SOME-THING!
DID IT HELP?
NOT AT ALL.

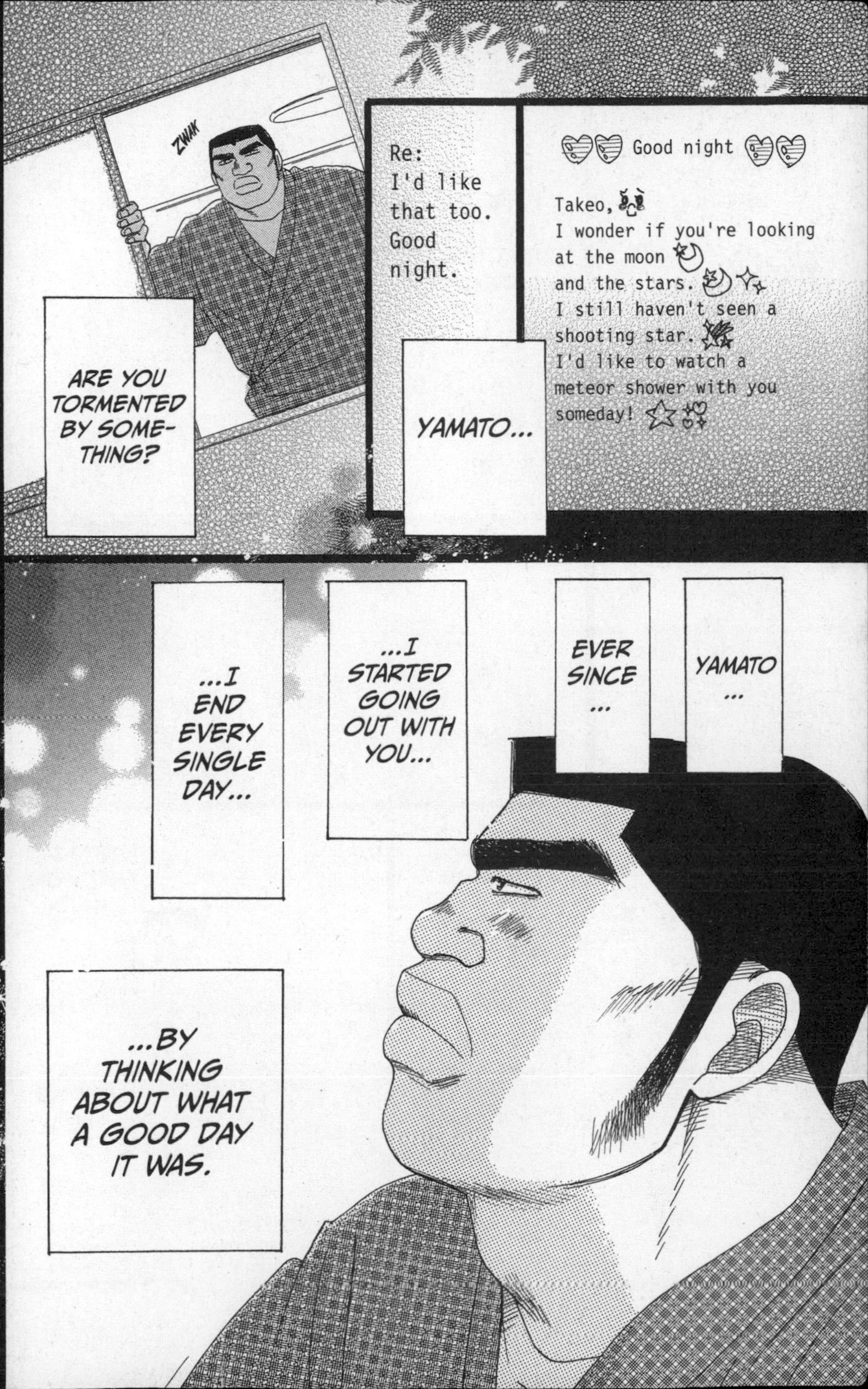

Good night
Takeo,
I wonder if you're looking at the moon
and the stars.
I still haven't seen a shooting star.
I'd like to watch a meteor shower with you someday!
Re:
I'd like that too.
Good night.
YAMATO...
ZWAK
ARE YOU TORMENTED BY SOME-THING?
YAMATO...
EVER SINCE...
...I STARTED GOING OUT WITH YOU...
...I END EVERY SINGLE DAY...
...BY THINKING ABOUT WHAT A GOOD DAY IT WAS.

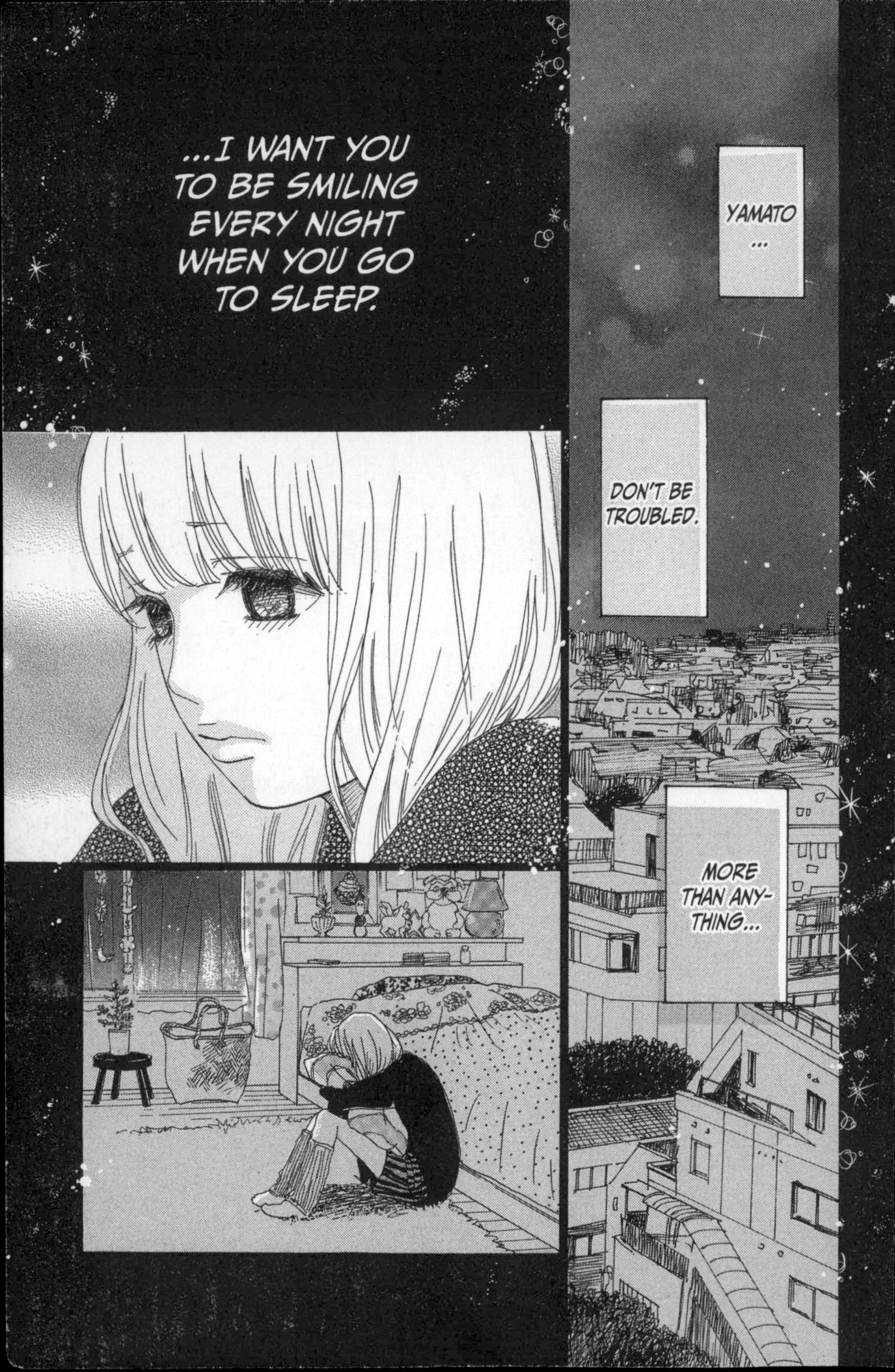
YAMATO ...
DON'T BE TROUBLED.
MORE THAN ANY-THING...
...I WANT YOU TO BE SMILING EVERY NIGHT WHEN YOU GO TO SLEEP.

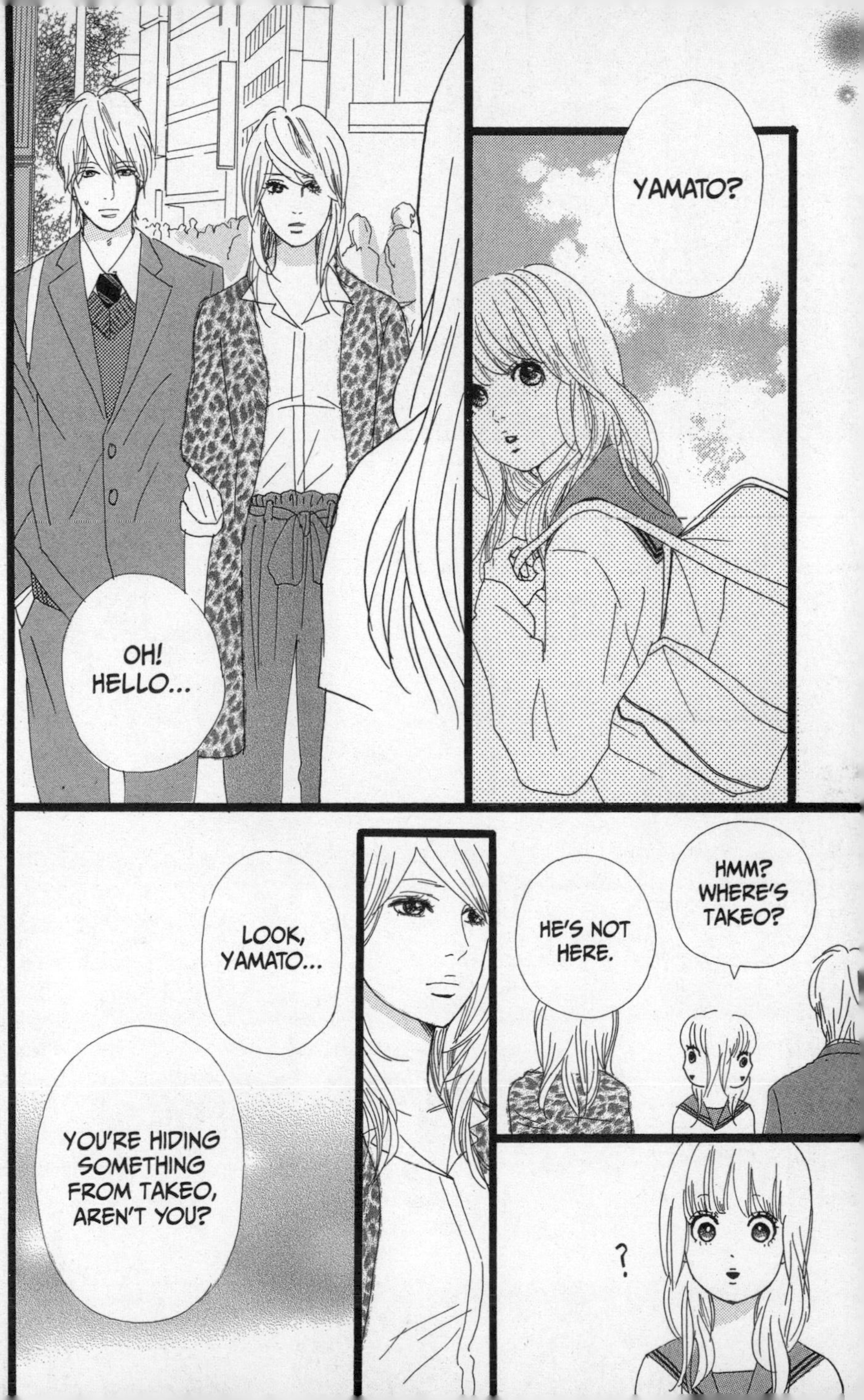
YAMATO?
OH! HELLO...
HMM? WHERE'S TAKEO?
HE'S NOT HERE.
?
LOOK, YAMATO...
YOU'RE HIDING SOMETHING FROM TAKEO, AREN'T YOU?

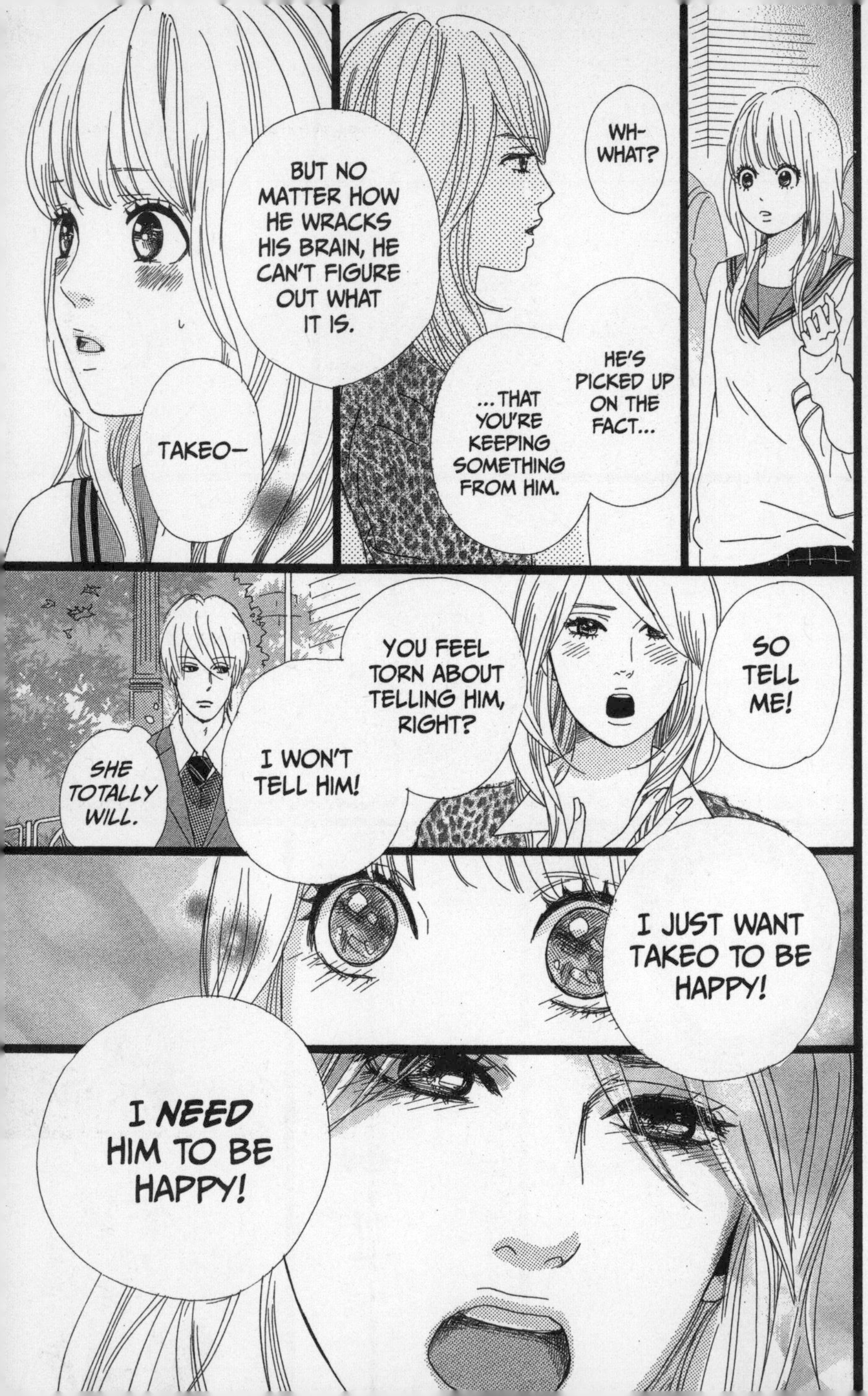
WH-WHAT?
HE'S PICKED UP ON THE FACT...
...THAT YOU'RE KEEPING SOMETHING FROM HIM.
BUT NO MATTER HOW HE WRACKS HIS BRAIN, HE CAN'T FIGURE OUT WHAT IT IS.
TAKEO—
SO TELL ME!
YOU FEEL TORN ABOUT TELLING HIM, RIGHT?
I WON'T TELL HIM!
SHE TOTALLY WILL.
I JUST WANT TAKEO TO BE HAPPY!
I *NEED* HIM TO BE HAPPY!

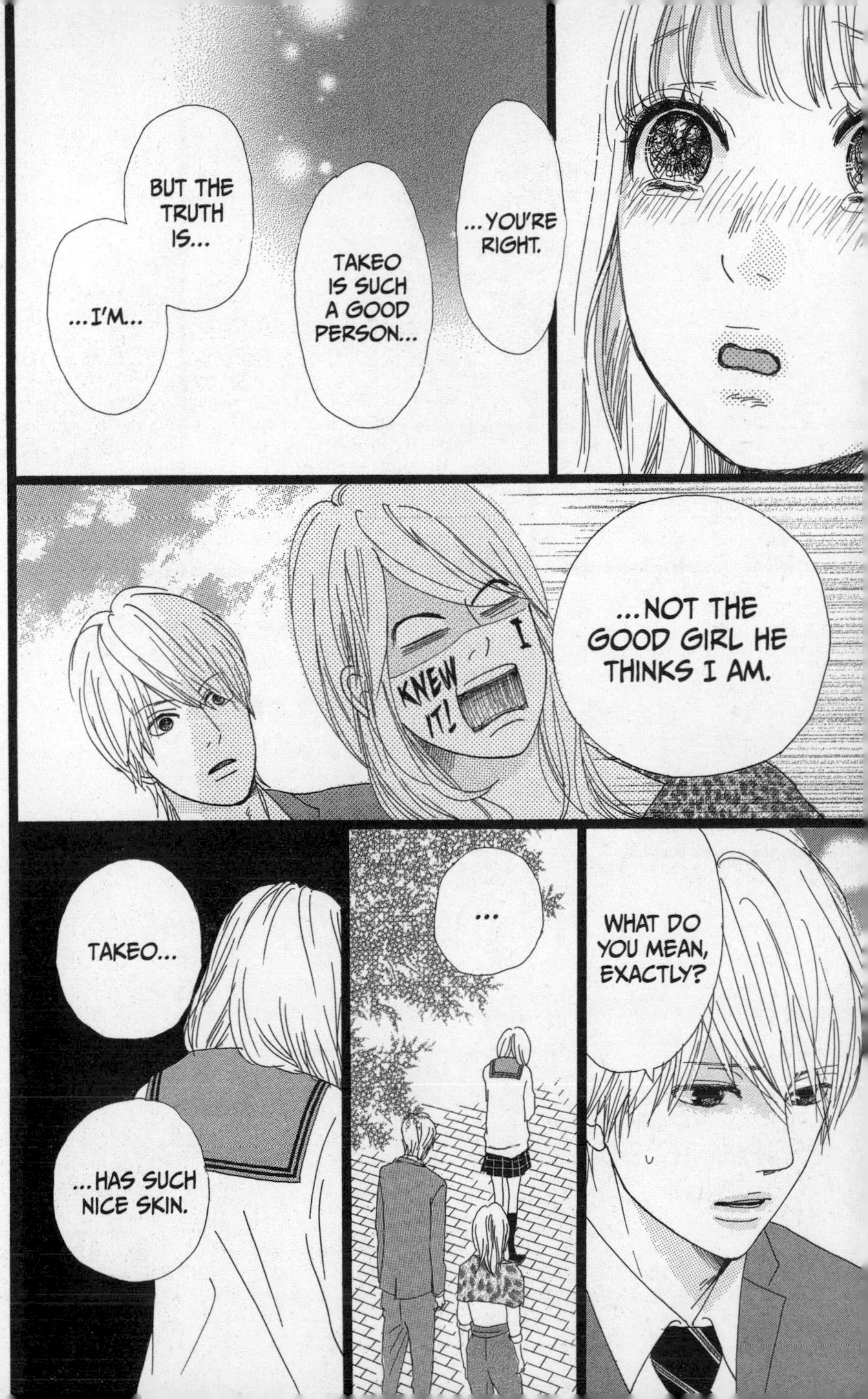
...YOU'RE RIGHT.
TAKEO IS SUCH A GOOD PERSON...
BUT THE TRUTH IS...
...I'M...
...NOT THE GOOD GIRL HE THINKS I AM.
I KNEW IT!
WHAT DO YOU MEAN, EXACTLY?
...
TAKEO...
...HAS SUCH NICE SKIN.

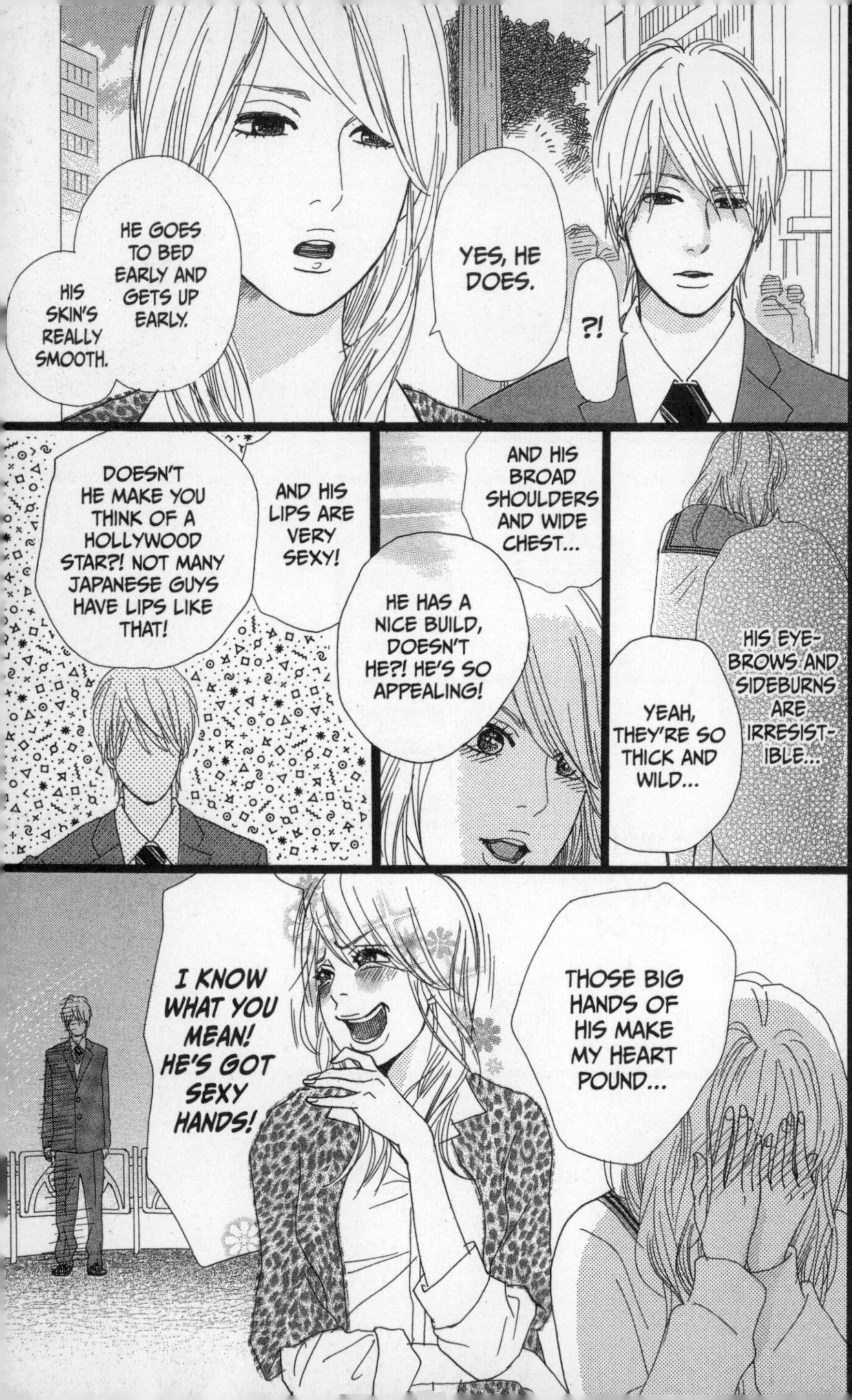
YES, HE DOES.
?!
HE GOES TO BED EARLY AND GETS UP EARLY.
HIS SKIN'S REALLY SMOOTH.
HIS EYE-BROWS AND SIDEBURNS ARE IRRESIST-IBLE...
YEAH, THEY'RE SO THICK AND WILD...
AND HIS BROAD SHOULDERS AND WIDE CHEST...
HE HAS A NICE BUILD, DOESN'T HE?! HE'S SO APPEALING!
AND HIS LIPS ARE VERY SEXY!
DOESN'T HE MAKE YOU THINK OF A HOLLYWOOD STAR?! NOT MANY JAPANESE GUYS HAVE LIPS LIKE THAT!
THOSE BIG HANDS OF HIS MAKE MY HEART POUND...
I KNOW WHAT YOU MEAN! HE'S GOT SEXY HANDS!

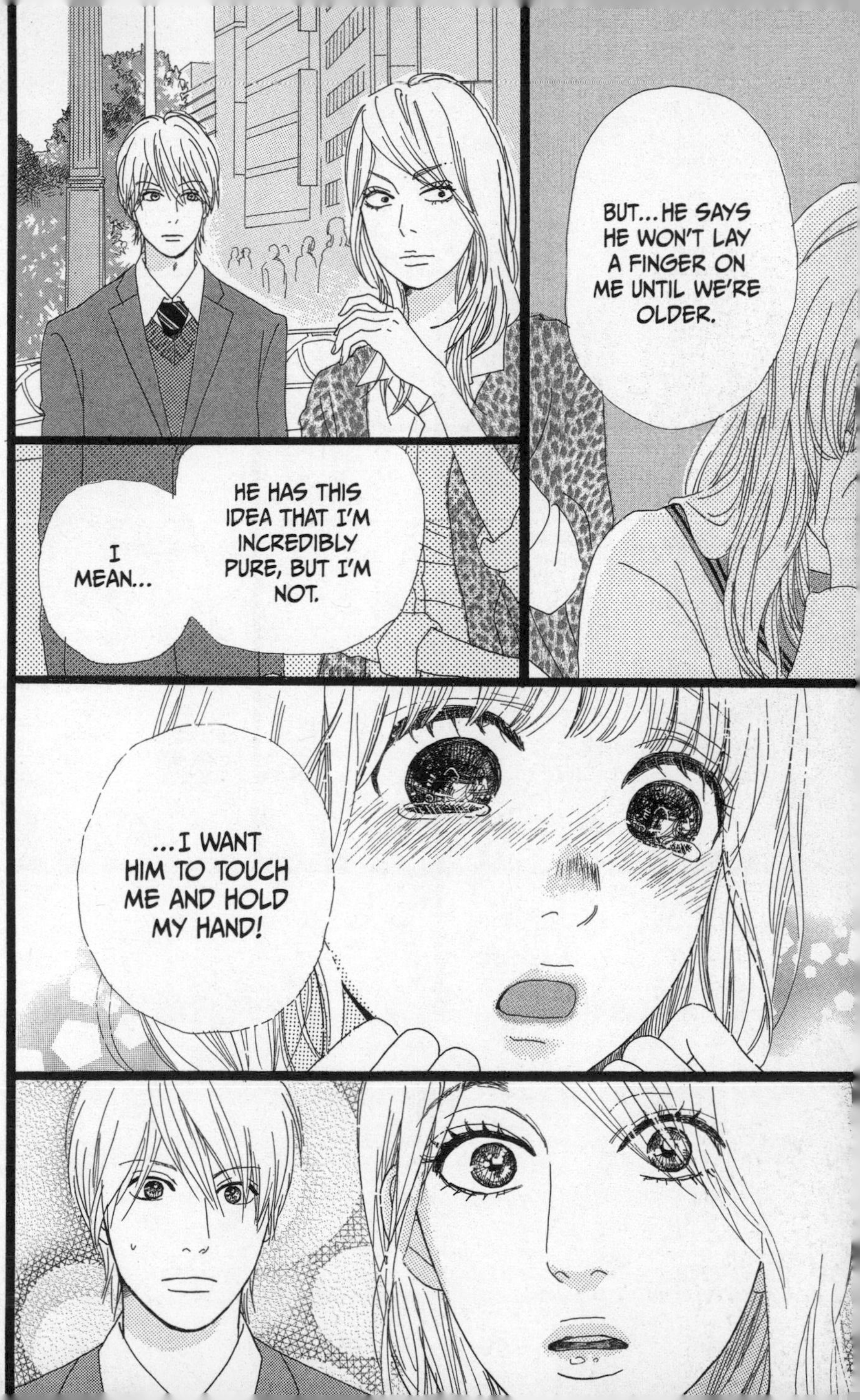

BUT... HE SAYS HE WON'T LAY A FINGER ON ME UNTIL WE'RE OLDER.
I MEAN...
HE HAS THIS IDEA THAT I'M INCREDIBLY PURE, BUT I'M NOT.
...I WANT HIM TO TOUCH ME AND HOLD MY HAND!

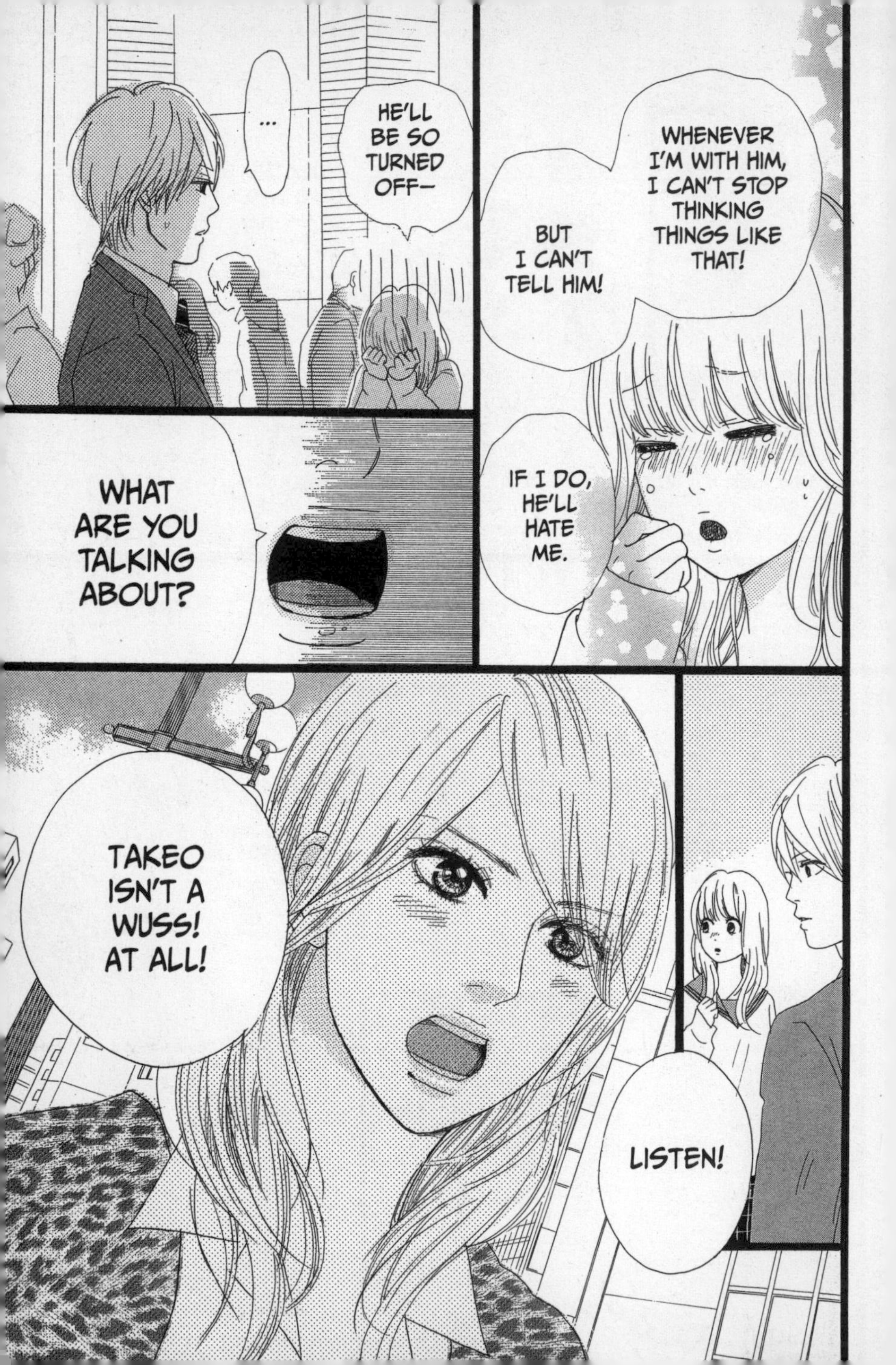
WHENEVER I'M WITH HIM, I CAN'T STOP THINKING THINGS LIKE THAT!
BUT I CAN'T TELL HIM!
IF I DO, HE'LL HATE ME.
HE'LL BE SO TURNED OFF—
...
WHAT ARE YOU TALKING ABOUT?
LISTEN!
TAKEO ISN'T A WUSS! AT ALL!

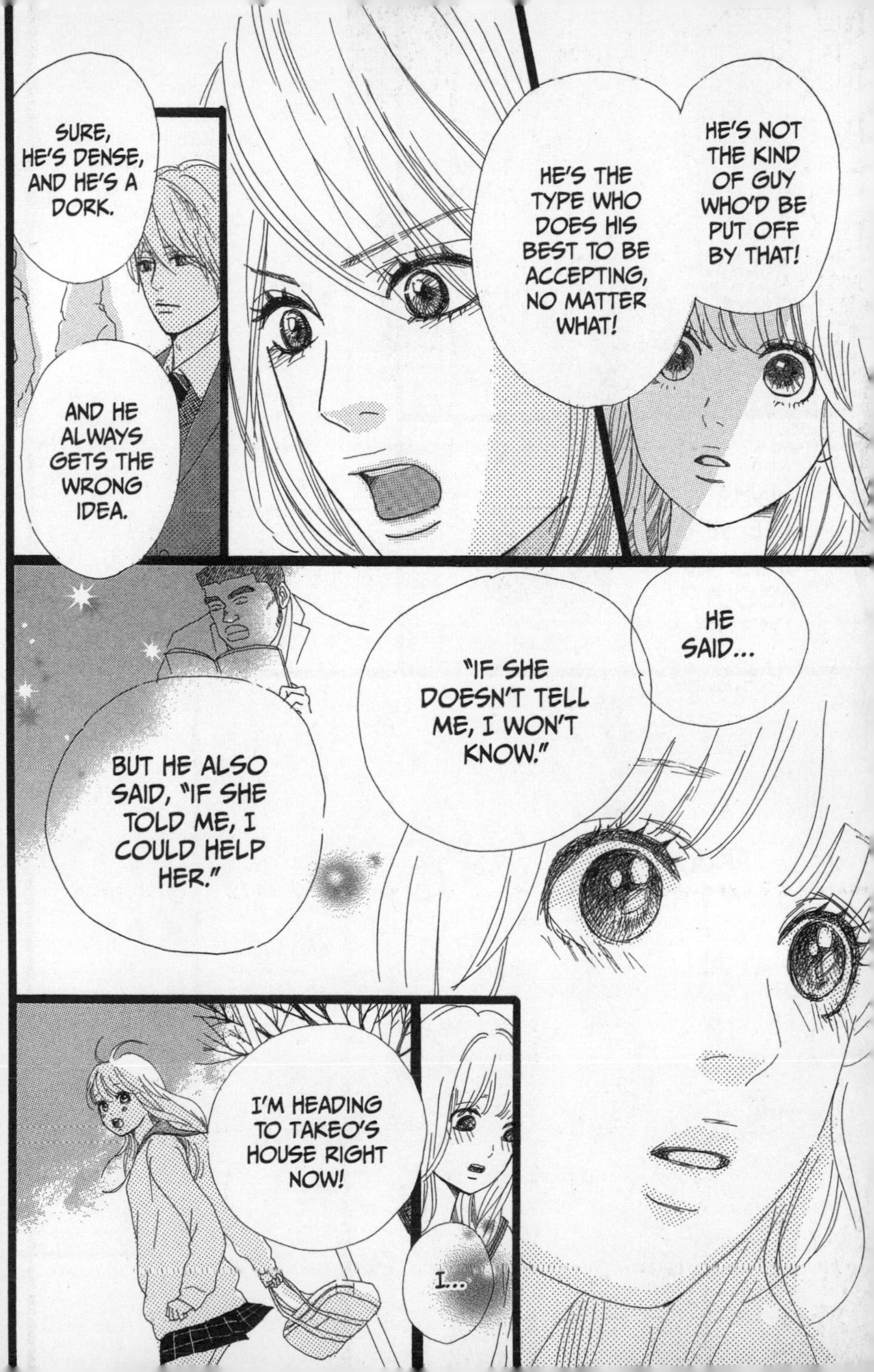
HE'S NOT THE KIND OF GUY WHO'D BE PUT OFF BY THAT!
HE'S THE TYPE WHO DOES HIS BEST TO BE ACCEPTING, NO MATTER WHAT!
SURE, HE'S DENSE, AND HE'S A DORK.
AND HE ALWAYS GETS THE WRONG IDEA.
HE SAID...
"IF SHE DOESN'T TELL ME, I WON'T KNOW."
BUT HE ALSO SAID, "IF SHE TOLD ME, I COULD HELP HER."
I...
I'M HEADING TO TAKEO'S HOUSE RIGHT NOW!

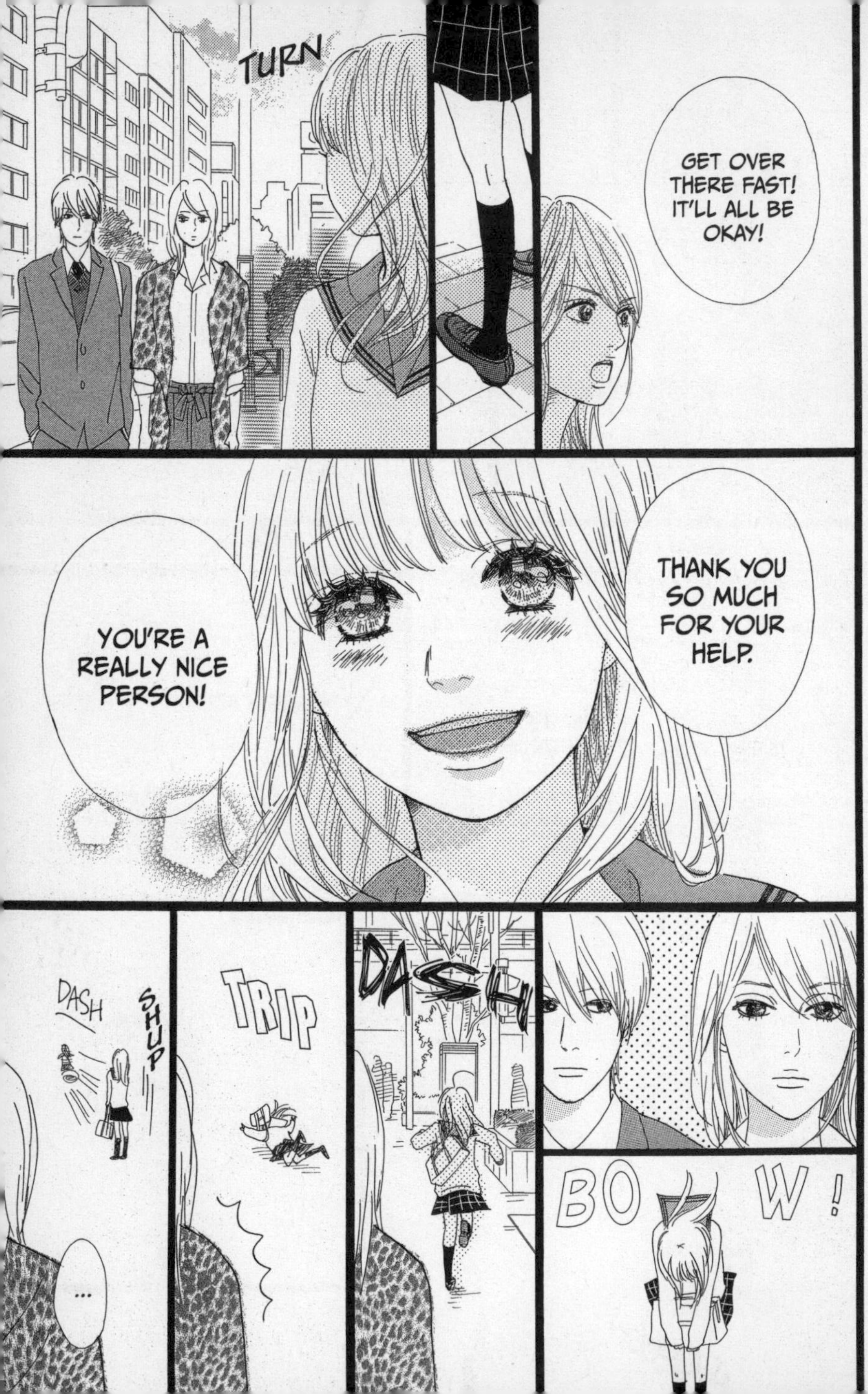
GET OVER THERE FAST! IT'LL ALL BE OKAY!
TURN
THANK YOU SO MUCH FOR YOUR HELP.
YOU'RE A REALLY NICE PERSON!
BOW!
DASH
TRIP
SHUP
DASH
...

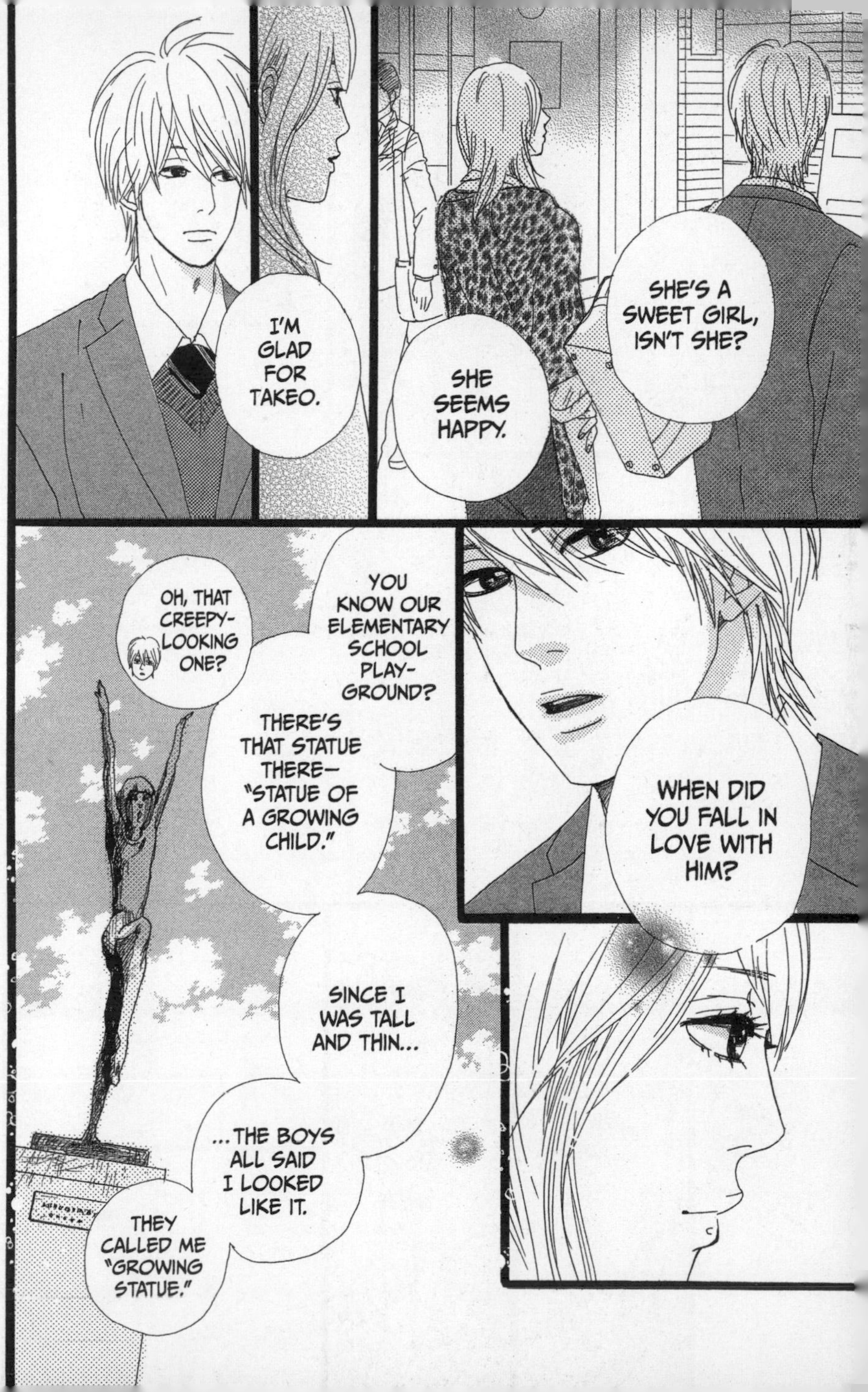
SHE'S A SWEET GIRL, ISN'T SHE?
SHE SEEMS HAPPY.
I'M GLAD FOR TAKEO.
WHEN DID YOU FALL IN LOVE WITH HIM?
YOU KNOW OUR ELEMENTARY SCHOOL PLAY-GROUND?
OH, THAT CREEPY-LOOKING ONE?
THERE'S THAT STATUE THERE— "STATUE OF A GROWING CHILD."
SINCE I WAS TALL AND THIN...
...THE BOYS ALL SAID I LOOKED LIKE IT.
THEY CALLED ME "GROWING STATUE."

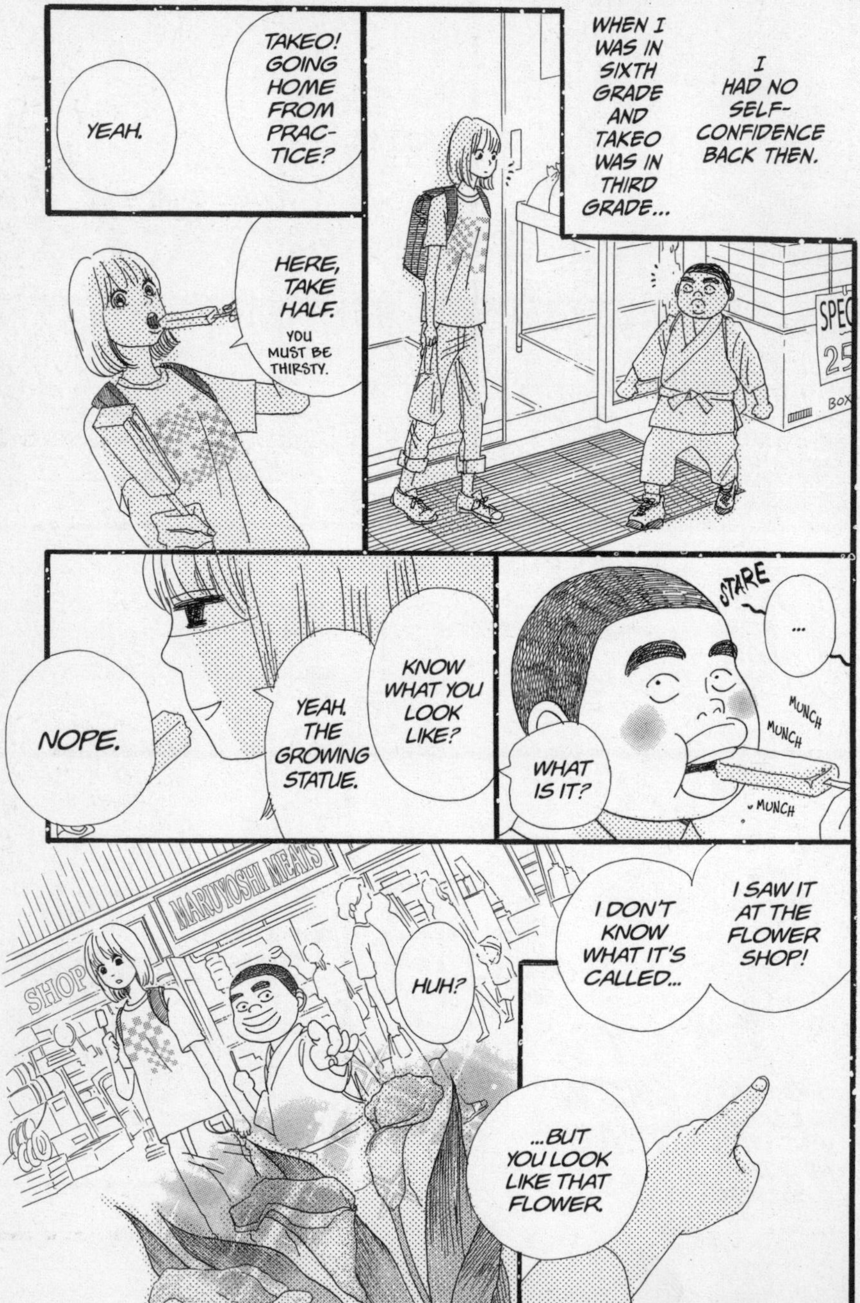
WHEN I WAS IN SIXTH GRADE AND TAKEO WAS IN THIRD GRADE...
I HAD NO SELF-CONFIDENCE BACK THEN.
TAKEO! GOING HOME FROM PRACTICE?
YEAH.
HERE, TAKE HALF.
YOU MUST BE THIRSTY.
STARE
...
MUNCH
MUNCH
WHAT IS IT?
MUNCH
KNOW WHAT YOU LOOK LIKE?
YEAH. THE GROWING STATUE.
NOPE.
I SAW IT AT THE FLOWER SHOP!
I DON'T KNOW WHAT IT'S CALLED...
HUH?
MARUYOSHI MEATS
SHOP
...BUT YOU LOOK LIKE THAT FLOWER.

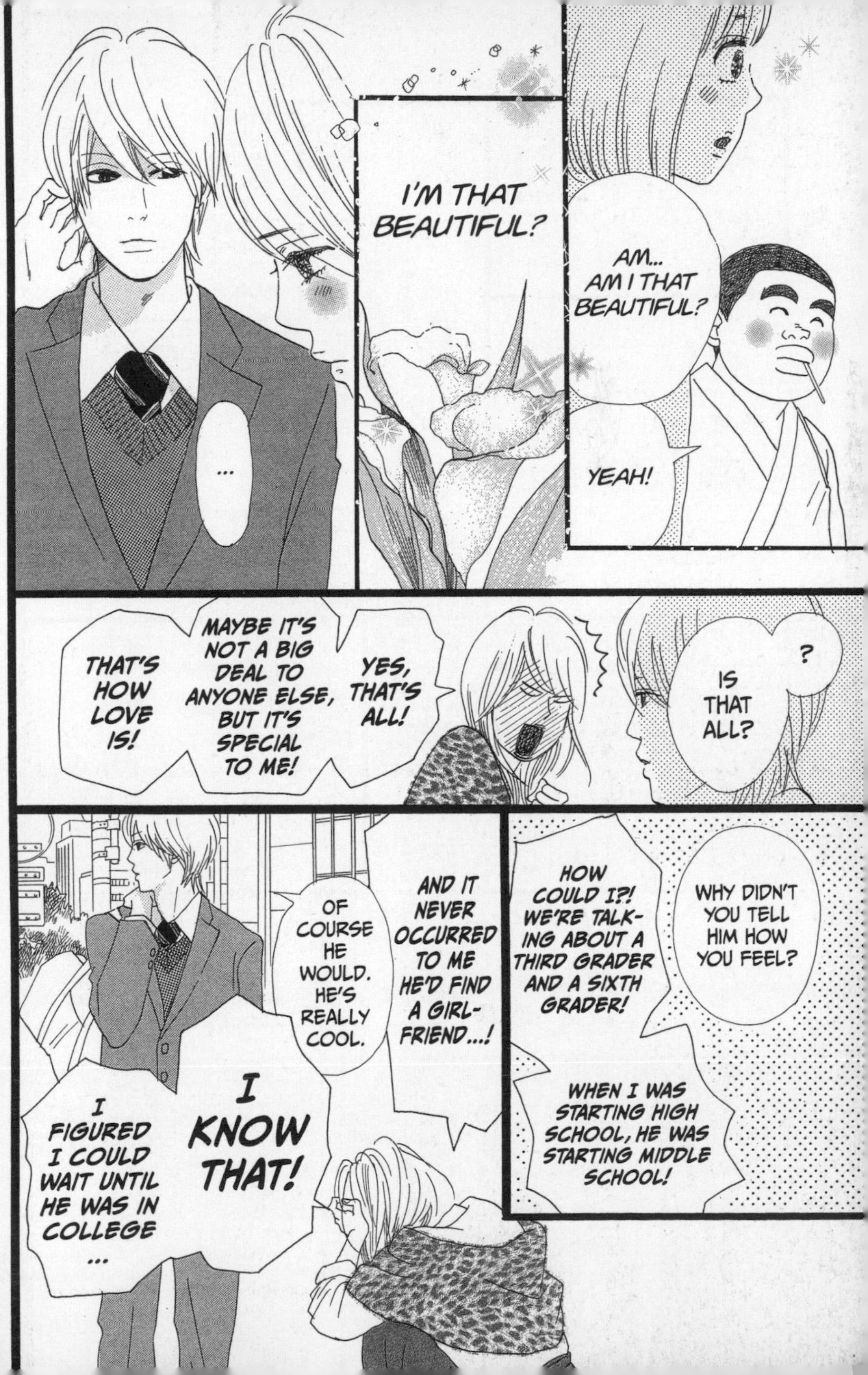

AM... AM I THAT BEAUTIFUL?
YEAH!
I'M THAT BEAUTIFUL?
...
?
IS THAT ALL?
YES, THAT'S ALL!
MAYBE IT'S NOT A BIG DEAL TO ANYONE ELSE, BUT IT'S SPECIAL TO ME!
THAT'S HOW LOVE IS!
WHY DIDN'T YOU TELL HIM HOW YOU FEEL?
HOW COULD I?! WE'RE TALKING ABOUT A THIRD GRADER AND A SIXTH GRADER!
WHEN I WAS STARTING HIGH SCHOOL, HE WAS STARTING MIDDLE SCHOOL!
AND IT NEVER OCCURRED TO ME HE'D FIND A GIRLFRIEND...!
OF COURSE HE WOULD. HE'S REALLY COOL.
I KNOW THAT!
I FIGURED I COULD WAIT UNTIL HE WAS IN COLLEGE...

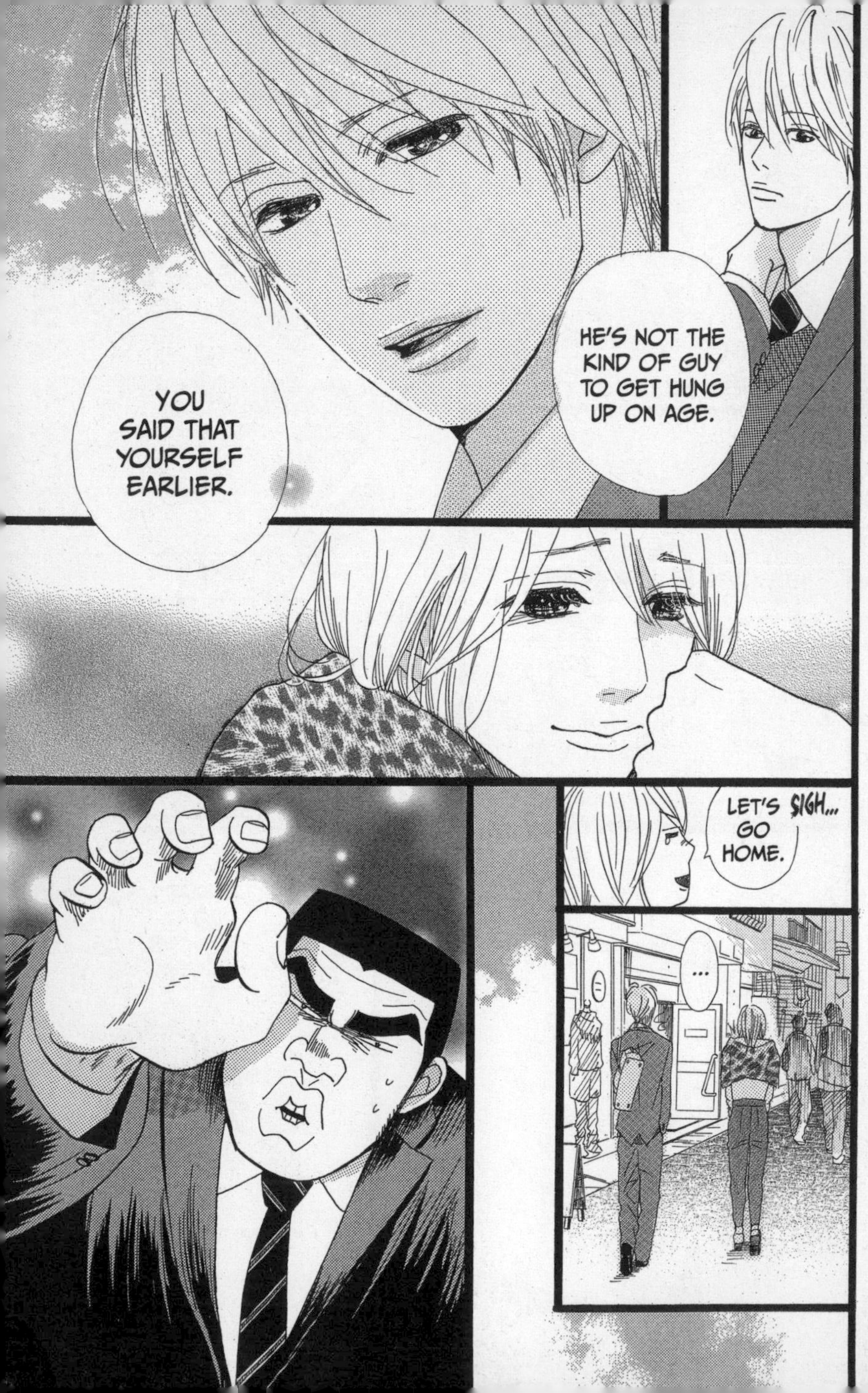
HE'S NOT THE KIND OF GUY TO GET HUNG UP ON AGE.
YOU SAID THAT YOURSELF EARLIER.
LET'S SIGH... GO HOME.
...

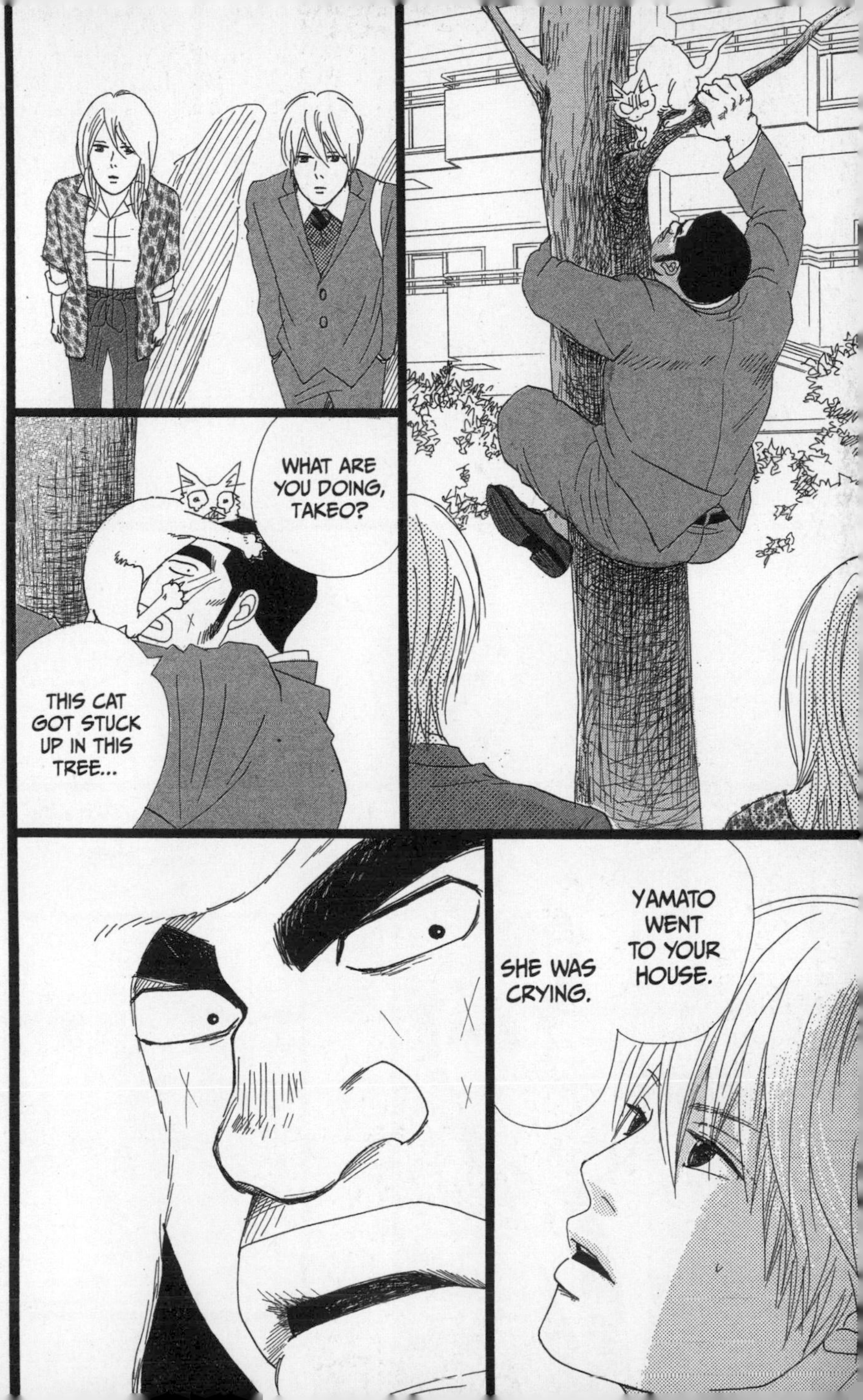
WHAT ARE YOU DOING, TAKEO?
THIS CAT GOT STUCK UP IN THIS TREE...
YAMATO WENT TO YOUR HOUSE.
SHE WAS CRYING.

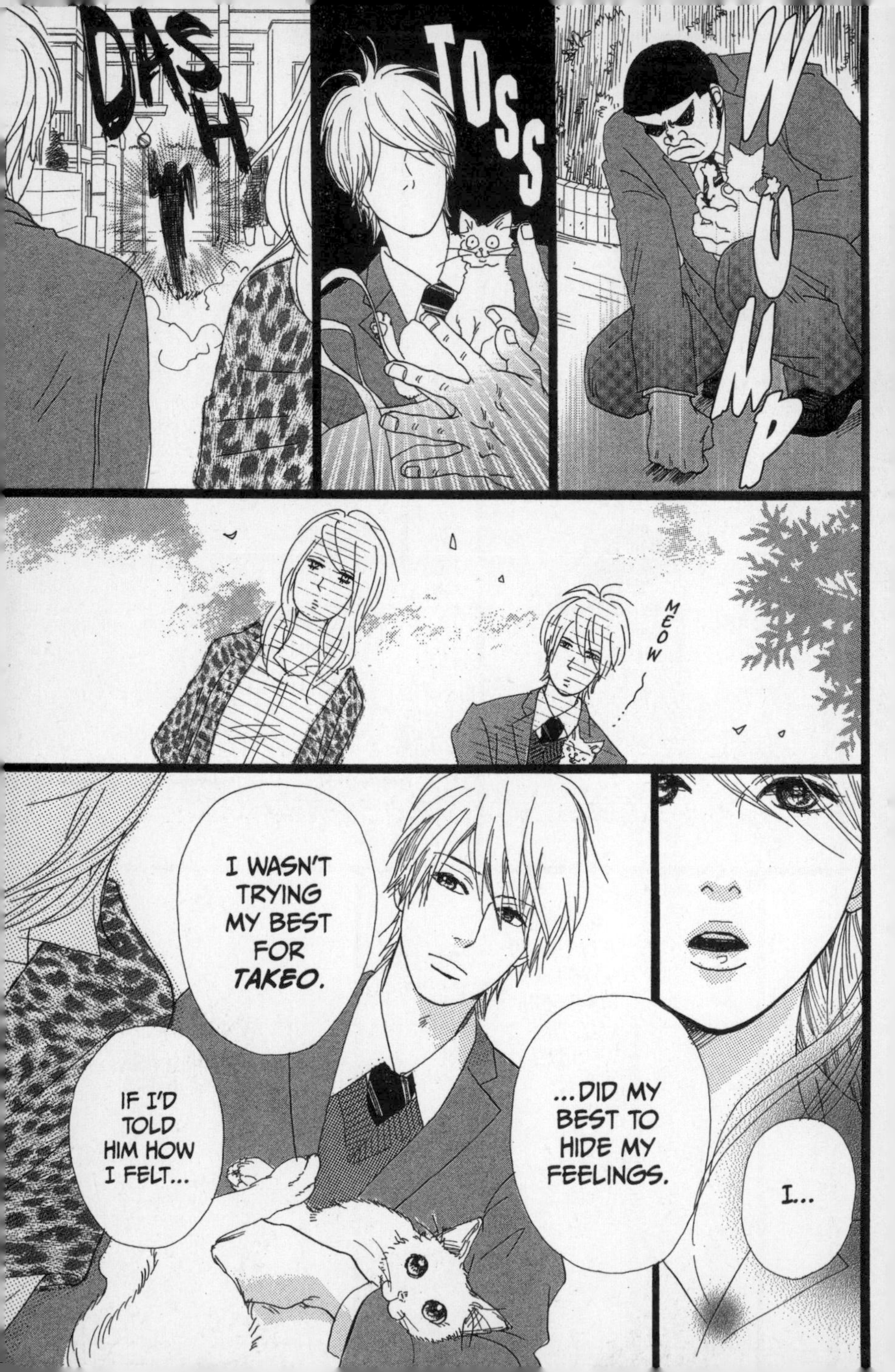
WUMP
TOSS
DASH
MEOW
I...
I WASN'T TRYING MY BEST FOR TAKEO.
...DID MY BEST TO HIDE MY FEELINGS.
IF I'D TOLD HIM HOW I FELT...

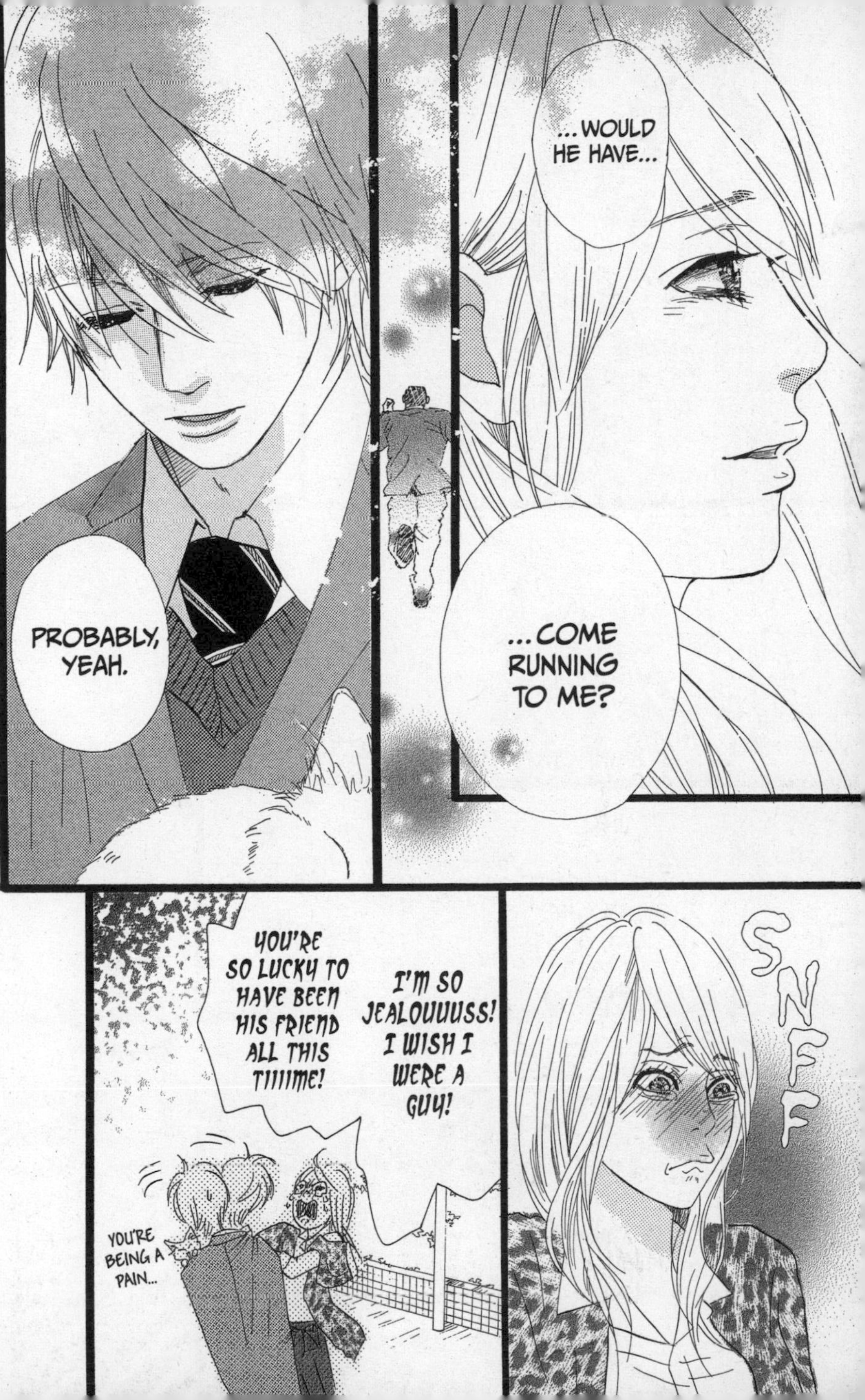
...WOULD HE HAVE...
...COME RUNNING TO ME?
PROBABLY, YEAH.
SNFF
I'M SO JEALOUUUSS! I WISH I WERE A GUY!
YOU'RE SO LUCKY TO HAVE BEEN HIS FRIEND ALL THIS TIIIIME!
YOU'RE BEING A PAIN...

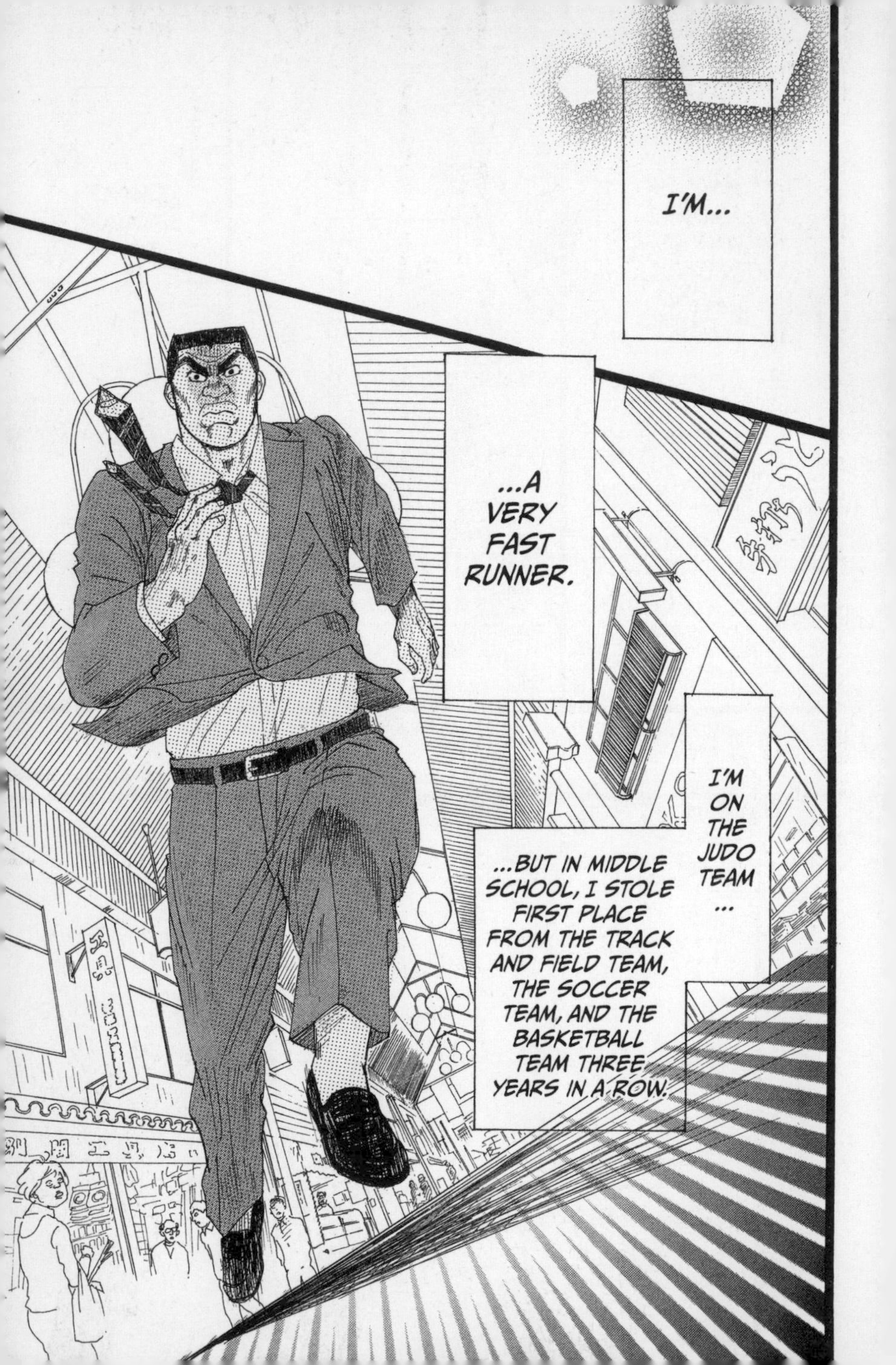
I'M...
...A VERY FAST RUNNER.
I'M ON THE JUDO TEAM...
...BUT IN MIDDLE SCHOOL, I STOLE FIRST PLACE FROM THE TRACK AND FIELD TEAM, THE SOCCER TEAM, AND THE BASKETBALL TEAM THREE YEARS IN A ROW.

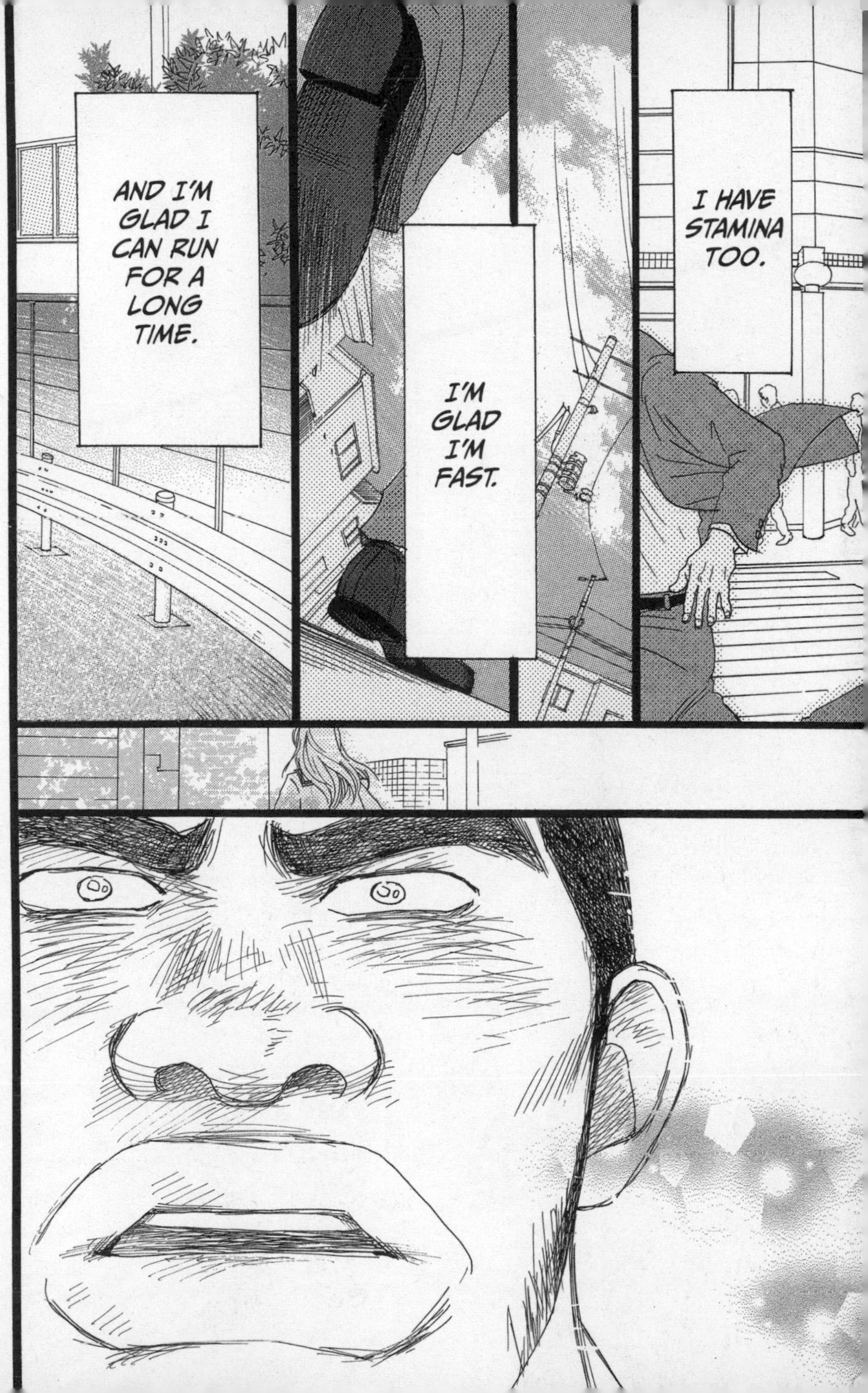
I HAVE STAMINA TOO.
I'M GLAD I'M FAST.
AND I'M GLAD I CAN RUN FOR A LONG TIME.

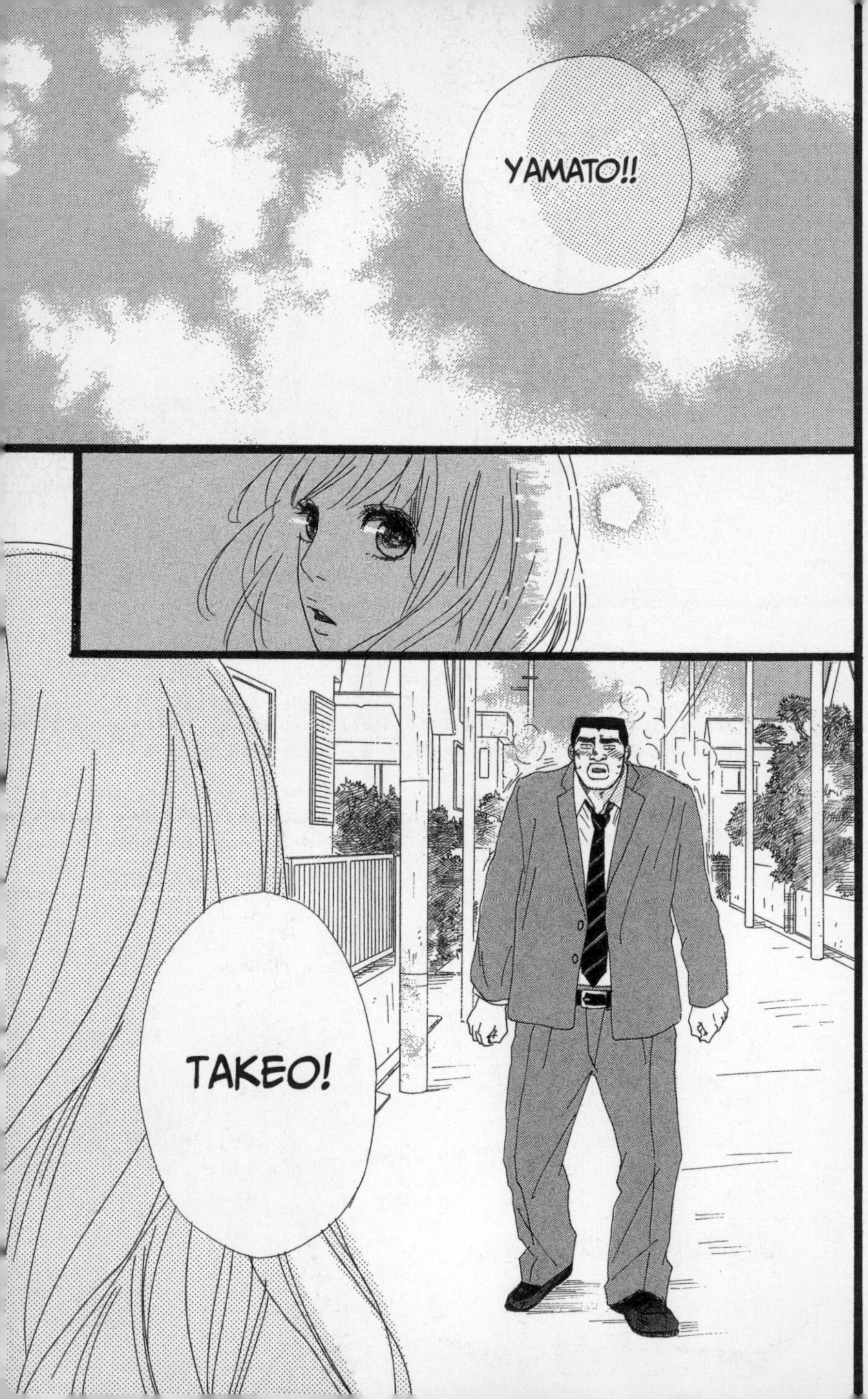
YAMATO!!
TAKEO!

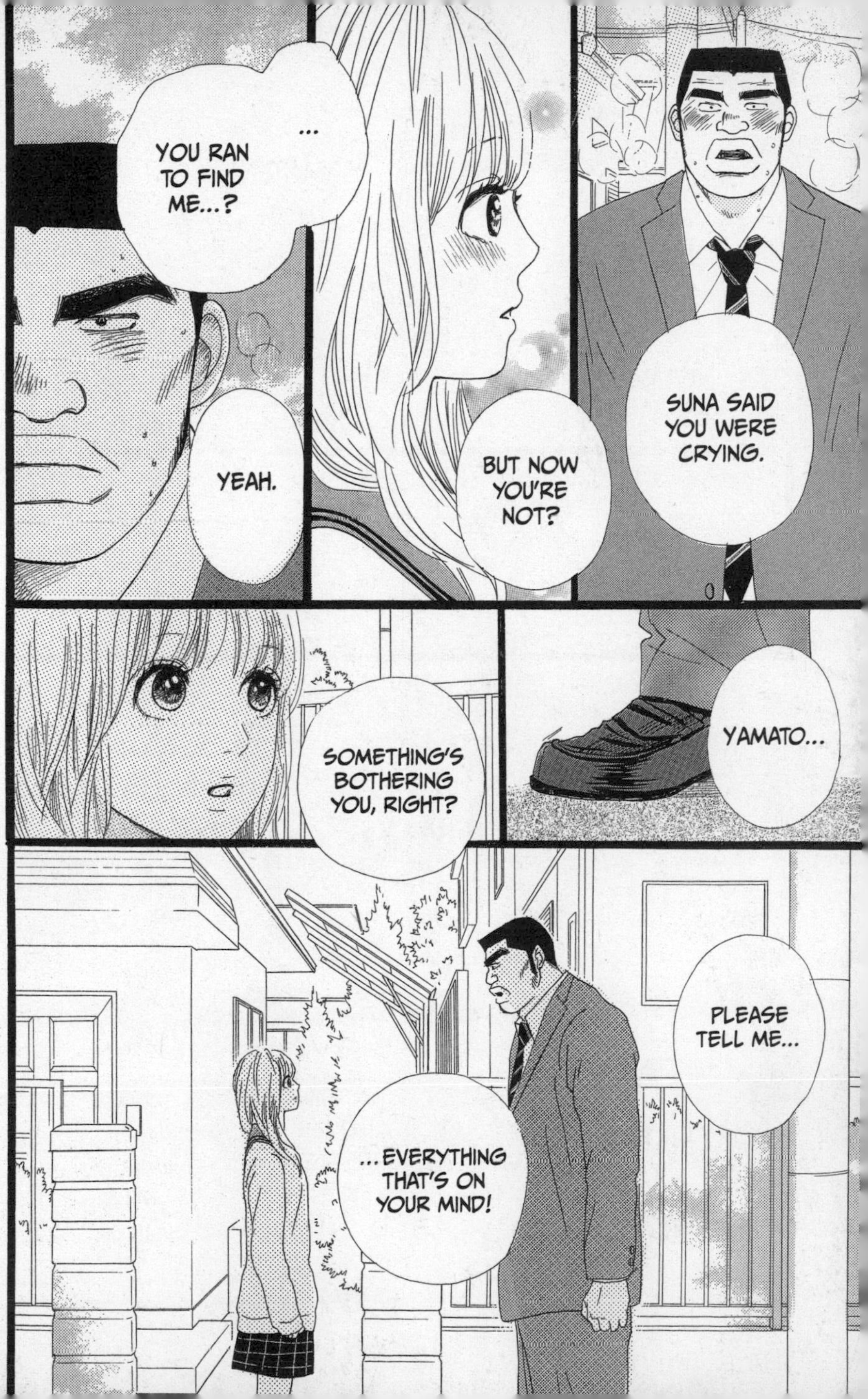
SUNA SAID YOU WERE CRYING.
...
BUT NOW YOU'RE NOT?
YOU RAN TO FIND ME...?
YEAH.
YAMATO...
SOMETHING'S BOTHERING YOU, RIGHT?
PLEASE TELL ME...
...EVERYTHING THAT'S ON YOUR MIND!

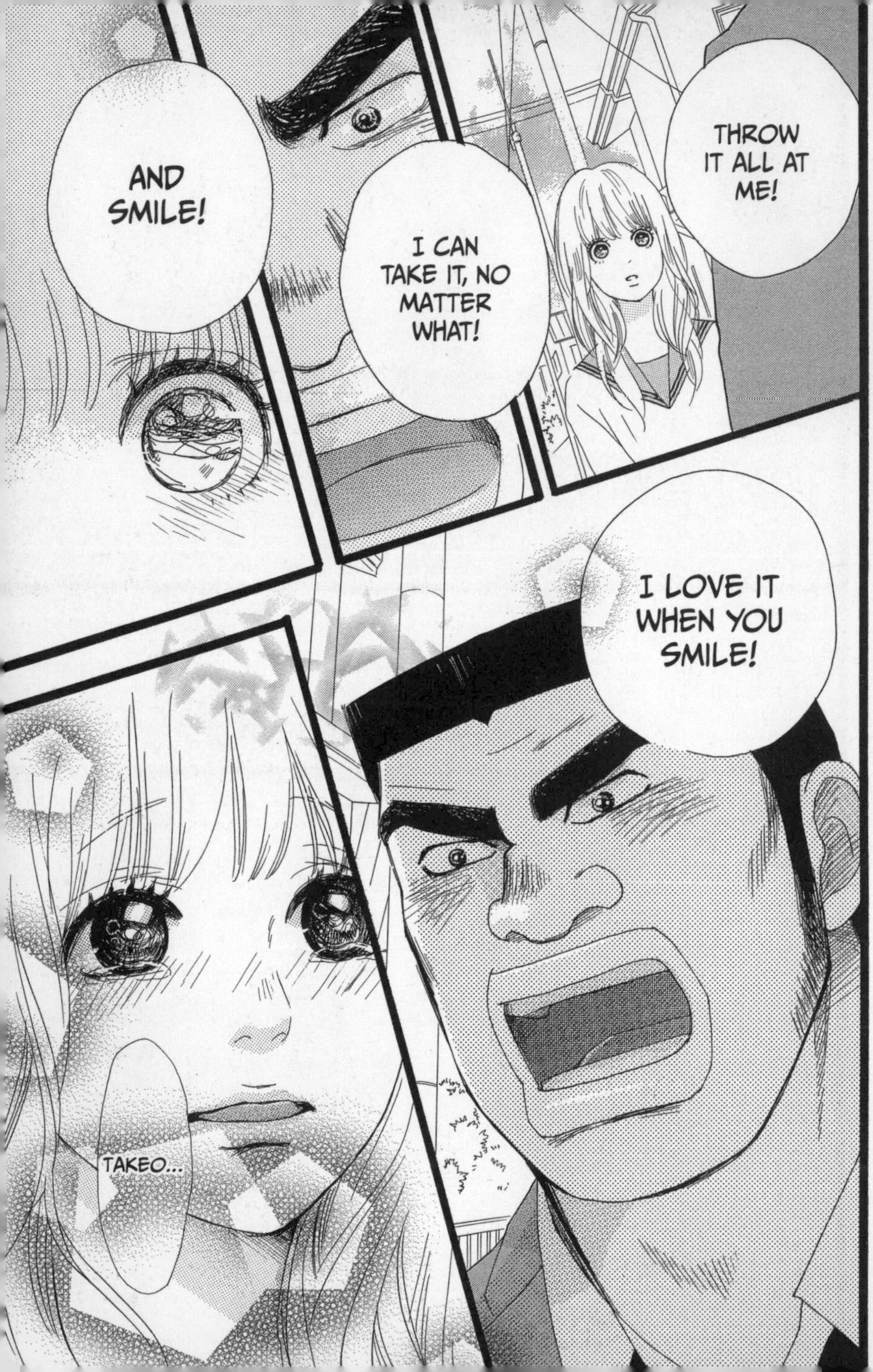
THROW IT ALL AT ME!
I CAN TAKE IT, NO MATTER WHAT!
AND SMILE!
I LOVE IT WHEN YOU SMILE!
TAKEO...

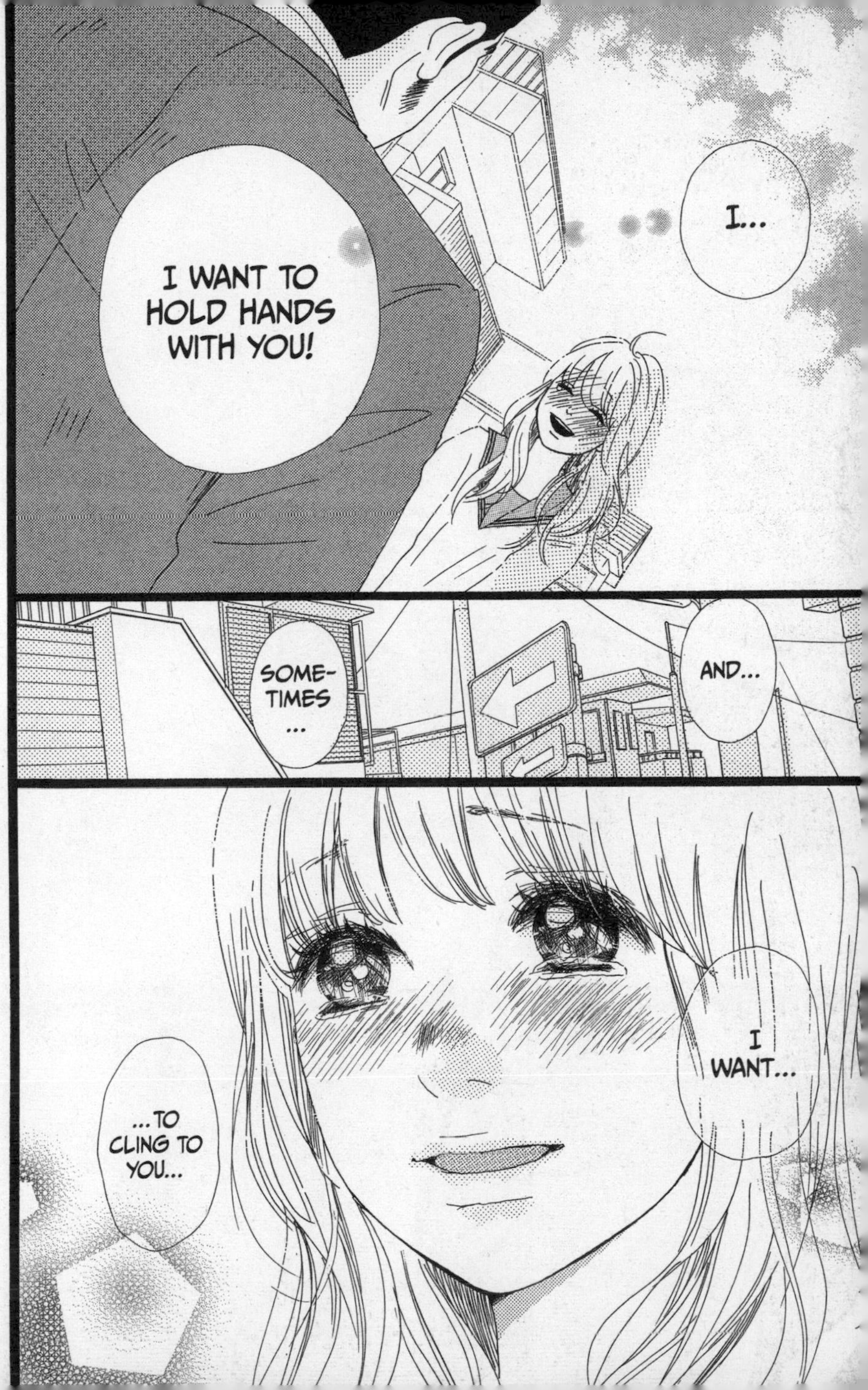
I...
I WANT TO HOLD HANDS WITH YOU!
AND...
SOME-TIMES ...
I WANT...
...TO CLING TO YOU...

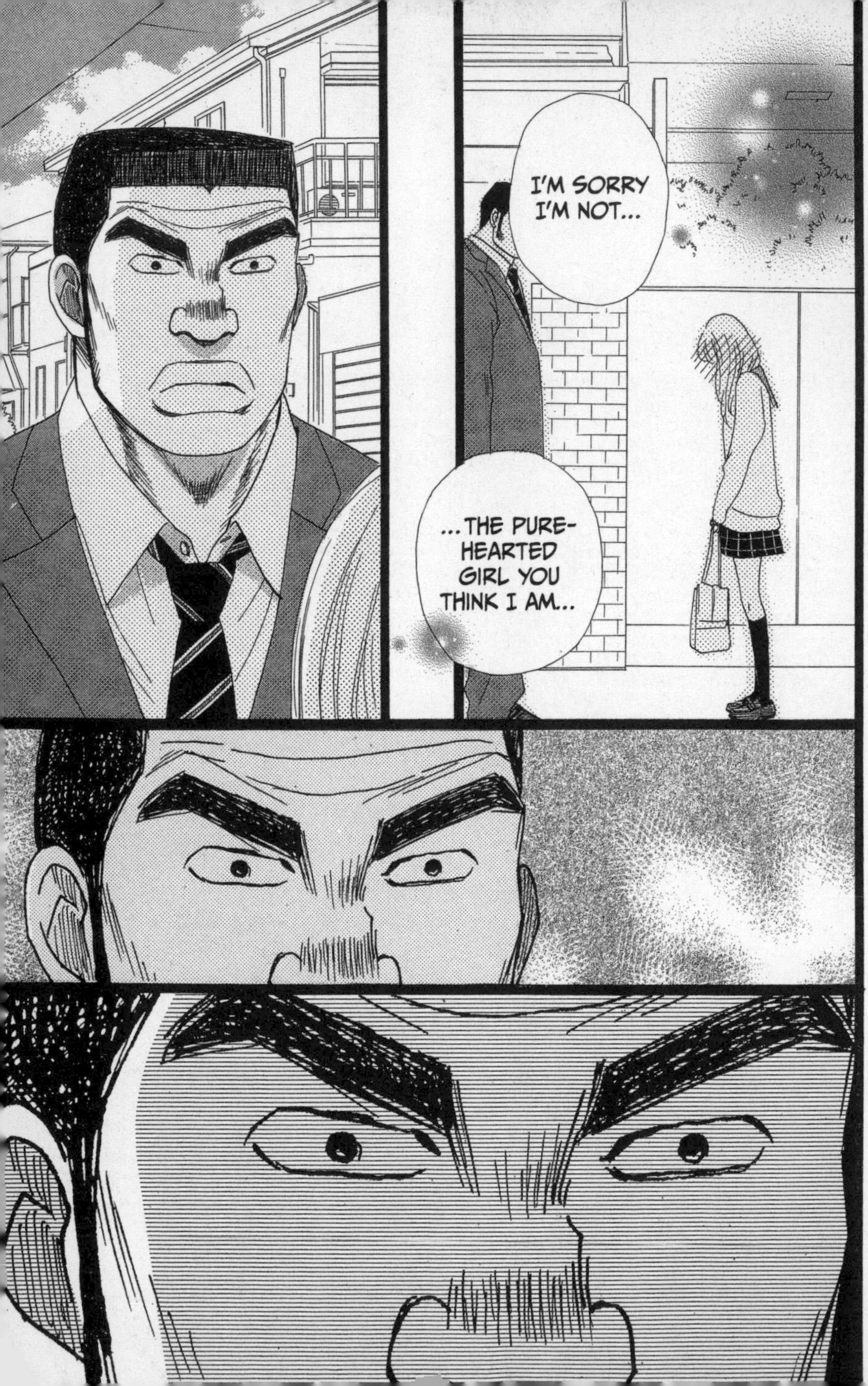
I'M SORRY I'M NOT...
...THE PURE-HEARTED GIRL YOU THINK I AM...

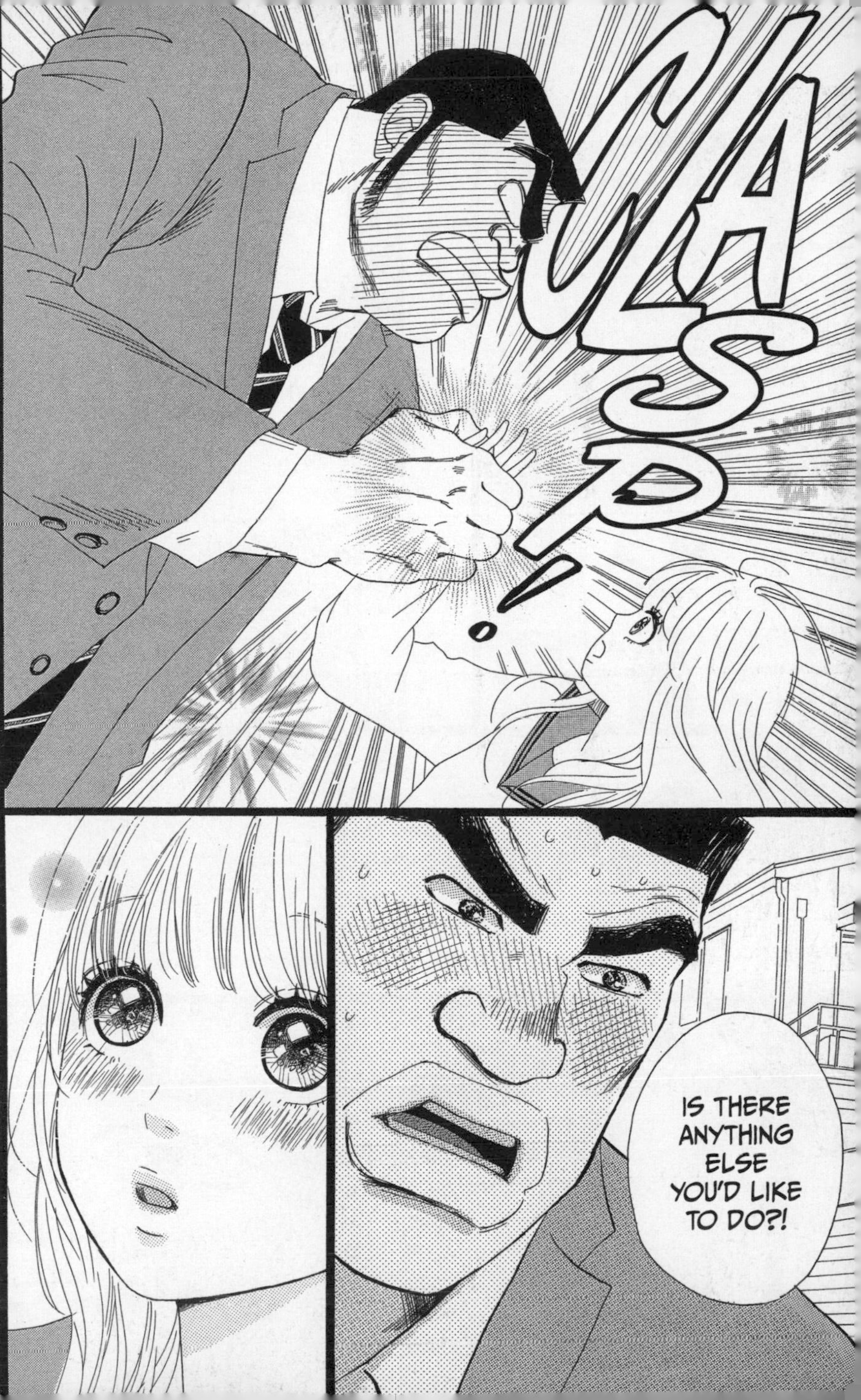
CLASP!
IS THERE ANYTHING ELSE YOU'D LIKE TO DO?!

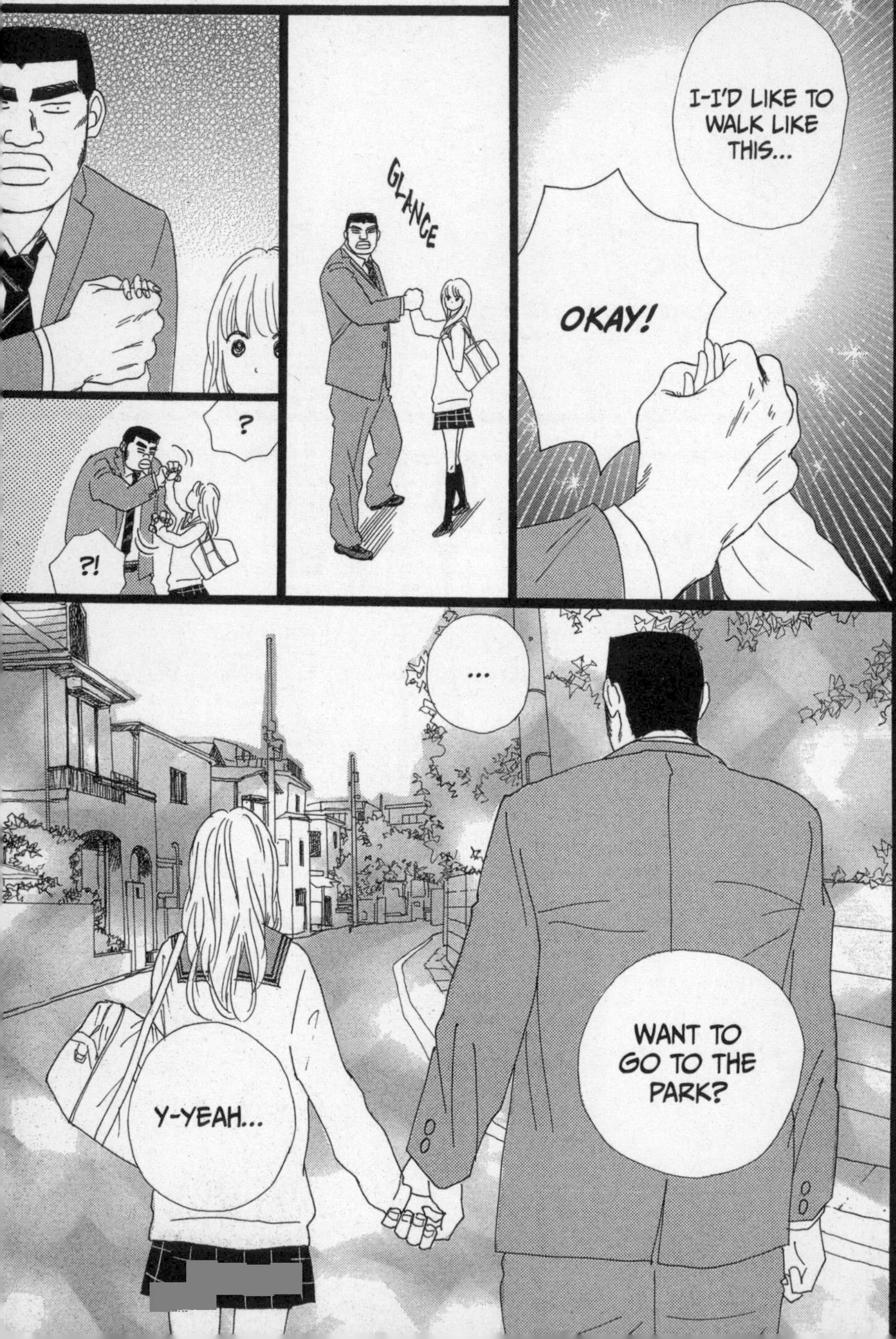
I-I'D LIKE TO WALK LIKE THIS...
OKAY!
GLANCE
?
?!
...
WANT TO GO TO THE PARK?
Y-YEAH...

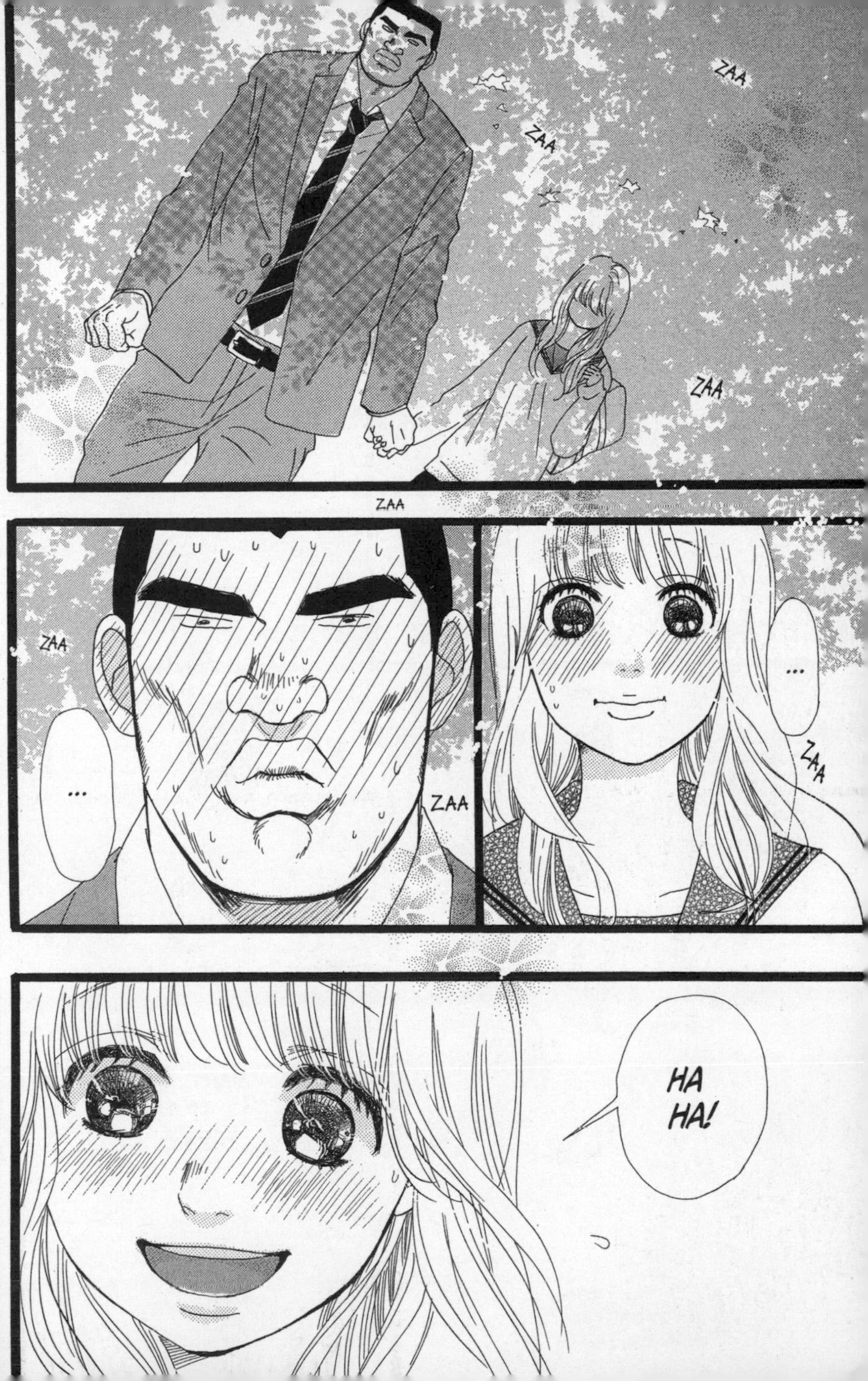
ZAA
ZAA
ZAA
ZAA
...
ZAA
ZAA
...
ZAA
HA HA!

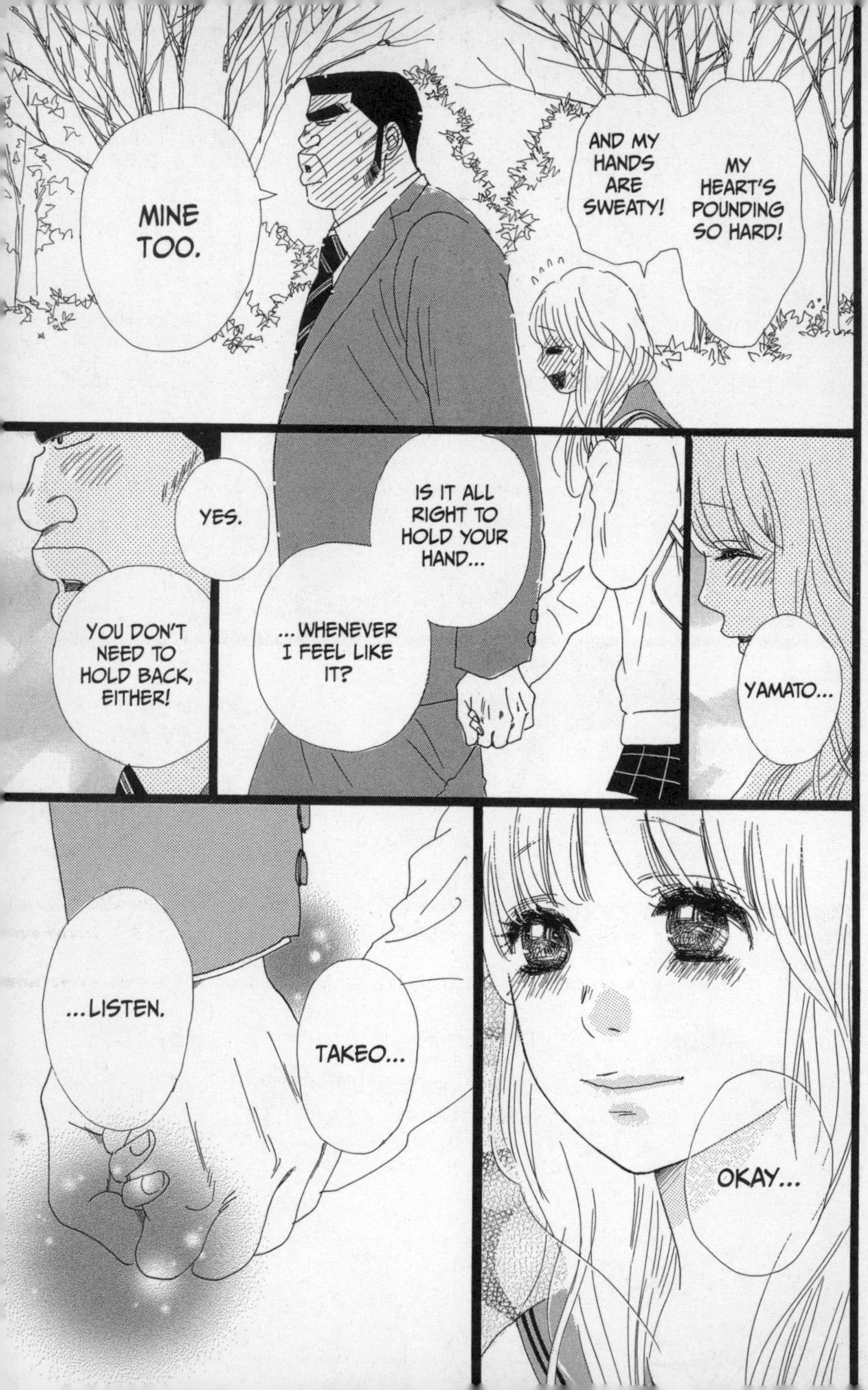
MY HEART'S POUNDING SO HARD!
AND MY HANDS ARE SWEATY!
MINE TOO.
YAMATO...
IS IT ALL RIGHT TO HOLD YOUR HAND...
...WHENEVER I FEEL LIKE IT?
YES.
YOU DON'T NEED TO HOLD BACK, EITHER!
OKAY...
TAKEO...
...LISTEN.

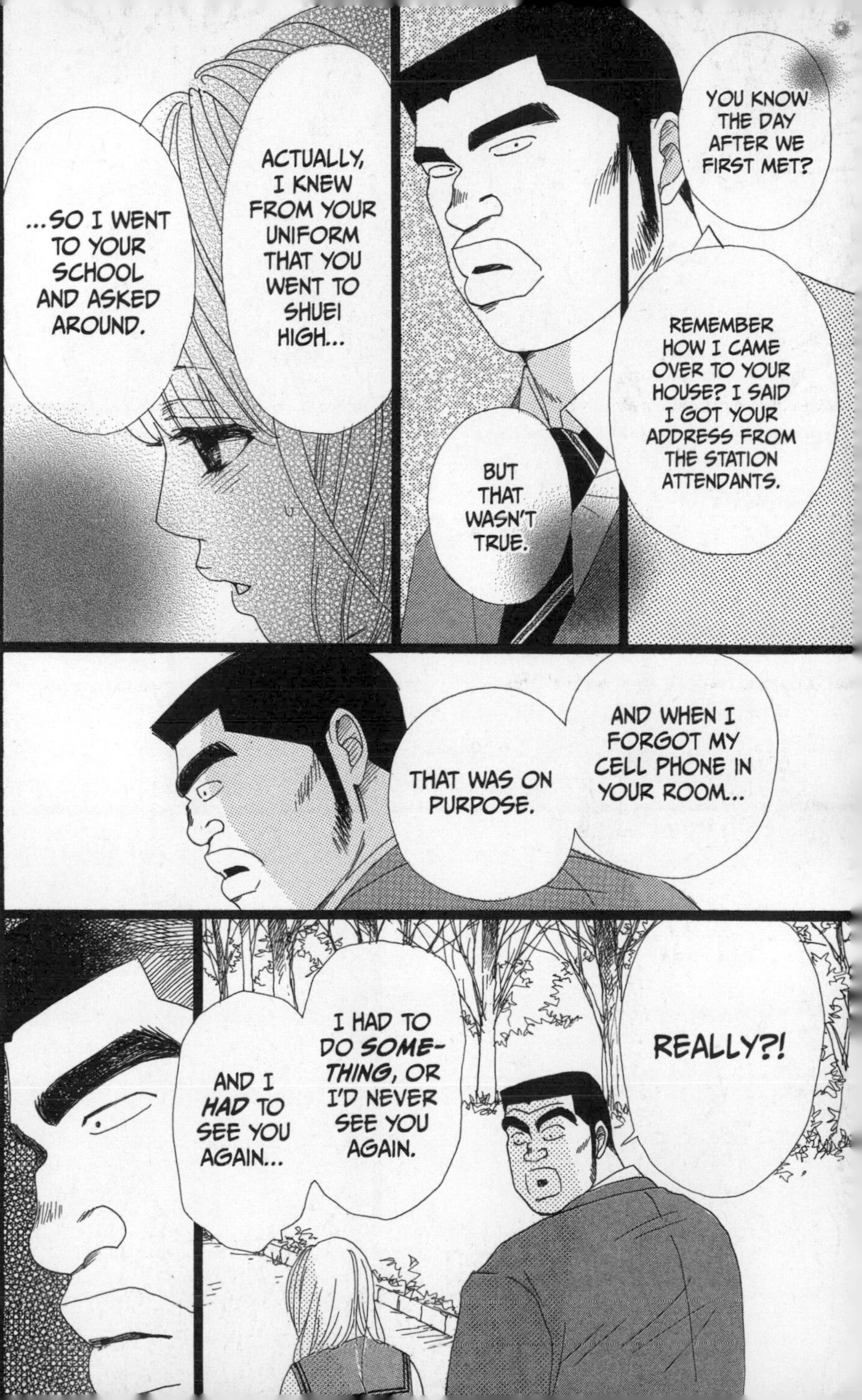
YOU KNOW THE DAY AFTER WE FIRST MET?
REMEMBER HOW I CAME OVER TO YOUR HOUSE? I SAID I GOT YOUR ADDRESS FROM THE STATION ATTENDANTS.
BUT THAT WASN'T TRUE.
ACTUALLY, I KNEW FROM YOUR UNIFORM THAT YOU WENT TO SHUEI HIGH...
...SO I WENT TO YOUR SCHOOL AND ASKED AROUND.
AND WHEN I FORGOT MY CELL PHONE IN YOUR ROOM...
THAT WAS ON PURPOSE.
REALLY?!
I HAD TO DO *SOMETHING*, OR I'D NEVER SEE YOU AGAIN.
AND I *HAD* TO SEE YOU AGAIN...

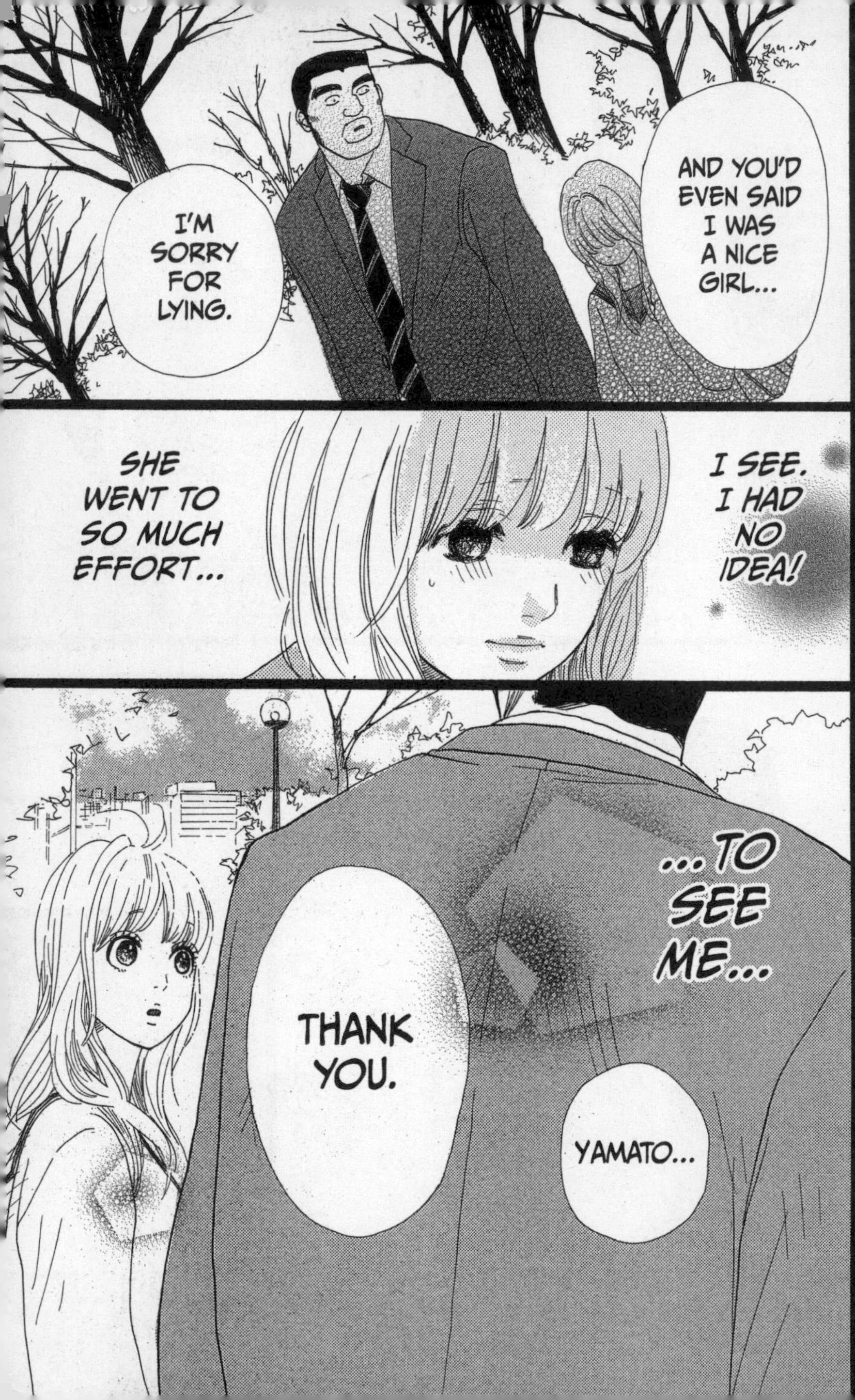
AND YOU'D EVEN SAID I WAS A NICE GIRL...
I'M SORRY FOR LYING.
I SEE. I HAD NO IDEA!
SHE WENT TO SO MUCH EFFORT...
...TO SEE ME...
THANK YOU.
YAMATO...

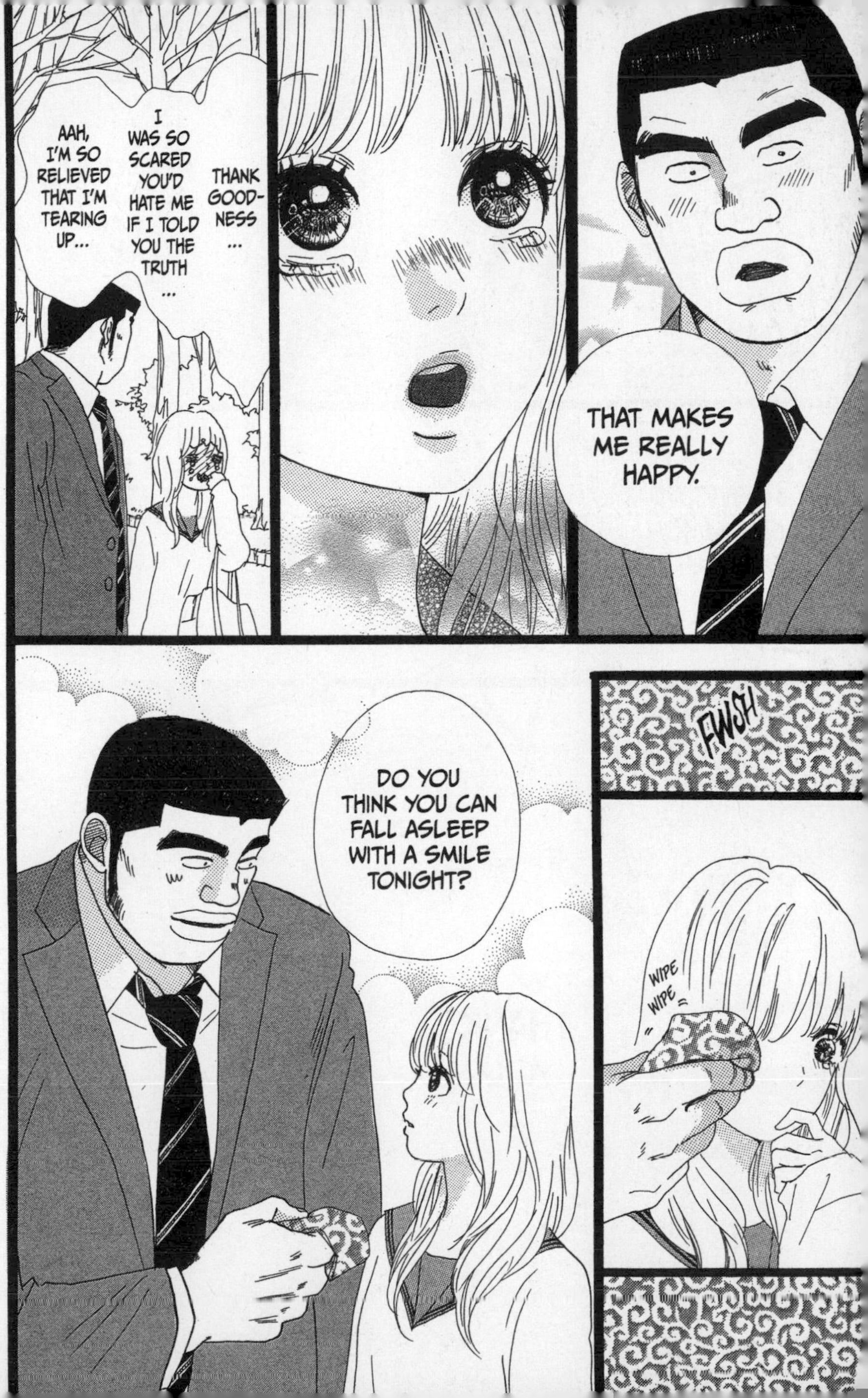
THAT MAKES ME REALLY HAPPY.
THANK GOODNESS...
I WAS SO SCARED YOU'D HATE ME IF I TOLD YOU THE TRUTH...
AAH, I'M SO RELIEVED THAT I'M TEARING UP...
FWSH
WIPE WIPE
DO YOU THINK YOU CAN FALL ASLEEP WITH A SMILE TONIGHT?

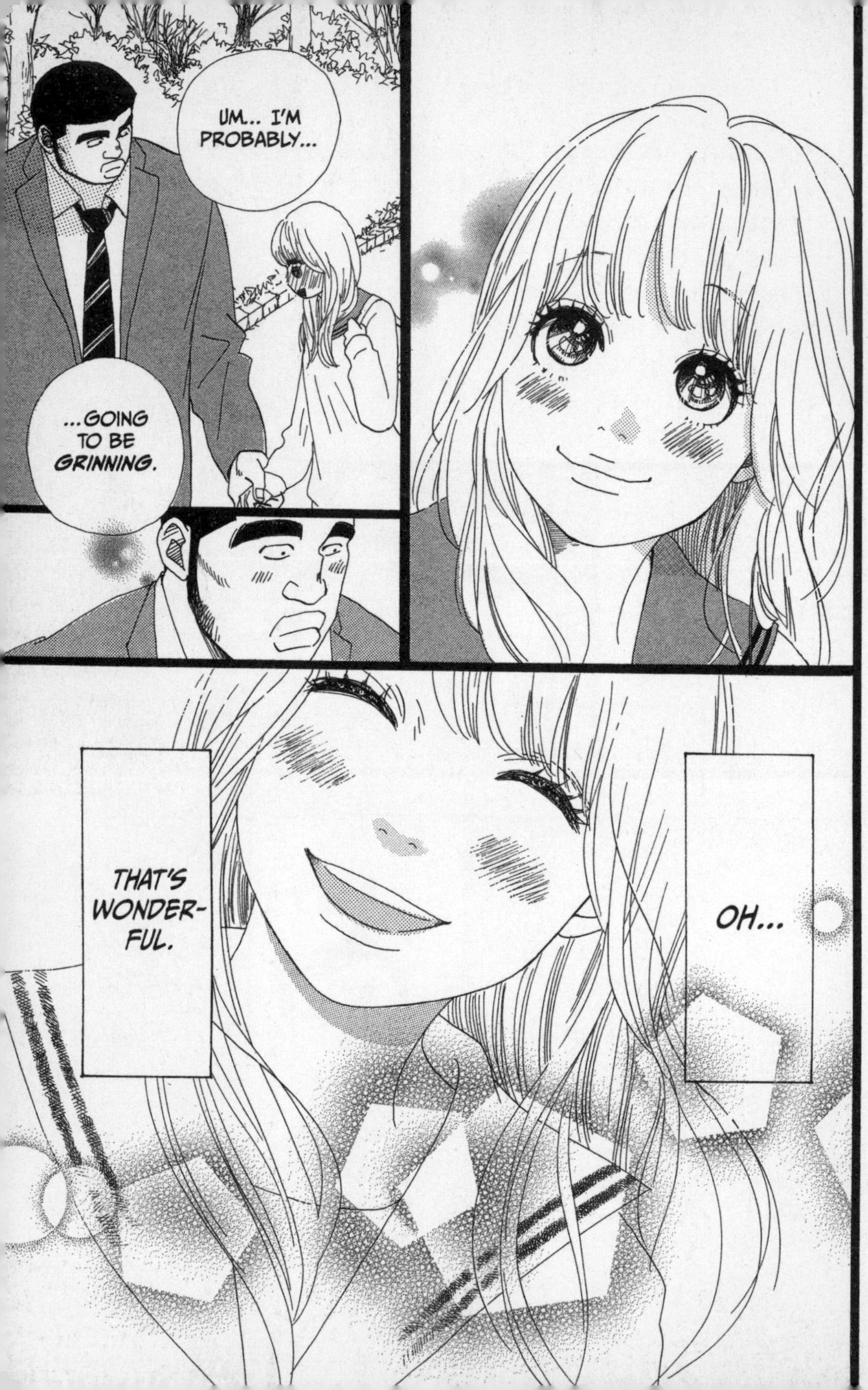
UM... I'M PROBABLY...
...GOING TO BE GRINNING.
OH...
THAT'S WONDER-FUL.

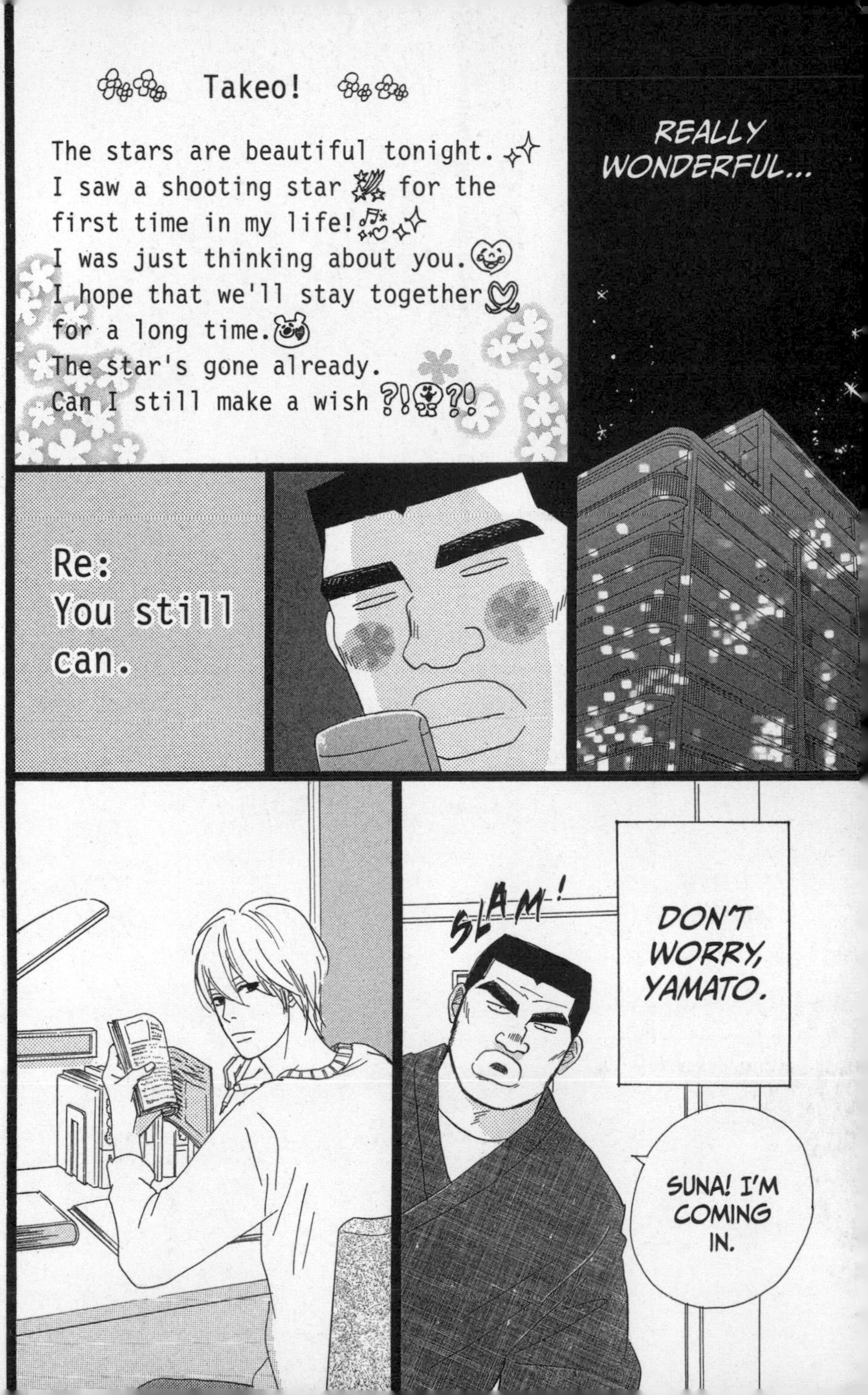
REALLY WONDERFUL...
Takeo!
The stars are beautiful tonight.
I saw a shooting star for the first time in my life!
I was just thinking about you.
I hope that we'll stay together for a long time.
The star's gone already.
Can I still make a wish ?!?!
Re:
You still can.
DON'T WORRY, YAMATO.
SLAM!
SUNA! I'M COMING IN.

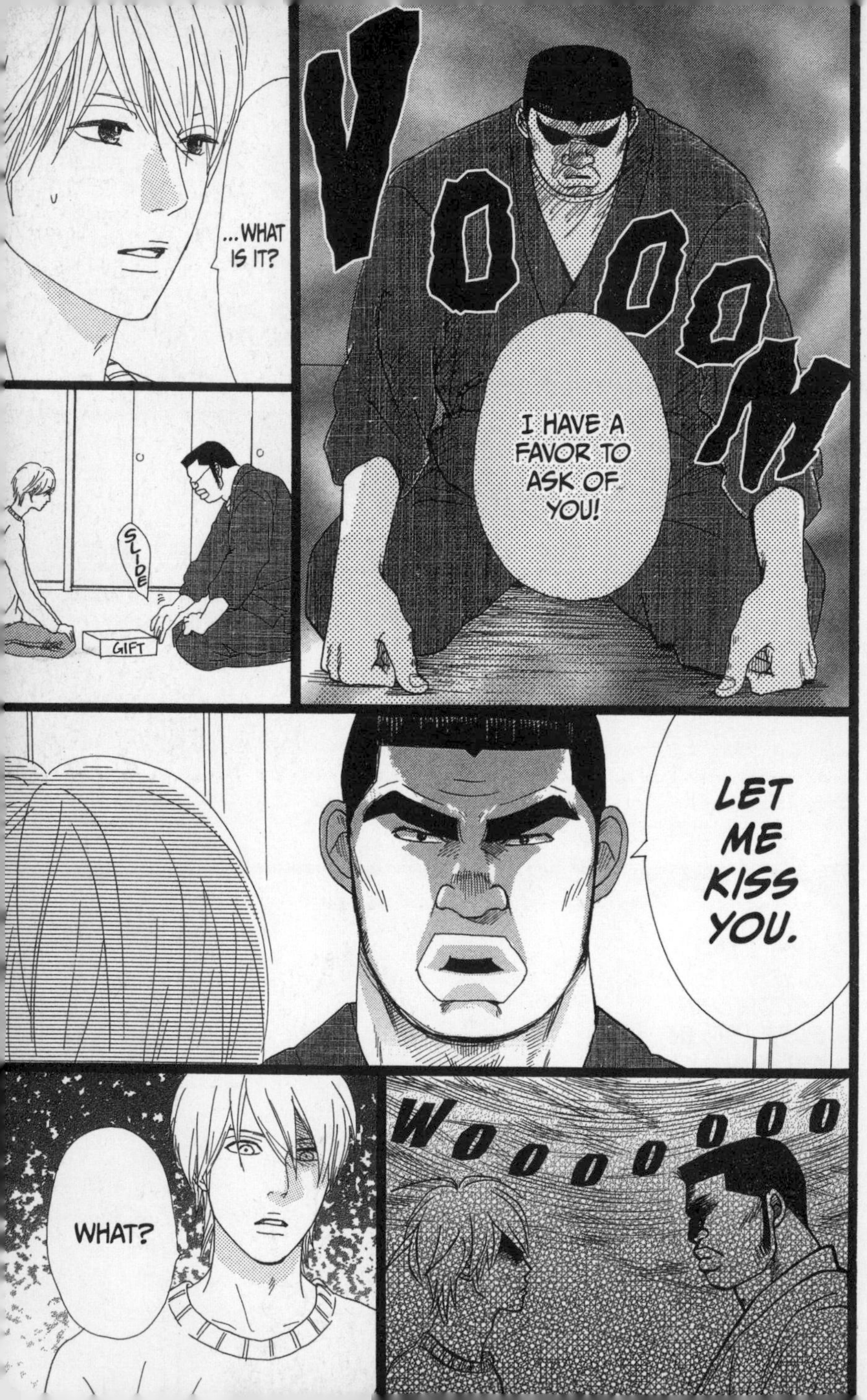
VOOOOM
I HAVE A FAVOR TO ASK OF YOU!
...WHAT IS IT?
SLIDE
GIFT
LET ME KISS YOU.
WOOOOOOOOO
WHAT?

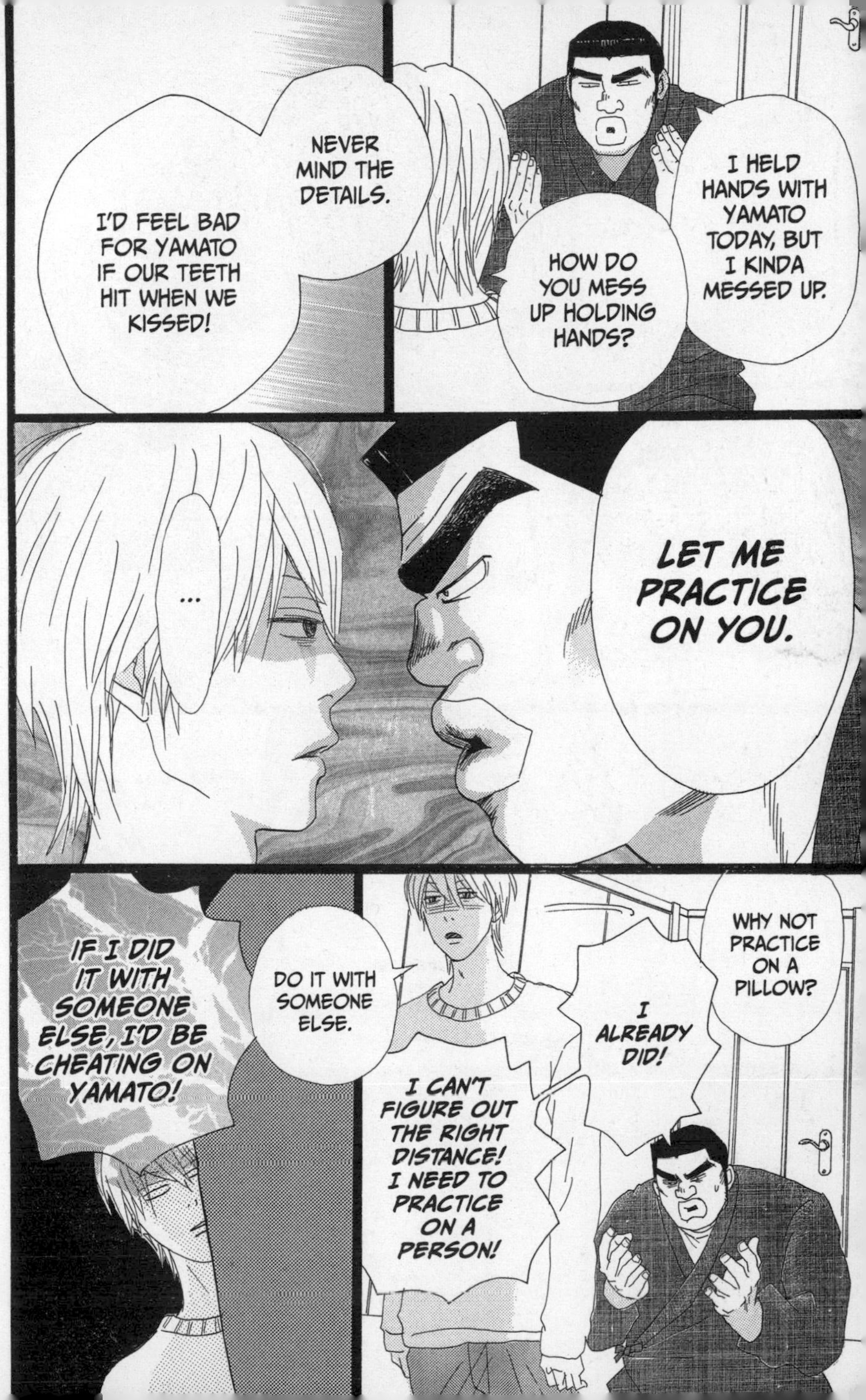
I HELD HANDS WITH YAMATO TODAY, BUT I KINDA MESSED UP.
HOW DO YOU MESS UP HOLDING HANDS?
NEVER MIND THE DETAILS.
I'D FEEL BAD FOR YAMATO IF OUR TEETH HIT WHEN WE KISSED!
LET ME PRACTICE ON YOU.
...
WHY NOT PRACTICE ON A PILLOW?
I ALREADY DID!
I CAN'T FIGURE OUT THE RIGHT DISTANCE! I NEED TO PRACTICE ON A PERSON!
DO IT WITH SOMEONE ELSE.
IF I DID IT WITH SOMEONE ELSE, I'D BE CHEATING ON YAMATO!

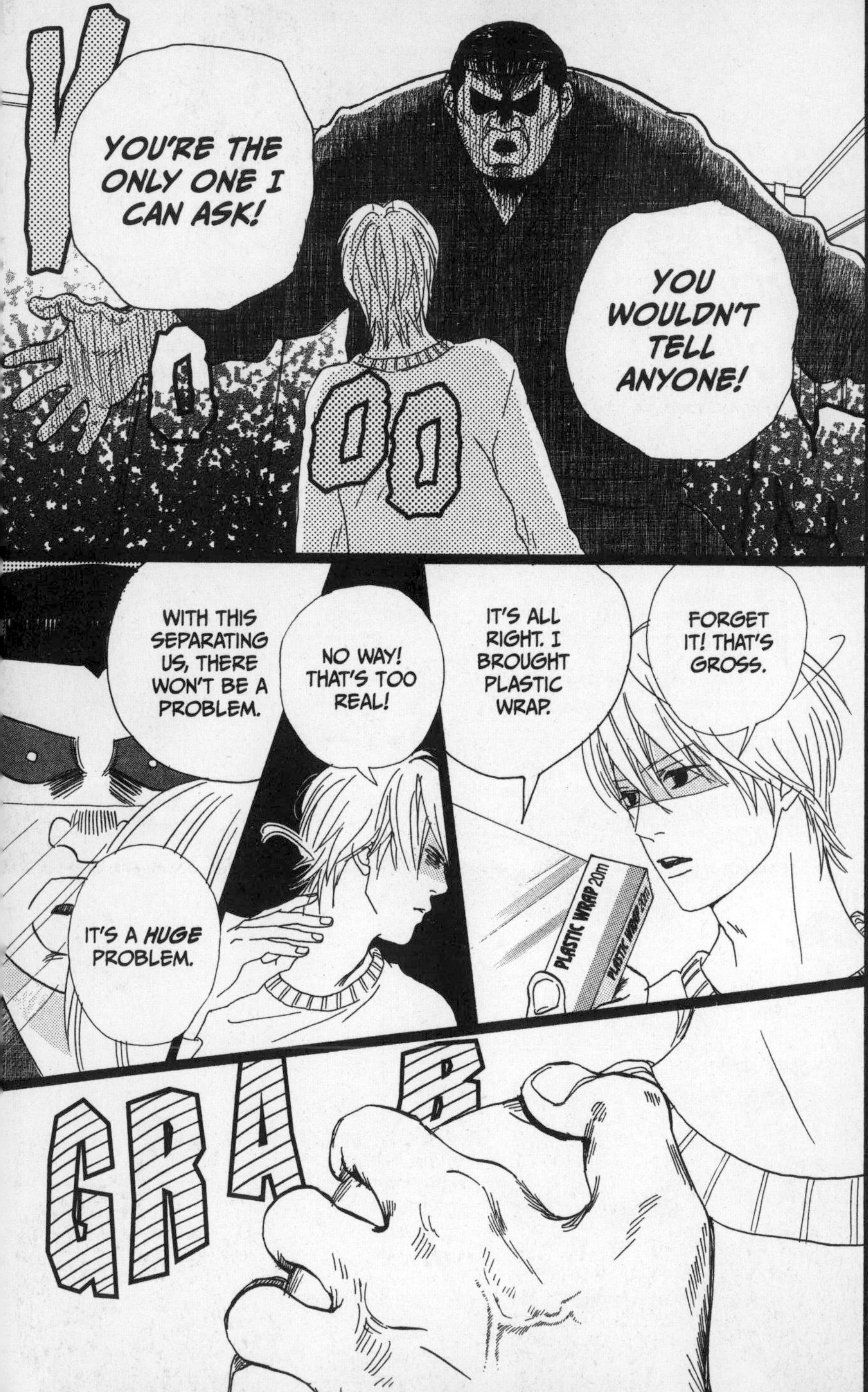
YOU'RE THE ONLY ONE I CAN ASK!
YOU WOULDN'T TELL ANYONE!
FORGET IT! THAT'S GROSS.
IT'S ALL RIGHT. I BROUGHT PLASTIC WRAP.
PLASTIC WRAP 20m
NO WAY! THAT'S TOO REAL!
WITH THIS SEPARATING US, THERE WON'T BE A PROBLEM.
IT'S A *HUGE* PROBLEM.
GRAB

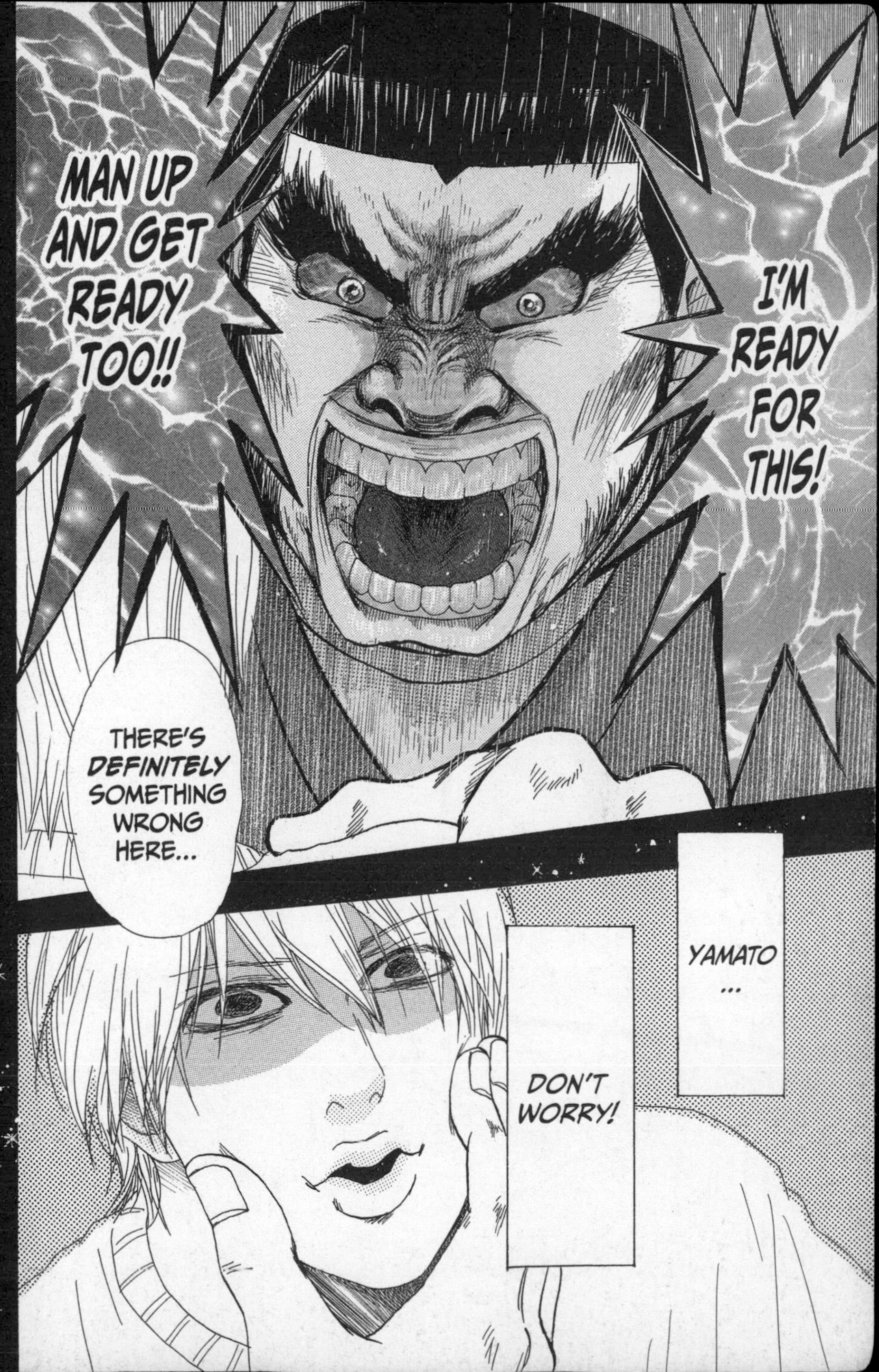
I'M READY FOR THIS!
MAN UP AND GET READY TOO!!
THERE'S *DEFINITELY* SOMETHING WRONG HERE...
YAMATO ...
DON'T WORRY!

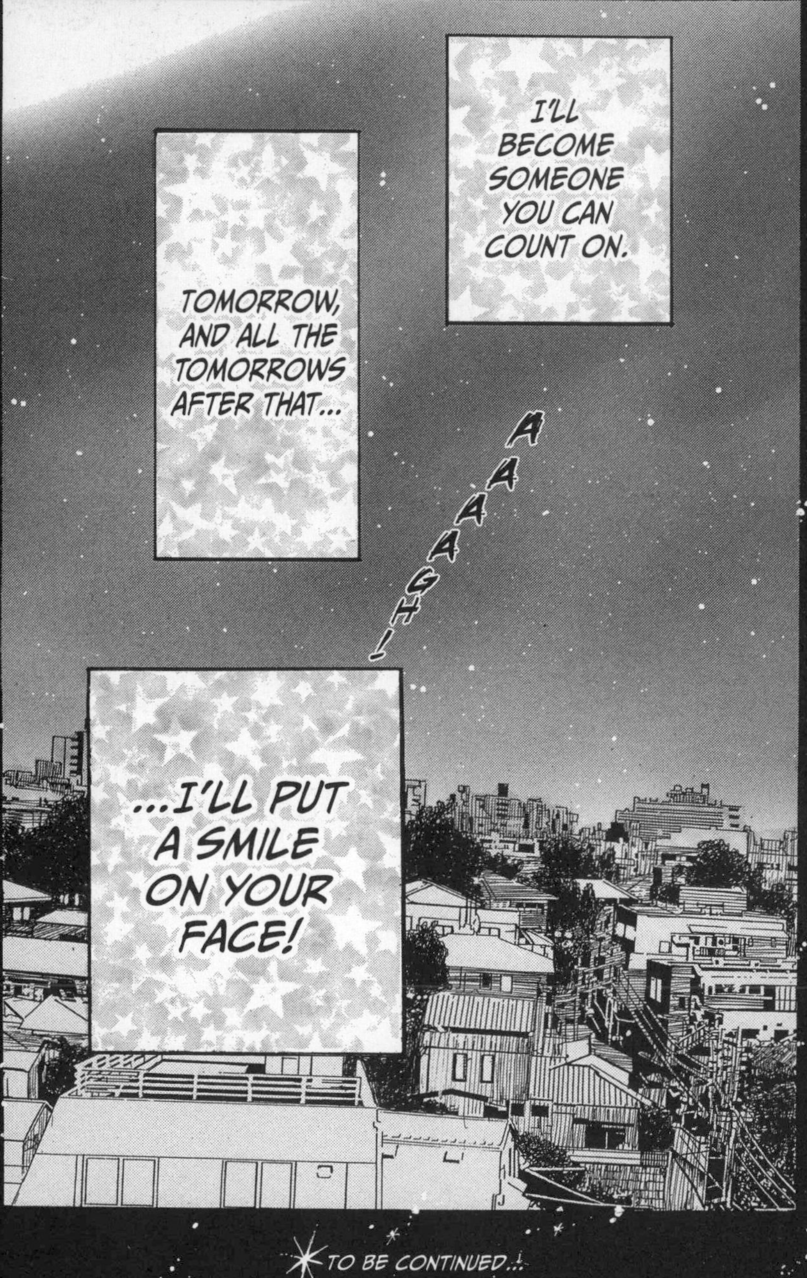
I'LL BECOME SOMEONE YOU CAN COUNT ON.
TOMORROW, AND ALL THE TOMORROWS AFTER THAT...
AAAAAGH!
...I'LL PUT A SMILE ON YOUR FACE!

TO BE CONTINUED...

Hello. I'm Kawahara, the author. After I sent in my story, I was excited to see what kind of manga Aruko-san would create. It was better than I anticipated. It came as a shock to me and brought me to tears. Thank you very much, Aruko-san.

– Kazune Kawahara

Ⓚ

ARUKO is from Ishikawa Prefecture in Japan and was born on July 26 (a Leo!). She made her manga debut with *Ame Nochi Hare* (Clear After the Rain). Her other works include *Yasuko to Kenji*, and her hobbies include laughing and getting lost.

KAZUNE KAWAHARA is from Hokkaido Prefecture in Japan and was born on March 11th (a Pisces!). She made her manga debut at age 18 with *Kare no Ichiban Sukina Hito* (His Most Favorite Person). Her best-selling shojo manga series *High School Debut* is available in North America from VIZ Media. Her hobby is interior redecorating.

This is the first time I've worked on something that already had a story, but despite being in awe of Kawahara Sensei's greatness, I had fun drawing it. I thought the original story was interesting, I thought drawing it was interesting, and I even thought what I had drawn was interesting. I would like as many people as possible to discover this series.

– Aruko

Ⓐ